Support the Troops

OXFORD STUDIES IN GENDER AND INTERNATIONAL RELATIONS

Series editors: J. Ann Tickner, American University, and Laura Sjoberg,
Royal Holloway University of London

Support the Troops

*Military Obligation, Gender, and the Making
of Political Community*

KATHARINE M. MILLAR

OXFORD
UNIVERSITY PRESS

OXFORD
UNIVERSITY PRESS

Oxford University Press is a department of the University of Oxford. It furthers
the University's objective of excellence in research, scholarship, and education
by publishing worldwide. Oxford is a registered trade mark of Oxford University
Press in the UK and certain other countries.

Published in the United States of America by Oxford University Press
198 Madison Avenue, New York, NY 10016, United States of America.

Library of Congress Control Number: 2022913778

ISBN 978-0-19-764233-7

DOI: 10.1093/oso/9780197642337.001.0001

1 3 5 7 9 8 6 4 2

Printed by Integrated Books International, United States of America

For Mom, Dad, and Carrie
I love you

Contents

Preface

Picture a small town in Canada, about 800 people. The average size of a high school graduating class is 25; the entire junior and senior high school has fewer than 200 students, grades 7–12. As the cliché goes, everyone knows everyone, whether they want to or not. The town is fairly close to a major city, but it's rural. The students at the high school take over the farm or go work in the oil fields. Maybe the young women go into teaching or nursing.

The town, like many in rural Canada, is a fairly reliable source of recruits for the Canadian Armed Forces. Not every year, but every couple of years. Enough that the band the military sends around to high schools to promote citizenship and enlistment shows up regularly. Remembrance Day is well marked; everyone in town knows where the grandparents and town leaders and farmers in the coffee shop served. There is an Army Cadets group in the high school; the principal runs it and encourages students considered heading for "trouble" join.

And so, everyone knows, or knows of, a few young men—always men—who joined the military after graduation. Some joined the navy or the coast guard; one, whose picture was still hanging in the high school, joined the air force and was killed in an accident in the 1960s. Most enlisted in the army. They were boys who had played on the hockey team, coached sports, did well or less well in school, sometimes went out on the weekends, mostly went to church, were well-liked, and were looking for a way out of town. Their parents owned farms, worked at the school, or the gas station.

After September 11, 2001, Canada joined the coalition forces in action against Afghanistan. The young men who had joined the army that year, and in the years before, suddenly had very different job descriptions. The Canadian military's central mission had shifted from peacekeeping to its first active war since 1953. The meaning of a military career quickly transformed from something that could plausibly (though unreflectively and neo-colonially) be understood as a form of international public service to something riskier.

The town saw the early years of the invasion of Afghanistan through the lens of their service. On April 17, 2002, four Canadian soldiers were killed, and eight injured, by the US military in a friendly fire incident. This was a big deal—the first soldiers killed in a war since Korea. Flags flew at half-mast; it amplified the unease of those who were not entirely convinced "we" should be in Afghanistan at all.

The news didn't come out all at once, and the town waited. At first, all that was known was Canadian soldiers had been hurt, maybe killed—and that it was possible some of the young men were in that battalion. The TVs were on most of the day in the high school as everyone waited for updates and thought about their parents trying to get through the day across town. Eventually, though it was probably only a day, or maybe two days, the town found out: the young men had been on leave.

Shortly after that—though it could have been before or long after—the families of the young men gave out yellow ribbon ("support the troops") magnets for people to put on their cars. Yellow ribbons weren't a huge thing, nothing like you'd see in a military town, or in the US, but there were some. A few in front yards, on the trees by the World War II memorial at the fire station. There were more flags around, suddenly.

My parents received one of the yellow ribbon magnets for their car. I remember them considering what to do about it. They weren't torn up about it or anything; it was a pretty matter-of-fact discussion. They were reluctant to put it on their car because they disagreed with the war in Afghanistan (and were not, I suppose, great fans of the military overall). They weren't convinced by the "support the troops, not the war" idea, which didn't have much traction there anyway. It was pretty clear, in my hometown, that you were meant to support the war and the troops. Obviously, you'll put up the ribbon. And they didn't want to do that—but they cared for the young men in the military. They had watched them grow up. It's hard to remember now, but we think my dad taught some of them in elementary school. And they wanted to support the families, who were very worried. What I remember happening is that the yellow ribbon magnet went onto the car for a while. And, eventually, it disappeared. (Something about a car wash?) I was never sure whether it was lost, or it was allowed to . . . fade away once the temperature went down. It was not replaced.

I've been turning that scenario over in my mind on and off for years. The push-pull of my parents' discussion—we don't necessarily agree with this, but we have to (or, actually, maybe we should), at least for a while—animates this book. What does it mean to "support the troops"? What do you do about those you care about in a war you oppose? Can you oppose a war while living in community? I thought about all those tiny interactions, with people balancing politics, their perspectives on war, their feelings about the military, and their social ties, added up, across the coalition forces states. What does it do to politics and to war when we support the troops? And, actually—the thing that's been bothering me for 20 years—why do we think we have to?

I'm not entirely sure about telling the story above, though I've blurred some details. There are large parts of it that aren't mine. And my hometown's experience of the global war on terror is nothing like that of towns, neighborhoods, cities, and families that sent (and lost) more people. It's so far from the loss and devastation that is still experienced by so many people in Iraq and Afghanistan. I'm wary that it plays into the idea that in order to write, and think, about the military you need to have a personal stake in it.

And, after all that, the book isn't about Canada: it's about the US and UK. I wanted to see how this played out in countries with larger militaries, fighting the war in Iraq, which Canada declined. The rest of the book—which is more analytical, more structured, and more diagnostic—reveals that my initial intuition of similar dynamics, intensified, basically holds. It's also a lot more complicated.

Acknowledgments

As the saying goes, it takes a village to raise a book. In my case, this includes the literal village in the preface and the many other metaphorical villages, communities, and spaces I've been fortunate to travel through and belong to as the book developed. While I have benefited from the advice of innumerable people, any errors contained within are mine alone. I would like to acknowledge the many scholars, named in the bibliography, whose research challenged, informed, and inspired this project.

Research doesn't happen without material support. I am grateful to those agencies whose generous funding supported the doctoral research (and doctoral education) that became this book. I would like to thank the Social Science and Humanities Research Council of Canada for awarding me a Doctoral Fellowship; the Government of Alberta for the Sir James Lougheed Award of Distinction; the Oxford Department of Politics and International Relations for a doctoral bursary; and the Maple Leaf Trust for a Canadian Centennial Scholarship. I also thank Somerville College, Oxford and the Rothermere American Institute for their generous financial contributions toward my research materials and travel.

I also thank the many people associated with military charities and antiwar groups who facilitated my access to uncatalogued primary research materials, gave me their time, and occasionally drove me home after letting me go through old boxes in their basements. Thank you to Wendy Chmielwski (Swarthmore Peace Archives), Debra Brookhart (American Legion), Donald Davis (American Friends Service Committee), Tom Kilgannon (Freedom Alliance), Carol Turner (Labour Against the War and CND), Joe Davis (Veterans of Foreign Wars), Anne Ascioti (PGA Tour/ Birdies for the Brave), Lisa Bogle (DAV), Juliet Chaplin (SSAFA), Stefan Dickers (Bishopsgate Institute), and, last but not least, Jeremy Corbyn, MP (Labour Against the War and StWC).

The majority of the research for this book took place during my doctoral studies at Somerville College, Oxford. I thank the faculty and staff in the Oxford Department of Politics and International Relations for challenging my intellectual boundaries, pushing me to think ambitiously and write specifically, and supporting me in getting here. In particular, I thank Eddie Keene, Todd Hall, Jennifer Welsh, Janina Dill, and Jonathan Leader Maynard for their insightful commentary on (very) early drafts of this project. I also thank Andrew Melling for helping me print my doctoral dissertation, in a panic, on the very last day.

I would also like to recognize my academic mentors, W. Andy Knight (U. Alberta), my undergraduate dissertation advisor; Elisabeth Prügl (IHEID) who taught my first feminist politics course; and Keith Krause, my master's supervisor (IHEID), for their belief in my ideas (and all the reference letters!). I also thank Kim Hutchings (QMUL) for not only examining the doctoral dissertation version of this book but also for her encouragement and advice in refining this project as it continued to transform.

The greatest thanks are due to my doctoral advisor, Elizabeth Frazer. As I revised (and revised!) this study and completed this final draft, I realized more and more how much her guidance informed my thinking, sharpened my analysis, tightened my writing, and bolstered my faith in the merits and contribution of this work. Liz's patience, open-mindedness, and feminist insights have made this a far stronger project and me a far more confident scholar. I learned how to be an academic by watching Liz, and I'm grateful to have had such a teacher.

This project was finished during my first years in my first job, as an assistant professor in the International Relations Department at the London School of Economics. I thank Tarak Barkawi, Mark Hoffman, John Sidel, Bill Callahan, Karen Smith, Milli Lake, and Peter Trubowitz for their support for me as a new colleague and their enthusiasm for this project. I particularly thank Nivi Manchanda and Chris Rossdale for their friendship, moral support, and solidarity as I became a working academic. They also helped me be intellectually, analytically, and politically braver—and change my mind about pacifism.

Over the past 10 years, I've presented my work in incredible academic and practitioner spaces. They are too numerable to recount here, but I am grateful for the opportunity these discussions have offered for collegial debate, external insights, and casual conversations built into friendships. I've benefited so much from my involvement in the critical war/military studies scholastic community through all stages of not only this book but also my academic career. I am also so grateful for the welcome, support, and sustenance of the feminist and queer security and militarism studies community as I honed my feminist analysis and praxis. I've learned so much from so many people—including my students, who remind me in every class why I do this.

I also thank the LSE IR Department for generously funding a final workshop discussing this manuscript. The feedback, encouragement, suggestions, and generous critiques offered by the participants in that workshop—who gave so much of their time, energy, and expertise—were foundational to the book you are reading now. I am indebted to Megan Mackenzie, Laura Sjoberg, James Eastwood, Tarak Barkawi, John Sidel, Peter Trubowitz, and Rachel Zhou for their kind, incisive, and generative engagement with my work.

Parts of Chapters 2 and 5 have appeared in the *Review of International Studies* and *Security Dialogue*, respectively. I'm grateful to those editors and reviewers for helping refine the ideas contained here. Eleanor Knott supported with me exceptional epistemological therapy—helping me quell the inner positivist and bring across the full contribution of my work. Hannah Tomlinson turned my half-notes into a functional and professional bibliography. My mom, Meg Millar, has copyedited everything I've ever written, including this entire book (twice), and loves me even though I still don't use "however" correctly.

I am also grateful to the editorial team at Oxford University Press—Laura Sjoberg, J. Ann Tickner, and Angela Raynor—for seeing the potential in my work and the importance of my argument. I'm so appreciative of the OUP anonymous reviewers who were so kind and so thoughtful.

Thanks are also due to my colleagues who have read and commented upon the various iterations of this dissertation—and heard not a small portion of it out loud: Aiko Holvikivi, Nivi Manchanda, Chris Rossdale, Nora Stappert, James Shires, Tina Managhan, David Mutimer, Joanna Tidy, Paul Kirby, Quentin Bruneau, Saliha Metsinoy, Yuna Han, Tristen Naylor, Carrie Millar, Meg Millar, and Ellen Ravndal. I particularly thank Julia Costa Lopez for her incredible, above-and-beyond investment in my work; she could likely reconstruct it from memory.

I also just need to thank my friends. Thanks to the not-so-secret 2011 Oxford IR "brain trust": Julia Costa Lopez, James Hollway, Ellen Ravndal, and Michael Sampson. Thanks to my fellow assistant professors at LSE for their solidarity, sense of humor, and commitment to change. Thanks to the 2020 COVID group—particularly but not only Milli Lake, Dan Berliner, Ellie Knott, and Blake Miller—for making the best of the worst year. Yuna Han hangs out with me at work on the internet every day. Thanks to Audrey Reeves for assuring me the future is bright. I thank Annie, Hannah, Max, and

Vanessa for being there. Thanks to my feminist fellow traveler and HLP Aiko Holvikivi for everything.

And, finally, I thank my family: my dad, Lorne; my mom, Meg; and my sister, Carrie. None of this would've been possible without out. I'm so grateful for all your love, support, and understanding. I can't wait to see you soon.

Abbreviations

ABF	Army Benevolent Fund (now The Soldiers' Charity)
AFSC	American Friends' Service Committee
BftB	Birdies for the Brave
BLESMA	Blind and Limbless Ex-Servicemens' Association
CND	Campaign for Nuclear Disarmament
CP	CodePink
DoD	US Department of Defense
DVA	Disabled Veterans of America
GWoT	global war on terror
H4H	Help for Heroes
IAVA	Iraq and Afghanistan Veterans' Association
MFAW	Military Families Against the War
MFSO	Military Families Speak Out
MoD	UK Ministry of Defence
OP	Operation Gratitude
PA	Peace Action
PSW	Peace and Social Witness UK
RBL	Royal British Legion
StT	Support the troops
StWC	UK Stop the War Coalition
UfPJ	United for Peace and Justice
VfP	Veterans for Peace UK
VFW	Veterans of Foreign Wars
WBC	Westboro Baptist Church
WILPF UK	Women's International Leave for Peace and Freedom UK

1

Introduction

Today is the expression of a wide felt, but so far unstated feeling that we need to do something . . . In my parents' generation normal people got involved in war—horribly in many cases . . . We all knew the suffering of war. Then after WWII war became, once again, a professional activity for a small number of dedicated people, often far from the public eye and mind. Iraq & Afghanistan have changed that. Large numbers of British forces have become involved in ferocious struggles far from home.

—Help for Heroes, 2007b

Sometimes they said: I support the troops but not the war. Or: Do you think we should be over there? Which is such a dumb question, Tanner, the Army captain, would think. Soldiers don't make those decisions . . . They bitch and moan, sure. But when the call comes, they pack their bags and go, knowing they may not come back. But Tanner doesn't say all that. Instead, he responds this way: "Oh, so you were over there? Because you said, 'We.' Because, I mean, I know I was over there."

—"Love the Troops, Hate the War," CodePink, 2010

During the wars in Iraq and Afghanistan, citizens of the invading states regularly thanked military personnel for serving in wars the citizens opposed. And almost no one thought it was odd.

One million people marched in London on February 15, 2003, to oppose the impending invasion of Iraq by the United States and coalition forces (BBC 2003). Antiwar rallies were held in at least 150 US cities the same day (Chan 2003). In the United Kingdom, majority support for the war lasted for only about a year; approval for military action fell below 50 percent in July 2005 and never recovered (Dahlgreen 2015). On the day of the invasion, US

Support the Troops. Katharine M. Millar, Oxford University Press. © Oxford University Press 2022.
DOI: 10.1093/oso/9780197642337.003.0001

support for the war in Iraq was 72 percent; it fell to 48 percent by November 2004 (Gallup 2010). By August 2005, a narrow majority of Americans consistently reported a belief that the invasion of Iraq had been a mistake (Gallup 2010). By 2014, 56 percent of UK citizens felt the war in Afghanistan "had not been worthwhile" (Chambers 2014). In the US, at the end of 2011, surveys found that though only 36 percent of Americans approved of the war in Iraq, while 41 percent approved of the war in Afghanistan (Peter 2016).

That same survey found that 76 percent of Americans reported thanking military personnel for their service (Peter 2016). This meant that "up to about a third of Americans thanked members of the military for volunteering to fight wars that they opposed" (Peter 2016). A later survey estimated that 90 percent of Americans had thanked active or retired members of the military for their service (Haddad 2019). Similar results hold in the UK. Though the wars in Iraq and Afghanistan were highly unpopular, nine in ten surveyed Britons voiced their support for the military personnel who served on those deployments (Gribble et al. 2020). The most remarkable aspect of these figures—that some substantial portion of Americans and Britons thanked people for fighting a war they opposed—is that it was utterly unremarkable at the time. Professional sporting events included tributes to military personnel (Fischer 2014), uniformed military personnel were applauded on airplanes (Bacevich 2005), and support the troops (StT) yellow ribbons adorned everything from trees to license plates to credit cards (Stahl 2009).

Though popular valorization of the military is strongly associated with the United States, the notion of "automatic" support for the troops is common elsewhere. Public commemorations of military sacrifice are increasingly visible in India (Parashar 2018). The formation of civil society organizations expressing solidarity with military personnel and their families (often with the yellow ribbon associated with the US armed forces) are emerging in Germany (Initiative Solidaritat 2018). Political discourses in Italy, France, and Denmark also increasingly frame civil-military relations in terms of support, obligation, and recognition owed to soldiers. Canada (Mirlees 2015; Richler 2012) and Australia (Soldier On n.d.; News.com.au 2015) fairly directly mirror the language and practice of supporting the troops. StT was a routinized component of British public discussions of Iraq and Afghanistan (Basham 2013; Dixon 2012). Many pro-military practices—such as "Armed Forces Day," an annual military awards, and the honoring of military personnel at sporting events—have become commonplace (Dixon 2012; Kelly 2012).

Even nongovernmental peace organizations, activist networks, and social movements, such as Pax Christi and the Stop the War Coalition, adopted the language of "supporting the troops" as a means of communicating their broader opposition to war. State officials frequently reference the phrase in public statements and policy launches. Militaries have developed "partnerships" with nongovernmental "support the troops" organizations, and engaged in active public relations campaigns encouraging communities to support "their military" (Whitehouse.gov 2012a; Armed Forces Covenant, n.d.).

Since its initial mass popularization in the United States during the First Gulf War, "supporting the troops" has become increasingly socially prevalent and transnationalized. In the US and UK, it was—and is—a broadly circulating form of common sense. Supporting the troops while opposing "the war" appears not only patriotic and moral but also logical.[1] Failing to support the troops, either through active opposition or a lack of overt supportive actions, is not only offensive but also potentially traitorous. It is obvious that, in the context of an unpopular war, people would, and should, support the troops.

Why?

Problematique

This book interrogates the political work performed by "support the troops" discourses and practices. It examines support the troops in the specific context of the US and UK during the early stages (2001–2010) of the so-called global war on terror and as a broader reflection of civil-military relations in contemporary liberal democracies.

What does it mean to "support the troops"? What do support the troops discourses and practices tell us about the relationship between the war, military service, and citizenship in liberal democracies? In other words: How is supporting the troops in a war you oppose produced as mandatory common sense? What are the consequences of that for democratic dissent and the use of force?

I argue that the normative structure of civil-military relations in the US and UK, as well as Western liberal democracies more generally,[2] is undergoing a process of transformation. Seemingly stable understandings of the relationship between military service, citizenship, and gender norms—particularly idealized notions of masculinity—are being unsettled by changes in the nature of warfare conducted by liberal democracies. This is producing a diffuse sense of uneasiness about the meaning of what it means to be a "good" citizen, "good" man, and "good" person in a context where neither war nor military service easily aligns with existing cultural myths about wartime obligations and collective sacrifice. "Supporting the troops" is an attempt to grapple with the gendered civilian anxieties regarding "good" citizenship and "good" masculinity in an era characterized by professional armed forces and (for people in the US and UK) distant conflicts. The unthinkability of an alternative position, of not supporting the troops, is the heart of this book—and a central challenge of contemporary politics.

Support the troops discourses, I will demonstrate, articulate several multilayered, ostensibly apolitical representations of society's implication in the collective use of force. StT shifts the locus of normative citizenship (and, with it, normative public masculinity) from the now uncommon experience of military service to the mandatory and easily accessible practice of support for the troops. Support is naturalized as the sine qua non of normative masculinity and, with it, political membership. It is implicitly though powerfully produced as both the foundational premise of the political community and its constitutive relational principle. To be in political community is to support the troops.

As a result, supporting the troops also serves to limit antiwar dissent that is recognized as socially intelligible and politically legitimate to the opposition of particular wars, rather than all wars or the underlying necessity of military support itself. In doing so, StT transforms wartime questions of political and normative legitimacy from the killing of distant others abroad to the maintenance of the appropriate structure of civil-military relations—and corresponding performance of gendered citizenship. In doing so, supporting the troops plays a distinct and important role in naturalizing the violence of the liberal state and transnational liberal order.

Context

This section outlines the cultural, ideological, and structural context— namely, a transformation in normative understandings of gender, citizenship, and liberal civil-military relations—that informs the analysis of the book. It is essential to understanding the politics and significance of supporting the troops and the argument outlined above.

Declining Military Service

Supporting the troops exists in a context where a small minority of the citizenry actively serves in the armed forces. In the United States, less than 0.5 percent of the population is in the armed forces (Eikenberry and Kennedy 2013). In the United Kingdom, the percentage of serving military personnel as a proportion of the overall population is even lower—approximately 0.25 percent (Office for National Statistics 2014; Library of the House of Commons 2014). The casualties of the wars in Iraq and Afghanistan—over 7,000 US and 600 UK military personnel (iCasualties. org)—are borne by a very small proportion of society. As a result, the public demonstrations of appreciation for the armed forces that typified the wars in Iraq and Afghanistan—and persist, though less visibly, in the US and UK to the present—are not necessarily grounded in an understanding of military practice or modern warfare (McCartney 2010). The surge in the social visibility and general popularity of the military comes at a time when distant "wars of choice" have reduced the collective experience of conflict.

This is not particularly unusual. Citizens of liberal democracies don't go to war anymore (see Blachford 2020). This is not to suggest that liberal democracies no longer go to war, there are many in recent memory.[3] But in an era of professional militaries and geographically distant conflicts, the vast majority of citizens of Western liberal democraciesonly indirectly interact with the military (Haltiner 2006).[4] Of the 88 states qualified as "free" in the 2018 Freedom House report (an imperfect approximation of liberal democracy, to be sure) (Foweraker and Krzaric 2000), 66 lack conscription (CIA World Factbook n.d.). Many former British colonies, in part due to the anti-conscription legacy of the English Civil War (Asal et al. 2017), have imposed a draft only during wartime emergencies.

The end of the Cold War saw a sharp drop in conscription, particularly within Europe. National service remains in only 10 democratic European states (Poutvaara and Wagener 2011; Sheehan 2009).[5] In most of these states, little of the eligible population is called for service, and even fewer of those conscripts participate in conflict. Military sociologists and policymakers often refer to this situation, with concern, as evidence of a growing "civil-military gap" (see Rahbek-Clemmenson 2012; Cornish 2012). Even Israel, which continues to employ conscription, has seen an increasing disconnect between the image of the heroic Israeli male combat soldier and the more mundane experiences that make up Israeli military service (Sasson-Levy

2008). In conventional national security terms, declining rates of military literacy and participation are a problem for strategic readiness and the rational institutional governance of the armed forces.

Military Service, Masculinity, and Citizenship

The decline of popular military service in wartime is also, however, a problem from the perspective of gendered notions of wartime obligation and ideals of normative citizenship. Both policy concerns over a civil-military "gap" and the pervasive claims to support the troops convey a subtle sense that society—and particularly able-bodied men—might somehow be "letting down" the military (and through it, the nation-state). Citizens of the US and UK seem to be expressing a latent concern that they are doing something wrong. The impulse to support the troops, therefore, should be read in the context of widely circulating and enduring Western cultural myths that teach us war is the preserve of all citizens, and if called, everyone ought to serve.

This is a central tenet of modern political membership: during wartime all "good" citizens—particularly "good" men—serve in the armed forces. Within liberal political traditions, this is often narrated in the idiom of obligation. In exchange for citizenship and its accompanying civil and political rights, and in accordance with the expectations of normative masculinity, citizens are obliged to serve in the armed forces during wartime. I refer to this general idea throughout the book as the "liberal military contract." The politics of this contract and its fraught relationship to liberal democracy are examined in Chapter 2.

For the moment, it is sufficient to observe that mass military service and (liberal) democracy "grew up together." Supporting the troops is a reaction to a slow transformation in an assemblage of gender norms, citizenship, and civil-military relations that dates to (at least) the mass "nation in arms" of the French Revolution. Marked by the *Lévee en masse* ("national" conscription), the Revolution saw a devolution of the burdens of warfare from professional long-service armies to society as a whole. This societal mobilization was based on nationalistic ideals and membership in the *patrie*; military service was exchanged for democratic citizenship and civil and political rights (Tilly 1995). The institutional structure of the mass army expanded across Europe throughout the nineteenth and early twentieth centuries, bringing with it the ideology of nationalism and concessions of citizenship required to legitimize mass conscription.

The transformation of civil-military relations toward a "citizen" military culminated in the First World War, when across Europe, "hordes of eager young men . . . flocked to volunteer and 'do their bit' before the fighting ended" (Bond, 1998, 96). By World War II, military service had been firmly entrenched as a normative obligation of democratic citizenship. The onset of industrial age "total war" involved all of society in war, through preparation, supply, or participation in battle (Overy 2005). Military service was "an experience shared by millions" (Sheehan 2008, 19–20). For the US and UK, the current state normative structure of civil-military relations stands in stark contrast to the mythical "good" wars of the past (see Adams 1994, 1998; Paris 2000), particularly World Wars I and II, when "men were men," and society pulled together as a whole. The "appropriate" relationship between society and the armed forces is one of shared sacrifice. Non-serving civilians, in the contemporary model of decreased/ing military service, are implicitly presented as shirking their obligations of political membership.

These obligations are gendered and gendering. The (ostensibly) universal citizen-soldier does not describe any given member of the polity. Instead, as put by a UK army major in an article arguing for the social benefits of national service, the military makes spoiled "mummy's boys" into "strong men" (Brown 2015). The universalized citizen-subject liable for military service was historically male and, in contemporary political thought and discourse, is masculine. The development of the mass army ensured that the majority of the male population engaged in state-sanctioned violence (or, in the case of volunteer militaries, were liable for military service). Military service was the "sacred obligation" of the male citizen—and the "right to impose it was the main source and expression of the state's legitimacy" (Sheehan 2008, 179). The ability and willingness to perpetrate violence became a requirement of masculine citizenship, wherein "the ultimate test of men's political obligation is his willingness to give up his life in defence of the state" (Sasson-Levy 2003, 322).

Women, in contrast, were assigned "support" roles, such as caretaking, reproduction of "the nation," symbolic potential victimhood, and so forth. They are a femininized "Other" to militarized masculinity. These historical empirical regularities have been transformed into stereotypical cultural narratives—frequently blurred and contradicted in practice, but ideologically powerful all the same. This paternalistic, heteronormative conceptual relationship is captured by Jean Bethke Elshtain's heuristic imagines of "the 'Just Warrior,' the male protector of home and hearth, and the 'Beautiful Soul,' the female innocent whose purity is to be defended" (cited in Kinsella 2005, 253–54; original Elshtain 1987). Modern liberal states rest upon a gendered/ing civil-military divide, between a protective, masculine military and dependent, feminine civil society. Civilian status is framed in terms of feminized/ing tropes of dependence and vulnerability and cast as inferior to military service. Civilian-ness sits uneasily with claims or aspirations to normative public masculinity (Millar 2019b).

Disconnect Between Gendered Military Expectations and Contemporary Service

These normative heteronormative gender roles do important work in legitimating the liberal military contract. When examined critically, there is nothing particularly liberal, nor necessarily democratic, about an arrangement wherein citizens are obligated to kill and die for the state. The notion of a gendered/ing "military contract" is awkward. It exists in tension with liberal ideas of, nonviolent conflict resolution, individual autonomy, and civic rights against arbitrary violence.[6] The masculinist (and heteronormative, middle class, White, cisnormative) constitution of the universal citizen-subject similarly belies liberal commitments to formal equality. Though the recourse to volunteer militaries has been posited by contemporary liberal thinkers—perhaps paired, in emergencies, with a conscript lottery—as alleviating the immediate problem of state coercion of individuals (Forrester 2014; Walzer 1970), it does not address the underlying normative obligation of service (Basham 2018). Rather, the duty of military service—owed to the political community—is taken on by a small group of volunteers.

The makeup of this small group of volunteers has also undergone changes relevant to understanding the politics of supporting the troops. The decline in overall military participation must be understood in the context of moves toward more inclusive service. Throughout the twentieth century, military service—both in conscript and professional armed forces—became a crucial means for marginalized groups, including women and sexual and racial minorities, to demonstrate belonging in the political community and demand recognition as citizens (Krebs 2006; Bristol and Stur 2017). The end of racial segregation in the US armed forces in 1948 is an important case in point. In the US, the contractual burden of the military during the global war on terror was/is disproportionately borne by the working and middle classes, those from rural backgrounds and poorer areas, and (with year-to-year variation), Black Americans, particularly Black women (Chalabi 2017; Lutz 2008; Melin 2016). Consequently, with the increasing inclusion of women in combat roles (Bradner 2015; BBC 2016) and the opening of military service to lesbian, gay, bisexual, trans*, and queer people in many liberal democracies (Sennott 2010), we can see this gendered, masculinized normative obligation of service further universalized and extended. The obligation to serve in the armed forces in wartime now potentially ideologically implicates anyone who would seek to be identified as a "good citizen." The duty of service remains masculine, but now (at least potentially) pertains to everyone.

The differential distribution of sacrifice along axes of gender, sexuality, class, race, and, often, region and nation of origin (Kelly et al. 2010; UK MoD 2014) violates democratic expectations of equality (Pateman 2007). The move toward a volunteer military, at the same time, does not extinguish cultural, ideological, and affective investments in the obligation(s) of all citizens to defend the whole. Indeed, moves toward open and inclusive service—and explicitly diverse militaries—implicitly underlines the non-service in wartime of those who more closely approximate the White, cis, heteromasculine citizen-soldier ideal. In the UK, non-officer recruits are typically from working-class backgrounds in disadvantaged areas explicitly targeted by the armed forces and are often under the age of 18 (Agerholm 2017). In 2012, one in ten UK military personnel were born overseas: 2,200 from Fiji, 3,680 Nepalese Gurkhas, and 8,505 soldiers from 38 different states (Beckford 2012).

In other words, the visible, voluntary military service of historically marginalized, minoritized, and/or feminized groups might be understood as making the non-service of those groups most proximate to the universal Western normative citizen, those with White masculine social privilege, somehow, ineffably, more pointed. Supporting the troops is thus articulated in a context of multilayered and intersecting anxieties relating to gender—but also race, ethnicity, sexuality, and the nature of the overall political community. Civilian anxieties are thus activated not only around the sense of doing something wrong—by not serving—but also around challenged privilege, insofar as a valorized institution (the military) and profession (soldiering) come to look less, in its public representations and aspirations, like the previously normative (and hegemonic) White heteromasculine citizen.

Overall, supporting the troops is produced in a context of disconnect between the idealized, mass-participatory liberal democratic military contract and the contemporary experience of volunteer service, distant wars, and quotidian normality at "home." This disconnect is characterized by a generalized, gendered "civilian anxiety" of non-service in wartime (Millar 2019b)—and the failure to live up to cultural myths. StT speaks to a broader set of questions regarding contemporary liberal democratic civil-military relations left radically uninterrogated by popular political discourse and academic inquiry. What happens when "we" no longer serve?[7] What does it mean to be a good citizen—and, indeed, good man and/or masculine subject—absent military service and/or war participation? How do "we" relate to the collective violence of the whole?

These questions, as well as the conditions that give rise to them, are crucial to understanding the compulsory and obvious nature of "supporting the troops" even—or particularly—in the context of a war one might oppose. I read "supporting the troops" as both an exigent political discourse of the US and UK experiences of the early global war on terror and as a lens upon the broader, underlying relationship between gender, citizenship, and violence within liberalism. As I argue throughout the book (and in Chapter 2 in particular), supporting the troops goes beyond what we might typically think of as militarism (i.e., the undesirable valorization of the military and military values within broader society). Rather, it actively constitutes normative citizenship, the boundaries of the political, and the socially intelligible. In so doing, supporting the troops, as a form of solidaristic martiality, makes the (liberal) political community.

The following section gives a brief overview of the logic of inquiry that I use to interrogate and interpret the politics of supporting the troops throughout the book. Those more interested in the substance of StT may wish to skip to the plan of the book, which signposts the development of my analysis and argument in more detail.[8]

Logic of Inquiry

This section outlines the logic of inquiry that underpins this book. It covers the broad conceptualization of "supporting the troops" as a social phenomenon, questions of method and sourcing, and the selection of the US and UK as the central sites of empirical analysis.

Point of Departure

I understand "supporting the troops" as a series of productive and pervasive discourses. Discourse not only provides a means of conveying knowledge and interpreting social reality—such as the liberal civil-military divide—but also actively *creates* it (Milliken 1999; Foucault 1984) through regularized patterns of communication, such as language, symbols, social practice, and so on (Edkins 1999; Foucault 1976a). It is an expression and working of power: diffuse, decentralized, and "productive of meanings, subject identities, their interrelationships, and a range of imaginable conduct" (Doty 1993, 229). Discourse constitutes broadly circulating notions of what is real (e.g., the state), legitimate (e.g., state-authorized warfare), and socially intelligible (e.g., heroic masculine sacrifice). It conditions social possibility not by rendering certain actions, such as standing at an intersection with a sign reading "Don't Support the Troops," materially impossible but by rendering them incommensurate with the current bounds of tasteful and recognizably political actions.

I pay particular attention to how these discourses are gendered. They communicate important, implicit understandings of normative gender roles—particularly masculinity—and their relationship to violence. As with most complex social phenomenon, supporting the troops is not uniformly gendered, nor does gender account for all of its political effects. While I employ feminist analysis throughout the book, gender (and sexuality, race, class, etc.) appears empirically only when most salient to the argument.

I take StT seriously as affective, sincere, and often very personal expressions of concern for and solidarity with serving military personnel. For many people, particularly those with friends and loved ones in the military, StT practices are deeply meaningful (Wegner 2021; Marsical 1991). In this study, however, I do not examine the individual intentionality of specific exhortations and practices of StT (i.e., what a person "really means"). Instead, I examine the way StT overall, as a discursive formation, serves to circulate and contest normative understandings of gendered citizenship and civil-military relations. Similarly, I attend less to the "intended" meaning of silences, or failures to explicitly articulate support for the troops, than the contextual meanings discursively projected onto such silences. In this way, I conceptualize "supporting the troops" broadly, as a form of martial discourse that (re)produces and negotiates the role of force in making the political community.

Method

To get at the politics of StT empirically, I employ a thematically organized discourse analysis of support the troops discourses in the United States and the United Kingdom across the initial phases of the global war on terror in Iraq and Afghanistan (2001–2010). The method allows for the consideration of a large volume of texts—and the identification of broad discursive patterns—within which to contextualize more specific interpretive claims (see Taylor and Ussher 2001).[9] For more details, please refer to Appendices 1 and 2.

In total, I examined an original corpus of approximately 9,000 pages of text and 3,258 paragraph units. The assembled documents are texts produced for public dissemination by national support the troops organizations (five pro-military charities per country case); peace and antiwar organizations (five NGOs per country case); the mass media; politicians; and government and military officials.[10] The texts were selected in accordance with the general principle (Hansen 2006; Weldes 2006) that robust and critical discourse analysis should be broadened beyond officially "authoritative" texts likely to participate in dominant discourses (e.g., policy documents and major newspapers). Consequently, the antiwar groups were included to avoid painting a falsely homogenous picture of the support the troops discursive formation and ensure potential contestation of the politics of the troops is captured within the analysis. While the inclusion of a different organization in any particular category would slightly alter the findings, the selected sources selected provide a useful snapshot of the discursive formation by representing the public culture of supporting the troops.

As with all discourse analysis, and appropriate to my interpretive argument, the selected materials do not capture all possible forms of resistance to the dominant politics of StT. Instead, they capture the politically salient and socially pervasive themes and patterns of meaning articulated within the discursive formation. Given the tendency of marginal voices and positions to be "reappropriated, ignored, and subverted . . . [within] the eventual hegemony of particular tropes" (Rao 2014, 202), it is reasonable to believe these texts convey the most significant contestations of StT that existed at the time.

Support the troops discourse had not, until this study, been the subject of a large thematic discourse analysis. It was instead examined in a more ad hoc and illustrative (though still insightful) manner (see, e.g., Stahl 2009). I assembled my large textual corpus to address this gap, identify overarching themes within the discursive formation as a whole and, in so doing, offer a "proof of concept" for the complex and political nature of StT. Given this volume of documents, working solely from the bottom up, in the manner of grounded theory, was impractical and risked missing key patterns. Deductive analysis alone, conversely, similar to content analysis, is limited in its ability to account for more implicit meanings and contestations. Using iterative, thematically organized discourse analysis enabled me to examine a large corpus of texts with an attentiveness to more contingent, complex, and subtle meanings at work in specific discursive articulations (see Taylor and Ussher 2001). The application of this method to two country cases (the US and UK) over a 10-year period (2001–2010) covering an array of social actors (media, government, and civil society) makes my work the most comprehensive treatment of support the troops discourses to date.

In practical terms, I first analyzed the texts according to a system of descriptive themes capturing more explicit (i.e., literal) uses of support the troops discourse. These first-cut themes were derived from my initial curiosities, informed by the literature, regarding broad patterns within the discursive formation. I interrogated the texts following a journalistic logic, asking: Who supports the troops? Why? Against what threats or dangers? How? The answers to these questions (e.g., people support the troops out of a sense of obligation, or to support the war, or to end the war) were derived from the texts themselves. I therefore moved from the initial organizing themes to more inductively derived categories requiring interpretation. For instance, identifying the reasons provided for supporting the troops typically requires reading the specific exhortation in the context of both the broader document and an awareness of specific tropes common to StT. The initial thematic interrogation of the text, organized using the qualitative analysis software NVivo, gave the empirics a rudimentary structure.

Next, I used the patterns revealed by my first-cut analysis of explicit questions to see key, more implicit subthemes—such as the persistence of liberal notions of soldiering obligation, and an absence of calls for conscription—that undergird the complex politics of StT. These themes were pulled out for more detailed, substantive interpretation, supported by a close-reading of key texts. The specific quotations analyzed throughout the book are exemplars of the overall, socially circulating discourse(s), conveying patterns of meaning often left implicit.

Paying attention to implicit meanings enables us to move from considering only the literal content of a text to its representation of underlying assumptions, normative structures, and significant silences. Given that the commonsensical nature of support the troops is the central question, even paradox, of the book, close analysis of implicit meanings, as well as their constitution of social and political reality, is essential. It is not possible to see, let alone interrogate, the politics of supporting the troops without it.

Cases

The United States and the United Kingdom during the initial phases of the global war on terror (2001–2010) were selected as the cases for the examination of the politics of StT on the basis of "political pregnancy" (Hansen 2006).[11] This principle holds that for critical, interpretive work, cases should be selected on the basis of their essentiality (which may be analytical or political) to the project according to "questions of (discursively constituted) influence" (Hansen 2006, 76). The cases are meant to be so influential the project would make no sense without them and also possess substantial political stakes. The US and UK "highlight more general characteristics of the [issue] in question" (Flyvbjerg 2006, 232): the relationship between supporting the troops and the underlying transformation in the gendered structure of liberal civil-military relations. They are empirically paradigmatic cases (see Della Porta 2012, 208, 216). The US and the UK were also selected on the basis of their (geo)political/critical importance: the conditions of political possibility for war within these states is of global significance.

The inclusion of the UK also sidesteps the US centrism of a good deal of contemporary scholarship on Western civil-military relations. This US-centric work has an implicit tendency to posit the US as exceptional—as exceptionally "bad," exceptionally "militaristic," or simply exceptionally powerful—in a manner that belies the entanglement of these exceptional practices with liberalism and the production of political community itself. The pairing also highlights transnational aspects of the StT, particularly with respect to what McCartney (2010, 426) calls the "transatlantic gaze": a tendency in the United Kingdom to explicitly refer to the United States as a model for relations between society and the armed forces.

The US and UK offer clear manifestations of supporting the troops, situated in a context of declining military participation, gendered anxieties, and distant conflicts shared by a variety of liberal democracies. The material and cultural power of Anglosphere militaries, globally and within recent coalition warfare, have led to a transnational diffusion of the Anglo-European "warrior" model of heroic masculine soldier-citizenship across contexts (Enloe 2007; Duncanson 2013, x). This suggests that though the explicit politics (and visibility) of supporting the troops varies from context to context, the insights generated by examining the transformation of gendered civil-military relations in the US and UK, as particularly influential empirical sites, are analytically generalizable.

Plan of the Book

The book begins with the primary conceptual chapter (Chapter 2). It provides a critical account of the relationship between gender, violence, and liberalism. I outline liberalism's innocent account of itself, as pacific, rational, universal, and so forth, and the role the corresponding concept of "militarism" plays in legitimating and upholding that story. I also introduce the notion of the "liberal military contract": all good men should defend the liberal state in war time. I then unpack the paradox of this contract—that to guarantee the protection of the liberal state one must kill or die for the state—and the ways a binary account of gender and sexuality helps smooth this over. The balance of the chapter introduces the book's central analytic—a discursive conception of the military that enables me to connect the gendered obligation to commit violence (i.e., the contract) with the making of liberal political community. This approach brings together the "politics" of military violence (i.e., war) enacted and contested in the formal public sphere with the bounding of the "political" (i.e., the underlying social and political order) via solidaristic violence. As the balance of the book demonstrates, supporting the troops operates at the intersection of politics and the political. It simultaneously reinforces and contests the nexus of masculinity, citizenship, and violence within liberal order.

Chapter 3 places the emergence of the troops in the historical context of US and UK civil-military relations. The "troops" first emerged in the context of the US invasion of Vietnam. StT was an attempt to generate support for the war effort at a time when conventional narratives of mass participation or heroic masculine soldiering were neither plausible nor resonant. The troops then became a staple of US discourse—though one that was relatively unchallenging through the First Gulf War, due to the limited and relatively popular nature of the intervening conflicts. In the UK, the military declined as an institution of popular veneration after World War II. The end of national service and the controversial martial violence in Northern Ireland lowered the social status of soldering. The Falklands/Malvinas conflict, however, followed by the First Gulf War, was characterized by an upswell in the social visibility and popularity of the military. It marked the emergence of "the troops" in the UK lexicon. Across the twentieth century, US and UK civil-military relations shifted from a suspicion of standing armed forces to the veneration of military service as a key component of citizenship and masculinity. This produced an expectation of apoliticized support for the troops, seen in the First Gulf War, that was then reinforced and challenged by the contested politics of the global war on terror.

Chapter 4 picks up with a detailed empirical examination of support the troops discourses and practices in the US and UK from 2001–2010. I examine constructions of (a) who is expected to support the troops; (b) why people are meant to support the troops; (c) how people express their support for the troops; and (d) the primary factors that cause the troops to need support. The dominant US narrative encourages everyone to support the troops out of a sense of obligation (underscored by strong support for the war) against, alternatively, the government or the uncontrollable social outcomes of war. Support is typified by, conversely, a contestation of conflict or the provision of material goods. The UK narrative is characterized by an expectation that everyone is obligated to support the troops against the government, expressed by calls for an end to war. Each element of these narratives, however, is subject to contestation by a range of social actors. The typical narratives—reflecting some key aspects of gendered notions of liberal martial obligation—do not reflect a stable consensus, but rather an ongoing process of negotiation and fragmentation of the meaning of supporting the troops.

Chapter 5 begins my detailed examination of the politics of supporting the troops. It looks at the meanings attributed to the troops as a distinct cultural figure. The troops are predominantly characterized by their collective nature, which precludes "them" from being reduced to existing, related figures of war such as the military, veteran, or soldier. This groupness means they may take on, or refuse, the meanings typically associated with the soldier (e.g., masculine bravery), the veteran (e.g., vulnerability) through discursive associations or contrast. The troops' groupness also enables them to incorporate all possible substantive identities (e.g., gender, sexuality, race, class, etc.) political orientations within the social relations of support. The troops, moreover, are not figured as actively involved in the violence of war. Instead, they are constructed as dependent on society for their well-being. As a result, support for the troops, rather than conflict legitimacy, becomes the central normative concern of war.

Chapter 6 continues with the politics of supporting the troops, shifting slightly to examine contestation over the meaning of "support." I find that dominant contractual, stereotypically liberal notions of support for the troops—that is, individuals "owe" the troops support—fail to reconcile cultural myths and expectations of masculine martial service with the contemporary experience of conflict. Liberal StT discourses demonstrate a clear "gendered civilian anxiety": a sense that non-serving civilians are doing something wrong. The balance of the chapter identifies two alternative logics of support within broader StT discourse. The first reflects a communitarian logic of martial obligation, characterized by fidelity to a holistic form of political community and war participation shared by all. The second reflects an altruistic logic of apoliticized obligation, wherein (ostensibly) private individuals support the troops as a form of charity, discursively divorced from the context of conflict. In both cases, the alternative supportive logics work to (re)masculine supportive civilians through a gendered process of contrast and association with both the troops and the hypermasculine combat soldier. Together, these three logics do not supplant the mythical martial contract but amend it. Support, not military service, is now constituted as the hallmark of normative masculinity and, with it, citizenship.

Chapter 7 examines the relationship between supporting the troops and the political—the foundations of social order. When the basis of normative citizenship has shifted, how does the polity hang together? I argue social relations of gendered, violent solidarity are as important to making up the political community as externally oriented dynamics of exclusion and enmity. Masculinized martial solidarity bounds the liberal polity and, when executed "correctly," redeems the normative status of the liberal polity. The chapter also examines the implications of StT for the warfighting of liberal polities abroad. I demonstrate that the gendered, political obligation of solidarity transcends the territorial boundaries of the nation-state: support can be projected or imposed as a continuity of affinity and/or imperialism. I read transnational martial solidarity across the West as expressing not only liberal but also colonial, frequently White solidarity in the context of the global war on terror. Support is also demanded from civilians abroad but on unequal terms. For those whose racialization as "Other" equates to a presumption of suspicion or enmity, support is expected, but even actual martial service is not always sufficient for the reciprocal recognition of rights and political belonging. Support covers up the continued reliance of transnational liberal order on racialized martial sacrifice.

Chapter 8 brings together the two components of discursive martiality—the articulation of formal politics and constitution of the political—to examine what supporting the troops means for dissent. I examine the use of StT discourse by a variety of US and UK antiwar and peace NGOs. The chapter works through a variety of ways the idea of "politics" is empirically related to the expectation to StT. StT itself is represented as apolitical or beyond politics. Politics in turn, is attached to attempts to debate or contest the wars in Iraq and Afghanistan, whereas war support is naturalized as moral and obvious. Meaningful democratic debate is foreclosed, while unreflective support is lauded as an obligation of normative, gendered political membership. StT transfers the masculinized soldier's obligation to refrain from politics to the masculinized supportive citizen. As a result, pragmatic antiwar invocations of "support the troops, bring them home," though logical in attempting to get a fair hearing for their message, end up reifying the idea that the troops must be supported. Instances of resistance—confrontations of the naturalized assumption that one must/does support the troops—are written off as offensive instances of apolitical bad taste. Socially intelligible opposition to the use of force is constrained, as martial obligation makes it possible to contest one war, on behalf of the troops, but not the practice of war itself.

Finally, in the Conclusion, I make the case that a politics committed to opposing liberal wars abroad—and martial forms of liberal violence "at home"—must refuse to support the troops. This is not about denying material support or empathy for individual members of the armed forces; rather, it is about confronting the assumption that, no matter what, *we* must support the troops. StT discourses obscure the complicity of liberal society in racialized, neo-imperial wars abroad by shifting moral concern to a matter of internal loyalty and solidarity.

2

The Military, Gender, and Liberal Political Obligation

Supporting the troops (StT) is produced within a specific ideological, social, and political context: liberal democracies with professional armed forces fighting distant conflicts. Understanding the distinct politics of StT requires understanding the broader politics of the armed forces, as well as martial violence, within liberalism. This chapter sets out conceptual critique upon which the book is founded and the analytical approach upon which it proceeds.

Providing an account of the military within liberalism is, perhaps unsurprisingly, difficult. With few exceptions, academics (and not some small number of practitioners) "imagine that any military force simply exists, ready to be deployed at will, whenever military commanders and their civilian superiors wish them to be deployed" (Enloe 2015, 6). Popular discourses, often framed in the academic literature in terms of militarism, in contrast, emphasize the normative values associated with the military—bravery, masculinity, self-sacrifice, public service, and so forth—without engaging with the military's central mandate: to use violence against distant others. This bifurcated understanding of the military elides the fact that (a) members of the military are part of the "body politic" with their own claims to rights and security, and (b) members of "the public" are socially and political implicated in the state's acts of violence. The tensions produced by the military's dual status as a naturalized instrument of force and group of socially embedded individuals are largely unaddressed within either liberal political thought or popular discourse.

In this chapter, I analyze these disconnects in liberal civil-military relations and their connection to liberalism's shifting account of the relationship between politics and violence. To unpack the implications of the civil/military and politics/violence distinctions for how we understand supporting the troops, this chapter makes four analytical moves. First, I provide an overview of liberalism's "innocent," universal account of itself, examining the

Support the Troops. Katharine M. Millar, Oxford University Press. © Oxford University Press 2022.
DOI: 10.1093/oso/9780197642337.003.0002

state, citizenship, and liberalism's ostensible restraint and pacifism. This is how liberalism is supposed to work. Second, I re-narrate liberalism to demonstrate not only the ways it fails to live up to its normative and ideological promises but also, due to its reliance on gendered and racialized violence, that it cannot. I examine the dependence of liberal political orders upon externally oriented war and enmity—and the ideological elision of those same processes. Throughout, I examine militarism as a concept that reflects the shifting and complex modern relationship between politics and violence. I understand militarism, which may be an intuitive way of understanding supporting the troops, as a core component of the political operation of liberalism, key to its ideological self-legitimation, rather than an analytically independent diagnostic tool (see also Howell 2018).

Third, I examine how liberal polities are internally produced and organized through force—expressed in the need for military service. In that section, I (re)introduce the concept of the gendered liberal military contract. I highlight the importance of the political obligation to commit violence— the normative, relational, and gendered/ing terms upon which political community hangs together—to the maintenance of liberal social order. Drawing upon critical feminist and military studies, I understand the divide between ostensibly separate civil and military spheres as contested, contingent, and the effect of gendered (and sexualized) power.

Fourth, I argue for understanding the military—or martiality—as a discourse, rather than (solely) a formal institution or social relation. Understood this way, the military is the modern idiom for the expressing the organization, social relations, and gendered, sexualized, racialized obligations of statist violence. Martiality captures the solidaristic, internally oriented productive capacities of violence. The chapter thus sets up supporting the troops as a specific form of martiality. This conceptualization of StT—as a contested, political martial discourse articulating the gendered, violent "terms" of political belonging—informs the balance of the book.

Liberalism: The "Good Story"

This section outlines the "good story" of liberalism as a form of political philosophy, ideology, and mode of governance, ostensibly typified by values of liberty, equality, and progress. In recognition of the tension between classical liberal thought and the political practices of purportedly liberal societies

(Hindess 2001)—that is, the diversity of liberalism as a tradition with unclear boundaries—I treat liberalism expansively and rather schematically. To account for the self-mythologizing tendencies of liberalism(s), I refer to its broad contemporary interpretation popularly and academically, rather than the specific minutiae of any particular theorist (see Jahn 2013; Bell 2014).

Classically, liberalism is concerned with the liberty and rights of the individual—often, but not always, associated with the ownership of property—from undue interference by others (Jahn 2013). Within much of liberal thought, either the threat of physical harm or the desire to preserve property (or both) spur the creation of political community (Hobbes 1985; Locke 1980). Individuals give up (some of) their autonomy—or sovereignty—to the state in return for its protection from predatory internal violence and the anarchic international. In return, as the story of the social contract goes, individuals accept the authority of the state, notably in the form of the duty—or political obligation (Horton 2010)—to follow the law (and the implicit renunciation of the independent recourse to force) (Simmons 1981). The political community, in turn, is understood as the Hobbesian state, the Rousseauian aggregation of fellow citizens (Pateman 2007), or, more often in practice, some blurry combination of both. Institutionally, this is often expressed (though it is not a necessary feature of liberalism) (Jahn 2013) in the form of liberal democracy, typified by popular elections, constitutions, and equality before the law.

The viability of the social contract—and correspondingly limited role of the state—follows from liberalism's understanding of the individual (and potential citizen) as rational (Ashley 1989; Freeden 2009). In this view, individuals possess a shared capacity for reason deriving from the Enlightenment understanding of the human as capable of generating and communicating knowledge. The individual recognizes the social contract is in their best interest and subsequently relies on reason to preserve it. The state's capacity for coordinating/facilitating the pursuit of individual interest is often understood in terms of its role in creating the predictability (and, if necessary, coercion) required for the functioning of the capitalist free market (Jessop 2012). It also, however, supports broader values associated with liberalism, such as freedom of conscience, protections for minorities, and individual civil and political rights.

Crucially to liberalism's self-narration, this vision of the individual is universal and, often, implicitly perfectible (Hobhouse 1964). Liberalism—as a system of governance, model of politics, and set of normative principles—is therefore applicable to all peoples and societies in theory and, over time, in practice.[1] History, in this view, is "progressive, moving towards the constant improvement of the human condition through the (rational) universalization of liberal values" and institutions, which are characterized "by a long, imagined, and teleological historical trajectory moving away from the rule of kings" toward popular sovereignty (Millar 2016b, 175–76). This is where the classical version of liberalism comes into contact with the more contemporary variations with which we are familiar, characterized by values of pluralism, tolerance, and substantive commitments to equality and social justice (Freeden 2015).

There are, of course, some tensions in the principles that characterize liberalism(s) broadly. Liberal commitments, for instance, to economic productivity and the pursuit of human well-being, or individual freedom and minority protections all, to some degree, pull in different directions (Marx 1843). To account for (and obscure) these competing imperatives, liberal ideology is committed to the possibility of nonviolent conflict resolution within the polity (and, to some degree, internationally) through appeals to rationality, overarching universal values, and responsive institutions (Kant 1991; Oneal et al. 1996). Liberalism therefore relies on a hard line between the rational conduct of politics in the public sphere as the normatively sanctioned method of distributing power and resources within society and actions of violence. The use of legitimate force is reserved to the state in its mandate to enforce domestic law and defend the population against external aggressors (Hobbes 1886). The "private" use of violence is associated with anarchy, danger, irrationality, and, ultimately, the apocryphal state of nature from which liberalism offers an escape. The good story of liberalism starkly separates violence and politics. It also defines the meaning of that politics: the rational negotiation of interests within a formal public sphere.

Liberalism's Absent Military

Given this foundational separation between a formalistic public politics and violence, it is perhaps unsurprising that the liberal metanarrative of progressive improvement has, typically, had little to say about the military, civil-military relations, and the collective use of force. As argued by Howard, liberalism "regards war as an unnecessary aberration from normal international intercourse and believes that in a rational, orderly world wars would not exist: that they can be abolished" (2018, 137). The paradigmatic expression of this belief is perpetual peace (or, in its social scientific guise, democratic peace) theory, which holds due to liberal norms or democratic institutions or capitalist interdependence (or all three), citizens have an interest in avoiding military service and the economic burden of conflict (see, e.g., Choi and James 2003; Doyle 2005). In Kant's initial formulation, he argued that in a republic where citizens may be conscripted into the military, rational individuals would constrain their leaders from undertaking unnecessary wars (1991). The "liberal conscience" (Howard 2018, 11) is centrally concerned with the avoidance of war (and protection of the property of the body politic) (Moseley 2005; Cowen 2008a).

The military is naturalized as a statist instrument of defense, an implicit object of acceptable risk, and, frequently, a necessary evil. As argued by Houngnikpo, "republican and democratic states" are perceived to be "vulnerable to either being destroyed, overturned or subverted by their armies" (2010, 42). If left unchecked, the military may use its monopoly on organized violence to overthrow a legitimate civilian government; gain undue control over foreign policy, leading to unjust or ill-advised wars; and/or promote antiliberal values such as hierarchy, aggression, and/or obedience within the broader polity. This is the classic definition of militarism: the propagation of a "vast array of customs, interests, prestige, actors, and thought associated with armies and wars and yet transcending true military purposes" (Vagts 1959, 3). Militarism, in this reading, is a form of institutional pathology, wherein military leaders become inappropriately engaged in politics and supplant civilian authority over the use of force (Huntington 1981; Janowitz 1964; Lasswell 1941). Consequently, the civilian, political control of the military— in policy terms typically referred to as the democratic control of the armed forces (DCAF)—is understood as central to preserving the viability of liberal values and democratic institutions (Born 2006).

This impetus to stave off the "problem" of militarism also pertains to a broader definition of politics, wherein the values, ideology, and symbolism associated with the military come to pervade ostensibly civil liberal social life (Bacevich 2005; see also Johnson 2004; Dixon 2012). Each reading of politics (and thus militarism), insists on the separability of civil and military "spheres" (Jahn 2012)—as well as, of course, violence and politics, irrationality and rationality—as both the default setting and ethically preferential means of governing force. Though rarely an object of concerted theoretical interrogation or explicit political debate—absent points of crisis or transformation, which are often framed as pathological instances of militarism (Summers 1976)—a static conceptualization of the civil-military divide is foundational to liberalism. This divide is, as the aversion to the militaristic "leaking" of military values outside its appropriate institutional container reveals, produced as a good in and of itself. The liberal metanarrative of the progressive pacification of human relations through the preeminence of (democratic) politics over violence is subtly reliant upon a normative investment in maintaining the appropriate structure of civil-military relations. The good story of liberalism is reinforced by the "bad story" of militarism, which align in their understanding of a stark differentiation between violence and formal politics: militarism occurs when something goes wrong with the institutional and normative separation of the civil from the military.

War and the Making of Liberal Order(s)

As alluded to by that final twist of ideological legitimation, this schematic, positive narrative is not, of course, how liberalism—in any of its forms—"actually" works. The twentieth and twenty-first centuries, often hailed as moments of ideological and political ascendancy for liberal ideas and governance systems, have been "age[s] of extremes," economic inequality, conflict, racism, and colonial legacies (Hobsbawm 1994; Jabri 2006). This section, informed by critical feminist, war, and militarism studies, outlines the centrality of violence—particularly war, and social relations of enmity and exclusion—to liberalism. The good story of liberal restraint obscures the violent historical processes of colonialism perpetrated by ostensibly liberal states and justified by classical liberal thought (Cowen 2008a; on liberal imperialism, see Jahn 2005).

The seemingly universal tenets of classical liberal political theory, for instance, particularly those derived from the apocryphal "state of nature," romanticize, erase, and dehumanize Indigenous peoples in North America to establish the European model of the enlightened liberal citizen. This racialized notion of difference from non-European Others facilitated mass violence, dispossessions, and the differential application of human rights/recognition from colonialism to the present (Jahn 2016; see also Losurdo 2014; Hobson 2012). The "freeing" of the European subject depended ideologically, and frequently materially, on the exploitation, expropriation, and enslavement of peoples of color through colonial systems of ideologically legitimated systems of governance (see also Lowe 2015; Bhambra 2007; Césaire 2001). Perversely, the universalism of liberalism, when read through a racist hierarchy of "civilization"— with Europeans at the top—served to jus-tify violent colonialism and imperialism (see for instance Bell 2016; Mignolo 2011). The logic of democratic peace theory, after all, implies that force is necessary not only for defense against illiberal polities but potentially accept-able also as a means of bringing liberalism to uncivilized—irrational—peo-ples (Barkawi and Laffey 2001; Millar 2016b). The pacific self-narrative of liberalism relies upon a "willful amnesia"—supported by the reified distinc-tion between violence and politics cum war and peace and, in turn, domestic and international—of the ways the modern state system relies upon and reproduces racialized appropriation, genocide, and displacement (Krishna 2001; see also Cowen 2008b, 12).

The reliance of liberalism upon violence reveals the socially productive— and even generative—capacities of war (see Shaw 1988). Tarak Barkawi (2011), for instance, conceptualizes war as a social relation; Christine Sylvester argues for understanding war as a social institution comprised of the experiences of people, rather than states or governing elites (2011, 4). Contrary to the liberal, modern reading of war as simply destructive or dis-ruptive, war is constitutive of social order (Barkawi 2011, 705 and 710). This not to say that war is necessarily laudable or that it will produce normatively desirable forms of order. Rather, war is understood as dynamically consti-tutive of order, identity, actors, and, ultimately, social reality (Barkawi 2011; Brighton 2011; Jabri 1996, 3). As summarized by Jabri (1996, 22), "war is both a product and a constitutive part of the relationship between self (agency) and societal structures." Violence is understood as *political*—not in the sense of formal public contestation, but rather in terms of the production of social and political life, as intertwined with power, as containing meaning and tex-ture beyond intuitive ideas of physical destruction.

Take, for example, Barkawi's analysis of the legacy of the Vietnam War within American society. He suggests that the experience of Vietnam may be identified in "everything from Hollywood films to electoral politics to the subjectivities or people . . . play[ing] out in US foreign policies . . . and shap[ing] US use of force" (2011, 713). The social relations and effects of a foreign war extend across time and space to incorporate the traditional high politics of foreign policy and comparatively banal cultural practices of representation. These condition the political possibilities for future conflicts. War, in this reading, operates similarly to the feminist concept of militarization: ongoing, iterative, ideational, and material processes that implicate individuals, organizations, and social systems in martial value systems and societal preparations for war, often through normative understandings of sexuality and gender (notably, heteromasculinity) (Enloe 2004, 218–20; see also Woodward 2014; Rech 2014; Lutz 2002). War exercises social and political ordering effects beyond the physical, kinetic encounter of combat (Cowen 2008b, 8, 12).

Liberal Militarism, Liberalism and Militarism

Within this account of liberalism, then, the meaning of militarism shifts accordingly. Here, militarism—the "social and international relations of the preparation for, and conduct of, organized political violence" (Stavrianakis and Selby 2013, 3; Mann 1987)—is no longer a pathological departure from liberalism, but rather a broader social phenomenon from which liberalism is not immune. The relationship between violence and politics comes to be cast in terms of "liberal militarism," characterized by (a) the universalizing, legitimating narrative identified above; (b) an aversion to conscription; (c) a reliance on professional militaries; and (d) the entanglement of the military with domestic civil society and economic production (Edgerton 1991, 141; Wood 2007). This relationship is also framed as the obverse, noting not how liberalism has become militarized, but rather the ways militarism has been (re)forged as liberal via its entanglement with modern capitalist production and the normative separation of, again, the civil from the military (Mabee 2016, 246 and 255).

Within this account, the civil-military divide is no longer taken to be either objective or natural. The separation of the civil and military is, instead, a contingent effect of power that holds the line on the separation of violence from politics within liberal ideology (Basham 2018, 33–34). The civil-military divide is understood by feminist scholars as both discursively reinforced and experientially blurred through gendered, sexualized, classed, and racialized quotidian ideas, activities, and processes (see Enloe 2007; 2010; Khalid 2015). These range from buying military-branded foodstuffs (Tidy 2015a; Enloe 2000) to maintaining intimate and personal relationships with military personnel (Gray 2016; Hyde 2016) to negotiating military-enforced colonial and racialized (im)mobility in daily life (Ware 2014; Natanel 2016). In so doing, the liberal understanding of politics as limited to the formal public sphere is supplemented by an understanding of security (and violence) as it-self political (Wibben 2018).

We could leave the re-narration of liberalism here: liberalism is consti-tuted through a contingent but socially powerful reproduction of a natural-ized, gendered, sexualized, and racialized civil-military divide that, in turn, serves to stabilize a similarly false division between violence and politics (Baker et al. 2016). This social and ideological legitimation of the violence, as well as organization for its material conduct, is militarism (Rossdale 2019, 3–5). This is correct. It is also incomplete. It neglects one last step: the impor-tant role the concept of militarism, as itself a powered, socially and culturally embedded political construct, plays in the ideological legitimation of liberal violence(s).[2]

Consider the intuitive tendency to treat empirical activities commonly framed as militarism, such as flag waving, playing military video games, or supporting the troops as obviously militarism (see Butterworth and Moskal 2009). This is reflective of a presumption that militarism is an objective social phenomenon with an existence identifiable across contexts (Millar 2016b; see Mabee 2016). If we follow the logic of the mutual constitution of civil and military through to the end, however, we see that though these empirical practices associated with militarism have an independent material existence, their framing *as* militarism—as well as the *idea* of militarism per se—are constituted with reference to a particular understanding of violence and pol-itics, itself inflected by liberalism. This logic underlies Howell's critique of the related concept of "militarization." She argues that the processual, temporal logic of "militarization," by suggesting that people, spaces, ideas, and so forth *become* militarized, implicitly posits they were not militarized already (2018, 119). As a result, militarization reflects the assumptions of the good story of liberalism: individuals and the social are inherently peaceable prior to their contamination by militarism (119–20).

The final turn in the critical reappraisal of violence and politics within lib-eralism, then, is to observe that though it is frequently posited as an external analytic, militarism reflects and reproduces the tenets of liberalism (however assessed). From this perspective, whether or not liberal societies are really militaristic is somewhat beside the point (Millar 2020). The answer depends on the meaning (and ontology) attributed to civil/military and violence/pol-itics, concepts which are produced within liberalism. Liberal societies are militaristic, in the sense that they empirically manifest the values, practices, and social relations associated with "militarism"; they are not militaristic, in the sense that militarism is itself an ideologically loaded way of understanding the relationship between politics and violence within liberalism. The importance of militarism lies less in its ability to definitively diagnose particular dynamics of actually existing violence and politics than the way it operates vis-à-vis liberalism. The *idea* of militarism, as not only deviant but also existing at all (Millar 2016b), is politically essential to liberalism.

As expressed by Howell (2018, 121) in the concept of "martial politics," liberal societies are constituted by warlike relations domestically and abroad, expressed in the many violences of (settler) colonialism, chattel slavery, and White supremacy.[3] These tend to fall outside academic and popular understandings of militarism and, consequently, are normatively and narratively deprioritized in the evaluation of liberal violence(s)—when they are read as violence at all.[4] Militarism anchors an economy of violence that legitimates and depoliticizes the nonmilitaristic violence of the state (e.g. torture, policing, immigration detention) (Millar 2016b, 189). War is normalized as an unfortunate exception to the way liberal politics are supposed to work while serving as the underlying raison d'etre of the state itself: the security of the normative (masculine, heterosexual, cisgender, property-owning, abled-bodied, and White) citizen (Millar 2016b; Howell 2018).

Within the critical narrative, the liberal polity is exposed as reliant upon war—violent dynamics of enmity, antagonism, and exclusion—against both state-based foreign adversaries and minoritized and marginalized groups at home, often under the guise of formal politics (Howell 2018; Alves 2018; Perry 2013). Militarism functions within the good—and the critical—stories of liberalism not only as an analytic but also as a reflection of the shifting normative meanings of politics and violence. Perhaps inevitably, it also participates in the legitimation, reproduction, and invisibilization of liberal violence(s).

Liberalism, Gender, and Military Obligation

As liberalism's ideological sin eater, militarism is typically focused on identifying the (im)permissible violence of the liberal state against Others. Militarism, much like war and security, reveals an underlying of logic of opposition (Basham 2018). The re-evaluation of liberalism as dependent on the violent expropriation of racialized and colonized peoples hinges upon dynamics of enmity (Jabri 1996, 7). If nonliberal peoples are barbaric, irrational, violent, underdeveloped, and so on, then liberal polities must be rational, civilized, pacific, and so forth (Said 1978). The liberal political community is produced through violently drawn and policed boundaries between insiders/outsiders, us/them, and self/other (Walker 1990; Campbell 1992). War produces political membership negatively, through exclusion and contrast. Violence makes up the liberal community by enacting a gendered, colonial, racialized politics of who is deserving of security and who is not (Howell 2018; Basham 2018).

This account, articulated by critical feminist, war, postcolonial, and military scholars, though vitally important, is incomplete. It leaves open the question of how, once bounded, a polity hangs together and is organized. Violence is not only about risk and security but "also, and mainly, about sacrifice" (Bigo and Tsoukala 2008, 2)—of particular, gendered bodies on behalf of a group. How are people motivated to commit and risk violence for the group? What accounts for military service? After all, "to belong," as argued by Igantieff, is often taken as a synonym for safety (2010, 276 cited in Yuval-Davis 2010). Looking only at the exclusionary, oppositional dynamics of war (and militarized security) misses the intuitive importance of solidarity, positive feelings of belonging, loyalty, and duty to the practice of violence (Millar 2019b, 219).

This section examined the ways violence is *internally* constitutive of the liberal polity. I argue that participation in violence is a hidden political obligation of membership in liberal political communities, expressed (and obscured) in the tense relationship between military service, gender, and the archetypical social contract.

The Paradox of Liberal Citizenship

There is a paradox—just as contradictory as the near perpetual imperial wars of supposedly peaceful liberal states—built into the social contract (Basham 2018). Despite the liberal state's ideological dependence upon claims to pacify the polity,

> the formal political power of the liberal state is expressed in its assertion of the "national interest," . . . [enabling it to] pursue concerns higher than life. It is for "national security" and "national honor" that the state sacrifices its youth in foreign military interventions. (Brown 1998, 184)·

As Hobbes put it, in war, citizens must be called upon to "protect their protection" (cited in Westbrook 1990, 59). The critical account of liberal war above does not entirely address classical/ideological liberalism's tendency to treat the military instrumentally—as a functional appendage of the state, rather than as a group of people with their own claims to life and liberty. Logically, the realization of the state's monopoly on force requires that "citizen soldiers be prepared to kill and die" for the state (Asad 2007, 60–61). Liberal political obligations are not exhausted by the negative duty to follow the law and refrain from random violence; they also include an underlying obligation to commit violence and risk death through armed service. This is liberalism's dirty secret.

Though in practice the historical co-production of democracy and nationalism, as seen in the French Revolution's *levee on masse*, has helped culturally solidify the notion that all citizens "owe" service in wartime over the course of the nineteenth and twentieth centuries (Tilly 1995), this is a difficult circle to square for liberal ideology. It's not particularly liberal (or democratic, for that matter). Bentham attempted to frame conscription as a form of benevolent social welfare for the poor, enabling them to earn a living and contribute to society (Cowen 2008a, 190). Mill justified the military as necessary to secure internal liberties (Carter 1998, 77). Rawls, more creatively, suggested pairing a *volunteer* military with, in emergencies, a conscription lottery, to alleviate the state's coercion of individuals (and equity concerns pertaining to mandatory service) (79).

None of these solutions, however, address the paradox inherent to requiring individuals to potentially die in the service of a state whose ostensible reason for existence is the preservation of their liberty. (Indeed, even the restrictions to personal autonomy imposed by conscription violate the liberal commitments to individualism and liberty.) This contradiction is sufficiently stark that some have argued that an obligation for military service is actually incommensurate with liberalism (Westbrook 1990). In contrast to giving up some autonomy to follow the law, it is, after all, not possible to "die a little bit for the state" (Walzer 1970, 80). As with racialized imperial and colonial oppression, the good story of liberalism can't make this work.

When we consider the liberal metanarrative as a form of ideological, self-mythologizing power, however, we are able to see not only the commensurability but also the essentiality of military service to the operation of liberalism(s). Challenging the inclusive, progressive, and universal claims of liberalism to examine the particularistic, exclusionary, and gendered nature of political membership reveals that the metaphorical social contract is underwritten by a corollary bargain. It holds that "good citizens," as "good men," must accept that "to be protected from violence by the nation-state is to be exposed to the violence wielded by the nation-state" (Butler 2006, 26; Jahn 2009). Put differently, in contemporary liberal democracies, "war's injuring, killing, and dying are regarded as transgressive, regrettable, and even tragic, despite the fact that these things transpire *on purpose*" (MacLeish 2019, 275).

Parsing the Social Contract

As argued by feminist political theorists, the nature and purpose of liberal political community are bound to an "ethos of manhood" (Brown 1998, 7).[5] The rationality, autonomy, agency, and (latent) potential for violence of the contracting liberal citizen are also the characteristics associated with hegemonic constructions of Western masculinity (Pateman and Grosz 2013; Tickner 1988). Masculinity (as well, typically, as Whiteness, property ownership, heterosexuality, etc.) is a precondition for taking on the political obligations of liberal citizenship. The universalism of the liberal citizen, as an abstract ideal that theoretically pertains to all subjects—in order for the contract to logically hold as the basis for legitimate secular political authority, it must be open to all—obscures its masculinist underpinnings. It also constitutes a certain form of citizenship, again characterized by reason, self-restraint, and performance of collectively accepted public duties, as central to idealized, normative masculinity. Given the universalization of the masculine to the individual (or even human), good citizenship comes very quickly to be associated with what it means to be not only a "good" public man but also a good (public) person.

This somewhat heroic characterization of the implicitly masculine citizen relies upon negative contrast with those values, persons, and behaviors excluded from the formally political. The political and ideological coherence of the liberal state rests upon the now-familiar (contingent, yet socially powerful) division of society into gendered (as well as classed, racialized, and sexualized) public and private spheres (Connell 1990). Carole Pateman argues that the "liberation" of the citizen through the liberal social contract required the subjugation of women (and the feminine) via rigid and essentialist gender roles and its corresponding social relations of exploitation and dependence: the "sexual contract" (Pateman 1988; Frazer and Lacey 1993).

Charles Mills, similarly, observes that liberalism rests on a "racial contract" between White elites, wherein they collude to exclude and oppress people of color (Mills 2014; Jahn 2016). Each excluded Other is imputed with a parallel set of inferior, ostensibly private, feminized obligations to, very broadly, defer to the White masculine authority of the liberal individual (and state). Women are obliged to offer heterosexual sexual loyalty and familial labor; peoples of color are meant to produce material wealth through labor, expropriation, and, in the case of chattel slavery, their persons.[6] These obligations are political in the sense of constituting the state/community but are not produced as conventionally/formally public.

Correspondingly, Brown observes that while the extension—both empirically and within evolving liberal political thought—of individual rights to women and minoritized ethnic, sexual, and racial groups may have decoupled citizenship from a particular male (White, cisgender, heterosexual, property-owning) body, a universalized masculine, often normatively White, "public" subjectivity remains the hallmark of normative citizenship (1990).

The Liberal Military Contract

This conflation of normative citizenship with normative gender, sexuality, and race is key to understanding not only the operation and legitimation—but also frequent popular and ideological celebration—of the obligation to commit and risk violence as a condition of liberal belonging.

Masculine (heterosexual, White) normative citizenship and the gendered, spatialized binary between public and private upon which it rests also typify the structure of civil-military relations. The universalized citizen-subject liable for military service was, historically, a White, presumably straight, European man,[7] and, in classical and contemporary political thought, is masculine, heterosexual, and normatively White/Western. Through the physical performance of violence and symbolic association with the state, soldiers are constructed as protecting non-serving civilians. This gendered structure of warfare is writ large to the relationship, cast in the familiar terms of heterosexual kinship, between a masculinized, protective military and a feminized society (or nation) vulnerable to harm (see Stachowitsch 2013; Young 2003). The best-known formulation of this dynamic is Elshtain's contrast of the masculine "Just Warrior," charged with defending "home and hearth," with the feminine (or societal) "Beautiful Soul" whose virtue and innocent domesticity require protection (Kinsella 2005, 253–54; original in Elshtain 1995). As identified within the parallel narrative of militarism, the gendered division of "political" space underlying the social facticity of the liberal state both relies upon and constitutes a gendered civil-military separating feminized, dependent society from the protective, autonomous military (Khalid 2015; Tickner 2001).

The universal citizen, therefore, may be considered doubly masculine. The political aspect of citizenship is conducted in a public sphere constituted in accordance with stereotypically masculine, normatively White characteristics—particularly rationality and autonomy. The very possibility of this rational liberal politics relies upon the exclusion, expropriation, and oppression of racial and colonial Others (Mills 214; Lowe 2015)—or the capacity for organized, ostensibly legitimate violence exercised by the state (war). This, in turn, is dependent upon the underlying constitution of the citizen as a potential soldier, typified by masculine virtues of bravery, physical endurance, risk-taking, righteous aggression, self-sacrifice, and so on (Connell 1995; Hale 2012, 705; Woodward 1998). The heroic, ideally masculine soldier is the apogee of normative masculinity and aspirational citizenship (Sasson-Levy 2008, 317). As a result, normative citizenship is defined by the masculinized willingness to "die for something," namely, the state (and, often, racial/settler community), rather than being "willing to live for or through something" (Brown 1998, 182).

Though rarely explicitly stated, liberal political thought provides a subtle yet significant normative connection between liberal citizenship, masculinity, and military service: a "liberal military contract" (Millar 2016a, 20). The contract binds together—or mutually leverages—the formal political obligations of existing with the liberal state and the normative gendered and racialized expectations of White heteromasculinity in order to produce and stabilize the gendered civil-military divide. The gendered articulation of the contract elides the paradox at the heart of liberal military service by transforming it from a failure of liberal principles to an obligation of normative masculinity. The contract also reifies the existence of a binary, heterosexual gender order through its reproduction of a fairly conservative masculine logic of military protection of vulnerable feminized society (Young 2003). Consequently, individuals are interpolated as good citizens and good masculine subjects (and, often, good racial subjects)—and, ultimately, as good people—(at least potentially) liable for military service.

This is slightly different to what is sometimes referred to as the veterans' contract, or "soldiers' contract" (Schrader 2019, 9–16), understood as the agreement between military personnel and the state. There, the state agrees to provide certain benefits (e.g., support to a deceased soldiers' family) and uphold a certain standard of conduct (e.g., not taking undue risks with soldiers' lives), while soldiers defend and uphold the (democratic) social contract (Schrader 2019). This logic can be seen, for instance, in the UK government's 2011 Armed Forces Covenant: the state "owes" military personnel for their sacrifice. Though the soldiers' contract is also politically significant (discussed further in Chapters 6 and 8), the liberal military contract is its implicit precursor, outlining the gendered, classed, racialized, and so forth political obligation for military service that, if unmet or unequally distributed, sets the terms of the soldiers' contract in motion.[8]

The contract, of course, does not represent an actual moment/outcome of democratic decision-making or consolidation, nor was/is it enacted in ideal-typical form. But the notion of the military contract is a powerful shorthand representation of the complex and often contradictory cultural understandings regarding military service in the West. It is "the last full measure of devotion" to the polity and a coercive expropriation of violent labor—and, potentially, the lives—of citizens (and, frequently, and with far less moral angst, those not recognized as citizens).[9] It is a freely given gift of masculine heroic sacrifice and an irrefutable, universal obligation of living in political community. The use of violence on behalf of the group—articulated in the idiom of military service—is the foundation of the pacific, individual-regarding liberal polity (and the practical necessity for the imperial liberal way of war).

The liberal military contract is related to the processes and ideals we associate with militarism—the valorization of war and military service, connecting citizenship and masculinity to military service, and so forth—with a more precise understanding of how these factors relate to the making of political community. It zeroes in on the specific notion of gendered political *obligation* and the importance of its contextual articulation in a contractual idiom. Not unlike the good story of liberalism (or bad story of militarism), the liberal military contract functions as a cultural myth and powerful sociocultural narrative that smooths over ideological inconsistences. It imbues impressionist recollections of history and normative beliefs with affective valence—"all good men/citizens should serve in wartime!"—and projects them forward into the present (see Blieseman de Guevara 2016).

Analytic Approach: Discursive Martiality

The liberal contract and its expression of gendered political obligation reveal what the empirical operation of the contract obscures: the foundational continuity of not just war and peace but also violence and politics within liberalism (Jabri 2006, 55). The contract, through reference to a seemingly static gender binary, simultaneously belies and reproduces the apparent separability of the civil and military within the liberal polity (Peterson 2010; Enloe 2007; Basham 2018). It also points us toward the role violence plays in constituting the liberal political community via normative notions of personhood.

Informed by feminist militarism, security, and critical military studies, I conceptualize the military as a diffuse and productive discourse of gendered obligation and organized socially generative violence. I do this, drawing upon the work of Alison Howell (2018) and myself (2016), through the analytic of "discursive martiality." By this, I just mean reading the power dynamics, subjectivities, social facts, and normative structures associated with the military through the lens of a conventional poststructural account of discourse. As we'll see throughout the book, the liberal military contract and gendered political obligation are my animating substantive concepts, but discursive martiality—as an analytic/expression of the solidaristic dimensions of violence—is important to understanding how they relate to each other, and to the constitution of social reality. It is helpful for placing supporting the troops into conversation with the broader, underlying normative structures (e.g., the civil-military divide, the violence/politics distinction, the military contract, etc.) of liberalism and liberal polities.

In turning to the idea of discursive martiality, my aim is not to reinvent the wheel, nor to disavow the key insights into liberal civil-military relations highlighted by feminist and critical military scholarship—particularly those generated by the deployment of militarism as an analytic. The use of discursive martiality is a pragmatic choice, meant to capture the multilayered constitution of the liberal polity (and politics) via relations of violence, without importing militarism's subtle, though significant, autotelic account of the relationship between politics and violence within liberalism (Millar 2020). As a consequence, I am agnostic as to whether supporting the troops—the point of this inquiry—is militarism. StT can intuitively "feel" like militarism; it certainly looks like it. Examining StT in terms of discursive martiality isn't meant to deny its empirical similarities with what we typically think of as "militarism." Instead, it's an attempt to avoid reifying the inadvertent, normative loading of militarism as distinct from, and pathological to, liberalism. It sidesteps the "excess of meaning" held within the idea of militarism that implies too much politically—that we know what StT is, ontologically, and therefore what to do about it—and not enough analytically (Rech 2014; Millar 2020). A diagnosis of StT as militarism doesn't actually tell us anything about how it operates. Discursive martiality, as an imperfect alternative, is more normatively open and analytically precise.

More specifically, conceptualizing the military as a discourse enables us to see the mutual constitution of (a) the reproduction of the military as a socially real "thing"; (b) the reification of the civil-military divide; and (c) gendered and sexualized notions of normative citizenship. It also, crucially, enables us to see the deeply constitutive role solidaristic violence plays in producing the political community. This last point is the central contribution of my analysis, going beyond the (important) dynamics of normalization and legitimation excavated by militarism scholarship. Put differently, discursive martiality captures the relationship between violence and "politics" (e.g., public contestations over civil-military relations or the legitimacy of particular wars). It also catches the relationship between violence and "the political"—the deeply naturalized social order within which politics "and other spheres of social life" (Edkins 1999, 2) are produced and made meaningful. Discursive martiality brings the phenomenon associated with conventional militarism (e.g., clapping for the troops on airplanes, playing military video games, etc.) together with the foundational production of political community.

Discourse

Discourse, in this conceptualization, refers to the fairly conventional post-structural idea of

> a group of statements which provide a language for talking about—a way of representing the knowledge about—a particular topic at a particular historical moment. . . . Discourse is about the production of knowledge through language. But . . . since all social practices entail meaning, and meanings shape and influence what we do—our conduct—all practices have a discursive aspect. (Hall 1997, 291)

It not only provides a means of communicating knowledge and interpreting social reality but also actively *creates* it (see also Edkins 1999 and Foucault 1976a). Discourse is an expression, manifestation and working of power—diffuse, decentralized, and "productive of meanings, subject identities, their interrelationships, and a range of imaginable conduct" (Doty 1993, 229). The "substance" of power is not "found" in the material world but is (re)produced through regularized patterns (structures) of communication.

Individuals and collectivities do not pre-exist discourse, Instead, individuals and groups are created by discourse as subjects and placed in particular (social) relations to each other (Doty 1993, 303). Through the delineation of subjectivities, discourses not only arrange the social world but also constrain "what is thought at all [and] what is thought of as possible" (Neumann 2008, 62), shaping the field of social practice. Discourse is "both intentional and non-subjective" (Foucault 1980, 94) and therefore irreducible to a particular individual or collective "consciousness." The political effects of discourse exceed (and, indeed, may be entirely divorced from) the self-reported intentions of a particular individual, or group of individuals, who may be unaware of their contributions to, and constitution by, particular discursive formations (Foucault 1976a, 60). The discursive constitution of reality is about the play of power and limning of politics in the social *whole*. It produces both "the political"—the deeply normalized limits and nature of social life—and "politics," the intersubjectively recognized processes of negotiation over the governance of public life.

This is not to deny the materiality of the military as a formal organization or embodied, practiced, social institution. Rather, I suggest that the taken-for-granted permanence, inevitability, and *reality* of the military is itself the working of discursive power. It is a structural effect, similar to the deconstructed and disaggregated state theorized in the 1990s by critical international relations scholars. Borrowing from Mitchell, the military (and civil-military divide) is not an "actual structure" but rather the "powerful, metaphysical effect of practices that make [it] appear to exist" (1991a, 94). The military, like the state, seems to have an existence ontologically independent of the discursive practices and subject-positions that sustain and reproduce it. The military—as both a "specific" institution (i.e., the armed forces of the United States) and as a form of universalized organization of the material relations, gendered/sexualized/racialized assumptions, and normative obligations around violence (i.e., militaries)—is created and maintained through a variety of practices and discourse. "The military" is a highly stable yet discursively produced social fact.[10]

Gender and Martiality

The stability of this social fact relies upon its subtle references to gendered logics of protection—and the seemingly stable, natural foundation of a binary sex/gender order. Within queer and gender studies, gender and sexuality, in addition to highly powered performative discourses, are also understood as a form of (iterated and discursively reproduced) normative structure. While the gendered division of violent labor underlying the liberal military contract seems stable—and, indeed, must, in order for the parallel structural effect of the separate and legitimate institutional military to hold—the gender binary upon which it rests is neither inevitable nor timeless. Masculinity/femininity, heterosexuality/homosexuality, and cis- and trans*- gender identities operate as normative frameworks relating additional concepts, values, and identities to each other, rather than possessing substantively "fixed" content (Hutchings 2008). These structures are not static, but "flexible and shifting" (394). The boundaries of masculinity/femininity—and therefore the civil-military binary that rests upon them—are not deterministic, but the ongoing result of mutually constitutive and contingent processes (Wilcox 2009, 227).

With respect to normative citizenship, performances of gender and sexuality animate not an actually existing, objective "thing"—a natural, biologically determined heterosexual gender order—but rather a discursively constituted social ideal of mandatory, idealized, heterosexual masculinity that derives its regulatory authority from its appearance as ontologically real (Bell 1999, 137). The social facticity of the military is consistently, if imperfectly, (re)produced through gendered, performative martiality. As observed by Butler, "if performativity has often been associated with individual performance, it may prove important to reconsider those forms of performativity that *only* operate through forms of coordinated action" (2015, 9, emphasis mine). Martiality is a complex of discursive performativities that both produces and operates with reference to larger groups and/or structures (e.g., the liberal military contract, binary heteropatriarchal gender, etc.). It also reifies the dimorphic sex/gender order as itself found, natural, and "real." The civil and the military, as with the masculine and feminine (and, indeed, straight and queer, as well as a plethora of other seeming binaries), are intertwined and co-productive (Howell 2018).

Concretely, discursive martiality refers to the ways particular understandings of citizenship, gender (and sexuality, race, class, etc.), organized violence, legitimacy, obligation, and the (liberal) state are constituted and arranged—and, in turn, produce a range of normative subject-positions, expectations, and social structures. In practical terms, discursive martiality means analyzing "military processes and practices as the outcome of social life and political contestation" with reference to naturalized understandings of gender and sexuality (Woodward 2014, 51). As in militarism studies, the civil-military divide—and underlying ideological insistence on the separability of violence and politics within liberalism—is treated as blurry, contingent, and relational, rather than found or static (Mabee 2016). The civil/political is intertwined and co-productive with the martial/violent (Howell 2018). Their appearance as separate is a contingent, yet socially meaningful, effect of gendered, racialized, and sexualized power (Wibben 2018; Runyan and Peterson 2014). This emphasis on contingency lets us zero in on the productive nature of martiality—in conjunction with other axes of subjectification, such as gender, class, race, sexuality, gender expression, and coloniality—and its generation of normatively valorized ideals (and obligations) of public personhood. We are then able to connect processes of individual subject formation (e.g., the heteromasculine soldier-citizen) to these key, socially factual structures of violence (e.g., the military, the righteous liberal state, etc.).

Discursive martiality implies relations of loyalty and solidarity rather than opposition and exclusion.[11] It is a complementary—and frequently overlooked—logic of constitutive political violence. Martiality is not synonymous with war per se, but rather acts as the primary vehicle and idiom of its modern organization—and thus the politico-ethical relationship of society to the use of force. Though martiality is inflected by other processes of subjectification—such as the feminized/izing norm of vulnerability, and/or classed and racialized/izing respectability politics (see Stoler 1989)—it operates through constructions of substantive duty rather than ascribed enmity. Martiality is best understood as a historically specific, gendered (and racialized, classed, sexualized, abled, and colonialist) discourse of *obligation* to risk/commit organized violence. Obligation, or the "oughtness" of violence, is central.

This, I argue, is the defining feature of martiality as discourse: the normative connection between violence, relational solidarity, and being a "good person." Martiality is about how being produced via normative gender roles within a community serves to "automate" one's obligation to commit violence (regardless of one's ethical perception of either violence generally or specific conflicts). This is not to say that relations of violent solidarism are necessarily ethically or normatively desirable. Indeed, they may be more conservative than exclusionary relations of self/other distinctions. Being alive to the political potential and effects of relations of violent obligation—as in the case of the gendered liberal military contract—however, is key to understanding the making of political community and the corresponding conditions for war. Martiality, as relations of organized violence, sets the bounds of the political and, in so doing, informs the substance of the "politics" enacted upon this terrain. Liberalism relies upon wells of belonging, normative (racialized, gendered, sexualized, etc.) identity, affect, and solidarity that are not particularly liberal to make liberalism sensible and acceptable—to function.

Conclusion

Martiality is antithetical and essential to liberalism. The "good" liberal story of progress, rationality, and restraint—though only ever partially convincing—invokes a universal model of the human/citizen in order to obscure its foundations in particularistic identity (White, cis, heteromasculine property owners). Externally, this universalism serves to justify, even necessitate, war against racialized and colonized peoples for the defense of the liberal polity or, perversely, "their" own good. This is supported by the parallel "bad story" of militarism, which writes off the empirical failings of liberalism as either temporary aberrations or simply not liberal.

Internally, we see that the liberal social contract is subtly reliant on a secondary, foundational military contract, wherein men, as both good citizens and good masculine subjects, are required to risk and commit violence for the group. Liberalism relies on gendered notions of violent political obligation—that is, military service—as a constitutive ordering principle, distributing rights, recognition, and normative worth within the polity. This is built on a seemingly natural binary gender order, which smooths over the not-particularly-liberal nature of the masculine obligation to kill and die for the state. At the same time, the gendered division of violence naturalizes and consolidates the existence of binary, patriarchal, heterosexual sex/gender. "Supporting the troops," then, at one level, is a straightforward reflection of the ostensibly stable normative structure of the gendered civil-military divide and, with it, the exclusionary modern liberal political order.

But, as we saw in the Introduction, the gendered ideological expectations of liberal martiality—all good men, now all good citizens, should serve in wartime—are no longer met. In this context, I conceptualize "supporting the troops" as a *specific* form of martial discourse grappling with the now open questions of violent obligation, appropriate citizenship, and normative gender in wartime. The political stakes of StT are not only about who should fight, and what we owe those who do—though these concerns remain alive— but also how normative citizenship, masculinity, and even good personhood might be accessed in a social and cultural context where the expectations of the contract pertain but the practice doesn't. The relationship between violence and the political appears to be shifting. What, now, constitutes normative public masculinity?

Far from an apolitical "bumper sticker," supporting the troops is a distinct discursive formation. It produces and communicates normative understandings of violent obligation, articulating and contesting the gendered terms of the liberal military contract while attending to its apparent fracture. It is, as a consequence, also deeply implicated in the martial, solidaristic reproduction (or breakdown) of the liberal political community. The next chapter tracks this fracture in the liberal military contract empirically through a historical examination of the emergence of "the troops" as a distinct martial and political figure.

3

Supporting the Troops
in Historical Context

The previous chapter conceptualized "supporting the troops" (StT) as a specific form of martial discourse—communicating, reproducing, and (potentially) contesting the gendered political obligations of the liberal military contract. This chapter traces the discursive production of "the troops" in the US and UK, as well as attendant understandings of normative civil-military relations, across the twentieth century. StT represents both a continuation of enduring cultural myths regarding the relationship between liberal democracy, gender, citizenship, and military service and, simultaneously, a qualitative shift in the normative construction of political obligation in relation to collective force.

Groups of soldiers have long been constituted as a locus of national affect in war; consider, for instance, the positive representation of US GIs giving candy to children in World War II or the much-mythologized "betrayal" of German World War I veterans at Versailles (Kimball, 2008). The term "troop/troops" has described military personnel since the sixteenth century.[1] Until relatively recently, however, the term existed primarily as an empirical category—a description of a group of literal military personnel—rather than a distinct cultural figure, akin to the idealized soldier/veteran, conveying a broader assemblage of meanings, affects, and relationships. The public salience and political animation of the troops derives from their production within social relations of support.

There are substantial continuities in military support across the twentieth century to the present, ranging from micro-practices of wearing pro-military trinkets to more macro nationalist understandings of the masculine heroism of soldiers and feminine home-front loyalty. There are also important divergences. The emergence of the troops tracks the shift from a conscription-based military, fighting seemingly existential conflicts characterized by mass participation, to professional armed forces engaged in

Support the Troops. Katharine M. Millar, Oxford University Press. © Oxford University Press 2022.
DOI: 10.1093/oso/9780197642337.003.0003

distant wars of apparent choice. "Support" is transformed from a nearly ir-relevant fait accompli of mass participation wars to a ritualized normative relationship between non-serving civilians and the troops, now constructed as a distinct object of public concern. The chapter thus provides important historical context for understanding the contested politics of supporting the troops—and transformations in gendered political obligation—during the global war on terror.

The chapter begins with a broad, conceptual account of the "liberal military contract" in Western liberal democracies to the specific twentieth-century histories of civil-military relations—and the production of the troops—in the US and UK. The discussion is organized around key conflicts that came to inform the structure of civil-military relations, gendered experience and expectations of war, and terms of military service in each state. It begins at the turn of the twentieth century, works through World Wars I and II, Vietnam, Northern Ireland, the Falklands/Malvinas and concludes with the First Gulf War—a watershed moment in supporting the troops.

Early Twentieth Century Civil-Military Relations: From Suspicion to Participation

The obviousness of supporting the troops in the US and UK today was not a foregone historical conclusion. In contrast to much of Western Europe, UK civil-military relations were long characterized by a "sturdy independent dis-like of standing armies" (Summers 1976, 105). For much of its history, and definitively in the nineteenth century, the UK relied on naval forces for its national defense (Best 1998; Kier 1999). The military's primary activity was "to garrison a world-wide empire" (French 2005, 72) with (ostensibly) recruited volunteers. Though military officership was regarded as a respectable (and relatively secure) occupation for the younger sons of landed gentry (French and Rothery 2019), it was not entirely prestigious. The absence of a domestic military presence, combined with poor working conditions, rendered the social status of the average enlisted soldier quite low (Kier 1999; Spiers 1992). Positioned at the wrong end of enduring UK regional and class hierarchies, enlisted soldiers were frequently regarded as degenerate and inappropriately masculine: ill-educated misfits and criminals (Sheehan 2008). These "deviant" enlisted soldiers existed in a complicated relationship to not only more "gentlemanly" officers but also the military personnel raised within UK colonies, some of whom, such as the Nepalese Ghurkas and Punjabi Sikhs, were positioned within racialized colonial hierarchies as excellent "natural" soldiers: "martial races" (Streets 2017).

The UK armed forces underwent a period of reforms from the Crimean War up to the First World War intended to "domesticate" and civilize military personnel (Summers 1976; Cowen 2008a) while also redeeming their masculinity (and with it, the racialized superiority of the White British Empire). These reforms posited the individual soldier as an unfortunate in need of saving, foreshadowing the privatized, altruistic politics of supporting the troops in the present. Organized military charity and provision of material "troop comforts" at this time was "patchy" (Grant 2008, 68–69). During the Anglo-Boer War, for instance, a staff officer was "against the whole idea of parcels being sent out for individual soldiers by their families . . . because they often contained 'inappropriate items' such as bottles of brandy or beer, inflammable wax matches or even a decomposing pig's head" (Grant 2008, 68–69). At the time, the Red Cross similarly noted the uncoordinated nature of military charity, inadvertent competition, and risks of profiteering (Grant 2008, 68–69).

Despite this uneven material and social investment in the armed forces, the perceived humiliation of the British Army—and with it, the Empire—during the Anglo-Boer War resulted in a popular fervor for military reform and expression of mass anxiety over the masculine character and "fighting fitness" of British men (Fremont-Barnes 2003; Searle 2004). At the turn of the century, "the soldier" was moving ideologically closer to the figure of nationalist (or, rather, imperial) investment and masculinist belonging underscoring the liberal military contract—but in a context of ongoing material, social, and political marginalization of actual service members.

The early United States was also skeptical of standing armies and their perceived threats to freedom. The post-independence United States built its national defense institutions and strategies around citizen-soldier militias (although it accepted the pragmatic need for small standing forces) (Stevenson 2006). The US was characterized by a rejection of the seeming "machines" of mass European armies, instead valorizing the citizen-soldier as an enlightened, rational amateur (Grant 2009, 283). From 1650 to 1750, the composition of the colonial militias, however, had shifted to "the dissolute and unemployed" and those racially and economically marginalized by society (Shy 1990; Grant 2009, 241). Although the citizen-soldier—and his colonial iteration in the revolutionary Minuteman—continued to be figured as the apogee of settler masculinity and citizenship, actual members of militias and the armed forces were greeted with suspicion and suffered poor working conditions and social status (Grant 2009). Early US ideals of the soldier were, as in the British Empire, tied in up classed and racialized understandings of normative "civilized" subjects—and contestation over what it meant to be "appropriately" White (see Isenberg 2017).

This anxiety regarding the social status of soldiering carried through the aftermath of the US Civil War. The Civil War was initially greeted with vol-unteerism and approval on both sides, but this waned with the introduction of (lightly implemented) conscription (Vinovskis 1989). In terms of mate-rial civil-military relations, the war resulted in the founding of a number of publicly supported military charities—particularly state-funded old soldiers' homes for destitute veterans in the South—and the inception of the veterans' social security system in the North (Skocpol 1993; Green 2006). Socially, however, though individual veterans experienced the hardships, mental and physical health struggles, and bouts of local valorization that follow most wars, demobilization and Reconstruction fairly quickly removed the armed forces from the popular consciousness (Marten 2011). Consequently, the Revolutionary era citizen-soldier, as a less controversial and troublesome figure of White settler masculinity and enlightened citizenship,[2] came to overwrite the Civil War era armed forces in the popular imagination (Grant 2009). Nineteenth-century US civil-military relations largely nostalgically echoed the central commitments of the Revolutionary War era: a refutation of the conscript (and liberty-constraining) mass armies of the Old World; a reluctant reliance on a small standing armies of borderline social respect-ability; and the romanticization of a White, individuated, autonomous masculine citizen-soldier who volunteers for local defense and eschews in-ternational wars.

The World Wars

The ambiguous social standing, already shifting at the turn of the twentieth century, of the armed forces and the figurative soldier in the US and UK was transformed by the two world wars. Widespread volunteerism, eventu-ally combined with conscription, rendered both war and military service a mass experience of all classes. It was also a transnationalized experience of the empire—although the millions of people who served as "colonial troops" during this time have come to be popularly acknowledged within the UK (and West) only recently.[3] Approximately 25 percent of all male US citizens aged 18–31 served in World War I; 16 million US citizens—or 9 percent of the total population—served in the armed forces in World War II. In the UK, approximately 58 percent of all Scots, English, and Welsh men between the ages of 18 and 49 served in the First World War (Winter 1977, 450); 5 million British men, or approximately 10–11 percent of the total population, served in the Second World War (BBC 2003–2005). Although the social, economic, and political experiences of war differed between the two states—particularly during the First World War, which the US formally entered three years after the onset of major European hostilities—by the end of the Second World War, both societies engaged in collective sacrifice and war participation.

In each conflict, civil society and business were mobilized to produce essential war goods, maintain farms, and generally assist in the war effort (Proctor 2010; Jeffries 2018; Harris 1992). The extent of this effort is evidenced by the well-known feminization of the US and UK workforces during this era. Women entered the workforce in previously unseen numbers to offset the loss of (literal) manpower to the armed forces (Goldin 1991; Greenwald 1990). In the UK, during World War II, childless women between the ages of 20 and 30 were conscripted for industrial work; by 1943, 90 percent of single women and 80 percent of married women were engaged in work categorized as essential to the war effort (Harris 1992, 23; Harris 2011). In the US, approximately 22 percent of all married women were employed in 1944; for women with an absent husband, the figure rises to 52 percent (Goldin 1991, 742). At the time, women's labor force participation was explicitly framed as both extraordinary and temporary (Proctor 2010). The (provisional) contradiction of heteronormative patriarchal gender roles was made palatable through the continuous framing of work as war participation—and an aberrant response to an emergency. Women, similarly, were largely responsible for managing the impact of rationing of food stuffs and consumers goods; many civilians, particularly the working class, suffered from sporadic food insecurity (Proctor 2010).

The First and Second World Wars were, of course, far from uniform experiences, both between and across the US and UK. War experiences differed by nationality, class, gender, geography, race, age, and sexuality; although (eventually) popular, neither conflict was greeted with universal enthusiasm or approval (Keene 2014; Hallifax 2010). At the time, public officials often decried the reluctance of civilians to alter their typical attitudes, values, or patterns of consumption (Leff 1991). The specter of conflict, however, cast daily life in the US and UK as a function of war, and enabled quotidian activities—from family meal-planning to agrarian labor—to be constituted as "doing one's bit" (or, conversely, as shirking). This, in conjunction with the "homeland" attack on Pearl Harbor in 1941 and mass bombing of the UK (in World War I, and notably the 1940–1941 Blitz) (Grayzel 2012) contributed to a shared sense of vulnerability, sacrifice, and war contribution. The First World War "blurred the nascent cultural and legal distinction between civilian and combatant" (Jones 2014, 85)—a process intensified by the scale of participation and destruction of the Second World War (Keegan 1999).

The world wars brought the structure of civil-military relations in the US and UK in line with that of the mass armies of continental Europe—and the tenets of wartime service-for-citizenship that founds the liberal military contract. The expansion of voting rights in both countries literalized this connection. In the UK, the mass participation of men of all classes in World War I, as well as women's contribution to the workforce, created pressure for the 1918 Representation of the People Act, which resulted in the vote for all men and for women over the age of 30 (with some property restrictions) (Ogg 1918). (Women achieved fully equal suffrage in 1928.) In the US, de jure (although certainly not de facto) universal suffrage for men was formalized in 1870, following the Civil War; women achieved the right to vote in 1920. As in the UK, the discourse of women's suffrage had become militarized and frequently referenced women's contributions to the war, both as military participants (nurses, support personnel, etc.) and as economic actors (Jensen 2008; Kerber 1998). The US policy of racial segregation within the armed forces—reflecting the activism of Black political leaders, bolstered by a sense of Black contributions to World War II and lack of recognition upon return—officially ended in 1948 (Krebs, 2006; Jefferson 2008).

The world wars continued a patterning of leveraging war contributions and military participation for increased citizenship rights and recognition of marginalized and/or minoritized groups that, arguably, commenced with the *levee en masse*. This continues through to the present, as more groups, notably women; people of color; lesbian, gay, and bisexual people; trans* and genderqueer people; and migrants have sought social and political legitimacy through military service. World War I and, particularly, World War II saw the ideological investiture of the liberal military contract, as well as the notion of citizenship as premised upon masculine military service in wartime.

It also marked a notable expansion of the notion of who might be constituted as a full citizen, and thus potentially liable under the contract.

The tenets of the liberal military contract were, of course, previously present in both societies. The US's republican understanding of the citizen-solider was premised upon a willingness to participate in organized violence and membership in the polity; military service was considered, at least symbolically, a respectable and honorable position for the British upper classes. The mass experience of the world wars, however, as well as the expanded notion of citizenship, opened socially honored military service and war participation to virtually all of society and saw the elevation of the masculine soldier to the apogee of citizenship.

Publicly valorized masculinity shifted from previous, romanticized revolutionary, independent frontier or cowboy masculinities (Kaplan 1990) and chivalric, stoic, and self-restrained Victorian "gentlemanly" masculinities (Tosh 1994) to center military service.[4] During World War I, particularly in the UK (World War II was arguably more crucial to this process in the US), "the soldier became a wartime citizen primus inter pares, often taking on metaphysical qualities in public discourse" (Jones 2014, 89). In contrast to the society-military relations of the past, soldiers were perceived to be heroes and liberators (McGarry and Walklate 2011) fighting for a cause (Sheehan 2008), rather than suspicious mercenaries or migrant degenerates motivated by money and a lack of alternatives. Though "the troops" had yet to emerge as a distinct figure of public concern, "the citizen-soldier . . . took on a transcendent spiritual role in public wartime discourse and commemoration, while ordinary civilian status became associated with lesser significance" (Jones 2014, 89). The combat soldier is an idealized figure that constitutes a particular form of idealized, martial masculinity as both the hallmark of citizenship and the values and identity of the nation-state (Sasson-Levy 2008, 317).

The heroic, de facto male and normatively (White, heterosexual) masculine soldier expressed, simultaneously, a new standard for political belonging and a form of citizenship. This is reflected, for instance, in the now-infamous presentation of white feathers of "cowardice" to non-serving, able-bodied young men by young women during World War I, reinforcing the normative expectation that male citizens perform military service (Gullace 1997). Emmeline Pankhurst, a leading UK suffragette, suspended "militant" advocacy and began publicly supporting both the vote and men's mass enlistment (Proctor, 2010). The efficacy of this shaming stems from the gendering of the civil-military divide and the corresponding feminization of apparently non-serving men, calling their masculinity and sexuality into question (Stevens 2016). World War II propaganda campaigns echoed these themes. US recruitment campaigns emphasized the heroism, patriotism, and manliness of military service to men and "attractive uniforms" and "prospects for romance" in persuading women to join auxiliary military units (Howell 1997, 802). The public discourse of the era reinforced not only martiality but also heteropatriarchy as a component of citizenship—as well as the expectation of women's home-front loyalty to the nation's war effort.

These gendered expectations of masculine military service and feminized support did not coalesce into the form of support the troops discourse we would recognize today. Though "support our boys" existed as a phrase (see Jensen 2019)—and appeared in some US propaganda materials (Field 1987)—it was not the primacy affective or political locus for relating to the military and war it is today. The soldier, rather than a collective entity known as "the troops," embodied the fortunes of the collective. Nowhere is this more apparent than in the figure of the Unknown Soldier, the anonymous individual soldier, entombed with honors as a stand-in for the sacrifice of the entire nation (Anderson 2006, 50–1). Between the relative popularity of the wars (Howard 2009) and the virtual pan-societal experience of war, support for the troops was both materially omnipresent and ideologically irrelevant.

That said, though given a different social inflection, many of the practices we now associate with supporting the troops originate in this period. World War I in Britain saw a "golden age" for charity writ large and military and war-associated charitable activities in particular (Grant 2014). The First World War led to the "birth of 18,000 charities," including the Blind and Limbless Ex-Servicemen's Association, St. Dunstans (now Blind Veterans UK), and the Royal British Legion to provide veterans' care. This created a social and political norm of private, charitable organizations caring for veterans out of a sense of obligation, gratitude, and compassion, alongside (and often in place of) the state. The British military came to somewhat grudgingly accept the necessity of care packages for "troop comforts," though records note that, as today, the donated items often failed to align with military personnel's actual needs and desires (Grant 2014, 56).[5]

On the home front, symbolic support for the war proliferated. On September 5, 1915, the Bristol Red Cross held the UK's first "Flag Day," which sold lapel pins to benefit refugees displaced by the German invasion of Belgium (Moore 2008). This was an early instance of the fusion of capitalist consumption, charity, and patriotic symbolism that imbues much of StT discourse and practice—particularly the yellow ribbon campaign—in both the US and UK. "Our Day" of 1915, a charitable campaign that sold flag lapel pins to benefit British troops further underlines this connection, as does the World War I practice of throwing coins at Nelson's column to, again, show support for the military (Moore 2008). Similar sentiments accompanied the launch of the now-ubiquitous poppy campaign in the interwar period by the Royal British Legion, as a way of demonstrating "gratitude to the dead by helping to support those who survived the war" (Moore 2008, 48; Gregory 1994). As observed by Grant, engagement in charitable activities became a public marker of "doing one's bit" (2014, 7)—particularly for women, as voluntary work was often the primary locus of their war participation (Proctor 2010). Through World War II, military charity became a regular component of war contribution and a demonstration of the feminized, frequently maternal, expectation of home-front care.

The US similarly saw an expansion in military and war-related charity during World War I. Major US military charities, such as the American Legion and Disabled American Veterans were founded from 1917 to 1919. Organizations such as the Red Cross and YMCA provided recreational activities and supportive services to US soldiers on domestic bases; the same organizations also cared for military personnel deployed overseas, though official reports decried inefficiency and duplications of services (Bremner 1988). Interorganizational and even religious rivalries led to "some areas being oversupplied with facilities, while others received not so much as a baseball, chocolate bar, or magazine" (Bremner 1988, 126). The United War Work Fund was considered the "largest voluntary offering in history," raising $200 million to ease the postwar transition of demobilization (Bremner 1988, 127). Although the early US World War I effort was dedicated more toward humanitarian aid for Europe, after the United States' formal entry, US women took up military-related voluntary work akin to their UK counterparts— knitting socks for deployed military personnel en masse (Orwig 2017).

The social commandeering of women into the war effort, not only as industrial and agricultural labor but also as housewives and mothers in accordance with heteropatriarchal feminine norms (Cornell 2010), similarly continued through World War II. Foreshadowing StT discourses of the global war on terror, advertisements for World War II war bonds aimed at women encouraged them to make theirs a "victory home" and help "bring them [the boys overseas] home to you" (Cornell 2010, 37). Women were encouraged to support the Red Cross, Salvation Army, and an interesting organization called Bundles for Blue Jackets, which pivoted in 1941 from sending aid to European refugees to sending material "comforts" to naval personnel in the Pacific fleet (Erenberg and Hirsch 1996; Coronado Eagle and Journal 1941). The world wars also saw the inception of blue and gold star family iconography, wherein families with a male relative deployed overseas would display a blue star banner on their window—or a blue star cut out from patriotic newspaper advertisements—to publicly recognize their service (Cornell, 2010). If the servicemember was killed, the blue star was replaced by a gold star (Young 2018; American Legion). This symbolism—and centering the military family as both a major source of support and a site of broader social/charitable support from the community—persists to the present.

Business was similarly involved in the war effort and visible charity. This was both a reflection of patriotic commitment and a recognition of the prestige conferred by association with the armed forces—and its subsequent potential to generate postwar consumer loyalty and profits (Leff 1991, 1310). This speaks to a complex intertwining of business, charity, and state war engagement, as well as support for the armed forces, that continues to the present. As noted by Cowen (2008b), the post–World War II GI Bill marked a shift in the structure of financial support for veterans from the volunteerism/charity of the post–Civil War era to state-guaranteed benefits, which servicemen were presented as having "earned" during the war. In the UK, the inception of the National Health Service and state welfare system was universal but premised on the same logic—shared sacrifice and contribution to the war effort (Cowen 2008b).

Though "the troops" did not emerge as a discrete cultural figure during this time, the World War I–World War II era marked an important shift in the social regard of the mass membership of the armed forces. The normative elevation of the masculine citizen-soldier and scale of war participation transformed enlisted personnel and wounded veterans from morally suspect members of the itinerant poor, requiring civilization or saving, to heroes entitled to state and philanthropic support (Skocpol 1995). In the UK, this centering of the soldier in national memory and identity is evident in Remembrance Sunday and wearing red poppies, commenced in 1919 to mourn the losses of the First World War (Imber and Fraser 2011, 385). As Remembrance Sunday is observed with services conducted by the Church of England, it marks a sacralization of the relationship between the soldier and the public.

In the US, similarly, the world wars marked the consolidation of previous civic commemorations of war dead—notably those of the Civil War—into the generalized remembrance now known as Memorial Day (Hammond and Curran 2002). 1919 also saw the inception of Armistice Day (now Veterans Day), which, by World War II, came to honor all military veterans (rather than solely war dead) (Piehler 2004). Though the commemorative days in the US and UK were initially somber events intended to warn of the horror of war (Newell 1976), they have come, as the politics of troop support has evolved across the twentieth century, to valorize military service and contemporary veterans (Basham 2016; Piehler 2004). Soldiering—and the associated masculine practices of heroism and sacrifice—was (and is) upheld and ritualized as the highest form of public service.

This era—particularly World War II—looms large in the popular imagination as "the last good war" (Paris 2000, 238–39). Though the scale of sacrifice, contribution, and deprivation within the US and UK were not particularly comparable (Leff 1991), the cultural mythologizing of World War II was remarkably similar.[6] Mass participation and the (relatively) uncontroversial nature of the war led to an emphasis on war effort rather than "troop support." This expectation of "doing one's bit" (and its fusion with postwar understandings of national identity) domesticated the liberal military contract experientially, affectively, and ideologically within the US and UK. It solidified the valorized image of the heroic combat soldier as the model for normative citizenship and public masculinity—further reifying the gendering of violent political obligation that provided the context for the emergence of the troops.

The Cold War and the Necessity of Support

The postwar period, once again, saw a shift in the structure of civil-military relations and the cultural context of war. The US sought to solidify its superpower status through a series of proxy wars and the UK attempted to manage the violence(s) of a declining empire. This context—of changeable terms of military service, heroic World War II soldiering imagery, and controversial wars—challenged the experiential and material equity of the liberal military contract while solidifying its normative expectations of gendered political obligation. In doing so, it gave rise to the first explicit articulations of the support the troops discourses traceable through the present.

The US and Vietnam

The mass public proclamation of support for the troops derives from the US experience of the Vietnam War (1965–1973). As is now common knowledge, the US was deeply divided over the Vietnam War, and many Americans— particularly women, Black Americans, and, during the later phases of the war, college graduates—were opposed to the conflict (Lunch and Sperlich 1979). These attitudes toward the military and Vietnam marked a significant departure from those accompanying mass societal mobilization in World War II. From 1940 to 1941, for instance, survey data indicate that Americans' approval for "helping out England" in the war hovered at around 70 percent; the statement "every able-bodied man should serve in the Armed Forces" also received slightly more than 70 percent approval (Berinsky et al. 2011).

Although both World War II and Vietnam involved the draft, conscription policies in World War II were widely considered fairer (Adams 1994). The World War II selection drew pan-societally and resulted in an older average age of service (27 in World War II, 19 in Vietnam) (Adams 1994, 76). In Vietnam, in contrast, service and sacrifice were differentially distributed. Less affluent and rural states had the greatest casualty rates (a reversal of World War II) (Willis 1975). Roughly 33 percent of all US casualties were draftees (New York Times 1970). Not everyone had the same chance of being drafted. When faced with a shortage in manpower, the Department of Defense, under "Project 100,000," opted to reduce standards for service rather than decrease deferments, resulting in the disproportionate draft of poorer, less educated and (by the questionable standards of the time) "less intelligent" men (Hsiao 1989).[7] The vast majority of the draftees were assigned to the army, suffering disproportionate casualties (Isaacs 2007). Young Black, Hispanic, and Asian American men, similarly, were disproportionately assigned to infantry units (Greiner 2014). Educated and affluent men, should they wish, were often able to avoid military service—or, if serving, combat—through education deferrals for college students (Card and Lemieux 2001) and domestic assignments to the National Guard.[8]

The liberal military contract was effectively exposed as fractured. Military service differentiated by education, class, region, and race belied the egalitarian premise of universalized service for citizenship at work in democratic martial myths. Home-front sacrifice, similarly, was unequally distributed. For households without a loved one serving abroad, social and economic life continued without systematic disruption (Lau et al. 1978). As observed

by Garner et al., Vietnam "lacked the full-scale mobilisation, industrial con-
version, and social dislocation to the degree associated with the two world
wars and Korea" (1997, 673). Criticism of administration war policy gained
greater coverage in print and television media (Sparrow and Inbody 2005).
The experience of Vietnam existed, as it continues to in memory, in strong
contrast with the "good wars."

The political currency and public saliency of "support the troops!" stems
from its initial invocation in this context of unpopular war, widespread protest, and inequitable terms of military service. To combat the war opposition
mounted by the peace movement, the US government deployed an astroturf
"support the troops" campaign in 1967 (Coy et al. 2008, 167–69). The Johnson
administration founded the "National Committee for Peace and Freedom in
Vietnam, which organised demonstrations and letter-writing campaigns to
'Support Our Boys in Vietnam'" (see Stahl 2009). A 1967 Support Our Boys
in Vietnam parade drew a crowd of 70,000 (Small 1988, 101). It was this "silent center" of support for the war—and the boys in the war—that later became Nixon's "silent majority" (Small 1988, 102,163). Concern for the troops
was politically instrumentalized by state officials to bolster support for the
overall war effort (Stahl 2009, 552–53).

The construction of "our boys," as well as its invocations of particular, idealized notions of masculinity, was important to how this discourse functioned
politically. The heroic combat soldier typical of World War II persisted as an
ideological ideal; military recruitment campaigns, particularly for the army
and Rangers, continued to feature conventionally attractive young White
men who were framed as "choosing" to do more, to "be number one," and to
do "man's work" (see LaSalle University digital archive). The contested nature
of the war, however, and real and perceived dodging of service by privileged
(generally, White, upper- and middle-class) elites stymied a straightforward
transposition of the romanticized heroic World War II soldier to Vietnam.
Many of those whose embodied identity aligned with the expectation of idealized heroism were constructed as either shamefully shirking or righteously
refusing to serve in an unjust war. Conscription, as well as the misalignment
of the racialized and classed ideals of elite leadership with the preponder-
ance of marginalized and minoritized soldiers in the military, made it difficult to simply transfer this understanding of the citizen-soldier to those
actually serving. The idea of normative masculinity as White, middle class,
and self-sacrificial persisted but as a relatively unmet ideal. As illustrated
by the valorization of John McCain's famous decision to refuse preferential

repatriation as a prisoner of war, this model of service was burnished by its apparent rarity.

The framing of soldiers as "our boys" produced another understanding of masculinity that shifted civil-military relations from a frame of war approval or popular participation to support for a sympathetic group. References to "our boys" constructs the soldier as "innocent": a paragon of youthful virtue whose boyishness underscores his potential for heroism under duress and the symbolic power of his transformation, via combat, to a man (Managhan 2011a, 452). The Vietnam conscript is framed as let down by civil society—and, in popular discourse, an irresponsible administration—and yet managing to maintain, or even improve, his personal character and morality (Boose 1993). This sense of martyr-like martial transformation underscored Project 100,000, which was disingenuously framed as a poverty-oriented social program, following in the footsteps of Johnson's Great Society, that would "salvage" underprivileged, racialized, and marginalized men through the cultivation of skills and social status (Worsencroft 2011). "Our boys," as victims overcoming a bad war to become "good men," ennoble the conflict—and the nation—through their embodied idealism. They also refute a parallel, contemporaneous construction of Vietnam martial masculinity, characterized by sometimes addicted, potentially hedonistic soldiers, who, trapped in a senseless war, dispense violence savagely (Kimmel 2017; Huebner 2011).

Given the ambivalence of soldiering masculinity, "the troops" begin to emerge as a distinct figure. In contrast to the future uses of support the troops discourse (discussed in Chapter 5), the meaning of troops is fairly literal. Though it begins to roll military roles and ranks together (Beamish et al. 1995)—an important characteristic of the discourse going forward—"troops," here, refers to a specific group of soldiers located in a particular place and time. "They" are a fairly straightforward synonym for "our boys," directly referring to the young, innocent conscripts who bear no culpability for the war.

The call to support the troops as imperiled young men was bound up in the complicated construction of the Vietnam era protestors as "anti-troop" (Beamish et al. 1995, 345), endangering not only the soldiers but also the war effort. US state officials, including future president (then Governor) Ronald Reagan, made assertions that the movement "'len[t] comfort and aid' to the enemy" (in Coy et al. 2008, 168; Small 1988, 67, 86). The distinction between "our boys" and the protestors reflected the gendered civil-military divide. The protestor was frequently represented in the figure of a civilian woman betraying her feminine obligation to support the masculine soldier (Boose 1993, 80, cited in Managhan 2011a). "Inappropriate" civil-military relations were cast in the language of the heteronormative family, wherein those opposing the war were constituted as either delinquent parents (particularly mothers) or fickle lovers. Framing the protesters as a threat furthered the state's construction of "our boys" as, despite their structural positioning as the violent agents of the state, dependent on support from the public "at home"—potentially for their survival. Even Nixon's "Vietnamization policy was supported as far as that policy was understood as bringing the boys home" (Small 1988, 213).

The Vietnam era marked "the troops'" initial political activation as a distinct collective subject. The troops became identifiable in their own right, imbricated in a complex web of institutional and social relationships. It also reflected the onset of what Brown (2012, 23–25) has identified as a 1970s so-called crisis in masculinity within the United States, produced by a combination of humiliating war defeat, corresponding decline in the social prestige of conventionally masculine soldiering, and the rise of progressive civil rights movements. In response to the operational defeat and blow to its public imagine, the Vietnam War set off a generation of soul searching among military leaders. The military was subsequently professionalized in 1973, ending national service in the United States (Bacevich 2005). This enabled the eventual rehabilitation of the US military's image and, by the 1990s, the popular resurgence of the romanticized World War II–style citizen-soldier. The professionalization of the military also, however, exacerbated tensions between the experience of war and the mythical liberal military contract, as the vast majority of eligible citizens no longer serve.

The UK and the Lead Up to the Falklands/Malvinas

Though the United Kingdom did not undergo a "shock" akin to Vietnam, the military operations involved in winding down the empire led to a similar lowering of the profile and prestige of the armed forces. Operations in Malaysia, Palestine, Suez, and Kenya, although often considered effective from an operational perspective, came to be perceived as moral and political failures (French 2012; Dixon 2012). Palestine, in particular, was quickly viewed as a disaster, wherein the British military was unable to manage violence between Palestinians and Jewish settlers and suffered humiliating, high-profile deaths of British personnel in "terrorist" incidents (Dixon 2000, 103–104). The "thankless" task of regulating the mandate led to public pressure for withdrawal and, reportedly, mothers to demand the government "bring their boys home" (British Foreign Secretary Ernest Bevin quoted in Carruthers 1995, 61 in Dixon 2000, 104).

Paris (2000) argues more broadly that in both popular culture and public opinion, war lost its appeal shortly after World War II. National service was again replaced by a professional army in 1960 (UK Parliament n.d.), returning to a version of the "lighter," externally oriented military that characterized the imperial age. By 1963, the armed forces were reduced to just over 417,000 personnel (or less than 1 percent of the total population) (DataBlog 2011). Mid-century "British political culture" exemplified a "notably lowered profile of the citizen-as-soldier" (Enloe 2000, 25). In a 1976 survey conducted by Inglehart, only 6 percent of Brits listed a "strong defence force" as first or second of their political priorities (Sheehan 2008, 176). In this context, military recruitment campaigns shifted slightly to mirror broader transformations in British normative masculinity, which emphasized the modern, white-collar, rational man (Roper 1994). Though such adverts continued to frame the military as an institution for men that produces men, they also emphasized professionalism, skill development, and technology oriented positions (Dodd 1973)—key hallmarks of "new" military masculinity (Brown 2012; Barrett 1996).

During the Troubles, the UK armed forces banned wearing military uniforms in public due to a perceived threat of Irish Republican Army targeting. This lowered the public visibility of the services (BBC 2013). Although the idealization of the World War II soldier, to some degree, persisted, actual practices of military valorization declined (temporarily, it would prove), diminishing the connection between normative public masculinity and soldiering. As a result of this disconnect, the UK civil-military tradition placed "less emphasis on the service-exchange relationship" than did the blurred liberal and republican tradition of the US (Janowitz 1991, cited in Basham 2013, 40–41). There was little exigency in dealing with the tensions between liberal democratic ideals and military service that accompanied the move to the use of professional militaries in "small wars."

Enloe (2000, 24) suggests that this "relative lack of national emotion" attached to the military was due to the diminishment of the British Empire and the "unappealing character of soldiering most visible to an ordinary British citizen watching the evening news . . . soldiers patrolling the streets of Belfast." During the Troubles, 21,000 military personnel were deployed to Northern Ireland (MacAskill 2015). The deployment lasted from 1969 to 2007, despite opinion polls consistently demonstrating support for withdrawal since 1971 (Dixon 2000, 2012). "Bloody Sunday," when British forces fired on a civil rights march in Derry killing 14 people and wounding 13 others (National Army Museum n.d.), contributed to demands for withdrawal and the social diminishment of soldiering. It was received wisdom at the time that the controversial conflict, combined with what was perceived to be an unjustified risk of death or injury, worried the parents and wives of potential enlistees and posed a problem for recruiting (Dixon 2000).

Constructions of soldiering masculinity, though not particularly socially prominent, tended toward two poles: somewhat naïve, innocent recruits, or violent, potentially abusive, occupying forces. Though the soldiers deployed to Northern Ireland were volunteers, they were frequently framed as victims in a manner not dissimilar to those of Vietnam. The first UK military casualty of the Troubles in 1971 was explicitly framed as a victim of terrorism (McGarry and Ferguson 2012). A year after his death, tabloid headlines expressed concern for deployed military personnel, stating: "ULSTER: HOW MUCH MORE CAN THEY TAKE?" (McGarry and Ferguson 2012, 26). Discourse around the conflict also came to invoke the figure of the boys as a distinct object of social concern. A 1973 campaign was launched to "Bring the Boys Back from Ulster" by parents of a serving soldier (Dixon 2000, 112). This prefigures the language of "support the troops, bring them home" that typified similar military family/peace advocacy of the global war on terror and continues the framing of civil-military relations in the idiom of heteropatriarchal family dynamics.

Significantly, however, although the troops emerged as an important figure within UK political discourse around the Troubles, it was not (as in Vietnam) a synonym for "our boys." Instead, "the troops" emerged in the context of the anti-occupation, pro-peace (and self-determination) Troops Out Movement (TOM) organized by anti-imperialist activists (Renwick 2016). The movement's twin demands (and key slogans) were "Troops Out Now! Self Determination for the Irish People as a Whole" (Renwick 2016, 116–18). The movement had approximately 1,200 members (and 10,000 affiliate) members by 1976, advocates within the Labour Party, and (particularly by present standards) relatively robust press coverage (Renwick 2016, 118–20). The meaning of "troops" here—and the movement's acronym,

TOM, which alludes to "Tommy," the British colloquial term for an enlisted soldier—is much closer to the conventional military usage of "group of soldiers" than victimized, collective boys. Far from soliciting support or solidarity, "the troops" rhetorically stand-in for imperial oppression and the contested policies of the British government. In the 1970s, British civil-military relations were thus characterized by substantial ambivalence, as individuated soldiers were framed as victims, the troops were presented as the violent instrument of the state, and martial concerns generally receded in importance.

This began to change with the Falklands/Malvinas War of 1982, which, in a precursor to the First Gulf War, was widely mediatized. The conflict was portrayed as a redemption of Suez (Paris 2000), with UK soldiers constructed as heroic and (inaccurately) outnumbered (Paris 2000; see also Dodds 1993). Supported by a tabloid press that disseminated chauvinistic, militaristic, and nationalist discourse and imagery, the Thatcher administration experienced a 16-point gain in popular approval during the conflict (Norpoth 1987; Lai and Reiter 2005). Individuals displayed posters indicating their approval of the war and respect for the military, bearing slogans such as "Thank God the most professional armed forces in the world are BRITISH," "Britain does not appease dictators," and "Congratulations to the Royal Navy" (Gray 1982, 10). Billig (1995, 124–5) observed that "when the British troops returned victorious from the Falklands War, they were met at the harbour by crowds, singing, swaying, chanting and waving flags, as if they were celebrating a football team returning with a silver trophy."

Though comparatively few photographs were produced of the conflict, in those that were, soldiers were in uniform and "in action," either (ostensibly) defending the country or interacting with the settler-citizens of the Malvinas (Brothers 1996). These images invoked long-standing tropes of military masculinity and individuated soldiering heroism, including bravery, endurance of hardship, physical strength, and (appropriately governed) violent aggression. The Falklands, in other words, resuscitated some aspects of the heroic World War II combat soldier—combined with some modern twists, including an emphasis on the Special Forces, specific skills and expertise, and (limited, contextual) autonomy (Woodward and Jenkings 2011). Postwar representations of the Falklands, particular in memoirs, demonstrated a desire to constitute the conflict as "real" soldiering and as a meaningfully heroic (as well as legitimately traumatic) experience (Woodward and Jenkings 2011).

This normative martial masculinity was bolstered by an outpouring (again, led by the tabloids) of gendered and sexualized support for the armed forces. *The Sun* declared itself "the paper that supports our boys." This may be the first major UK discursive merging of existing notions of our boys—who appear, here, to be constituted as a group of heroic soldiers, rather than the unfortunate victims of the Troubles—with the compulsory "supportive" politics that characterizes troops discourses of the present. This tabloid emphasis on support was accompanied by the promotion of "page three girls" who patriotically took off their tops for the boys, and accounts of wives, mothers, and girlfriends who waited for their deployed men (Anderson 2011, 190). Though cast in a more positive vein than that of the US in Vietnam, civil-military relations were framed in terms of mandatory heterosexuality—and the patriotic (read as sexual) loyalty of both literal civilian women and feminized society as a whole. Together, these gendered constructions of soldiering and the home front constituted a particular—normatively White, necessarily colonial—Britishness (Anderson 2011, 190) that facilitated the resurgence of the citizen-soldier and the possibility of legitimate warfare.

The Falklands/Malvinas represent a rapprochement between the military and society. It was the beginnings of a shift in the normative structure of civil-military relations that harkened back to the popular military engagement of the two world wars and foreshadowed the global war on terror. Significantly, as the British military transitioned to increased professionalism and decreased size, "the political/moral obligation upon commanders not to expose soldiers to risk needlessly actually became more keenly felt" (Cornish 2003, 565). The Cold War thus saw the nascent, yet increasing, constitution of soldiers—if not the troops per se, who were largely presented functionally, as strongly associated with the military institution—as in need (and deserving) of care, protection, and sociopolitical consideration.

The First Gulf War: Support as Common Sense

The First Gulf War (1991) was the first conflict where "the troops" formed the locus of normative civil-military relations. Though differing according to national context, these constructions of the troops as a distinct collective subject briefly succeeded in reforging a consensus around the liberal military contract and collective use of force in both the US and UK.

The United States and the Redemption of Vietnam

In the United States, the First Gulf War was met with an unprecedented level of enthusiasm. Public support for then-President Bush reached 83 percent (Tuleja 1994, 29), while between 76 and 79 percent of surveyed Americans indicated support for the operation (Clymer 1991). For political elites, it was an opportunity to put to rest the "Vietnam Syndrome"—public aversion to major US military commitments abroad—that had characterized US foreign policy since the "fiasco" of Vietnam (Simons 1997). Popular discourses—and approval—of the war were characterized by widespread acceptance of the idea that both peace activists and general society had betrayed the troops returning from Vietnam. Supporting the troops was framed as a key means of "making amends" (Beamish 1995, 345; Heilbronn 1994). Similar to previous administrations, Bush called on the nation to "support our boys and girls," unambiguously indicating that "support for the troops also meant support for the war" (Coy et al. 2008, 170). Tuleja (1994) understands this process as an attempt to "bury" Vietnam and "correct" the mistakes of the past without politically examining the grounds upon which they were made. This time, the call to support the troops occurred in a radically different context, characterized by a swift, popular war prosecuted by a (comparatively small, at approximately 1 percent of the population) professional, volunteer military.

The composition of the military during the First Gulf War is important. Women's military participation increased from just over 42,000 in 1973 to approximately 200,000 in 1991 (Patten and Parker n.d.). The overall military was comprised of approximately 60 percent White personnel, 30 percent Black personnel, and 10 percent personnel from other racial and ethnic backgrounds (Wilkerson 1991). Black personnel, particularly Black women, were overrepresented in the forces, as Black Americans made up approximately 12 percent of the total population (Wilkerson 1991). The mediatized nature of the Gulf War—and public discussions of women's proximity to combat—reflected this diversity. In so doing, more (though not all, as LGBTQ+ citizens were still formally excluded, though many served) citizens were symbolically constituted as eligible to take up the idealized, masculine mantle of the citizen-soldier, even as broader military participation declined.

The characteristics associated with the soldier, as observed by Brown (2012), although retaining ideals such as bravery, patriotism, and so on, also reflected a subtle transformation in the nature of normative masculinity. In keeping with broader shifts in social, or civilian, masculinity toward managerialism, rationality, technological competence, and computer and technology skills, martial masculinity also came to emphasize the skills and positions associated with "technowar" (Niva 1998, 1999; cited in Brown 2012, 27). It also came to incorporate—if not without contestation and tension—an ideological commitment to liberal ideals of gender, sexual, and racial equality and inclusivity (Brown 2012). The soldier existed in conversation with new US (and, increasingly UK/globally hegemonic) ideals of "tough and tender" masculinity (Niva 1998).

More specifically, the Gulf War soldier was constituted as a reluctant but willing purveyor of violence—an active and informed volunteer, unimpeded by the feminized tropes of victimhood and failure that characterized the Vietnam veteran (Papaynis 2010). The First Gulf War updated the World War II soldier ideal and resuscitated its political, social, and ideological standing after Vietnam (Watson 2010). This revivification depended upon a rhetorical strategy of aggregation and abstraction, wherein all soldiers were constituted as heroes, less on the basis of specific actions than the sheer fact of their deployment (Papaynis 2010). Archetypically, if everyone in Vietnam was posited as a victim, in the Gulf War, "everyone comes back a hero" (Papaynis 2010). This shift in the qualitative grounds of martial "heroism," combined with its application to all deployed personnel, represents an important change in US civil-military relations. It was a key step in an evolving detachment of war and violence from martial discourses, ideals, and military service that, as the balance of the book will show, reaches an apogee in global war on terror support the troops discourses.

This (re)heroification of the soldier was accompanied by an increasing ubiquity of support the troops discourse and symbolism. Yellow ribbons—a folk symbol of vigil made popular by the wife of the captive American ambassador during the Iran hostage crisis (Parsons, 1981, 1991; Tuleja 1994, 23–30)—proliferated as a sign of support for the troops, adorning homes, cars, public buildings, and consumer products (Larsen 1994; Santino 1992). The US Postal Service issued a yellow ribbon stamp; the city of Reno, Nevada, was wrapped in 25 miles of yellow ribbon; and "school curricula were designed around the phenomenon" (Coy et al. 2008, 170). The slogan "support the troops" appeared "on T-shirts and bumper stickers, emblazoned on magnetic yellow ribbons, on banners at charity events, in public debates, in church sermons, on advertising billboards, and just about everywhere in between" (Stahl 2009, 534). The largest US ribbon manufacturer "saw sales increase by 10000 percent in one year" (Tuleja 1994; and Larsen 1994 in Coy et al. 2008,

171). Due to the end of national service, most Americans did not serve in the military, and many did not personally know anyone deployed overseas. Yellow ribbons communicated a generalized affective identification with the troops (Heilbronn 1994), compounded by the unprecedented mediatization of conflict through live television broadcast (Taylor 1992).

Despite the comparative remove of the general public, peace groups faced enormous pressure to publicly support the troops or risk the demonization of their Vietnam era predecessors (Beamish et al. 1995; McLeod et al. 1994). Coy et al.'s (2008) study of US antiwar groups finds that they consistently engaged in StT discourse, framing the soldiers as victims of policy. For instance, the Fellowship of Reconciliation's stated Gulf War position was:

> To those who say that now that the war has started we must support the president, we say this: "We support and share the deep concern for our servicemen and women who were so abruptly and cruelly uprooted and sent into the desert to fight a war that never should have been. But we can never support the bankrupt foreign policy that sent them there. We want them home." (1991, cited in Coy et al. 2008, 172)

"The troops," in this quotation, have not yet supplanted "the soldier" within activist and war discourse or become the center of antiwar activism. War is opposed in and of itself—or for the sake of innocent civilians in the theater. The logic of supporting deployed, victimized personnel despite political disagreements with the government, however, is very clear. This requirement to support the troops, in combination with the brevity of the conflict, meant that organized opposition to the war struggled to get off the ground. Correspondingly, the peace groups contributed to the development of an important political expectation that antiwar dissent should, essentially, honor the military contract—opposing particular policies, but never the troops (Coy et al. 2008).

During the 1991 Gulf War, support the troops came to perform an actively regulative function in the United States. It constructed ostensibly apolitical support for an abstract, yet sympathetic, entity: "the troops" as the political norm. This solidified the troops as a legitimate collective subject. Appeals to visibly support the troops, drawing on a societal legacy of Vietnam era guilt (Marsical 1991), were successful in papering over the normative dissonance of a liberal democratic deployment of a professional military to fight a distant conflict.

The United Kingdom and the Making of the Troops

In the UK, the rebound in the social and cultural prominence of military discourse and symbolism continued through the Gulf War, which also saw the (tentative) emergence of "the troops" as a distinct subject. Following the invasion, the war received between 80 and 88 percent support for "allied military actions" and between 60 and 79 percent considered the mission to liberate Kuwait worth risking British lives (Shaw 1996, 128). As noted by Shaw, each subgroup of the British population evidenced majority support for the war, and Prime Minister Major enjoyed a 74 percent approval rating (128, 134).

The model of normative martial masculinity promoted within these discourses continued to develop along the lines of the Falklands hero (and resuscitated World War II era heroism), with a few updates. First, paralleling broader cultural trends in "new man" masculinity that increasingly incorporated an ideological commitment to equality and inclusivity (Ashe 2007; Edwards 2003), UK martial masculinity began to incorporate an emphasis on other-regarding protection through human rights and peacekeeping, as opposed to solely belligerent aggression (Higate and Hopton 2004). The UK soldier was, as elsewhere, a "reluctant warrior"—but also a force for good, bringing aspects of normative (White, liberal, middle-class) civilian masculinity together, if not always easily, with the more traditional characteristics of valorized soldiering.

Second, as in the US, the increased participation of women in the UK armed forces, in a greater variety of roles, with a good deal of public visibility, similarly detached normative martial masculinity from literal embodied maleness (Higate and Hopton 2004). The gendered political obligation of heroic (citizen) soldiership that underscores the liberal military contract was now in line with the increasing inclusivity of liberal social and political norms, extended to encompass women (though not in combat roles) (Dandeker and Segal 1996). As in the US, those previously marginalized or exempt from the racialized and gendered strictures of the liberal military contract were now, at least symbolically, similarly subject to the gendered expectation of idealized military service. The expansion of this expectation to a broader portion of society—while largely preserving the constitution of the soldier as normatively White, masculine, heterosexual, and so on—would be further consolidated in the global war on terror. (Service formally opened to lesbian, gay, and bisexual personnel in 2000 and trans* personnel in 2014, further expanding the technical inclusivity of the military contract—though, obviously, many LGBTQ+ personnel served prior to this time). The First Gulf War's reflection of initial moves toward greater symbolic inclusivity provides important context for the first substantial emergence of the troops within UK discourse. The gendered distinction between a feminized, supportive home front and a masculinized, righteous armed forces was largely maintained.

As in the United States, the British Gulf War effort received immense media coverage, with camouflaged BBC reporters embedded with UK military units providing live updates (Wyatt 2012). The tabloid press promoted aggressive patriotism and support for the military, publishing, for instance, a front page depicting a giant Union Jack with a soldier's head in the middle, under the banner "Support Our Boys and Put This Flag in Your Window" (Shaw 1996, 98). This became a daily header for the *Sun*, which once again proclaimed itself "the paper that backs our boys"; the *Star* employed a similar motif that proclaimed "go get 'em boys" (Shaw 1996, 98–99). The same tabloids again published photos of scantily clad female models displaying patriotic imagery for the titillation of deployed soldiers—a framing that underlined the continued gendering of the heroic, patriotic citizen solder as male (and heterosexual) (Shaw 1996, 98–99). In the *Star*, "topless Starlets" sold "giant yellow ribbons" (Shaw 1996, 99).

Though the balance of the press demonstrated greater restraint in their coverage of the war,[9] the troops also gained prominence among established social and political elites. Hansard includes references to "support/ing our troops," and shows evidence of initial contestation regarding the phrase's meaning. Member of Parliament Margaret Ewing, for instance, stated:

> The motion mentions strong support for the troops in the Gulf. Some hon. Members seem to think that the only way to support the troops is to rant and rave and make pacifist speeches. That is not a line that I pursue. The best way to support our troops is to argue the case for diplomatic means to bring our men home as quickly as possible. . . . I know about the worries of the families of service men. They ask us to send messages of support but also to do everything possible to avoid mass killings. They all want to see their families safely home, but they recognise the responsibilities of members of the armed forces. (Ewing 1991)

Here, the speaker contrasts a "pacifist" notion of supporting the troops with engaging in conflict and bringing them home quickly. She clearly identifies the troops as a distinct corporate entity, embedded in social relations, with a claim to consideration independent of their function as "the military." They also possess responsibilities as citizen volunteers of a professional military.

This sentiment dramatically differs to that of Labour deputy leader Denis Healey, who stated, "We all made clear, including me, that once the fighting started we'd support our troops" (Castle 1991). This framing of StT as an obvious obligation, and fait accompli following the onset of hostilities, foreshadowed the public discourse surrounding the 2003 invasion of Iraq. In 1991, however, in contrast to the US, it was not the political elite pushing support for the troops. This was evidenced by the Conservative Prime Minister Major's rebuke to his own backbenchers for their "ritual . . . harangue about the BBC's decision to refer to 'British troops' rather than 'our troops'" (quoted in Shaw 1996, 34). "The troops" accrued a social facticity as a collective subject with definite political stakes but with a blurrier meaning and less elite acceptance than in the US. It is worth noting, however, that even Major's suppression of jingoistic discourse was publicly framed by Tory MPs as a form of support, observing: "The public wants us to support the troops, and not get in the way. They wouldn't want it any other way" (Pienaar 1991).

Public approval for the war, combined with the conflict's brevity and concern for the troops, undermined the efficacy of the antiwar movement (Shaw 1996, 60 and 176). Unlike their US counterparts, the UK antiwar groups primarily framed their activism in terms of a "just peace" and concerns regarding civilian casualties—a message that received scant media coverage (Shaw 1996, 61) The continuation of the UK antiwar movement's engagement with the troops, commenced during the Troubles, however, re-emerged and gained complexity.

The Campaign for Nuclear Disarmament's (CND) belief that military casualties would result in greater opposition to war and participation in the peace movement, for instance, indicates a reading of military personnel, if not the troops per se, as an object of broader social concern, rather than solely an instrument of force (in Shaw 1996, 61) Similar to the military family campaigns of the Troubles, CND began to frame enlisted personnel as potential victims of the conflict. Similarly, the National Executive Committee of the Campaign Against the War and CND, in a prewar emergency resolution, expressed concern regarding the risks to British armed forces placed under US command and control (National Executive Committee 1991). The Campaign Against the War in the Gulf, conversely, referenced the troops in their materials—"US and British Troops out of the Gulf!" (Campaign Against the War 1990)—in a manner directly reminiscent of TOM and the Troubles. The troops were not to be removed for their own sake, but as a means to ending the conflict (or illegal occupation/neo-imperial military presence). The UK peace and antiwar movements thus reflected the unsettled meaning of "the troops" through a combination of increasingly visible concern for military personnel while still promoting a more radical politics of implicit opposition to the troops as a force of foreign aggression.

In contrast to the struggles of the peace and antiwar organizations, military-related charitable organizations experienced a substantial increase in donations and "engaged a significant minority of the population" (Shaw 1996, 132). Again akin to the US, spontaneous and uncoordinated practices of support also arose, as, for instance, "25,000 letters and parcels were posted simply addressed to 'a soldier in the Gulf' and blood donations increased from 9000 to 14,000 pints per day" (Shaw 1996, 132). The Soldiers', Sailors' and Airmen's Association (SSAFA) reported that more than 20,000 people "responded to national and local appeals for volunteers" (1990, 3). These practices mark a continuation of the quotidian practices of military engagement of World War I and World War II, now read as "support" rather than war participation. Though the troops did not become the object of hegemonic concern in the UK they did in the US, the First Gulf War represents an important inflection point in UK normative civil-military relations and the early articulation of an explicit political obligation of military—if not always literally "troop"—support.

The UK experience of the First Gulf war should forestall contemporary presentism, which often reads the UK Armed Forces Covenant and Cameron Conservative government's moves to raise the social profile of the armed forces as (a) an unprecedented break with a UK tradition of military skepticism and/or (b) a phenomenon wholly distinct to that evolving in the US. The call to support the troops and associated popular practices of support for the military—and valorization of the ideally masculine combat soldier—have a long, if discontinuous, history in the UK. By the end of the twentieth century, the historically reviled, colonial era figurative soldier had been largely replaced by stories of individual masculine valor and a creeping concern for an aggregate troops. As in the US, concern for the troops became a regular, if contested, component of public discourse.

Conclusion

With important contextual differences, the twentieth century saw a shift in US and UK civil-military relations from suspicion of standing armies to expectations of heroic masculine war participation to a more generalized, (a)political norm of support for members of the armed forces, increasingly constituted as a distinct cultural figure: "the troops." The rise of the troops paralleled a largely unnoticed but meaningful disconnect between normative, gendered understandings of mass sacrifice, masculinized military service and the actual experience of warfare. Despite substantial differences in historical trajectory, the structure of civil-military relations, as well as the variable social stature of "the soldier," by the conclusion of the Gulf War, US and UK military institutional structures and military-oriented political culture had begun to converge. Each exhibited a professionalized military, popular regard for the troops, a mid-century experience of military disappointment, and a strong cultural mythology of heroic soldiers and "good wars." The relative popularity of these key conflicts—the 1982 Falklands/Malvinas War, the 1990–1991 Gulf War, and various peacekeeping missions—as well as their short duration, helped solidify the "commonsensical" nature of StT. Together, these factors may have forestalled a more robust reckoning with the political and ethical implications of unconditional troop support and declining military service. Instead, despite occurring over decades, the fracture of the military contract snuck up on us.

This is reflected in the fact that, although the global war on terror was, in important ways, distinct from the earlier conflicts of the twentieth century, support the troops rhetoric and symbolism remained as prevalent in the US and much more so in the UK as that of 1991. The September 11, 2001, attacks on the Pentagon and World Trade Centre shook the US, allies and the world. It was a shock to long-held beliefs in US exceptionalism and the ideological triumphalism of the liberal West in the post–Cold War era (Ralph 2013, 3). The aftermath of 9/11 saw a "rally round the flag" effect in the US, wherein national mourning combined with overt displays of patriotism across the government, formal media, and general public (Carruthers 2011, 2014; Mueller 1973). In contrast to many of the past conflicts, the US was suddenly positioned as the victim of attack (Esch 2010, 373). This created an ideological climate conducive to a retaliatory war (Carrruthers 2011, 214) and increasing restrictions upon US civil liberties. The UK, along with other US allies, expressed solidarity in response to the 9/11 attacks, keen to maintain its political relationship with the US through support for the invasions of Afghanistan and Iraq (Ali 2005, 2–4). It is easy to see how, post-9/11, the idea that everyone would support the troops became obvious.

The war on terror also offered a relatively novel discursive and information context, wherein frontline war reporting was increasingly "embedded," and therefore vetted by the Pentagon, restricting the access of US (and UK) publics to objective war reportage (Carruthers 2011, 224–26). At the same time, the collapse of the battlefront and home front via the increasing use of social media (i.e., blogging, Facebook, chat forums, and Skype) by individual military personnel gave domestic US and UK audiences direct access to the personal, humanizing accounts of the servicemembers constructed as "the troops" (Youngs 2010, 925–26). The early years of the war on terror were characterized by relatively minimal material sacrifice by US and UK civilians, a comparative dearth of stories of the wars' impact on Afghan and Iraqi civilians, and an intense focus on the experiences of the troops.

As the war on terror drew on, however, particularly after the invasion of Iraq, the increasingly controversial nature of the Bush and Blair administrations' foreign policy sparked a proliferation of differing interpretations as to what, precisely, it meant to "support the troops." It remained clear that "everyone" supported the troops, but exactly how, or even why, was suddenly unsettled. StT reflected, once again, the normative status of civil-military relations, as the tensions of the liberal military contract—namely unequal service and frustrated ideals of normative public/martial masculinity—were exacerbated. The political ambiguity inherent to the disparate, purportedly apolitical and exhortative nature of support the troops that, during the First Gulf War, facilitated a (relatively) homogenous narrative, as well as smoothed over the growing fractures in the liberal military contract, now lent itself to a "fragmented and collective discourse" of contestation, (re)appropriation, and (faltering) resistance (Stahl 2009, 557). The next chapter unpacks this process, providing an empirical overview of the post-9/11 articulation of supporting the troops in the US and UK.

4

Contemporary Support the Troops
Discourse and Practice

In the context of two contested wars and the ongoing fracture of the gendered liberal military contract, contemporary support the troops (StT) discourse is complex and contradictory. It changes over time, shifts in meaning—often within the same utterance—and, despite protestations to the contrary, is deeply political. This chapter is a descriptive analysis of contemporary StT discourse in the US and UK: how it works, where the internal fault lines lie, and what it doesn't say.

While StT discourse broadly rises and falls with the key events of the wars in Iraq and Afghanistan, its explicit content (and implicit meaning) has become unmoored from the wars and questions of their legitimacy. Supporting the troops is constituted, in line with the contractual logic of liberal political obligation, as something "everyone" must do—but not without contestation. There are many reasons, explicit and implicit, provided for supporting the troops. Most of these reasons are complementary (e.g., not only due to a sense of obligation, but also to conduct the war), although some are actively contradictory (e.g., to win the war, to end the war). The top-level consensus that "we" must StT is holding, but the proliferation of justifications for that "must" suggests the foundations are crumbling.

As StT becomes more pervasive, its substantive meaning is simultaneously expanded and hollowed out. Virtually any practice or social action (e.g., holding a bake sale, buying helicopters) can be framed as a way to support the troops. Against what, though, is somewhat unclear. As StT becomes unmoored from war, it is apparent that "the troops" need support more in response to government policies, people who *don't* support the troops, or nebulous social forces than an external enemy. The discursive formation is self-referential in a way that facilitates its (re)production as natural, obvious, and apolitical. From the perspective of assessing silences—that is, what is unsaid in relation to particular themes, as well as the failure to utter a form of

Support the Troops. Katharine M. Millar, Oxford University Press. © Oxford University Press 2022.
DOI: 10.1093/oso/9780197642337.003.0004

troop support at all—this complexity in the guise of default compulsion is an analytical challenge.

All of which is to say— StT discourse is imperfect and messy. It's difficult to capture and bound. Any discussion of "supporting the troops" will, inevitably, leave something(s) out. As mentioned in the Introduction, to examine key articulations of US and UK StT discourse, I looked at state (i.e., legislative, executive, and defense departments), media (i.e., major print newspapers), and civil society (i.e., five pro-military and five antiwar NGOs) discourse. This is a stratified data collection strategy that captures the commonsense and socially pervasive meanings of StT. It also means that discourses articulated by smaller organizations (or individuals)—such as Reddit forums calling out people for not supporting the troops or protestors handing out anti-military flyers—are not visible. I follow the typical conventions of discourse analysis in capturing salient contestations of StT discourse in the US and UK without exhaustively mapping all instances of resistance.

Even limiting my scope to these more conventionally authoritative actors and organizations returned an enormous volume of materials. To keep the interpretive analysis manageable, I sampled several strata of the US data. Specifically, while I explored US media use of StT discourse exhaustively, I examined a random sample of 20 percent of all StT discourse use, per year, for US government and NGO documents (see Appendixes 1 and 2). This enabled me to reduce the corpus to a manageable size while preserving the depth and diversity of the discourse captured. Sampling was not necessary for the UK, as StT discourse, though on the rise and politically significant, has not reached the level of social pervasiveness it has in the US (and thus a similar level of textual reproduction). With fewer uses of StT discourse overall, sampling in the UK risked missing salient, if infrequent, contestations of conventional UK StT discourse.

The trade-off inherent to this choice—to consider as much of each case as practically possible—means that the specific frequency (i.e., number times used) of particular themes are not directly comparable between the US and UK (even with the sampling of some strata, the US totals typically outstrip those in the UK). Please remember that StT is far more widespread in the US. By including as many texts as possible within both the US and UK cases, I provide the most accurate picture of the discursive formation and corresponding social narratives of troop support within each state. Comparisons of these *narratives* between the two states are also more accurate, as the depth and breadth of StT discourse in both the US and UK is preserved. It also enables me to identify continuities in the underlying assumptions and implicit meanings of StT across and between the two cases, as plausibly related to the transformation of gendered liberal civil-military relations more generally.

Concretely, I organize the discourse into descriptive themes tracking fairly explicit language use (e.g., who supports the troops), then broken down into subthemes (e.g., everyone, Brits, etc.) I identified through the close-reading and interpretation of the texts. To succinctly convey patterns and contestation, this chapter sometimes uses graphs. They are a visual shorthand rather than exhaustive. The graphs convey themes *within* my corpus, which is plausibly, but not definitively, illustrative of empirical trends beyond these specific texts (see Appendix 1). The illustrative nature of my analysis is partially to account for the analytical difficulty in bounding the discursive formation, reflected in the pragmatic messiness of a textual corpus collected from a variety of social actors (the media, government, and NGOs) that each used slightly different StT idioms and institutional archiving practices (see Appendix 2).

My analysis also reflects the fact that StT discourse—even small articulations at the paragraph and sentence level—can mean more than one thing simultaneously. This is obviously a challenge for simple visual representation of patterns, rather than single articulations, of meaning. Consider the excerpt below, from a 2007 op-ed written by the US NGOs Veterans of Foreign Wars and the American Legion:

> This is not a Democrat or Republican issue. This issue is about American men and women who we sent to war and who now some want to pull back before they finish their job. The time to debate the war is not in the funding bill that keeps our troops alive. If they need funds, it is the responsibility of Congress to provide them the money so that they can accomplish their mission. The sooner their job is done, the sooner they come home. That's how you "support the troops." (Kurpius and Morin, 2007)

This statement contains two explicit suggestions as to how the troops should be supported: providing them with funds and equipment and bringing them home. It also, in tone and the context of the balance of the op-ed criticizing Democrats' resistance to authorizing further military funding, suggests the troops should be supported by supporting the war. The passage not only conveys the typical sense of obligation to support the troops (particularly by Democrats) but also a sense that supporting the troops protects them. Each of these meanings—and the similar layering of meaning in each of the 3,000-plus paragraphs I considered—is captured by the thematic organization of the corpus. The charts therefore express patterns of *meaning* across the US and UK discursive formations, rather than tracking mutually exclusive linguistic "units" of troop support.[1] The graphs are intended to aid comprehension of StT discourse as an aggregate phenomenon, to help contextualize subsequent analysis of particular quotations, rather than offer a definitive empirical landmarking of all possible iterations.

Practically, this means multiple utterances/themes within the same passage are represented within the graphs. For the above example, both the ideas of providing money and bringing the troops home are represented within the "why support the troops?" graph. This chapter is a pragmatic exercise balancing the presentation of the overall discursive formation in more empirical detail than has been done previously and accounting for nuance. The "neatness" inherent to representing these layered and non-mutually exhaustive patterns of meaning via graphs is unpacked and made messy in the balance of the book. The way the logics, themes, and patterns initially outlined here constitute, contest, and blur each other is the central point of interrogation in Chapters 5 through 8.

The chapter proceeds by looking at the way StT discourse changed during the early years of the global war on terror (2001–2010). Next, I examine the ways war and conflict legitimacy are produced in relation to StT discourse. The chapter then plays out the main descriptive themes in StT discourse: who supports the troops, why they support the troops, how they support the troops, and the challenges (or threats) that render the troops in need of support.

Support the Troops Discourse and the Wars in Iraq and Afghanistan

Support the troops discourse during the so-called global war on terror (GWoT) demonstrates an interesting tension. Its overall pattern of articulation aligns with key events (e.g., battles, funding disputes, etc.) of the war, but its substantive content is disengaged from the wars, violence, and questions of conflict legitimacy.

Figure 4.1, which represents the change in the use of the StT phrases in the Google NGram English-language database, shows that the contours of the discourse follow the events of the wars in Iraq and Afghanistan. "Support the troops" increases after September 11, 2001, and the invasions of Iraq and Afghanistan; there is, after all, less call to support the troops absent an ongoing war. (Though the failure of StT to completely decline following the First Gulf War suggests it is coming to comprise a more routinized baseline of English language.) StT also broadly mirrors the height of the conflict in Iraq, with peaks in 2005–2006, and a decline as the war in Iraq (and, for the UK, Afghanistan), began to wind down.

This "close contact" in the articulation of StT discourse and broad trends in the wars also characterizes trends in the UK and US respectively.

UK Trends in Supporting the Troops

Figure 4.2 breaks down the use of StT within my UK textual corpus by year and social actor. The included texts were identified by their use of the phrase "support the troops" or an analogous expression expressing the normative relationship between the armed forces and society. What counts as an articulation of "supporting the troops" is purposively drawn very broadly. This accounts for context-specific iterations of the exact phrase, such as Help for Heroes (the branding of a UK military charity) and the inclusion of more ambivalent, yet clearly relevant discourses articulated by antiwar groups, such as calls to "bring them home."[2]

Figure 4.2 demonstrates two things of note. First, the discourse, as the NGram above, follows the broad trends of the UK experience of the GWoT. Reflecting the relative social acceptance of the war in Afghanistan, StT discourse is low in 2001–2002, before a sharp peak with the invasion of Iraq. In 2006, when violence in Iraq resulted in high numbers of civilian casualties and near civil war, the discourse demonstrates a slight increase (BBC 2015a; Reuters 2015). In 2008, StT begins to increase again, as the UK experienced its deadliest year in Afghanistan, the death of the 100th British service person, and continued to hold responsibility for operations in Helmand province (BBC 2011a). The continued prevalence of StT in 2009–2010 coincides with the end of combat operations in Iraq in 2009 and a shift in focus to Afghanistan (BBC 2009a).

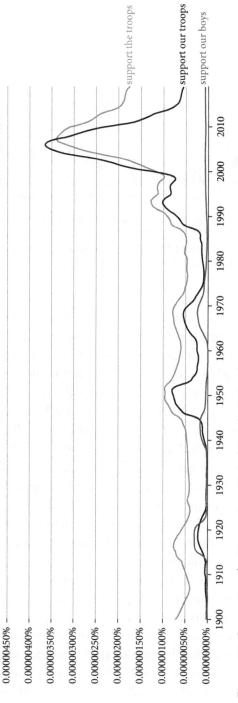

Figure 4.1 Supporting the Troops Over Time (Google NGram)

Note: The NGram corpus is millions of volumes scanned into the Google Books online database and made keyword searchable. The y axis is the change in the proportion of the various phrases as a percentage of the English corpus as a whole (hence the small percentages). (See Michel et al., 2011.) Figure 4.1 represents the *entire* English-language corpus, not just the US and the UK. It represents the occurrence of the literal phrase "support the troops," etc. and not variations such as "Support the Troops" or "supporting the troops."

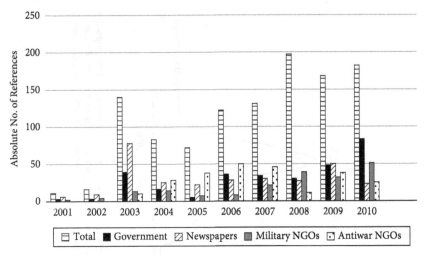

Figure 4.2 UK Support the Troops Discourse by Year, 2001–2010
Note: Texts that could not be dated were excluded.

Second, Figure 4.2 shows that with the (logical) exception of the media, UK social actors' participation in StT discourse is not a uniform response to the war. The discursive formation is produced differently at different times, as the social and political context changes. From 2001 to 2002, the discourse was informed by (a) the press commenting on the upsurge in StT discourse in the United States following the invasion of Iraq; and (b) subsequent press commentary regarding the ethics of the media (and, occasionally, politicians) opposing UK participation in Iraq (see Fletcher 2003; Freedland 2003). It was less an articulation of "organic" UK support for UK troop than a discussion of *US* troop support practices, their ethics, and their applicability to the UK—a continuation of the mild transnationalization of StT discourse seen during the First Gulf War. This conversation, in reporting US StT practices, however, also began to reify them as (a) existing and (b) at least potentially desirable (see Reese and Lewis 2009, 787).

StT discourse began to be more grounded in the UK context in 2003, as the Labour government (and opposition politicians) debated the invasion of Iraq. At this time, the mainstream media was increasingly disciplined to support the war. Of the major papers, only the *Guardian, Mirror* and *Independent* expressed skepticism regarding the invasion (and articulated solidarity with the troops after it was done) (Ali 2005, 25). StT discourse, however, did not entirely "come home" to the UK until 2005–2007. Help for Heroes, a major military charity, was founded in 2007 and strongly engaged in StT discourse, raising its profile overall and "setting the tone" for troop support organizations (Help for Heroes, n.d.). In its wake, older charities, such as the Royal British Legion, adapted their public discourse to more directly refer to normative civil-military relations. Antiwar groups, interestingly, were a major proponent of StT discourse. The newer mass organization Stop the War Coalition (StWC) and older antiwar groups, such as the Campaign for Nuclear Disarmament (CND), organized a series of rallies and campaigns opposing the war in Iraq and calling for the troops to be "brought home." The mainstreaming of StT in the UK is seen in the government's 2009–2010 discourse. In 2009, a shortage in military equipment, notably military helicopters, became a major scandal for the governing Labour Party (BBC 2009b). In 2010, the new Conservative administration made civil-military relations a key component of its governing agenda and public messaging (Taylor-Norton 2009).

Although the overall trends in UK StT discourse align with the events of the wars in Iraq and Afghanistan, its politics and social uptake do not. This contingent relationship between the wars as context for StT discourse and its articulation by particular actors is also seen in the US.

US Trends in Supporting the Troops

As expressed in Figure 4.3, US StT discourse also reflects key events of the wars. It was relatively low, as in the UK, following the invasion of Afghanistan before increasing in 2003. The subsequent period of substantial StT use included the capture of Saddam Hussein in 2003, heavy fighting in Fallujah in 2004, the 1,000th US military casualty, and the first Iraqi elections in 2005 (New York Times 2011). The 2007 jump coincides with the announcement and deployment of "the surge" of US military personnel to Iraq (Abramowitz and Wright 2007). The later decline aligns with a shift in emphasis in US military operations from Iraq to Afghanistan. In 2009, Obama announced a timeline for removing troops from Iraq and deploying additional personnel to Afghanistan; in 2010, Iraq combat operations ended (DeYoung 2009; Office of the White House Press Secretary 2010).

In the US, in contrast to the UK, the arc of StT discourse is closely aligned with the war in Iraq rather than Afghanistan. This is logical: UK political discourse was highly engaged with the legitimacy of the war

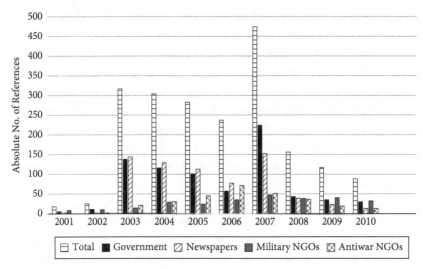

Figure 4.3 United States Support the Troops Discourse by Year, 2001–2010
Note: Texts that could not be dated are excluded.

in Iraq, but the UK military's material commitments were greater in Afghanistan. In the US, Iraq remained at the forefront of the experience of the war on terror. The mainstream US media, including Fox and CNN, moreover, adopted a pro-military lens on Afghanistan, declining to report on civilian casualties or the costs of war in detail (Carruthers 2011, 222). The war aspect of the war in Afghanistan soon vanished. Relatedly, following Vietnam and the First Gulf War, "support the troops" was firmly common sense in the US. The relative declines in StT in relation to Afghanistan reflect an inattention to that conflict and the intensity of StT discourse at the height of the war in Iraq. The baseline of StT discourse in the US far outstrips that of the UK.

The patterns in which social actors, in response to which events, were driving StT are particularly interesting. The (relatively) low early engagement with StT discourse in 2001 and 2002, for instance, is a departure from the First Gulf War that, though similarly brief (and popular), was fairly immediately characterized by troop support. This may be due to the invasion's temporal proximity to the 9/11 attacks. Military operations in Afghanistan were not an instance of US post–Cold War triumphalism, but a response to a more direct threat. Established military charities, such as Disabled American Veterans (DAV) and Veterans of Foreign Wars (VFW), which were founded and operated by the Vietnam generation of veterans, began advocating for StT as both a response to 9/11 and to, again, forestall public apathy.

From 2003 to 2005, StT discourse was strongly informed by government (and opposition politicians') statements (and their coverage in the press). In the post-9/11 environment, the US media, even more so than that of the UK, adopted a pro-war stance (Reese and Lewis 2009, 778). In contrast to the UK, however, where the major political parties took a (relatively) uni-fied line on the wars in Afghanistan and Iraq,[3] the GWoT was a major point of contention for the Republicans and Democrats. The Bush Department of Defense (DoD), for instance, commissioned a broad public relations cam-paign (not unlike those of the Vietnam era) to generate community support for the troops. The 2004 presidential election saw Bush and Democratic can-didate John Kerry compete over who was more supportive of the troops. In Congress, this discourse stems from (a) habitual statements by individual members of Congress as to their generalized support and admiration for the troops and (b) debate regarding the best means of funding operations in Iraq and Afghanistan. Democrats engaged in the discourse slightly more than Republicans, often to soften criticism of the Bush administration.

The Iraq surge subsequently informed StT discourse, as politicians debated its wisdom and antiwar groups mobilized to oppose the war. Though older antiwar groups, such as Pax Christi and Peace Action, experienced similar challenges to established UK peace organizations in quickly responding to the invasion, by 2006–2007, new GWoT-specific organizations, such as CodePink and United for Peace and Justice (UfJP), had filled the gaps. Their use of StT discourse was less ambivalent than their UK counterparts, as they explicitly proclaimed their support (even love) for the troops.

StT's subsequent return to something closer to a US baseline reflects the Obama administration's antiwar platform and governing priorities. It also coincided with the peak of the late 2000s financial crisis, reflecting a broader change in public and legislative priorities. By the end of this period, in 2009–2010, military charities such as DAV and the Iraq and Afghanistan Veterans' Association (IAVA) become significant proponents of StT as the tenor of "troop support" moved from the promotion of battle morale to veterans' care.

The US thus demonstrates the opposite pattern to the UK. StT discourse was initially driven by government/state actors and then maintained by mil-itary charities (though the 2004 election is really important to this pattern). While the UK went through a process of consolidating the requirement to StT in formal politics during the GWoT, in the US it was already business as

usual. The articulation of StT was informed, but not mechanistically determined, by the onset and fortunes of the wars in Iraq and Afghanistan.

Support the Troops Discourse and the Recognition of War

Despite StT discourse tracking the events of the wars in Iraq and Afghanistan,
the substance of StT discourse has an ambivalent relationship to the wars
themselves. Somewhat surprisingly, it does not always reference a particular
war or, in content, engage with the practice of making war.

In the US corpus, StT discourse explicitly references the war in Iraq approximately 13 times more often than the war in Afghanistan. It also, however,
references either both wars—or fails to explicitly specify a war, leaving the context ambiguous—just as often, (actually, slightly more), than the war in Iraq. In
the UK corpus, references to Iraq specifically are only 20 percent greater than
references to Afghanistan, while references to both, or unspecified, wars are
greater still. This is logical. At one level, these trends reflect the pattern above,
wherein the more politically salient war informs StT discourse. Iraq was (then)
more important in the US; Iraq and Afghanistan were alternately at the center
of UK political conversations. There's a case to be made that this is how the
instances where the conflict is unspecified should be interpreted: if Iraq or
Afghanistan isn't mentioned, assume it was the more contextually contested/
central one. I argue, however, that the prevalence of references to both (or neither, and thus ambiguous) wars is more reflective of the intertwining of Iraq
and Afghanistan into the overarching global war on terror.

The global war on terror was the frame for not only Iraq and Afghanistan,
but also myriad smaller operations conducted globally (including counterterrorism "at home") (Youngs 2010, 931; Reese and Lewis 2009, 781). There is
a difference in discussing the "war against Afghanistan" or "war against Iraq"
and a territorially and temporally ill-defined "war on terror." The vagueness of the war on terror meant as an experience of war and politics, Iraq,
Afghanistan, and other operations were not easy to separate (Youngs 2010,
931). Consequently, even articulations of "support the troops" that explicitly reference Iraq inform the war on terror context in which Afghanistan
is interpreted (and vice versa). The simultaneity of the two wars intertwines
their politics and relationship to civil-military relations. The failure to specify
a particular war in much of StT discourse further reifies the nebulousness of
the specifics, and politics, of the war on terror. It also, subtly, (re)produces

StT not as a reaction to the GWoT, or even contested conflicts, but a normalized component of contemporary warfare generally.

Consider the quotation in the introduction to this chapter—it firmly connects funding "the war" with supporting the troops but does not specify which war. The balance of the piece (and its timing) makes it clear the funding in question is for the 2007 troop surge in Iraq. It also, however, references the overall context of the GWoT. Most importantly, the emphasis upon the "men and women we sent to war" elevates StT to a general principle. Veterans of Foreign Wars and the American Legion are asking Congress to recognize their duty to "support the troops" in *any* war. The specific vote or even fortunes of Iraq are not the source of this obligation, but a context that makes it relevant.

Much of StT discourse pushes this trend further by underplaying, or failing to mention, war at all. The UK military charity uk4uThanks!, which provides Christmas packages to deployed UK military personnel, for instance, encourages Brits as follows:

> Get your kids and family involved and help uk4u Thanks! make a difference for our troops. It's not just adults that want to get involved and make a difference—get the whole family involved with raising money to help our troops on operations at Christmas. (2013)

The closest this passage gets to engaging with war is the mention of "operations." The clear concern of the group is the implied hardships the troops experience being away over Christmas—the specific conflict does not matter.

This constitution of StT as a general principle—as a foundational political obligation—is also reflected in a discursive ambivalence regarding the legitimacy of the wars in Iraq and Afghanistan. In much of US and UK StT discourse, it was not possible to assess a perspective on conflict legitimacy. The uk4uThanks! quotation, through its generic reference to operations, avoids engaging with, or evaluating, the legitimacy of the GWoT. Sending care packages to troops abroad could be taken as implicit endorsement of the war, just as the failure to explicitly state support for the war could be taken as evidence of opposition.

Where I could plausibly identify positions of conflict legitimacy, the pattern was indeterminate. In the US, discourse constructing the war in question as legitimate are slightly more common than discourses critiquing the war as illegitimate. In the UK, the pattern is reversed. This reflects the (slightly) greater contestation of the legitimacy of both wars in the UK, as well as the centrality of antiwar groups to UK StT discourse. In both states, however, constructions of the war as legitimate and illegitimate are at a near draw; neither emerges as a dominant frame.

A very small minority of discourse explicitly frames the legitimacy of the conflict as "irrelevant" to supporting the troops—directly articulating the underlying obligation to support the troops no matter what. A US military official recounted his interactions with members of the public, stating: "You know what was really amazing? The people who said, 'Chris, you know, I don't support the cause, but no matter what the cause, I'm always going to support the troops.'" (Washington Post 2006, A10). Though the officer expresses his pleasant surprise at this sentiment, it's actually an unusually explicit articulation of the way the entire discursive formation functions with respect to conflict legitimacy. From the perspective of StT, it does not matter.

Supporting the troops neither aligns with a particular evaluation of conflict legitimacy nor meaningfully engages with the substance and practice of war per se. The ambivalence toward war naturalizes StT as "obvious"—but also unmoors the normative demands of troop support from the practice (and legitimacy) of war. Support the troops discourse is oriented inwards, towards itself.

Who Supports the Troops?

The chapter now unpacks the internal workings of support the troops discourse, starting with the question of who supports the troops (and who is *supposed* to). Unsurprisingly, given the exhortative nature of the call to support the troops, the discourse holds that everyone is meant to StT. A plethora of specific constituencies, however, are also named as enacting (or failing) troop support.

Everyone Supports the Troops

Figures 4.4 and 4.5 outline each group that either produced materials supporting the troops or was explicitly named supporting the troops. The all-encompassing nature of the discourse is reflected in the prevalence, in the US and UK, of the idea that everyone should support the troops. "Everyone" refers to discourse that uses language such as "we," "all," "us," or "everyone"

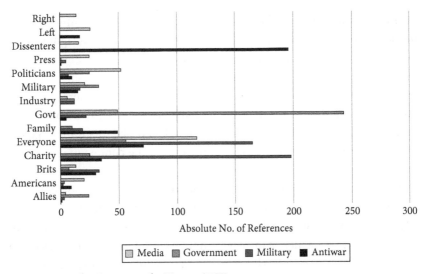

Figure 4.4 Who Supports the Troops? UK

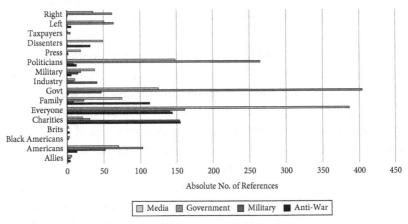

Figure 4.5 Who Supports the Troops? US

without specifying the group as American, or British, or veterans, and so forth. Consider, for instance, this Royal British Legion appeal, which asks:

> Can you help us? . . . [Our work is] . . . funded by the kind donations and fundraising efforts of our supporters. But for every person we reach, there are many more who are still struggling alone. Please help us be there for all of our brave heroes. (2003)

One could infer the "you," here, to means Brits, or patriots, or military families, and so on—but the failure to designate the group at hand is significant to how the discourse operates politically. It is just open-ended enough in target that it is, always-already, about everyone. The difference between "everyone" and "British" or "American" is important. It alludes to a difference in the meaning of StT discourse when the nation-state is explicitly invoked. This difference suggests a relationship between StT and liberalism more generally, related to, but distinct from, its animation in the context of specifically "American" or "British" nationalism.

This broad interpellation is more obvious in the substantial portion of the discourse that exhorts an unspecified audience as, for instance, in the use of protest signs or bumper stickers with the decontextualized slogan "Support the Troops!" The practice of displaying military-related symbols and slogans proliferated during the GWoT. In the US, "it was difficult to drive more than a few miles through middle America without seeing a car displaying a magnetic yellow ribbon" (Ward 2007). Berwick Offray, a US ribbon wholesaler, reports that "absolutely we saw an increase in yellow ribbon demand—any type/style we carried flew off the shelves" (Joaquim 2016, personal communication). At the height of demand, Magnet America, the largest purveyor of car magnets in the US, sold up to USD$1.2 million per month (Ward 2007). Local military charities and craft retailers across the US reported yellow ribbon shortages in the immediate aftermath of the invasion (Swanson 2003).

In the UK, Help for Heroes, the most prominent of the post-9/11 military charities, offers items ranging from branded clothing and jewelry to dog coats to delivered flowers to men's cologne (Help for Heroes 2016). Public uptake of this form of charitable engagement—and corresponding dissemination of these banal, decontextualized declarations of StT—was facilitated by tabloid sponsorship of Help for Heroes (Help for Heroes 2009a). These quotidian practices work as a personal declaration of support for the troops, a call for others to do the same, and, depending on the context, an indictment of others who fail to act similarly or support the troops "enough." They contribute to a generally circulating sense that everyone supports (or should) the troops.

A number of other groups are framed as StT—industry, military brass, antiwar protestors (i.e., "dissenters"),[4] taxpayers, even noncitizens (i.e., "allies").[5] The key takeaway is that there is not really a social constituency left out. The range of entities who StT span the public/private divide and encompass formally political actors, such as politicians,[6] and ostensibly apolitical actors, such as charities and military families. The construction of other groups as StT is not an indication of contestation of the idea that everyone should StT, but rather "everyone" scaled down to a particular context. Military families, for instance, are not constituted as StT *instead* of everyone but as *part* of everyone.

Identity and Experiential Support

It bears reiterating that the groups contained within Figures 4.4 and 4.5 are those *explicitly* referenced within the discourse itself. Methodologically, this follows: it constrains the analysis to meanings circulated within the discourse, rather than making assumptions as to either the embodied identity of the speaker or the intended audience. As a result, however, some key variation within "who" supports the troops is not visible within Figures 4.4 and 4.5. Notably, they don't give an indication as to how gender, sexuality, race, and class relate to troop support.

This is accurate to how the discourse is constructed. The gender, race, sexuality, and so forth of troop supporters is mentioned vanishingly rarely, and so does not appear in the inductive analysis of the texts.[7] StT discourse collapses difference into a universal relation of obligatory, mandatory support—helping elide the inequities of military service and sacrifice under liberalism. The construction—or lack thereof—of particularistic identity within StT discourse is discussed in Chapter 5. The *implicit* ways in which troop supporters are gendered, racialized, and so forth via conceptual associations and relational power dynamics are interrogated in Chapters 5–7.

Empirically, however, particular groups and communities certainly experience both the expectation of troop support and the practice(s) of troop support differently. Marsical (1991, 109–13) examines, for instance, the complex civil-military experiences of Latinx communities within the US, who disproportionately risk their lives in military service and are simultaneously frequently targeted by racist state (police and immigration) violence. This positions the family and community members of Latinx military personnel into politically and affectively contradictory, though heartfelt, relationships of support to the troops—who are often parsed from the state and military institution. Strachan (2003) notes that military service in the UK is classed, with enlisted military personnel frequently recruited at age 16, without continuing education, from working-class backgrounds. Conversely, "most

Britons now see themselves as middle class, and that means that they expect to join the armed forces as officers or not at all" (50). Though "everyone" in the UK supports the troops, it is safe to infer that the experience of military deployments and troop support is highly classed, as well as racialized and regional. These disparities in the lived experience of supporting the troops, though not visible via the methodology of this study, are an important avenue for future work.

The State Supports the Troops

Returning to the discursive construction of who StT, the insistence that everyone supports the troops exists in an interplay with the next most prominent group framed as StT—the government. "Government," here, is straightforward: it captures discourse that frames actors speaking, implicitly or explicitly, for/as the government as StT. (Unsurprisingly, most, though not all, of this discourse is produced by the government itself.)[8]

The state use of StT reveals again the salience of the expectation that everyone—particularly governing elites—will StT. It also points to the pragmatic deployment of StT discourse to generate support (or at least tolerance) for the wars. A Conservative MP (member of Parliament), for instance, called on the legislature to pass a government motion expressing support for the troops by arguing that serving military personnel had said to him, "Come off it, we're out here doing a mission; support us! Don't just say, 'We support you.'" (Stewart in Hansard 2010, c496). Supporting the troops is read as supporting the war is read as supporting the government—made all the more powerful by rhetorically locating that sentiment in military personnel themselves. These overt framings of the government as StT, however, do not exhaust the state's involvement in cultivating a sense of "who" ought to StT. The state also reifies the notion that everyone ought to support the troops through explicit campaigns to magnify grassroots troop support.

From 2005 to 2009, for instance, the UK marked Veterans Awareness Week (BBC 2006a) to honor and remember the sacrifices of UK veterans of all conflicts. This was is in addition to the continuation of commemorative poppy sales by the Royal Legion and observance of Remembrance Sunday by state and Church of England ceremonies throughout the war on terror (Basham 2016). In 2009, Veterans Awareness Week was changed to Armed Forces Day. Its mandate was extended to showing appreciation for all serving personnel and their families. The event, marked annually, now involves co-ordinated, state-funded events across the UK, including parades, family activity days, museum visits, military demonstrations, concerts, and air force fly-bys (UK Ministry of Defence 2022).

The state has also promoted an Armed Forces Covenant between society and the military. The covenant, originally framed in a 2000 army pamphlet, refers to the moral obligation of society to support and provide for those who have risked and sacrificed a great deal for the nation—soldiers and their families (Army Doctrine Publication 2000 1–3). It includes a Community Covenant, in which local politicians, voluntary sector workers, and other public officials pledge to support the Covenant and raise awareness of the armed forces (UK Ministry of Defense 2012a). Aspects of this agreement are codified in the 2011 Armed Forces Act. Successive UK governments have sought to make the normative status of the civil-military relationship not only a matter of public concern but also of active, daily social practice by a range of social actors—of everyone.

State promotion of support for the military is more pronounced in the US. Post-9/11, pre-existing civic commemorations and valorizations of the military, notably Memorial Day and Veterans Day, continued—now entangled with the militaristic legitimation of the war on terror (Hammond and Curran 2002). The flagship of state-promoted troop support was America Supports You (ASY), a Department of Defense program launched in 2004:

> To showcase and communicate to U.S. military members defending our freedom around the globe what thousands of individual citizens, community groups, corporations, businesses, and others are doing to support them and their families. (Inspector General 4)

The website listed hundreds of NGOs involved in military-support activities and encouraged citizens to write messages of support for the military (America Supports You 2004). Many of the activities of the public relations organization that ran ASY, particularly those soliciting, as opposed to communicating, sponsorship and/or support, were subsequently found to be ethics violations of DoD regulations (Inspector General 2008, 4).[9] ASY was not the only such government program. A 2015 report found that the DoD paid over $53 million to 50 professional sports teams to publicly promote the armed forces—and recruitment (Carpenter 2015)—during games from 2012–2015 (Quandt 2015). Though similar documentation is not available for 2001–2010, comparable pro-military activities, from audio visual presentations on sacrifice to public re-enlistments, occurred at professional sporting events (Butterworth and Moskal 2009, 420; Fischer 2014).

The DoD presents yearly Freedom Awards to "to publicly recognize employers who provide exceptional support to their Guard and Reserve employees" (Secretary of Defense Employer Support Freedom Award 2016), extending StT into the private sphere. In 2011, the Obama Administration replaced ASY with the Joining Forces initiative, which "call[s on] all Americans to rally around service members, veterans, and their families and support them through wellness, education, and employment opportunities" (Whitehouse.gov 2012). Though the emphasis shifted from supporting troops in the field to supporting military families at home, the overall aim of fostering "greater connections between the American public and the military," similar to the UK Armed Forces Covenant, remains the same.

The state's reinforcement of the idea that everyone must (and does!) support the troops is similar to the Vietnam era astroturf campaigns of the Johnson and Nixon administrations. As then, though there is certainly a strategic, propagandistic aspect to these state-propagated discourses (Dixon 2012; Chomsky 2002), they also reflect the broader, underlying structures of normative civil-military relations. Military service, through sheer repetition, is elevated as the apogee of citizenship, producing gendered demands for support, care, and recognition by protected and dependent civil society. The Covenant, and similar initiatives such as Joining Forces, make the subtextual implications of the liberal military contract text. These moves towards formalization and overt institutionalization also, somewhat counterintuitively, reflect the contract's ongoing fracture. The expectation that everyone StT—apparently—needs explicit restatement and retrenchment.

The idea that everyone StT is reified by state discourse and programs, and it is furthered by many social actors. "Everyone supports the troops" is the closest thing to a point of consensus within contemporary StT discourse. It also has an implicit corollary that is just as important to understanding the politics of StT: if everyone supports the troops, no one is exempt.

Why Support the Troops?

The relative consensus that everyone supports the troops does not extend much further into the discursive formation. In contrast to the broader substantive agreement at the end of the First Gulf War, it is no longer clear what support means. The reasons provided for supporting the troops are a matter of significant contestation. The fracture of the liberal military contract is visible, even at this macro-discursive level. Though "obligation" is constituted as the main reason for StT, the meaning of obligation is internally differentiated. Contractual notions of support sit alongside contending constructions of political obligation.

Figures 4.6 and 4.7, which provide an overview of the many reasons provided for supporting the troops, are quite busy. They convey contestation of the liberal military contract through the sheer proliferation of rationales. (Multiple rationales may also, recall, be present within the same text.) Contradictory goals—to support the war, to end the war—are both presented as reasons to StT. It is possible, however, to discern some patterns within the noise.

Obligation

"Obligation"—references to the typical (liberal) understanding of support as owed, in pseudo-contractual form, to those serving in the armed forces—is the main supportive rationale in the US and UK. The UK government document laying out the vision for the Conservative-Liberal Democrat coalition administration, for instance, states, "We are agreed that the first duty of government is to safeguard our national security and support our troops in

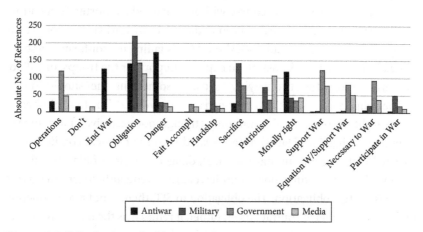

Figure 4.6 Why Support the Troops—UK

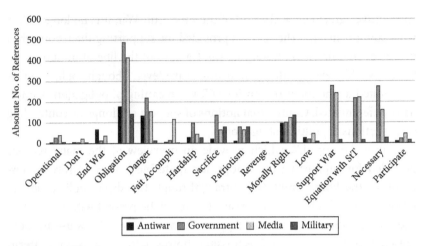

Figure 4.7 Why Support the Troops—US

Afghanistan and elsewhere—and we will fulfil that duty" (UK Government Coalition 2010, 8). This mirrors the logic of the military contract; the relationship between the state, political violence, and citizenry is articulated in terms of reciprocal expectation and obligation. (It also highlights the paradox of the liberal contract, insofar as national security and supporting the troops—who theoretically, are the instrument of that national security—are both incommensurably listed as top priorities.)

There is texture within the way "obligation" is articulated. Much of StT discourse doesn't give an explicit reason for StT but simply conveys a sense of compulsion, that is, one "must" support the troops. Similar to the way that "everyone" includes StT discourse without a named supporter, "obligation" encapsulates unspecified exhortations directed outward (i.e., "support the troops!") that imply the audience should (or is failing to) conform to a social obligation. It's nearly impossible to express support for the troops, or call for others to do so, without conveying a sense it's something one "should" do.

The obligation to StT is also specified and concretized. The four subthemes to the right of "obligation" commonly (though not exclusively) accompany a sense of obligation. Hardship (associated with the physical conditions associated with war and military service), danger (the risk of life and injury), and sacrifice (of life, time, opportunities, etc.) are frequently constituted as the *grounds* for this obligation. The obligation to StT, then, is not a reproduction of the liberal military contract itself; rather, it reifies it as the normative structure of civil-military relations from which obligation is derived. The contract is the reason for support. This is best expressed in the fourth category associated with obligatory StT—"fait accompli"—which captures discourse that *explicitly* states that, in wartime, there is no choice but to support the troops. In the UK, the Scottish National Party's stance of opposing the war, but accepting that, once it began, it was "necessary to support our boys," is paradigmatic of this position (Massie 2004). The obligation to StT does not bear debate.

Support the War

The next substantial theme from Figures 4.6 and 4.7 posits "supporting the war," as well as associated categories, as the reason to support the troops. This is much more common in the US than the UK, where themes of "obligation" and "morality" (see next section) appear more prevalent. This reflects the greater level of public contestation regarding the war in Iraq experienced in the US vis-à-vis the UK (where public opinion turned against the war quite quickly[10]) and a greater degree of elite division. In the UK, all three major political parties, once hostilities commenced, broadly supported government policy (and the war). The majority of contestation regarding the legitimacy of the war on terror—particularly in Iraq—was contained within the governing Labour Party, rather than spanning partisan lines. In the US, though there was broad initial support for the invasions of Iraq and Afghanistan, prominent Democratic politicians, including presidential candidates during the 2004 election, voiced more frequent and explicit opposition. By approximately 2006, the supportive consensus for the war on terror within the US political elite had broken down, with Republicans largely for the war in Iraq and Democrats against.

In this context, the meaning of the "support the war" rationale is straightforward: discourse that posits supporting the troops as logical in the context of supporting the war. A 2003 congressional statement regarding war appropriations, for instance, conveys this casually: "we have to really focus on what this is all about, my colleagues . . . and understand that the most important part about this [funding bill] is to support our troops and support the war in Iraq" (Delay 2003, H3204). In a departure from the balance of StT discourse, much—though not all—of this theme at least implies an understanding of the military as the instrument of state security.

There are differentiations in "support the war" represented in the three categories to the right of "support war" on the graphs. Discourse that equates

StT with supporting the war goes further than discourse that frames StT as a *means* of supporting the war. It makes StT and supporting the war indivisible. A participant at a 2005 Freedom Walk event—intended to commemorate 9/11 and veterans, but contextually read as also supporting the war in Iraq—for instance, stated: "What I've never really understood is how someone could say they support the troops but they don't support the war . . . Because the troops want to win the war" (Montgomery 2005). They construct StT and supporting the war as being logically (and ethically) indivisible. The idea of StT as "necessary" is another twist on supporting the war, constituting support as essential to the war effort/operational success. "Participation" includes StT discourses that frame supporting the troops as a way civilians can contribute to the war effort.

Though they aren't mutually exclusive—one can feel obliged to support the troops and support the war—"supporting the war" suggests a reason for StT that doesn't solely derive from the liberal military contract. Instead, it alludes to either an independent, non-contractual relationship to the war or, more interestingly, an acceptance of the illiberal elision of military service within the "good" story of liberalism. "Supporting the war" contests the obligations arising from the liberal military contract by both bypassing it and refusing to interrogate its underlying paradoxes.

More Reasons to Support the Troops

"Obligation" and "supporting the war" do not exhaust the supportive logics produced within StT discourse. One can support the troops because they want to end the overall war ("end war"), as part of ongoing military operations (e.g., "the air force will support the troops on the ground"), and as an expression of pride about specific nation-state ("patriotism").

There is also a substantial portion of StT discourse—the third most common supportive theme in the UK—that expresses a sense it is "morally right" to support the troops. This discourse frames StT as good and/or appropriate without a sense of obligation, a specific reason, or a feeling of common cause. Though this sense of morality infused StT is expressed by all social actors, its prominence within the discursive formation reflects the remarkable post-9/11 growth in the military-related charitable sector in the US and the UK (not unlike the UK post–World War I charitable boom) (Millar

2016a, 11). The number of UK charities established to support the military tripled every year between 2005–2011 (Telegraph 2011). In the US, the rapid growth of the veterans' charitable sector since 2000 (a 77 percent increase compared to a 43 percent sector average) and 2008 (up 41 percent compared with 19 percent across charities overall) indicates the prioritization of "the troops" as a locus for charitable giving (Hrywna 2013).

As an example, the public was encouraged to purchase a charity single by the Military Wives Choir because "military families are ably supported by both The Royal British Legion and SSAFA Forces Help so we are delighted to be donating to them all proceeds from this heartfelt song. These women support our troops and now it's your chance to support them" (Stafford Branch 2010). The two levels of support constituted here—by the Military Wives Choir (Cree 2020; Baker 2018) and the purchasing public—imply that supporting the troops is a generous and prosocial but *voluntary* ("now it's your chance") thing to do. The liberal military contract doesn't come into it.

There are lots of reasons to support the troops. Obligation, reflecting the cultural dominance of the myths of the liberal military contract, remains the most prevalent rationale, referenced by all social actors. It is also, reflecting the experiential fracture of the contract, subject to contestation. With very few exceptions,[11] however, the mandatory nature of StT is unaffected; while people may StT for a variety of contradictory reasons, the troops must still be supported.

How to Support the Troops?

Contestation over why one should "support the troops," combined with the insistence that "everyone" support the troops, has made StT socially pervasive and substantively ambiguous. In this context, literally anything can be (and is) justified as somehow supporting the troops. "The troops" offer an ur-rationale for social action (e.g., pay your taxes to support the troops) and a get-out-of-jail-free card for controversial opinions, such as war support or opposition. As seen in the heterogeneity of actions listed in Figures 4.8 and 4.9, anything you can do, you can do for the troops.

The sentiment that as long as the troops are supported, anything goes, is encapsulated by a fundraising appeal by the UK military charity Help for Heroes (2008):

Baking cakes may not be your thing, despite being amazingly successful and profitable; you may prefer a quick assault on Everest or a jog across the Kalahari, a marathon, a tandem parachute jump or a sponsored leg wax; it doesn't really matter, as long as you do something.

The US DoD America Supports You program, similarly, listed a range of opportunities for people to StT on their website, ranging from donating frequent flier miles and phone cards to providing teddy bears to service members' children to job retraining for veterans to conventional care packages to religious counselling to sewing patriotic pillows (America Supports You 2005).

These excerpts, and the graphs above, reveal that activities conventionally read as both private and public—from prayer to supporting the government—can be called into service as StT. Activities that are conventionally masculine, such as actual military operations, and that are conventionally feminine, such as supporting troops' families and providing veterans' care, are all available to be framed as StT. The civil-military divide and its underlying, gendered division of violent labor are blurred by the appropriation of all forms of social and political activity as a form of StT. Support can be active (i.e., holding morale activities like parades), passive (e.g., displaying a symbol), or negative (e.g., abstaining from dissent).

This means that opposing stances—ending the war and supporting the war—may be justified with reference to StT. In the UK, references to "protest" and "ending the war" make up a plurality of StT practices. In the US, references to providing material goods, from care packages to congressional funding to military equipment, are most common. Combined with explicit declarations of support for the war and the government, war-facilitating practices are more common in the US than the UK. This is an important contrast, reflecting the greater influence of antiwar groups in the UK discursive formation, as well as the sheer volume of StT discourse produced by the US government. In both countries, however, neither ending nor supporting the war made up a majority (or even a particularly substantial plurality) of StT discourse.

In contrast to questions of "who" and "why" we support the troops, "how" largely lacks an identifiable center. Everything can read/justified as a form of support. This suggests that absent explicit declarations of opposition to the troops, the failure to perform troop support may not be socially read or recognized as a form of contestation or resistance. If anything can support the troops, the bar for meaningful contestation of the obligation to StT is raised substantially.

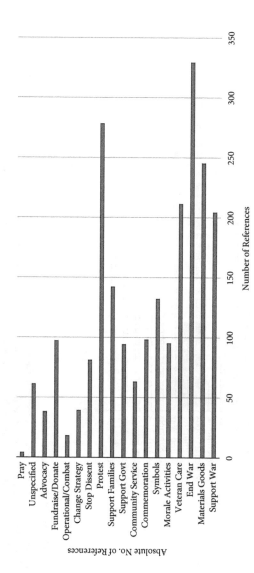

Figure 4.8 How to Support the Troops—UK

Note: "Operational" refers to discourse related to the active practice of war (such as "supply convoys support the troops in country"); "community service" suggests either: a) StT is a form of community service or b) that community involvement, such as volunteering, is a means of StT); "commemoration" references remembering fallen soldiers of past and present conflicts, honouring veterans, or formally noting contemporary service; "symbols" captures references to the display (as signs, apparel, adornment, etc.) of symbols associated with the military (and, frequently) the nation.

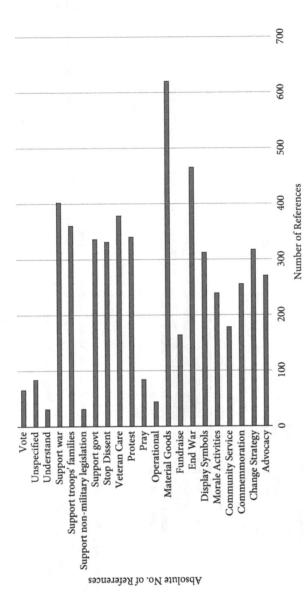

Figure 4.9 How to Support the Troops—US

Note: as in Figure 4.8, "operational" refers to discourse related to the active practice of war (such as "supply convoys support the troops in country"); "community service" suggests either: a) StT is a form of community service or b) that community involvement, such as volunteering, is a means of StT); "commemoration" references remembering fallen soldiers of past and present conflicts, honouring veterans, or formally noting contemporary service; "symbols" captures references to the display (as signs, apparel, adornment, etc.) of symbols associated with the military (and, frequently) the nation.

Why Do the Troops Need Support?

Given the unmooring of StT from war, and its inward rotation as a mandatory discourse implicating "everyone," it is not surprising that the reasons the troops need support are typically vague or unspecified. Looking at the quotations referenced in this chapter, from the declaration that the legitimacy of war is irrelevant to supporting the troops to the idea that care packages "make a difference" to troops at Christmas, the factors that render the troops in need of support are unstated.

When the reasons the troops need support can be identified, they contradict what we might expect for a military entity in wartime. The sources of threat are rarely presented as "the enemy" in combat. A "Loyalty Day" speech by Veterans of Foreign Wars (which engages with war and fighting within StT more than most military charities) states that the organization "supports our military leaders and our troops as they endeavor to preserve and protect our way of life" in the context of "a grave threat from the Iraqi regime that threatens American security and the people and nations of that region" (2003). The troops are supported in their role as, essentially, the instrument of state force, threatened by battle and the specific conditions of the war on terror as a result.

Most StT discourse, however, sidesteps the question(s) of war and instead frames the government, or broader social forces, as the reasons the troops require support. In the UK, the government was commonly constituted as a source of threat to the troops, predominantly, but not exclusively, by antiwar groups, led by the Stop the War Coalition. (In the US, antiwar groups and military charities also frequently critiqued the government for imperiling the troops, as did Democrats.)[12] A Stop the War Coalition protestor, for instance, characterized a local antiwar protest as aimed "at the government for putting [the troops in] Afghanistan." He argued, "We are saying we do support the troops but the best way of supporting them is to bring them home. They are ill-equipped, they have been put in a completely impossible situation, in a war they don't understand" (Harrison 2009). The troops require support against the neglect of the state they ostensibly serve. This construction reveals the underlying paradox of the liberal military contract, wherein the state risks the lives of citizens in war, but stops short of refuting it entirely. It instead implies that a more legitimate conflict, better military provisions, or more responsible government would assuage these concerns.

The troops are also commonly constituted as requiring support due to "social conditions" or "social forces"—diffuse and unspecified harm, suffering, or danger. In the context of a US Senate debate on "Honoring our Armed Forces," a Republican senator stated, after noting that he had visited a wounded service member at the Walter Reid veterans hospital, that

> [I]t is also comforting for those in the field to know their loved ones back home are being taken care of when push comes to shove. I think Operation Homefront [an NGO that supports deployed service members' families] will be an excellent tool for getting information out to people. Supporting our troops is something we think about every day. We appreciate their risks and the sacrifices they are making. (Burns 2003)

The source of challenge to the troops' well-being is not particularly clear. It seems to be "risks and sacrifices," but those could arise from separation from their families, from material deprivation at home, or perhaps from battle during deployment. As in this passage, the troops are frequently framed as imperiled by situations unattributed to particular social actors. The idea of "social forces" encompasses discourse that constructs the troops as vulnerable to amorphous (ostensibly, as constituted empirically) "agent-less" harm, ranging from PTSD to physical injury to homelessness.

Reflecting the divorce of StT from the wars in Iraq and Afghanistan, the troops are posited as requiring support because things "just happen." The discourse could be taken to imply that it's obvious why the troops need support (a useful indeterminacy). The corollary of this, however, is that the troops are constituted as definitionally in need of support. This challenges the gendered constitution of society within the patriarchal civil-military divide as inferior and dependent—as feminized. The implications of this generalized sense of peril and potential harm for the constitution of the troops are taken up in detail in the next chapter.

Conclusion: The Meaning(s) of What Isn't Here

StT discourse is characterized by a specific form of indeterminacy. In contrast to the past, wherein StT was produced as synonymous with supporting the war (and the government), the StT discourse of the early war on terror was heterogenous. Opposing goals and commitments—such as, end the war, win the war—can serve as reasons to support the troops. Any banal practice can be produced as a form of supporting the troops. The troops' need for support derives from a vague sense of peril, rather than conflict. The vagueness of the war on terror facilitated a counterintuitive detachment of supporting the troops from the politics (and contested legitimacy) of the wars in Iraq and Afghanistan. Supporting the troops, as a wartime discourse of solidarity, is self-referential. Its major point of normative reference is itself.

This ambiguity and tautology, however, should not be taken as an indication that StT is somehow meaningless. "Everyone" remains subject to the expectation that the troops are supported. The flexibility in the rest of StT facilitates its dissemination and naturalization. The meaning of StT is subject to substantial contestation; the idea that the troops must be supported is not. The gendered division of violent labor underlying the liberal military contract appears to be blurring and shifting, but the valorization of military service is not.

The compulsory and pervasive nature of StT discourse has political and analytical implications. Most importantly, when everyone is assumed to StT, for any given reason, by doing nearly anything, silences in the discourse become difficult to see and interpret. It is challenging to identify ironic, or half-hearted engagements in supporting the troops. The failure to articulate StT, overall or in a given context, could be read as resistance but may also convey acquiescence, disengagement, or naturalization. The analysis of StT in this chapter provides the context within which silences around StT are made meaningful. Silence enters a tautological, self-justifying discursive formation that both reflects the notions of gendered political obligation at work in the liberal military contract and contests them. Support is discursively projected upon silence as a presumption, and explicitly socially disciplined as an expectation of good conduct.

This rendering of StT discourse also points toward specific silences: the unsaid, rather than the absent. It is notable that joining the military—the most obvious possible form of supporting the troops—is one of the few practices not commonly offered as a means of StT. It also important that key axes of substantive identity—gender, sexuality, class, race, and so forth—are not explicated within these broader relations of support. Though the group of supporters may be scaled up and down, the universality of liberal political belonging remains intact, even as the power dynamics, as well as gendered social relations, of the heteropatriarchal civil-military divide are challenged.

Understanding the substantive political meaning of the complexity and contestation identified in this chapter—the dissociation of StT from war, the apoliticization of support, the multiplicity of reasons for StT, the tricky relationship between antiwar groups and StT– requires further interpretation. The balance of the book unpacks the politics of StT articulated within this chapter, beginning with the meaning of "the troops." It also examines StT as a reflection of liberal civil-military relations: the gendered dynamics of violent political obligation that make up the political community.

5

The Politics of the Troops

This chapter begins the book's detailed interrogation of the "politics" of the troops as a manifestation of discursive martiality: the way in which the troops operate within discourse to inform the terms of social intelligibility and "normal" conduct. I zero in on the meaning(s) of "the troops" as a distinct figure of war.[1] "The troops" function counterintuitively within the discourse. Based on the way Western wars—particularly the "good" wars, World Wars I and II—are typically narrativized, we might expect them to be constituted like the soldier: heroic, ideally masculine, agential, sacrificial, and protective (Dahl Christensen, 2015). Alternatively, thinking about the angst that accompanies contested wars, such as Vietnam or Northern Ireland, we might expect the troops to be framed as the wounded veteran, with themes of victimization, betrayal, and failure (Achter 2010). As this chapter will demonstrate, however, "the troops" mean something different.

First, the troops are a group. In contrast to the soldier, the veteran, or the institutional military, which have fairly stable substantive meanings, this makes the "content" of the troops difficult to pin down. They are abstract; "the troops" can discursively stand-in for a variety of subjects, including the military, civilians, family members, and so forth, simultaneously and without contradiction. The troops may convey some of the meaning(s) associated with the soldier or veteran, but they are not reducible to those common narratives. Instead, they have an ambivalent relationship to the existing gender dynamics and politics of the liberal military contract: "the troops" can reinforce myths of soldiering heroism while also acknowledging the harms and vulnerability experienced by military personnel.

Second, the troops are produced as vulnerable to harm—a reversal of the typical gendering of the liberal civil-military divide. Rather than the troops, as the military, protecting society from foreign adversaries and the violence of war, supporting the troops (StT) discourse produces the troops as victims of war or circumstance, reliant upon a supportive society for their well-being

Support the Troops. Katharine M. Millar, Oxford University Press. © Oxford University Press 2022.
DOI: 10.1093/oso/9780197642337.003.0005

(and even survival). Violence is presented as incidental to war, as something that "happens" to the vulnerable, structurally feminized troops, rather than an active practice of the political community. The central normative concern of war shifts away from questions of legitimacy and the ethics of killing distant civilians to maintaining the morale of the troops.

Third, the "groupness" of the troops enables them to include, rather than elide, substantive differences (e.g., race, gender, sexual orientation, etc.) within the polity. As "everyone" is obliged to support the troops, the entire polity is produced as potential supporters and/or potential troops; no individual and no socially meaningful group is left out. The compulsory, affective obligation of support absolves society, through deflection, from engaging with violence, democratic decision-making, or even the institutional military. The obligation to support the troops overrides all other political considerations, from the deaths of individuals to the articulation of differences within society.

The chapter works through each of these characteristics of the troops—groupness, dependence/vulnerability, and ability to incorporate difference—in order. Overall, the troops produce a new, internally oriented politics of war (or war avoidance) more engaged with the maintenance of normative civil-military relations than evaluating the legitimacy of externally oriented violence. The troops displace public affective investment in war from identification with the increasingly inaccessible heteromasculine soldier to the support of the dependent, vulnerable, and feminized troops. "They" draw upon logics of gendered contrast and association to elide the ideological inconsistencies at the heart of liberal war. This depoliticizes war within formal politics, while, as a corollary of broader discursive martiality, "papering over" the ongoing fractures in the liberal military contract.

The Soldier and the Legitimation of Liberal Violence

To excavate the distinct politics of the troops, this section first provides a brief overview of the role of the soldier in the typical legitimation of liberal violence. As outlined in Chapter 2, the paradox of the liberal military contract—that citizens are required, normatively and practically, to kill and die for a state whose sole reason for existence is their protection—is resolved by fusing committing violence for the state with normative masculinity. Martial violence, as an instrument of liberal war and a condition of liberal citizenship, is legitimated and elided through broad social regard for the armed forces.

"The soldier" is a key figure of this liberal martiality, condensing "distillations" of shared meaning, background understandings, normative orientations, and so on toward violence into a seemingly stable "image" that evokes more than it literally represents (Weber 2016, 28). "He" is less a description of an actually existing individual—or even profession or social role—than shorthand for the complex narratives, myths, and assumptions that make up contemporary liberal notions of "good wars," gender (sexuality, race, nationality, etc.), citizenship, and civil-military relations. By conveying these unspoken but socially and culturally resonant understandings of legitimate violence and normative gender, the figurative soldier grounds the liberal military contract (Hurcombe and Cooper 2009, 109).

First, as seen in Chapter 2, the figurative soldier is elevated as the universal ideal of public personhood to which all citizens may identify and aspire. The soldier mirrors and reproduces the universalized masculine (White, cis, heterosexual) public subject of the modern West (Basham 2013, 13). "He" is aggressive yet judicious, physically brave yet technologically adept, and courageous yet disciplined (Hale 2012; Connell 1995; Barrett 1996; Higate 2003, 30 cited in Duncanson 2009, 64). Like the liberal individual, he is autonomous and rational: heroic. This is reinforced via gendered contrast with the non-serving civilian: "the brave wear a uniform, the coward wears a suit" (Sands 2008). The soldier serves as a "triumphalist image . . . that give[s] us the idea of the human with whom we are to identify . . . the patriotic hero who expands our own ego boundary ecstatically into that of the nation" (Butler 2006, 145). The valorization of the soldier legitimates the violence of the nation-state, while the state fulfills the soldier and renders him (and his potential sacrifice) meaningful. Martial violence and the underlying military contract are legitimated through a relationship of universalized interpellation between individual citizens and the idealized heteromasculine soldier.

Second, the efficacy of this legitimation is bolstered by a related process, wherein the soldier also comes to represent the nation-state itself. The body of the individual soldier frequently stands in for the body politic (Hass 1998). In instances of national triumph, the "soldier becomes a proponent for a society's whole set of values," an embodiment of virtue and heroism (Dahl Christensen 2015, 355). Following collective shame or loss, the wounded body of the soldier—the veteran—comes to represent the trauma and failure of the nation (Sturken 1997). This process of legitimation operates

differently than that above by metaphorically negating the distinction between the nation-state and the soldier. As argued by MacLeish, when "the
soldier stands for the nation, then to question the worthiness of the soldier's
death [or killing] . . . is to perform a parallel manoeuvre on the nation itself"
(2005, 81).

Mapping the soldier onto the nation obscures the state's exposure of its
citizens to violence—the central tension of the liberal military contract—
by treating their figurative stand-ins as if they were one and the same. The
potential tension and trauma of war is reconstituted into an affective relationship with the figurative soldier whose death is not only accepted but
also lauded, thus securing the social order and legitimating the use of force
(Millar 2015). This is one of the ways the liberal state gets away with risking
the lives of its citizens. The soldier conveys a specific politics of violence. He
frames martiality as an obligation of citizenship, an idealized form of masculinity, *and* an individual choice while, through the figure's social valorization,
legitimating the use of force against external antagonists. The soldier makes
the gendered political obligations of the liberal military contract look not
only normal but actively desirable—hence the social and political tensions
accompanying its fracture.

Aggregating Legitimation?

Given the affective and political power of "the soldier," it is tempting to read
"the troops" as operating the same way: a further valorization of sacrificial
public martial masculinity and corresponding legitimation-by-association
of liberal war. The plain language meaning of "the troops," after all, is a group
of soldiers.

This is the approach taken by many existing analyses of support the troops
discourse. Stahl, for instance, suggests that supporting the troops works to
"transfer[] guilt from policy makers to an embattled individual soldier in
need of forgiveness" and "fuse lower-rank soldiers together with the leadership" (2009, 549). He argues, in essence, that StT aggregates the socially laudable characteristics of the soldier and gives them to the institutional military.
The legitimation of violence depends on the relationship between the heroic,
individuated soldier and the institutional military, itself a stand-in for the
state. Managhan (2011a, 449), similarly, in her analysis of the troops and antiwar dissent, argues that "what was ultimately being protected was the figure

of the soldier who had come to embody no less than the promise of the nation." The troops are again assumed to be an aggregation of the soldier, who retains its association with the nation-state.

This interpretation of the troops, however, misses a key slippage in the way the troops are constituted within StT discourse. In the above analyses, the soldier is read figuratively, while the troops are read literally, as an aggregation of either figurative soldiers or actual military personnel. In both instances, of the soldier-as-troops and troops-as-state, the aspirational pull of the figurative soldier on individuals, and corresponding gendered legitimation of liberal violence, is assumed to hold. But the troops, unlike the soldier, are a *group*. The one-to-one interpellation between the individual citizen and the figurative soldier is disrupted. Analytically, "the troops" is a single concept, yet one constituted as a corporate—in the sense of being comprised of many distinct parts—entity. The troops are a *collective* figure characterized less by a substantive identity, or "content" (e.g., heroism, masculinity, etc.) than a sense of groupness.

Consider the relationship between the worker, class, and labor. Analytically and experientially, we regard class as both a corporate entity composed of workers and as a monolithic subject, such as "the working class," about which it is possible to generalize. The working class may be understood as made up of individual people, or figurative workers, but it also signifies a particular assemblage of affects, material production, social relations of exploitation, gender, race, and so on that cannot be inferred from the worker or deduced from labor. The working class, as a unique social category, rather than just a bunch of workers or subcomponent of the structural division of labor, makes a certain form of politics possible. Correspondingly, the troops mediate and intervene in the typical gendered legitimation of violence within liberalism. They facilitate a distinct form of politics that requires taking their groupness, and corresponding conceptual abstraction, seriously.

The Troops Are Not (Just) the Institutional Military

The "groupness" of "the troops" challenges a straightforward extrapolation of the characteristics of "the soldier"—and associated logics of legitimation based upon individuated interpellation of citizens—to the collective figure. This section begins to unpack the sociopolitical implications of the troops as a *distinct* figure of liberal war by empirically parsing them from the institutional military and the soldier. This is something of an analytical challenge since, due to this groupness, the troops are "irreducible to specific 'contents'" or substantive identities (Dean 2016, 116). I therefore examine the social dynamics within which the figurative troops are made meaningful, rather than (futilely) attempting to fix them to concrete characteristics (e.g., bravery) or a given, actual referent group (e.g., citizens).

As a first step, examining discursive constructions of the troops' agency stymies the notion that the troops might be (just) the institutional military (or even military personnel). Broadly, where the troops are constituted as active (i.e., portrayed as engaging in any form of activity, as *doing* something),[2] they are also constituted as the military. A transcript of US Republican presidential candidate John McCain's nomination speech illustrates this framing:

> When it came time to support our troops fighting to protect our freedoms and way of life, my opponent said he'd never deprive them of the funds they needed to fight—and then he did just that. Barack Obama voted against funding the equipment our troops rely on as they fight to protect us. That is not putting the men and women of our military first. (McCain 2008)

The troops in this passage are clearly active: they are "fighting to protect our freedoms." The reference to agency-as-fighting reflects broader patterns in constructions of troops in the US and UK. When the troops' activities are specified—which is not always the case—combat is their primary activity.[3] The troops are also unambiguously linked to "the men and women of our military," as a sexed, corporate entity, but also, via the military, to the state. The agential, combat-oriented troops are primarily identified with the formal military institution.

The use of the troops as a stand-in for the military is even stronger in the "operational" strain of StT discourse (see Figs. 4.6 and 4.7), which refers to the provision of assistance to deployed military personnel *within* the military. A 2010 speech by the UK minister for defence personnel, for example, observes: "The excellent medical support to our troops is truly a joint effort [of the armed forces] and sustaining such deployed operations depends on moving people and materiel by air and sea as well as overland" (Robathan 2010a). This aligns with the existing tropes of the military/soldier. Together, the explicit references to war operations and "protecting our way of life" serve to structurally distinguish the troops from society through a connection with the military's institutional structure and practice of combat. When the troops act, the figure refers to the (actual) institutional military or its constituent personnel.

The troops therefore *can* stand in for the military; the association is politically useful insofar as it supports the quick reading of the troops as "obviously" enlisted personnel. But they do not have to. In both the US and UK, the troops are constituted as passive about three times more often than they are as active. Constructions of the troops as passive include decontextualized references, such as bumper stickers proclaiming "support the troops," and instances where the troops are not framed as doing anything. This is a significant departure from the way we tend to think about the military and military personnel in wartime. Perhaps unsurprisingly then, when the troops are constituted as passive, they are rarely also constituted as synonymous with the institutional military.

A White House blog post by Dr. Biden, spouse of President Joe Biden, for instance, noted: "As a military mom myself, this is personal—but it's also the duty of all Americans to support our troops. It can be as simple as saying 'thanks'" (2009). Though the troops are contextualized by the balance of the text—Biden was commenting on a visit to military families—nowhere are the troops framed as *doing* anything. Their sole action in the discourse is the implicit receipt of support. A UK Campaign for Nuclear Disarmament statement on the deaths of British military personnel in a helicopter crash follows similar lines: "All life lost in this conflict, either by accident or design, is a tragedy. As some of the placards on the anti-war protests have said, 'Support our troops, bring them home'" (CND 2003). The rest of the text expresses CND's dismay over the extent of civilian casualties and condemns the war. Nowhere are the troops presented as active. They are neither blamed for the conflict nor are they constructed as implementing it. In contrast to the StT rhetoric of the First Gulf War, this passivity facilitates, though does not necessitate, a "dissociation" between the warriors and the war (Silvestri 2013, 109).

The troops' meaning, then, does not center on what they do, but rather their relationship to others. Biden's call for Americans to show "appreciation for our troops and their families," for instance, despite its framing within an official White House visit, shifts the primary identity of the troops away from the military toward the private sphere, as family members. CND's messaging, similarly, separates the troops from the military (and state) by reading the helicopter accident into a broader loss of predominantly civilian life. This framing is reinforced by the call to bring the troops home—as opposed, for instance, to withdrawing the troops or bringing home the military. It inflects the troops with domestic, even familial, connotations of private social positioning.

These passages demonstrate that the troops are neither wholly synonymous with the implicitly masculine military as the statist instrument of force, nor with frequently femininized "civil" society as family members or citizens (Elshtain 1995). Instead, the troops may refer to many subjects at once. Consider the following statement, by a US senator, recognizing the "commitment and sacrifice of Tennessee citizen soldiers. One thousand Tennessee National Guard troops and airmen have been deployed to participate in Operation Iraqi Freedom . . . These men and women leave full-time jobs and their families to serve their country and protect our liberty" (Frist 2003). The troops are identified as members of the military and explicitly placed in the context of the war in Iraq while simultaneously constructed as employees and family members (Silvestri 2013, 112). The relevant group with which the troops are identified oscillates between the military, the nation-state, and the family.

The troops' groupness mediates substantive identity. It enables disparate subjectivities aligned with competing collectivities—for example, the military, nation-state, citizens, and the family—to be collected in a single, seemingly coherent figure whose meaning, at least superficially, seems obvious. Politically, this serves to diffuse potential normative (or even ideological) tensions between the groups. The troops' lack of substantive content allows the figure to recognize the social embedding of family members and citizens beyond the military institution without constituting those groups as alternative sources of belonging, affect, or meaning. Instead, the transitivity of the troops makes it a vector for martiality into ostensibly civilian spaces and relationships (Millar and Tidy 2017, 5) and vice versa. The troops constitute a multiplicity of public and private subjects within martial discourse(s), including those, like the family, that might in other guises offer a normative and affective challenge to both the military contract and war.

The Plural of Soldier Is Not Troops

The effective exercise of agency also differentiates the troops from the soldier. Within the "good" story of liberalism, within which the figurative soldier resides, the decision to risk significant harm by enlisting posits him as freely choosing to renounce the rights to which the democratic citizen is otherwise entitled (MacLeish 2013, 144). By volunteering, the soldier exercises the same autonomy that characterizes the universal, rational liberal-democratic political subject.[4] In joining, he demonstrates a future-oriented temporality. Volunteering for military service is a form of war preparation, done in anticipation of securing the polity during a future conflict.

The troops, in contrast, are constituted in the context of a present war—absent conflict, there is no need to support the figurative troops—but passively and without directionality. They are figured in something of an ahistoric ever present, a trope that, again, distances the troops (and through them, war) from political questions as to the conduct and legitimacy of violence. The soldier's futurity is oriented toward combat. His violent agency communicates a particular spatialization—the battlefield—and a relationship of antagonism toward the imagined enemy (Basham 2018). The troops, however, as a consequence of their passivity, do not act violently (for they frequently do not act at all). Together, these factors parse "the ultra-agency of the masculine combat soldier" from the "passive, objectified—almost fetishized—collective subject of the troops" (Millar 2016a, 17).

This conceptual distinction between the soldier and the troops, however, does not mean the two are entirely disconnected. The contextual meaning of the troops is frequently played off of commonalities and contrast with the soldier. The interplay between portrayals of (literal and figurative) individuals within StT discourse and the collective troops illustrates this dynamic. A UK MP's remembrance of deceased individual soldiers, for instance, states:

> I am sure that the whole House will join me in paying tribute . . . to those members of our armed forces who have lost their lives in Afghanistan since the House last met: from 1st Battalion the Royal Welsh, Fusilier Jonathan Burgess; from 1st Battalion the Mercian Regiment . . . We salute their bravery, we honour their sacrifice and we remain steadfast in support of our troops . . . We will genuinely work with the Government in support of our troops, their wives and families. (Harman 2010, c39)

The deceased are constructed through the tropes of hegemonic soldier masculinity; they are brave, risk-taking, and, by implication, involved in combat. They are also, in contrast to the anonymized, collective troops—named. As observed by Parry, the practice of naming individuals creates a sense of immediacy and identification (2011, 1192). It is a process of recognition compelled, under the liberal military contract, by individuated sacrifice.

This recognition, however, is immediately followed by a distancing and displacement, as the speaker quickly moves from saluting the bravery of the deceased to supporting the troops. The positive characteristics of the combat soldier—bravery and sacrifice—are read into the collective troops. The troops are also, by association, implied to be heterosexual via reference to "their wives." The contrast between the soldier and the troops thus separates the masculinity of the combat soldier from the passivity of the troops, while still serving to distance the deceased individuals from the actual practice of violence. Their bravery partially derives from this association with the troops, rather than a particular practice of warfare. It is also unclear which troops are being supported—the dead, in remembrance, or the remaining troops. This is another crucial characteristic of the troops: as they are not reducible to a group of particular individuals, they cannot be killed. The slide from the deceased individual to the troops preserves the viability of the *figure* of the hegemonic combat soldier, even as the individuals interpellated by it die, through its attachment to a structurally invincible collective subject.

This analysis suggests that in the context of the ongoing transformation of normative liberal civil-military relations, the liberal military contract is not solely maintained by the idealized soldier's relationship with the nation-state. The intelligibility and (purported) stability of that relationship—the good story of liberal martiality and heteronormative masculinity—is dependent upon its embedding in a series of associations and contrasts with the troops, a collective, ambivalent figure. The figurative troops convey, as described by Scarry, "the fact that the fate of the overall army, or overall population, and not the fate of single individuals, will determine the outcome" (1985, 71).

The oscillation between the troops, the soldier, and the deceased normalizes war. The "authority of soldiers" may be invoked (Tidy 2015a, 226), but in the context of a blurry "massification" that "draw[s] attention away from individual body counts" (Stahl 2009 cited in Fischer 2014, 214). The troops, in their passive ever present, absorb the tension between the future-oriented heroism of the figurative soldier and the empirical consequences of combat—the deaths of real people for whom time stops. This insulation of the universal soldier with(in) the troops precludes the deaths of individuals from undermining the ideological viability of valorized military service and with it, the underlying gendered martial contract itself.

Dependence and Vulnerability

The role of the troops in distancing risk and death from the figurative soldier, though key to upholding the gendered political obligation of military service, does not exhaust the figure's entanglement with vulnerability. As a further entailment of the troops' passivity (and lack of substantive identity content), the meaning and political effects of the troops are also informed by their production within relations of dependence.

A *Washington Post* article, for instance, describes an NGO called "Soldiers for Truth" that advocates "the best available training, leadership and equipment for our kids" (Shulte 2006). The organization's mandate is to "protect" the troops against an unresponsive military brass that endangers soldiers' lives by failing to provide them with appropriate body armor (Shulte 2006). Antiwar groups employ similar frames, with the general secretary of UK CND, for instance, stating, "Yesterday saw the 100th British combat death in Afghanistan this year, yet the Government wants us to stay . . . How many more will die by then? . . . We need to end this bloody war and bring the troops home now!" (CND 2010) In this example, the war—and government— as we saw in the previous chapter, are posited as threatening the lives and well-being of British troops. The troops are not represented as doing anything other than implicitly suffering harm. Their safety is connected to, and dependent upon, the government heeding the desires of antiwar activists to "bring them home." Throughout the war on terror, this understanding of the troops as imperiled was intensified by mainstream war reporting that emphasized themes of survival and existential threat to military personnel. Such coverage constructed "invading forces as . . . not as aggressors themselves inflicting harm, but as beleaguered *victims*" (Carruthers 2011, 229; see also Woodward et al. 2009).

These constructions illustrate a common theme, wherein the soldier is regarded as "innocent"—a paragon of youthful virtue whose boyishness serves to underscore his heroism and the symbolic power of his transformation, via combat, to a man (Managhan 2011a, 452). In the US, this sentiment is encapsulated in the figure of the Vietnam era conscript, let down by both civil society and an irresponsible administration (Boose 1993). In the UK, soldiering innocence is invoked by the young, White, working-class "Tommy" of the First World War, whose youth is stolen by incompetent politicians and military leaders (Bell 2003, 73). The troops are also constructed as innocent (and implicitly victimized by the state and/or war).

As a passive collective, however, the troops are not figured as undergoing a gendered process of normative metamorphosis, from guileless child to righteous man (or citizen). Instead, the impression left by such constructions is that the troops are dependent upon external support for their well-being (and, potentially, success), through the implication that should support not be forthcoming, they would be worse for it.

Uk4uThanks! articulates this formula, citing a UK Ministry of Defence endorsement: "Knowing that the public are behind them when they are working in often very difficult conditions, especially at this time, is a real morale boost for our Servicemen and women" (2010). The polemical slogan articulated by strongly pro-military Americans, "if you don't stand behind our troops, please feel free to stand in front of them" (MacLeish 2013, 212) takes this logic further. This allusion to violence against non-supporters counter-intuitively constructs the troops as vulnerable to some indeterminate harm at the hands of those who do not support them. Not only are the troops dependent upon support, but its absence is construed as a threat. The reception of support is a constitutive condition—at two levels—of the troops' existence. It is essential to the survival of the literal military personnel intuitively read into the troops. It is also the premise of the figuration of the collective entity of the troops itself. Though the various groups represented by the troops—the military, service personnel, family members, and so forth—would exist independent of support, the intelligibility of the figurative troops is inextricable from this sense of vulnerability. Unlike the boyish soldier, the troops cannot help themselves. Consequently, despite the typical representation of both the figurative soldier and veteran, as well as empirical military personnel, as men, the troops are relationally feminized through their dependence upon civilian society for their protection. The gendering of the liberal civil-military divide is contextually reversed.

Forestalled Betrayal

The figuration of the troops as dependent upon support stems from the "discursive legacy" of Vietnam (Coy et al. 2008, 163) and the subsequent desire in US political culture to redeem society's apocryphal "betrayal" of conscripted personnel (Beamish et al. 1995, 345 and 351; Enloe 1993, 176). The subsequent offering of unqualified support during the global war on terror (GWoT) is inflected by the belief that "national unity and citizen support for the troops has a critical operational value" that will "maximize the soldier's chances of survival" (Huiskamp 2011, 291). The cultural memory of Vietnam furthers this narrative by making the source of morale, the civilian population, explicit. It shifts the morale factor from its historic constitution as a reserve of empowerment and strength to a source of vulnerability. A Veterans of Foreign Wars statement condemning an antiwar vigil outside Walter Reed military hospital articulates this logic:

> The political protesters of the '60s didn't end their war and neither will this new generation. They will, however, achieve the same result: they will devastate troop morale . . . Morale means everything on the field of battle, but good morale starts at home. (2005a)

The troops are dependent upon morale on the home front and construed as physically endangered—via an unspecified mechanism—by antiwar dissent. Coverage of a StT rally, for instance, quoted a Vietnam veteran as stating, "I'm here to support the troops because I know what it was like when people didn't" (Associated Press 2003). StT discourse is "haunted" by the betrayed Vietnam veteran, who hovers, as a "living ghost," in contemporary "pledge[s] of never again" (Managhan 2011a, 456).

The specter of Vietnam also features in UK constructions of the troops. In 2010, for instance, a Plaid Cymru MP invoked Vietnam in relation to Afghanistan as an analogy for a failed military operation. MP Llywd stated, "Some of us said at the beginning that it was another Vietnam. At the time, we were laughed at, but I am afraid we are rapidly getting there" (2010, c226). He follows, however, this "quagmire" framing with a paradigmatic recitation of the post-Vietnam redemption script:

> As long as the troops are there, they deserve every possible support. They deserve the best kit, they deserve our support, and they deserve every comfort and care when they return to the UK . . . It is not the people out there who are the authors of foreign policy. We . . . are the authors of this unfortunate foreign policy, but it is they who daily have to stand in harm's way. We should respect them for that and give them every possible credit.

Llywd refutes each of the United States' perceived failures of the Vietnam era conscripts: (a) lack of proper equipment; (b) inadequate veterans' care; (c) inappropriate assignation of blame for an unpopular war; and (d) a general failure to venerate their military service. Though, in a literal sense, the "Vietnam veteran" exists at a remove from the British social imaginary, its metaphorical sense of betrayal, abandonment, and alienation have transnational resonance. The cultural memory of Vietnam is a specific manifestation of a broader sense of forestalled and imminent betrayal of the military—now figured as the vulnerable troops.

Again, however, this does not mean the veteran may be directly extrapolated or aggregated to the troops. The veteran invokes an assemblage of other meanings, such as physical and psychological disintegration, military failure, national impotence, and neglect that do not pertain to the troops (Managhan 2011a). As Managhan (2011a, 454) points out, the elevation of the troops as the locus for popular affect, ideology, and myth-making regarding war actually works to efface the veteran by displacing civil-military relations to a more amenable subject. It also halts the politico-affective engagement with conflict in the present, rather than engaging with war's traumatic afterlives. "The troops" and the "veteran" exist in a cautionary juxtaposition. The troops are frozen in an unchanging, constant rehearsal of the refusal/redemption of the past. If the troops are (re)produced by support, they cannot be the betrayed veteran, who was/is defined by its absence.

"The troops" illustrate yet another tension in the liberal military contract, wherein ostensibly separate, feminized society is dependent upon the masculine and protective military—yet success in war is considered to be premised upon "morale." This morale, in turn, connotes a dependent relationship with society. In doing so, these countervailing gendered/ing dynamics expose the limitations of relying on heteronormative patriarchy—and a binary gender order—to anchor the civil-military divide (and with it, normative public masculinity). Instead, the troops highlight the existence of far more ambivalent gender relations. They serve as a site for the negotiation of the dual subjectification of society to the protective military and the passive, victimized, yet somehow-martial troops to society. War is presented as something that happens to the troops, rather than a practice in which the troops—and with them, the (supportive) polity—are actively engaged.

The Troops and the Veteran

Consider the following exchange from a US Department of Defense news story commending Homes for Troops, a small NGO and partnering developer for building homes for disabled veterans. The developer states, "As a company, we never could have given what Pisey (Tan) did, but we can at least try to make life a little bit easier for him . . . We can make sure he knows that this country supports him, and we'll try to be there for him" (Kruzel 2007). This quotation invokes several of the tropes associated with "veteran"—sacrifice followed by dependence and hardship. The shade of Vietnam is also present in the forestalled betrayal underlying the declaration "try to be there for him." The individual veteran (Tan) is subsequently quoted as stating that such organizations are "truly a blessing" (Kruzel 2007). He performs the "thanks" required by his receipt of philanthropy and implicitly accepts the invitation (Millar 2016a, 19), inherent to such rehabilitation programs, to resume his "normal" life outside the military (Achter 2010, 64).

The story goes on to juxtapose Tan with the troops, noting that while deployed, he wondered about "the level of public support for the troops." Upon his discharge, however, he was "introduced to a lot of the programs and to a lot of support . . . And it basically showed [him] that life can go on" (Kruzel 2007). The troops initially refer to military personnel, with whom Tan identified on active service. As Tan reimagines himself as a disabled veteran, the figurative troops travel with him. The troops simultaneously represent serving personnel and veterans, eliding the disjuncture of the switch from an agential, ideally masculine soldier subjectivity to the dependence and deficit that frequently accompany the veteran. The groupness of the figure facilitates both association and contrast, enabling several subjectivities and gendered dynamics of protection and dependence, to be "true" while, again, displacing the threat of ideological contradiction.

As a collective subject that cannot be injured per se, the troops naturalize the occurrence of injury while at the same time highlighting its rarity. In doing so, the troops represent injury as an "accidental or unanticipated" consequence of war (Scarry 1985). If Tan is encompassed within the passive, positive troops, his practice of soldiering is obscured, leaving his subsequent injury to appear accidental or as bad luck rather than a foreseeable, even likely, occurrence. The play between the veteran, the troops, and the veteran troops serves to "disrupt the connection between the state [and supporters] and the consequences of war" (Achter 2010, 63). Tan acquires a form of symbolic immunity to injury through his association with a broader collective figure. The groupness of the troops, their figuration (as passive, as dependent, as vulnerable, etc.), and their ambivalent reference to various collective subjects (i.e., veterans, the military, family members) integrate Tan into the social order by offering him identification with an entity that both is and is not a veteran.

The Troops and the Mediation of Difference

The collective troops cannot be analytically or empirically generalized from the soldier or the veteran. Instead, the troops distance heroic martial imaginaries from empirical experiences of vulnerability. They then transform this vulnerability into a source of implicit legitimation by reconstituting war as a matter of support rather than violence. This section plays out a final dimension of the troops' normalization of the liberal military contract: their ability to accommodate particularistic difference.

To recap, the soldier legitimates both martial violence and the obligation of military service by "calling" citizens to identify with, and aspire to be, a heroic ideal. Though the soldier is, at least implicitly, produced in accordance with the particular, substantive characteristics of the Western political subject (as masculine, heterosexual, cis, White, etc.), the figure is presented as universal. It elides difference within the political community through the production of all individuals as always-already (citizen)soldiers. The existence of the troops, as a group, disrupts this logic of universal interpellation. Materially and discursively, the existence of a group suggests the need for bounding principles, determinants of inclusion/exclusion, and, more basically, diversity. The troops, in contrast to the soldier, divide the polity into (at least) two groups.

We can see the significance of this internal differentiation by comparing the sex of the troops with their relational gendering. The previous section suggested that the figurative troops may be read as structurally feminized, due to their passivity and dependence, in a flip of the conventional gendering of the civil-military divide. Empirically, however, where sex was mentioned, the vast majority of the text referred to the troops as men and women (see the McCain speech). As a collective figure whose meaning is produced relationally, the gendering of the troops is distinct from the sex (and gender) of the subjects (e.g., military personnel) frequently understood as making it up.

Why does this matter? It indicates that though the troops are not constituted in a way that communicates socially stable identity content in a manner similar to the soldier, the troops may be inflected with substantive identity through their association with various collective and individual subjects. With this in mind, the description of the troops as male and female should not be dismissed as semantic or descriptive. Instead, it is a reflection of the mythical liberal military contract—and binary cisnormative hetero sex/gender order —that holds that all who aspire to "good," implicitly masculine, public personhood are liable to serve. In liberal democratic states where citizenship and military service are formally available to male- and female-identifying people, the troops *must* be substantively constituted as male and female. In other words, regardless of the sex/gender of the individuals empirically represented by the troops (who are predominantly men), the *figurative* troops, as a corporate entity, must include all genders to be consistent with its (re)production in a liberal democratic society. In contrast to the soldier, which interpolates all citizens in line with Western heteromasculinity, the troops can accommodate recognition of men and women *as* men and women: sexed/gendered persons expressing socially meaningful difference. This mediation of formal equality and substantive difference makes the troops, due to their collective nature, as an ideal vessel for popular empathy and identification. If the troops are men and women, they may also be, and encompass, (nearly) everyone.[5]

Difference and US Martiality

The flexibility of the substantive characteristics of the troops also pertains to other axes of difference, including race, sexual orientation, and gender identity. The troops' incorporation of difference contextualizes the complicated affective politics of US communities of color whose lives are disproportionately risked by the state in military service—and who are often deeply committed to supporting the troops (Marsical 1991). A member of the Congressional Black Caucus, for instance, stated: "I want all people to know that the Congressional Black Caucus wholeheartedly supports our troops . . . I move throughout my district . . . and hear Americans talk about their sons and daughters and friends that are overseas now fighting for us, my heart definitely goes out" (Cummings 2003). The statement begins with a typical declaration of support and invocation of the passive collective figure of the troops. The explicit framing of supporters as the Black Caucus, however, as well as references to the speaker's district and neighborhood, encourages a specified reading of the troops.

The troops, here, are not an aggregation of the universalized White masculine subject nor a literal description of military personnel. The troops, instead, are constituted as explicitly multiracial, men and women, and embedded in affective social relations. Congressman Cummings transitions from support for the troops to a discussion of social disparities "at home," observing the differential experiences and outcomes of access to medical treatment for Black and Latinx Americans compared to the national average (Cummings 2003). He implicitly connects this experience of America with the troops, constructing them as representing *both* the heroic ideals of service associated with universalized citizen-soldiering and an inegalitarian, racialized society. Through the troops both military service (D'Amico 2000, 105) and military support work to claim recognition for minoritized groups within the political community—as, crucially, Black Americans, rather than universalized, White, cis, heteromasculine citizens.

There are few explicit references to sexuality or gender expression within StT discourse in the US from 2001 to 2010, partially because the repeal of the discriminatory Don't Ask Don't Tell policy prohibiting open service by lesbian, gay, and bisexual service members did not occur until 2011. Subsequent discourse around inclusive service, however, reinforces this analysis. Arguments in favor of repealing Don't Ask Don't Tell were cast in terms of the need to support all the troops, not some of them (Coates 2011). This is supported by polls that indicated that in 2010, 75 percent of Americans supported open service (McCabe 2010). Seventy percent of Americans polled also support inclusive military service for trans people (Rodrigo 2019). Judicial rejection of Trump era discrimination against trans people in US military service, combined with President Biden's commitment to inclusive service (Dallas Voice 2020) suggests that the troops' incorporation and mediation of particularistic difference pertains to trans service members as well.[6]

Difference and UK Martiality

The UK troops similarly work to integrate particularism but following a slightly different logic to that of the self-avowedly liberal, multicultural (and unnoted settler colonial) US. StT discourse in the UK mirrors broader social silences surrounding "marked"—or minoritized and/or marginalized—subjectivities perhaps even more so than in the US. This is perhaps attributable to the fact that a variety of embodied identities, including sexual orientation, race, and ethnicity, are (at least legally) consonant with UK military service. In contrast to the US, as noted in Chapter 3, open service for lesbian, gay, and bisexual people was legalized in 2000, following a decision of the European Court of Human Rights (BBC 1999), followed by inclusive service for trans people in 2014. Though harassment and discrimination within the services continues (Basham 2009b), as in the US (Cahn 2016), LGBTQ+ people have been explicitly incorporated into the liberal military contract.

UK StT discourse similarly rarely makes explicit reference to race or ethnicity. This reflects the complicated racialized legacy of British martial imperialism, where White British officers often commanded "colonial" forces of color—in colonized territories and during the world wars—who were subject to substantial harm and discrimination (Sherwood 2018; Levine 1994). These soldiers of color, however, in keeping with the "good" story of UK liberal imperialism, have been largely excised from UK military mythology (Mycock 2014). Relatedly, in contrast to the US, people from minoritized racial and ethnic groups are slightly under, rather than over, represented in the armed forces (Government of the United Kingdom 2019; Greene 2016).[7] Correspondingly, race, when explicitly mentioned post-9/11, was (and is) often raised in the context of recruitment. Campaigns from 2005 to the present sought to increase the participation of Muslim, BAME (Black and minority ethnic), and LGBTQ+ people within the armed forces (Sengupta 2004). The need for such a recruitment push, however, also highlights the fact that while the troops and our boys must, ideologically, be pluralistic and diverse, the unpopularity of military service within many marginalized and minoritized communities indicates that the subsequent relationship of support, though affectively compelling, is not experientially mechanistic.

That said, the common theme running through the rare discussions of marked particularity is, similar to the US, a recognition of and insistence upon diversity. In 2009, the Ministry of Defence was criticized for commissioning and creating a line of 25 "HM Armed Forces" action toys (similar to GI Joe) that, while representing a variety of roles within the military, were all portrayed as White men (Townsend 2009). Observers referred to the figures as inappropriately "overtly macho," eliding women, and "offensive" in their exclusion of racial and ethnic minorities (Townsend 2009). The discourse, in other words, contested the model's fairly literal reproduction of the ideal-typical White male figurative soldier. Crucial to this contestation was the reading of the models as a *group*. They were not considered a single

"character" in different dress, but rather the body/ies of the armed forces—
"the troops" and the communities and identities they encompass.

As a group, the troops are able to accommodate and incorporate particularistic difference as socially embedded and meaningful. Instead of inter-
polating citizens as soldiers on the basis of universalized identification,[8]
the troops operate via the universalized social relation of compulsory support (Managhan 2011a, 451) and solidaristic loyalty. Individuals are constituted as both supporters *and* potential troops simultaneously, as an abstract
citizen-soldier and a socially embedded person existing in diverse relations
of power, community, identity, and affection. "We" might not all be the normative citizen(soldier), but we may all be, or know/love, or owe, the troops.
Through this integration of difference, the collective troops may be a more
effective avatar of the liberal military contract than the potentially alienating
soldier—and essential to the legitimation, depoliticization, and perpetuation
of conflict.

Conclusion

The troops are a distinct figure of war, characterized by abstraction, passivity,
dependence, vulnerability, and an ability to incorporate difference. These
traits, underscored by the troops' status as a group, enable them to absorb
and accommodate tensions between the romantic Western imaginary of war
that travels with the figurative soldier and empirical experiences of failure,
death, and injury. The fracture in the liberal military contract is displaced, as
its central myth—the heroic heteromasculine soldier—is discursively insu-
lated from ideological failure. The dependence of the troops transforms vulnerability from a source of potential opposition to war to a justification for
the use of force—to *protect* the troops from further harm.

In doing so, the troops facilitate a dissociation between those collective
subjects they contextually represent—including the military and enlisted
personnel, among others—and violence. This internally oriented tenor of
StT discourse reflects a broader societal disconnect from the GWoT in daily
experience and lack of civilian contribution (Eisenstein 2007, xv). Civilian
casualties and suffering were dramatically underreported, particularly in the
US, in during the first years of the war on terror (Carruthers 2011, 21–22).
There was a general sense, encapsulated by a 2001 televised comic performance, that the West was entirely disinterested in harms it enacted abroad.

During the telecast, a comedian led a US studio audience in a chant of "We don't want to know!," arguing that war details were "for you and your cocktail chatter at parties in DC. Leave our boys alone over there" (Kulman et al. 2001, 44 cited in Carruthers 2011, 216).

In that quote, as throughout the chapter, it is clear that "our boys," the troops, are not the agents of war, but its victims. Not only is war opposition or critique posited as a potential threat to the vaunted ideal of troop morale, so too, if satirically, is even *knowing* anything about the violence of war. Instead, the victimhood and vulnerability of the troops are centered in a manner not dissimilar to the victimization of the United States—and, with it, implicitly, the West, and/or "civilization" by the 9/11 attacks within the broader narrative of the GWoT. The troops take the previous place of society—while accommodating varying visions of that society—as the dependent entity requiring protection. This transformation in the gender dynamics of martial protection plays a powerful role in legitimating—or apoliticizing—the violence of the state. It shifts the politico-ethical calculus of war from responsibilities to distant civilians to a moral investment in the troops' well-being.

The ability of the troops to incorporate particularistic difference within the polity *as difference* is key to this process. It renders all identities, communities, and political positions on commensurate with the universalized/ing relation of support. The troops can be overwritten with (almost) anything, enabling the polity to simulate an experience of war without actualizing it, since, as a collectivity, the troops may never die. The troops are collectivized so that we can be them, kill them, love them, and ignore the fact that they (we) also kill. They facilitate a broader shift in the politics of gendered, violent obligation from individuated, universalized heteromasculine military service to a more open and ambivalent relation of politically and emotionally obligatory support.

Supporting the troops, it turns out, is not all that interested in war. The central political question of supporting the troops is not the legitimacy of conflict, or even the troops themselves, but the polity's normative relationship to itself. It's about the maintenance (or lack thereof) of the liberal military contract. From the perspective of discursive martiality, the troops maintain the relationship between violence and the political as the basis for liberal political community, even as the politics of war, and gendered terms of military service that operate on its surface, change. To unpack this relationship further—and its reliance upon visions of normative gender—the next chapter shifts to consider underlying ideas of gendered political obligation. It looks at "support."

6

The Meaning(s) of Support

It has been established that the troops must be supported. In this chapter, I return to the book's central problematique to ask: Why? Upon what grounds? How is this naturalization of support sustained and what are its implications? In asking these questions, I continue my investigation of the politics of discursive martiality, moving from the disconnect from violence produced by the troops during the early years of the war on terror to interrogate the meaning(s) of support.

"Support" constitutes the relationship between society and the troops. It contests and reproduces the normative structure of civil-military relations within the US and UK; it reflects and works to resolve the normative and experiential fracture(s) in the liberal military contract. The chapter argues that supporting the troops (StT) is a response to the gendered civilian anxiety that accompanies individual failures to serve in the military during wartime—particularly among those who closely identify with the cis, heteromasculine, White normative citizen ideal. Gendered civilian anxiety is tied to both the liberal military contract and a crisis in the meaning (and possibility) of normative public masculinity writ large. It suggests anxiety over the existence (or lack thereof) of a binary, cisnormative heterosexual patriarchal gender order, and its ability to continue to anchor the naturalized understandings of political obligation that make liberal politics and polities possible.

To make this argument, I identify and deconstruct three ideal-typical modes of gendered political obligation on the basis of two interrelated criteria: the normative dynamic of support presented within the discourse (i.e., why we owe), and the relationship between the troops, society, and war the dynamic implies. First, I identify a contractarian dynamic of support that reproduces the basic tenets of the liberal "military contract." It reflects an assumption of reciprocal public obligations: support is exchanged for service. This form of support most directly betrays gendered civilian anxiety. It continues to posit the heteromasculine combat soldier as the apogee of normative

Support the Troops. Katharine M. Millar, Oxford University Press. © Oxford University Press 2022.
DOI: 10.1093/oso/9780197642337.003.0006

citizenship (and masculinity) without an expectation that everyone will serve or even approve of the war. The gender dynamics of civil-military relations are ambivalent—exposing the fracture of the liberal miltiary contract and the contingency of binary sex/gender order upon which it rests.

The two remaining modes of political obligation respond to this crisis in normative public masculinity and attempt to resolve it in compatible, but opposing, ways. "Communitarian" dynamics of StT constitute support itself as a form of war participation—as an acceptable performance of normative martiality (and citizenship). Supporters are able to access normative public masculinity through participation in the war effort and contribution to the cause. "Altruistic" rationales for support, conversely, constitute support for the troops as private and a matter of paternalistic, ostensibly voluntary, charity. Through this gendered dynamic of power and dependence, society is produced as normatively masculine—as "providing" for the troops—while, via this support, able to access normative martiality. Together, the two logics address the ambiguities of gendered civilian anxiety by (re)masculinising society via the specific meaning(s) given to support and in so doing, collapsing the civil and martial spheres.

The chapter unpacks each of these three modes of gendered political obligation in turn. StT discourse is not an unproblematic or straightforward reproduction of the gendered liberal military contract. Instead, it contributes to the broader transformation in violent, gendered political obligation in liberal democracies. Neither the fracture in the liberal military contract nor the crisis in (priviledged) public masculinity can be addressed within the tenets of individualistic, universalised ideological liberalism. Together, however, the three supportive rationales shore up ideals of normative public masculinity, a binary sex/gender order, and the liberal military contract.

Contractarian Political Obligation

Contractarian support the troops discourse most closely approximates the mode of political obligation underscoring the idealized liberal military contract while also revealing its ongoing fracture. Unsurprisingly, contractarian StT discourse is by far the most common; it is derived from all the discourse (see Figures 4.6 and 4.7 in Chapter 4) that suggests people support the troops due to "obligation," "hardship," "danger," and a sense of "fait accompli." Contractarian StT mirrors many of the key components of the good story of martial liberalism, particularly an understanding of public, reciprocal obligation existing between individuals. It expresses what Schraeder (2019) refers to as "the soldier's contract"—the terms of service (and recognition) for miltiary personnel. Although the discourse is, in keeping with liberalism's formal commitments to universality and equality, ostensibly gender-neutral, it continues to reference the "heroic" soldier as the pinnacle of citizenship. This logic of individuated obligation, however, is independent of a sense of shared mission or investment in war.

This strain of StT discourse typified UK state messaging regarding the armed forces. MP Robathan's 2010 statement is a good example:

> The nation and the Government have a moral obligation to care for those who have made a commitment by joining the armed forces, and taking on the duties and sometimes the sacrifices that service requires . . . When we provide support, we must place the ex-serviceman or woman at the heart of what we do . . . One of the yardsticks by which a Government are [sic] judged is how well they treat their ex-servicemen and women. We are determined to treat them with dignity and respect and to reflect the huge debt . . . that we all owe to all of them. It is our moral duty to do so. (Robathan 2010b)

The statement explicitly references an "obligation" and a "duty" to care for and support the troops. The mention of "debt" underscores the contractual nature of normative civil-military relations: supporters "owe" the troops, as active service members or as veterans, their support for services rendered. The quotation goes further, suggesting the obligation of support is so central to the political community, it is the means by which "a government [is] judged."

This form of obligation, however, is increasingly articulated less in terms of a direct relationship between the troops and government than in a series of interlocking, contractual relationships between discrete individuals, akin to the imagining of the original social contract. Another quotation from UK Hansard makes this clear: "Our society should be more aware of the sacrifices that our armed forces make, and the problems that they face. Those of us in this country who enjoy the protection provided by our armed forces have a duty to support them" (Fox 2007). Support is owed to the troops because they accept hardship to protect not the community per se but the more individualized "those of us" who do not serve.

As observed by Kenneth MacLeish in his ethnography of a US military base, visiting civilians were prone to proclamations that "if you're American, you will always be 100 percent in debt" (2013, 184). Civilians are obliged to provide support because the troops are doing something on their (personalized) behalf. A press release by the US NGO Disabled American Veterans, publicizing military-oriented television programming, put this more directly:

> The channel's heartfelt gratitude and appreciation to the men and women who have served and currently serve in our armed forces . . . We salute their dedication and sacrifice, and we applaud their courage . . . We hope this will let them know we . . . recognize what they are doing for us all. (Disabled American Veterans 2004a)

Though the "obligatory" nature of this support is subtler, the civil-military relationship is framed as one of asymmetric obligation, wherein the troops are portrayed as undertaking military service in the place of the supporters. Sacrifice is vague and limited to the military; supporters are encouraged, implicitly or explicitly, to continue their normal lives (Cole 2005, 148).

This construction of support as a multilayered web of individualized, interpersonal—though still political—obligation facilitates the move to "support the troops, but not the war,"[1] an iteration of StT discourse that, for many, defines the overall phenomenon. *New York Times* coverage of a StT rally highlights this sentiment, with one demonstrator stating, "If you're going to fuss, fuss before the war . . . but now that the war is going on, stop and support the troops." Another demonstrator, the mother of a Marine reservist, echoed "Don't get me wrong . . . I'm against the war. But they are supporting us" (Gootman 2003). A clear distinction exists between StT and "fussing," which, as articulated by the first speaker, is self-evidently irrelevant once the conflict has begun.

This sense of obligatory support—but absence of common cause—was also present in the UK. Most (in)famously, Piers Morgan (then-editor of the *Daily Mirror*) and Liberal Democratic leader Charles Kennedy were criticized for their declarations that they opposed the war in Iraq but would support the troops once it began (Hall 2003; Burrell 2003). Upon the invasion of Iraq, Morgan noted he had "never seen such a switch in public opinion," stating that, in hindsight, "It's entirely down to the natural sense in this country—particularly among the tabloid readership—that once a war starts, if we're involved, we must unequivocally support our boys and girls" (Burrell 2003). This sense of popular obligation—and its connection to class, in terms of the tabloid readership—speaks to the centrality of obligatory support to the UK civil-military relationship.

The notion that the troops are owed support for their service mirrors the classical liberal narrative of civil and political rights being earned in military service. This parallelism, however, belies the tension in the discourse revealed above. While it conveys a clear sense of shared community between the supporters and the troops, this does not translate into a sense of common cause. This represents a substantial departure from the idealized understanding of the liberal military contract, wherein the fortunes of existential war are shared throughout the people, as heteromasculine soldiers and as loyal, feminine home-front supporters. Instead, this misalignment of martiality between the supported and the supporters reveals the fracture in the liberal military contract.

Gendered Civilian Anxiety

This fracture stems from a concern that non-serving, masculine-aspiring civilians are doing something wrong. Despite the all-encompassing nature of StT discourse, without universal service, a key component of the liberal contractual premise of equality is missing. Contractual StT discourse invokes the *idiom* of archetypical liberal political obligation, citizenship, and implicitly heroic masculinity, but it is unable to performatively fulfill it.

A *Baltimore Sun* columnist quoted in a VFW press release, for instance, observes:

> This is one of the most challenging and uncomfortable subjects in American society—the lack of shared responsibility, across all social and economic classes, in the nation's defense [*sic*] . . . We support the troops, but most of us have no interest in seeing our own families engaged directly. (Dan Rodricks cited in VFW 2006).

Similarly, the chairman of the UK charity Help for Heroes proclaimed at the opening of a rehabilitation facility:

We must act like heroes to support our wounded. *We do not have to join the Services, we don't have go into a minefield or risk our lives* under fire but we should act to support those who do, we can take part in something a little heroic . . . They are prepared to risk their lives for their mates, we should be prepared to look after them. They deserve the best we can give them. (H4H 2010a, emphasis added)

This quotation lays out the source of the obligation to StT: a sense of individualized indebtedness but also, crucially, of a potentially unfulfilled obligation of reciprocity. Contractarian StT discourse is undershot by a profound sense of "gendered civilian anxiety" stemming from idealized notions of normative martiality and "good," public, heteromasculinity.

According to Kierkegaard, anxiety stems from the relationship between the subject and a prohibition (often understood in terms of law) and the recognition that the subject has the potential to break the law (Millar 2019b, 342; Zevnik 2017, 238). It comes less from actual acts of transgression than the realization of a temptation to break the rules while still abiding by them (Zevnik 2017, 238; Kierkegaard 1980). This notion of anxiety maps well onto the understanding of the social contract—and the liberal military contract. To live in community, citizens agree to abide by the rule of law—the authority and prohibition—but retain the ability (and desire) to break the law, which results in anxiety. As put by Zizek, "the more rigorously we OBEY the law, the more we bear witness to the fact that . . . we feel the pressure of the desire to indulge in [transgression]" (Zevnik 2017, 238; Zizek 2007).

Gendered civilian anxiety does not arise from the negative prohibition of law (i.e., that we must not harm one another) but instead the positive obligation of military service/sacrifice: we must, at least potentially, harm others under the liberal military contract. It derives from the possibility of shirking an unwritten expectation of soldiering—and, further, the recognition of a desire to do so.[2] It incorporates the parallel normative expectations of feminine "home front" loyalty and masculine military service that undergird the gendered, protective logic of archetypical liberal civil-military relations (Young 2003)—and the unease that stems from the dual possibility of contravening intertwined gender and citizenship norms.

This anxiety can be seen in contractarian StT discourse's tense relationship with the hegemonically masculine combat soldier. At first glance, the idealized soldier seems to remain the model of normative citizenship. And, to a degree, this is true: the above quotations reference the troops' selfless-ness, acceptance of sacrifice, bravery, and so forth—all lauded character traits associated with archetypical Western military masculinity.

A member of the UK band *One Direction* (oddly) explicates this logic in a statement for the UK MoD:

> We're on a TV show and they're putting their lives on the line. We feel scared to go out on stage . . . but I'm sure that none of us could even step foot in these guys' treads . . . We met loads of guys at Headley Court, but the people who really struck me were the guys of my age who were injured soldiers. It was a weird way to think of it; they're my age doing things like that and fair play to them because I don't think any of us lads could do it. They're such brave people, made of strong stuff. (Liam Payne quoted in UK Ministry of Defence 2010)

The speaker is comparing himself, a young man of military service age, unfavorably to his peers on the basis of their military service and mascu-linity, which they perform by risking their lives, demonstrating bravery and strength. He conveys a sense of respect for their service as well as gendered civilian anxiety. His own gendered performativity, characterized by stage fright, a seemingly superficial career in entertainment, and a self-described inability to meet the masculine standards of normative martiality are presented as implicitly feminized—as lacking.

This gendered sense of "coming up short" pertains to all in the liberal polity—particularly, but not exclusively, those whose embodied identifica-tion more closely aligns with the normative Western political subject (and soldier), as White, cis, heterosexual, masculine, and so on. This extension of the contract is encapsulated in Help for Heroes' explanation that though its slogan says, "It's all about the blokes," the message is "intended to encom-pass both the men and women of armed forces," whom the founder encoun-tered "as individuals" (H4H 2009c). Both men and women, as citizens, are interpellated as liable for military service without challenging the gendering of either citizenship or martiality as masculine (or the cisnormative gender binary). This tension is "dialed up" by the military service of previously fem-inized Others—including women and LGBTQ + people—throughout the war on terror. The ideologically compelled inclusivity of the liberal contract heightens awareness of living as a civilian—and in a structurally feminized subject-position—and thus failing to perform not only normative citizenship but also normative gender and sexuality. It raises the specter of martial and masculine "wannabeeism."

At one level, contractarian StT discourse does exactly what we would expect. It anxiously reifies the binary gendered civil-military divide between a protective, masculine military and an endangered, feminized society, grounded in the affective and socio-political elevation of the combat soldier. As we saw in the previous chapter, however, the troops are not affectively, socially, or politically reducible to the archetypical soldier. The general displacement of violence from StT discourse—seen here in the refusal of a common cause in conflict and insistence on separating the "warrior from the war"—means that martial violence is not the entire story.

The Feminization of Heroism

StT discourse constructs "heroism" as the benchmark of idealized normative citizenship. A careful examination of the normative dynamics of support-as-obligation, however, reveals that this heroism derives from "the voluntary assumption of risk, and the corresponding exemption of the volunteer from the rights and protections to which they are otherwise entitled" rather than proximity to combat (Millar 2016a, 17; MacLeish 2013, 144; Cowen 2008b, 16). This voluntary renunciation of rights and acceptance of risk is reflected in the emphasis upon "danger" and "hardship" as reasons civilians are indebted to the troops (see Figures 4.6 and 4.7). The Iraq and Afghanistan Veterans' Association (IAVA), for instance, frames veterans' support as redressing the hardships, including physical injury and PTSD, endured by the troops as a result of their exposure to war. In the words of IAVA, "We owe it to these men and women," whom they construct as the "newest generation of heroes," to "get them the help they need" (2008; 2007). The UK Legion, similarly, emphasizes the danger of active military service, noting: "A career in the Armed Forces is unique. Those who join know that they will have to follow orders" (2007). This hardship and deprivation was also frequently reiterated in media coverage of the war on terror, humanizing military personnel and eliding stories of Iraqi and Afghan civilian suffering (Carruthers 2011, 230).

These examples allude to the fact that the troops' heroism lies not in their use of force but in their acceptance of the burden of military service. The US America Supports You program publicized Walmart's practice of posting the photos of all local residents serving in the military on a "Wall of Honor" (VFW 2005b). Veterans of Foreign Wars lobbied US airlines to eliminate luggage fees for "young enlisted troops" because "those who wear the uniform are a special class of citizen, and they deserve special treatment because they have earned it" (2008a). Similar programs recognizing the service of the troops as an undifferentiated entity are also found in the UK (especially since 2010). Tickets for Troops, much like US professional sporting spectacles, provides tickets for current and former military personnel to attend sports events. The troops are encouraged to wear their uniforms (a change in UK military tradition),[3] and they are applauded by the attending crowd (Kelly 2013). Heroism is (re)defined, in practice, as being/becoming the troops, rather than engagement in war.

This account decenters—without completely eliding—the combat soldier as the implicit model of masculinity and normative citizenship. If heroism resides in joining, then "at the time of the defining action, the figure in question is less a soldier than a citizen" (Millar 2016a, 17). The arc of the heroism story moves from autonomy, independence, and civic-mindedness to membership within a passive, vulnerable, and dependent group. In practice, improved medical technology throughout the war on terror led to a decline in military combat deaths—92 percent of wounded US personnel made it home alive (Vergun 2016)—but an increase in veterans with severe and traumatic injuries (Goldberg 2017; Penn-Barwell et al. 2015). The displacement of war from contractarian StT discourse means that "being the troops" is characterized less by glorious combat than the more mundane endurance of bodily and emotional hardship, compounded by dependence upon society. The heroism of the troops doesn't derive from masculine sacrifice for the state—dying for something—but rather feminized/ing forbearance, *living through* something (Brown 1998, 6).

The implicit feminization of heroism as forbearance complicates the typical gendering of the liberal civil-military divide. The discourse's emphasis on support as owed to the troops due to their military service in the place of others maintains the gendered, protective dynamic between the troops and civilians but severs the direct connection to violence. The troops continue to not only protect supporters from physical harm (as in conventional military masculinity) but also from the feminizing dependence and vulnerability that accompanies military service. The relationship between the troops and supporters is ambiguously gendered, as the structurally masculine troops protect feminized civilians not from war per se, but rather their own political obligation to serve. Part of the troops' heroism resides in renouncing their own claims to normative, autonomous masculinity on behalf of others.

This morass suggests that a key characteristic of the fracture of the liberal military contract is not just the normative and political difficulties raised when the vast majority of citizens no longer serve but also the blurring of binarism more generally. The troops are and are not masculine; they are and are not feminine. The heroic masculine citizen is and is not martial. With the displacement of the combat soldier, normative masculinity seems inaccessible to nearly all subjects caught within a tautological loop of dependence and unreciprocated obligation. Contractarian StT discourse reveals that strict gender binarism no longer meaningfully anchors the normative structure of a discretely spatialized liberal civil-military relations. "Civilian anxiety" may be read as not only deriving from a failure to live up to the heteromasculine expectations of the liberal military contract but also the exposure of the contingency of the gendered foundations upon which the contract ostensibly rests. Normative public masculinity is inaccessible but also, more unsettlingly, potentially impossible. In its absence, contractarian StT discourse is unable to address the fracture in the liberal military contract but instead projects it forward as a source of unanswerable gendered guilt (MacLeish 2013).

Communitarian Political Obligation

Communitarian StT discourses expresses one of the two ideal-typical attempts to resolve (liberal) gendered civilian anxiety through the (re)masculinization of society. This discourse contests the contractual articulation of gendered political obligation—and hierarchical (now, blurry) gender dynamics between a masculinized military and a femininized civil society—through the implicit constitution of an alternative. It stems from StT discourse that frames "support" as "necessary," "patriotic," akin to "supporting the war" and, most centrally, a form of "participation" (see Figures 4.6 and 4.7).

This form of gendered political obligation is not communitarian in a formal, political theoretical sense. But it does contain an account of civil-military relations, the relationship between society and warfare, and normative masculinity. I refer to this as "communitarian" insofar as the discourse reflects a sense that, contra liberalism, it is a holistic, indivisible community, defined by with values "rooted in communal practices" rather than individual choice, which is the central entity of political concern (Frazer and Lacey 1993, 2). Communitarian gendered political obligation articulates a model of normative masculinity based on collective action and civic participation.

Support as Masculinized/izing War Participation

Communitarian StT discourse addresses gendered civilian anxiety through the constitution of support for the troops as, itself, a form of masculinized/izing war participation. This can be seen in the passage below, wherein a service member thanks the US NGO Operation Gratitude for their care packages:

> [In Iraq] . . . Grizzly [sic] murders occurred every day. Today, thanks to the bravery and sacrifices of our soldiers—and to you for supporting them from afar—hundreds of criminals and terrorists have been killed or captured, the schools and hospitals have been rebuilt and are operating . . . In addition to this, our soldiers are winning a thousand small victories every month—glorious little triumphs that shine like stars against the blackest night . . . Your gifts, prayers and support have made a significant contribution in this just and worthy endeavour. (Maj. DCC, quoted in Operation Gratitude, 2006)

The support provided by ostensible civilians via Operation Gratitude is directly connected to day-to-day military violence, contributing to *killing or capturing* the enemy. The supporters are not represented as the feminized, passive home front that grounds the gendered (liberal) civil-military divide, but rather as part of a conventionally heteromasculine military "team." Civilians help prosecute war against racialized Others in Afghanistan and Iraq (Khalid 2014) (who typically go unmentioned) and, in the process of such support, serve to frame the conflict as an explicitly just war.

The UK NGO uk4uThanks!, which provides Christmas boxes to deployed military personnel, demonstrates similar constructions. Responses from the troops emphasize the operational utility of the items provided. Thanks for the 2008 Christmas box, for instance, noted: "The small mugs were great and something that soldiers will keep in their kit for ranges and other days away . . . The superbright keyfob torches are really good and regularly being used as signal torches between vehicles on convoys" (uk4uThanks!

2009). This quotation highlights that while the troops may be dependent upon civilian support, as exhibited by their use of quotidian items provided by civilians in the battle space, the purpose of this support is to further the troops' success in war.

Organizations such as the Law Enforcement Equipment Program (an associated group of America Supports You) and, somewhat surprisingly, the antiwar war group Military Families Speak Out go further, providing specialist military equipment, such as batons, body armor, and sniper scopes to deployed military units, stating, "I believe that it is our responsibility to assist our Armed Forces in any and all ways possible" (LEEP 2008; Oregon Military Families Speak Out 2009). Through the provision of war-fighting materials and the contribution to "killing terrorists" civilian support is constituted as a form of war participation by proxy (see Millar 2021). The gendered and sexualized anxiety of non-service is addressed through the reading of support as *itself* military participation.

The performative martiality of support-as-participation connects supporters—as aspirant normative citizens—to normative heterosexuality and masculinity. The normative masculinity produced through war participation more closely approximates "the [masculine] citizen-soldier ideal of the civic republican tradition, [which] fuses military service and participatory citizenship" (Sasson-Levy 2003, 321–22) than the individual, voluntary heroism of the liberal (citizen)soldier. The expansive notion of communal civic virtue makes normative masculinity far more available, via support, to civilians with no connection to the formal institution.

This is apparent in the common insistence that to really support the troops, the "warrior" cannot be separated from the war.[4] In a congressional debate regarding Iraq, for instance, Representative Ros-Lehtinen declared, "While urging a withdrawal, some state that they support the troops. But as leaders of the American Legion and the Veterans for Foreign Wars have stated, you cannot separate the warrior from the war" (2007, H1830). She then referred to her stepson and his wife, noting that both were Marine pilots who had served in action, praising their commitment and that of "their fellow service men and women," noting that "they are so confident in success that they are willing to risk their lives to secure it" (2007, H1830).

The traits associated with her family members—perseverance, confidence, willingness to accept risk, and proximity to combat—reproduce the hegemonic model of Western military masculinity, "associated with practices of strength, toughness and aggressive heterosexuality" (Duncanson 2009, 64;

Barrett 1996). That Ros-Lehtinen is offering up these warriors as a model to be emulated underscores the foundational connection between military service, heteromasculinity, and citizenship. The warrior troops are invoked to shame those who support a withdrawal for their apparent failure to meet this same level of commitment and appropriately perform their martial—and masculine—obligations.

The framing of a personal connection to the military via family members is important to how this works. The warrior-troops-as-family-members invokes the martiality—and good public personhood—of the son and daughter-in-law, and, in supporting them, the speaker herself. A similar dynamic can be seen in the Royal British Legion's (2010a) Take the Pledge campaign, which asked elected officials, electoral candidates, and the public to "take the pledge" to "to do [their] bit for the whole armed forces family." The gendering of the call is clear, as the references to "doing one's bit" evoke the World War I image of the small child asking their father, "What did you do in the war, Daddy?" (Victoria and Albert Museum n.d.) as an expectation of good citizenship and masculinity.[5] The heteronormative family ("the armed forces family," "Daddy"), not the gender-neutral, universalized individuals of the liberal political order, is constituted as the bedrock of public valor. A failure of support—of war participation—is also a failure of heteronormative kinship, either literal or as a component of good public personhood. Conversely, the good performance of support (and martiality) affirms both normative public masculinity and the binary sex/gender order upon which it ostensibly rests.

The (Re)Masculinization of Society

The (re)masculinizing dynamic of support-as-participation is redoubled through the constitution of the troops and supporters as engaged— equivalently—in a common cause. The founder of the UK charity Help for Heroes, for instance, states that the impetus for the charity was that "we knew that thousands of people felt the same as us; that something had to be done" (Dancy 2008). Contra the liberal military contract, the troops are a constituent aspect of the community, incorporated into a (presumably) pre-existing social network characterized by relations of "reciprocity, mutuality, and interdependence" (Frazer 1999, 1). They are not meaningfully distinct from supporters.

Communitarian normative masculinity is also produced by leveling the gendered hierarchy of the liberal military contract. This sentiment is reflected in the US Veterans of Foreign Wars' observation:

> We are in an era of persistent conflict where success is dependent upon our whole Nation working in concert. Your participation in this collaborative process counts immensely . . . You not only serve the living, but you honor the fallen and safeguard their proud legacy. (2008b)

Though the participatory aspect of support is foregrounded, the VFW posits both advocating for America's "all-volunteer force," an immediately martial activity, and preparing to care for new veterans, a practice associated with the feminized home front, as equivalent inputs to success. This is typical of mainstream articulations of the discourse, which preserve the logic of masculine citizen participation in the troops' mission but broadens what counts as a contribution. The explicit connection to war fades, further opening normative (hetero)masculinity to all.

The paradigmatic example of this expanded notion of war participation is Bush's famous speech announcing the global war on terror, wherein he answered the question, "What can I do to help in our fight?":

> All of us . . . mak[e] a commitment to service in our own communities. So you can serve your country by tutoring or mentoring a child, comforting the afflicted, housing those in need of shelter and a home . . . You can support our troops in the field and, just as importantly, support their families here at home, by becoming active in the U.S.O. or groups in communities near our military installations. (Bush 2001)

Bush's statement, as with the bake sales and bike rides and other quotidian activities outlined in Chapter 4 as means of "doing your bit," expands the practice and experience of warfare, albeit at a remove and divorced from its typical association with violence, into the everyday. With such a range of supportive activities on offer, everyone has the opportunity—or responsibility—to, if not engage in military violence themselves, functionally approximate the noncombat support personnel within the military (Millar and Tidy 2017, 11). We could ask whether it is ideologically possible, in this mode of gendered political obligation, to do anything that is not—or cannot be read—as a form of war input. The liberal spatial divide separating a masculine, protective military and dependent, feminized civil sphere is inapplicable. The "civil" is collapsed into an always-already martial whole.

Communitarian constructions of political obligation resist the structural feminization of supporters (as civilians) within the conventional gendering of the liberal civil-military divide. A holistic vision of the political community facilitates an absolutist approach to normative citizenship, wherein that which, under liberalism, would be culturally coded as feminine (e.g., civilian status, the civil sphere) is elided. Normative heteromasculinity is accomplished through the functional equation of civilian support with war contribution. This renders society, read as the heteronormative family, synonymous with martiality as the basis of the public/polity. Communitarian StT discourse alleviates gendered civilian anxiety by obviating the idea/possibility of a civilian at all. Both the first-order (non-service in wartime) and second-order (contingency of binary sex/gender order) aspects of gendered civilian anxiety are, at least superficially, addressed.

Altruistic Political Obligation

The final response to gendered civilian anxiety is found in altruistic constructions of support for the troops. This mode of politcal obligation is challenging, analytically, to nail down because it is largely characterized by a sense that it is good or appropriate to support the troops without providing a specific reason. Empirically, it encompasses discourse that holds it is "morally right," or a matter of "love," to support the troops (see Figures 4.6 and 4.7). This is altruistic not only because it's associated with charity but also because it presents StT as a moral good that is not mandatory, compelled by pre-existing social relations, or a function of common membership in a political community.

A US congressperson's statement that "it is really, really nice" when politicians cooperate to support the troops—"it is exactly the right thing to do" (Moore 2004, H1690)—is a good example of StT as a form of naturalized morality. Reporters covering the war on terror, similarly, frequently admitted to "loving" the troops both as a source of stories and personally (Boyer 2003). Altruistic gendered political obligation reflects private or apolitical understandings of citizenship, which eschew the liberal public sphere in favor of an idealized private constituted by a network of paternalistic, heternormative relationships (see Berlant 1997).

Support as Masculinized/izing Patronage

Contrary to what we might expect, the construction of support as a matter of private morality does not articulate in terms of a maternal dynamic of care; instead, it is a masculinizing relation of beneficent masculine/izing patronage. Throughout the GWoT, as we saw in Chapters 4 and 5, support was frequently framed as "protecting" the troops—from the elements, from the enemy, from unspecified harm. The production of the troops as dependent and vulnerable—as feminized—is compounded by the articulation of altruistic support in a charitable idiom.

The UK charity BLESMA illustrates this framing. When describing to potential donors "how you can help," it notes that while the state makes general policy, the organization "concerns itself with individual cases," asking, "will you make them your concern too?" (2008, 13). This is a moral indictment of the state's failure to provide support, but it works in a different register to that of the communitarian and contractarian logics. It (re)produces the troops as akin to any other needy group, an (ostensibly) apolitical social cause (Tidy 2015a, 221). They are "citizen-victims—pathological, poignant, heroic, and grotesque" (Berlant 1997, 1), marrying suffering with worthiness (see Cowen 2008b).

These construction of the troops as cause—and implicit framing of supporters as benevolent saviors—challenges the typical (liberal) gendering of civil-military relations. It is tempting, given charity's association with care to read altruism as a fairly stereotypical form of maternal support (Ruddick 1980). It is, however, as Hutchings reminds us, an essentialist error to further the "conflation of feminization with the absence of war" (2008, 395) or, conversely, the presence of care. The positioning of civilians as protecting the troops and economically supporting veterans produces a civil-military dynamic of hierarchicalized dependence. It is more akin to the operation of the patriarchal welfare state, or masculine head of household, than a maternal logic of care.

This is evident, for instance, in the 2010 statement of a Conservative MP:

> The help that charitable and voluntary organisations and—dare I say it?—the big society have given to people returning from warfare goes back a long way. It is not for the state to do everything, and the state is not necessarily best placed to do that. We all have social responsibilities, and service charities are an excellent example of the big society in action. (Colvile 2010)

This statement, referencing a Conservative plan to encourage the provision of social services and supports by nonstate entities (BBC 2010), explicitly highlights the paternalistic dynamic between the big society of supporters and the dependent service members returning from war. This passage attributes characteristics associated with stereotypical hegemonic Western masculinity (and, with them, citizenship) such as rationality, selflessness, independence (Connell 1995) as pertaining to civilians rather than the troops. The monetary transfers that typically accompany such charitable support,[6] moreover, as a capitalistic formalization of relations of dependence (and literal and moral indebtedness) are similarly "key for accomplishing masculinity" (Lainer-Vos 2014, 48; Millar 2019b).

The masculinizing capacity of altruism is also seen in the increasingly common recognition of civilian supporters, either in the press or through formal awards, for their service to the troops. In marking the careers of US public servants and politicians, it is commonplace to note their support for the troops—regardless of their formal connection to the armed forces. A former US senator, for instance, was praised as having "supported our troops fervently. Senator Bayh was not afraid to call out leaders when he felt an injustice was being done, and he spoke up often for our men and women overseas when necessary" (Reid 2010, S90s00). In speaking truth to power, the senator exhibited independence, risk-taking—"not afraid to call out"—and public action on behalf of others, attaching attributes of conventional Western masculinity to the speaking civilian rather than the troops. Similarly, support for the military—particularly disabled veterans participating in the Invictus Games—is framed as a crucial part of the personal maturation and redemption narrative of Harry Windsor of the UK royal family. The CEO of the Invictus Games has commented on Prince Harry's "real sense of humility," observing that "his is not somebody who is doing this because he needs attention" (Davidson 2016). Paternalistic, benevolent support, rationally measured and conducted without personal stake, is constituted as a component of implicitly masculine public virtue.

Support for the troops, cast in the masculine idiom of contribution to the community, is central to social recognition as, first, a good (masculine) person and, as a function of this recognition, a good citizen. In the UK, for instance, the founders of Help for Heroes were awarded a "Millie" (or Military Award) by the *Sun* tabloid to recognize their "invaluable help to the Armed Forces" (Iggulden and Newton Dunn 2008). The US National Military Family Association awards a Very Important Patriot for "exceptional volunteerism" to individuals who have "demonstrated out-standing service that contributes to improving the quality of life in their military . . . communities" (Armed Forces Press Service 2008). The Millie awards are a red-carpet event, attended by prominent citizens and celebrities. These attendees are photographed distributing awards and in the company of military personnel, reinforcing both the laudability of charitable support and the hierarchical imbalance of status (and capital) between the supporters and the troops (Earlam 2012). Philanthropy as a form of normative public masculinity, "as controlled sacrifice for human well-being, render[s] the man who donates to the public good a heroic figure" (Boon 2005, 309). The reading of support as charitable patronage resolves the gendered component of liberal civilian anxiety through the (re)masculinization of generous supporters.

The Elision of the Martial

This dynamic of paternalistic (re)masculinization only works if it is not something that supporters could be expected to do absent their masculine qualities of community mindedness and material beneficence. A key masculinizing aspect of altruism is—paradoxically, given the ways supporting the troops is naturalized as both presumed and compulsory—its apparently spontaneous quality (Jenkings et al. 2012, 361). The gendered structure of civil-military relations produced within altruistic StT discourse is, counterintuitively, defined by a denial that, as a matter of public concern or liberal politics, it exists at all.

Charitable support, as observed by Sylvester in relation to development workers, implies a normative dynamic wherein the benefactors are in, but not of, the communities they help. Donors may be "compassionate and show an admirable sense of urgency—as they hold themselves aloof" (2013, 105). Paternalistic support constitutes a structure of political obligation that, on the surface, is "a well-intentioned, altruistic and unconditional interaction, wherein one individual or group acts to benefit another without expecting anything in return" (Gronemeyer 2010, 56). Altruistic gendered political obligation is morally superior, here, to care provided by the state; it exemplifies a masculine logic of individualistic and agential voluntary contribution. Any potential civilian anxiety is resolved by the denial of its premise: the point of charity is that no one has to do it.

This structural collapse of gendered civil-military relations into an all-encompassing private sphere can be seen in the tendency of altruistic StT discourse to elide the relationship between the troops and the state—and, with it, supporters' masculine obligations of martiality. In contrast to communitarian and contractarian structures of political obligation, altruistic StT discourse constructs support as accruing to the private lives and activities of the troops as individuals and heteronormative family members. The UK Soldiers' Charity, in a fundraising appeal, stated:

> We support soldiers, former soldiers and their families whatever their age, whatever their rank, whenever they need it. We currently support over 6,000 individuals. Last year they ranged in age from 5 months to 107 years old. Here are just a few of their stories . . . It is thanks to your generosity that you make our work possible. (Army Benevolent Fund 2010)

Though the charity elsewhere frequently references military service, in this passage the primary identity of those being supported is private persons in need of welfare services. This positioning is brought home by the visuals of the webpage. Men in uniform—clearly active service members—are presented alongside women, the elderly, and disabled veterans in civilian clothes as equivalent beneficiaries of the charity. While martiality is the qualifying factor for support, it is constructed as private social relation rather than a public obligation or practice of warfare. Masculinized supporters are able to personally associate themselves with martiality without taking on the burden of service or complicity in state violence.

This dynamic is reinforced in discourse that associates the troops with other social entities, explicitly positioned against the state. A statement by the Stop the War Coalition, endorsing the NGO Military Families Against the War (similar to Military Families Speak Out in the US) stated: "All we want to do is to tell Tony Blair what we think which is he should bring the lads home—they need to be with their families. They don't need to be shot at in Iraq" (Stop the War Coalition 2009a). The quotation exemplifies the typical use of (fairly conservative) invocations of heteronormative kinship structures (see Silvestri 2013) to express support. A barber interviewed by the *New York Times* in 2005 put it succinctly, maintaining, "You've got to be there for them [the troops] . . . You can't stop loving the kids just because you don't like their father" (Kayal 2005, 10). Contrary to the way heteronormativity grounds the martial public of communitarian political obligation, however, here the family is a direct competitor to the state: the true unit of moral concern.

The sense of affective connection underlying paternalistic support is not limited to familial appeals. A parishioner quoted in an article examining religious responses to the invasion of Iraq declared, "As a Catholic, where you have an interest in human life, you have to support the troops . . . I definitely support the troops and everything they do, but inside I'm torn" (Davey 2003). The relevant structure of altruistic obligation is religious, as the speaker places her support for the troops in the context of a broader metaphysical moral duty (which, notably, privileges the troops' lives over foreign Others). This suggests that it is membership within the Catholic community, rather than the profane political community, from which this supportive impulse derives.

Gendered civilian anxiety is displaced through an appeal to nonstate sources of morality, transcending and subverting the obligations of the liberal military contract. Paternalistic support produces an altruistic structure of obligation that, paradoxically, is not socially recognized as political. Normative obligation exists, but the foundation of these responsibilities is not a public political contract between rational masculine subjects, but rather affective appeals to alternative, nonpolitical sources of morality and belonging. The martial is elided through its collapse, along with public politics, into an all-encompassing private.

The elision of the public reflects a need to address, albeit through a denial of its legitimacy, the figurative combat soldier as an exemplar of normative heteromasculinity (and citizenship). The normalization of the troops as a form of social cause reifies an underlying assumption that "military objectives are socially valuable" (Tidy 2015a, 224). Despite the vanishing of the soldier and warfare, normative heteromasculinity continues to function as a means of accessing martiality as a component of good public personhood. Altruistic gendered political obligation operates analogously to Sasson-Levy's account of the gendering of (some) non-combat soldiers in the Israeli military. Instead of accepting either a combat-based understanding of masculinity, against which they would fall short, or understanding themselves as feminized, the soldiers instead propose "alternative definitions for their masculinity, which are not anchored in military life," but are instead domestic, and emphasize "autonomy, independence, and responsibility in the private sphere" (2003, 320; see also Henry 2015).

Altruistic gendered political obligation also, finally, subtly bails out binarism. In continuing to leverage a particular notion of normative Western masculine subjectivity as the political ideal—going so far to resignify practices that would conventionally be considered feminine as masculine—the heteronormative sex/gender order is reified as an intelligible anchor for martial and political order. The multiple layers of gendered civilian anxiety are addressed, if imperfectly, through the continued valorization of heteromasculinity as the key to normative personhood and with it, martiality by association.

Intertwined Obligations

So far, I've demonstrated how each of the responses to the fracture of the liberal military contract seek to flee femininity and take on aspects of hegemonic masculinity (Agostino 1998, 565). On its own, the contractarian model is unable to square the situation of professional militaries and distant conflicts with the mythical cultural narrative of liberal military service as a universal obligation of (gendered) citizenship. Communitarian political obligation posits StT as a form of normative martiality—equivalent to military/war participation—and means of establishing implicitly heteromasculine normative citizenship. Altruistic support flips this dynamic by reversing the gendering of the civil-military divide through the articulation of a paternalistic, heteromasculine logic of care, demonstrating implicitly martial citizenship through normative gender performance. They each attempt to (re)masculinize society and re-anchor liberal heteropatriarchy.

Of course, this neat account is not how StT discourse really works. The three ideal-types are an analytical heuristic rather than an empirical description. The gendered constructions of civil-military relations they express are, in practice, messy, contingent, and intertwined. The politics of support derive from the coexistence and co-implication of these three logics of gendered political obligation (and readings of normative masculinity) within the same time, space, and, often, conversation. I wrap up the chapter by reading the politics and gendered dynamics of the three modes of political obligation together in, of all places, traffic coverage in the *Washington Post*.[7]

Dr. Gridlock Supports the Troops

In September 2004, the "Dr. Gridlock" column of the *Washington Post*, which typically covers local transportation issues like potholes, hosted a debate regarding what it means to support the troops. The discussion was spurred by the column's author—who establishes his own normative martially by identifying himself as a Vietnam veteran—asking where to get a yellow ribbon decal for his car (Schaffer 2004a). Initial responses articulated a paternalistic understanding of support, with a reader noting that she "just bought five" because "it is so important to show that we love and support our troops!" (Schaffer 2004b). The column also included, however, a more controversial statement:

> I hope your column does not encourage people to get these magnets. If you put one on your trunk, no troop will see it. No life will be saved. If someone does or does not have a magnet on their car, is the war closer to being won or lost? What purpose does empty, more-patriotic-than-thou symbolism serve? (Schaffer 2004b)

At first glance, this appears to be an argument against supporting the troops—and is responded to as such by Dr. Gridlock, who invokes contractual obligation, and underlying gendered shame, stating "They are serving for you . . . You can salute them, or not" (Schaffer 2004b). The affectively charged response to the specter of non-support is not only a rebuttal of not supporting the troops but also an anxious refusal of the possibility that some might be tempted to do so. Dr. Gridlock implies that since service cannot be refused, the salute is irrelevant. The writer may be a poor citizen and masculine subject (and thus bad *person*) but they cannot opt out of obligation. The letter writer might superficially fail to support the troops, but, as a member of the political community, they actually cannot.

A closer reading of the original statement, however, suggests that the writer is critiquing not the troops, but society for engaging in superficial symbolic gestures instead of making greater sacrifices—for a pretension to unearned normative martial masculinity. The communitarian critique of more moral modes of support raises the specter that charitable support *per se* might not be normative citizenship at all . . . but a means of evasion. Dr. Gridlock responds with a contractarian retort, highlighting the intertwining of differing sources of gendered anxiety of non-service at work within the discursive formation. What it really means to support the troops is indeterminate: a partial function of differing expectations as to the appropriate performative of masculine, martial political obligation.

Subsequent interventions in the debate reiterate this point by intertwining modes of obligation within the same response, rather than as differing interpretations of the same yellow-sticker practice. Endorsing the original critique of yellow ribbons, one reader argued:

> All fair-minded Americans support our armed forces because of the sacrifices they make for all of us, and just because some people choose not to "salute" the troops by displaying these images does not make them less supportive or less American. To imply otherwise is a bit like asking "Do you still beat your wife?" and stating you are un-American to not display a ribbon or flag. Patriotism is not defined by symbols. (Schaffer 2004c)

The reference to sacrifices for "all of us" invokes a contractual notion of obligation; framing the general practice in terms of "patriotism," and "being American" refers back to communitarian understandings of war as a collective practice. The heteropatriarchal parallels between the failure to support the troops and beating one's wife draw themselves.

Another reader later writes that they have procured a "red, white and blue 'Freedom Isn't Free' ribbon." The slogan references the contractarian notion that those serving in the military perform a service for those who do not, invoking the creeping feminization of martial heroism while simultaneously refusing it through overt references to patriotism through the use of the flag's colors. The reader goes on to state that "the best part is, my purchases actually support the troops in a double way because I bought them at the Marine Corps Museum Shop" (Schaffer 2004d), ensuring that charities supporting the troops benefit from the sale. The statement positions the reader in a position of masculine, altruistic patronage while affirming a normatively martial vision of the troops *and* acknowledging contractual notions of indebtedness.

A seen in these statements, StT addresses the fracture in the liberal military contract through gendered logics of contrast and contradiction. The ability to shift between the participatory, masculine citizen-soldier and the beneficent, empowered civilian patron construct a "network of [contrasting] permutations that may take masculinity in radically different directions, while still preserving a sense of continuity" (Hutchings 2008, 401). Each contains a differing construction of the troops, understanding of the political community, and acknowledgment of violence but are still articulated within an overarching martial discourse of masculinity and political obligation. This common register facilitates the (re)production of the society of the obligatory, liberal dynamic of civil-military relations as itself masculine—a shift in the "dominant mode of masculinity" (Hutchings 2008, 401; see also Mann 2006).

All three also unified by a central contradiction: the refusal of femininity. Each of the three ideal-types indicates a discomfort with the structural feminization within the liberal gendered civil-military divide. The foundation of normative citizenship in the figure of the masculine combat soldier continues to extend a hierarchy of military/ized masculinity beyond the formal institution, interpellating civilians. Rather than challenging this premise of normative citizenship, these discourses (imperfectly) resolve the problem of the combat soldier by replacing him with the troops. This enables all three discourses to draw social capital and intelligibility from martiality. As the troops are more easily resignified in relation to society—as aggregate idealized combat soldiers, as citizen heroes, as the institutional military, as dependent victims, and so on—the tension of maintaining good public masculinity in wartime is resolved by an endless series of potential contrasts between dominant masculinities unified by a central contradiction.

Together, the three ideal-types contest the gendered structure of violent political obligation. They do not, however, not challenge the central premise of the mythical liberal military contract: service grounds citizenship. Instead, via shifting logics of masculinization, they affirm its contractual corollary: the troops must be supported.

Conclusion

The gendering of StT discourse demonstrates an important double-move. At one level, through the continued reproduction of a hierarchical gender order grounded in martial masculinity, it seems to stabilize the liberal civil-military divide, the dimorphic sex-gender order, and binarism more generally. At another level, however, the contrast between supporters' structural association with (feminized) society and their performance of heteromasculine martiality "*implicitly reveals the imitative structure*" of the gendered and sexualized civil-military divide, "*as well as its contingency*" (Butler 1990, 137, emphasis added).

There is thus a form of "rump" anxiety within the discursive formation that the three ideal-types are unable to address or acknowledge. It stems less from the substantive content of a given statement or practice than the process of performing (and demanding of others) support itself. The very necessity of soliciting support—and of performing and seeking masculinity—acknowledges the possibility that civilians might *not* be doing their bit and, without prodding, might be tempted not to help, not to participate. That perhaps "we" are not masculine, not good citizens, not good people (Millar 2019b). This risks exposing the fact that the liberal military contract, heroic ideals of soldiering masculinity, and underlying heteropatriarchal order are impossible and unreachable. StT discourse, though it looks like a bumper sticker slogan, politically operates to forestall the realization that either we are perpetually failing normative subjects or if we are not, that the social and political order that produced the possibility of normative gender and sexuality was never, in fact, real in the first place.

StT discourse provides a series of gendered escape valves that offer a near-infinite array of possibilities for reiterating obvious support for the troops, and obvious masculinity, in a loop of societal reassurance. Supporting the troops doesn't refute or replace the liberal military contract but amends it. Normative citizenship is reconstituted as a universal, masculinized obligation to provide martial support, rather than war participation or military service.[8] In doing so, the lowest common denominator reading of StT—something akin to "support the troops because they are the troops" is naturalized as apolitical. In doing so, as I examine more in the next chapter, support, as well as the solidaristic relationship to collective violence it reveals, comes to bound the liberal political. Support is the new service.

7

Support and the Making
of Political Community

Thus far, we have seen that the liberal polity is produced internally via violence, articulated in the idiom of the gendered liberal military contract.
In theory (and ideology), all "good" men (now, citizens) ought to serve in
the military in wartime. With the rise of professional militaries and distant
wars—exemplified by the wars in Iraq and Afghanistan— however, very few
people do. The liberal military contract and related notions of binary heteronormative gender are fracturing. Concern for the troops directs attention
away from war toward the maintenance of civil-military relations as a matter
of normative concern. Support discourses, in turn, resolve the gendered civilian anxiety—how can someone be a good man (now, citizen) without military service—through a recasting of support as martial, masculine solidarity.
The politics of support for the troops imperfectly amends the terms of the
gendered liberal military contract.

As outlined in Chapter 2, discursive martiality, conceptualized as the
modern idiom of articulating violent obligations, contains two mutually constitutive components. It captures the politics of war, as we saw in
the meanings of "troops" and "support" and the constitution of the underlying political (i.e., normal social order) through relations of force. In this
chapter, I interrogate the relationship between supporting the troops (StT)
and the political. I examine what happens when the gendered foundations
of political obligation shift and the contingency of previously reified normative structures is (at least partially) revealed. *In the context of an amended,
gendered military contract, how does the liberal political community hang together?* (Or does it?)

Existing accounts of the relationship between violence and the formation
of political community tend to emphasize the creation of the boundary between inside and outside the polity. These analyses focus on internal security

Support the Troops. Katharine M. Millar, Oxford University Press. © Oxford University Press 2022.
DOI: 10.1093/oso/9780197642337.003.0007

and external relations of antagonism (Walker 1990, Campbell 1992). This is the bargain of the originary liberal social contract: the state exists to preserve individual freedom by protecting domestic society from the anarchic violence of the international. In naming/creating an Other, or enemy, the state legitimates its exercise of power. It creates an appealing narrative of national "Self" (Campbell cited in Sheehan 2008, 140 and 163) as a specific nation and a form of political community. This dynamic of making political community is supplemented by nationalism, as both a political ideology undergirding modern self-determination (Calhoun 1993) and an account of the (constructed) cultural, social, linguistic, and historical specificity of the resulting community (Anderson 2016, 5–6). The polity hangs together on the basis of a common constructed, but substantive, identity that differentiates it from other groups, which are excluded through relations of security and force (Campbell 1992; Said 1978).

These dynamics were present during the global war on terror (GWoT). The constructed distinction between ostensibly freedom-loving, gender-equal, and modern coalition states, as liberal democracies, and ostensibly oppressive and backward Iraq and Afghanistan, as religiously inflected autocracies, was a defining feature of the wars (Khalid 2017; Amin-Khan 2012). In September 2001, for instance, Bush announced that "we're going to find those evildoers, those barbaric people who attacked our country, and we're going hold them accountable" (cited in Carruthers 2011, 215). In another statement, Bush used Islamophobic tropes to insist the US "rejects hate, rejects violence, rejects murderers, rejects evil" (2001 cited in Richter-Montpetit 2007, 43; see also Esch 2010). UK political leaders, though, like US politicians, at times keen to parse extremism from Islam, used similar terms. Blair noted that "the terrorists base their ideology on religious extremism—and not just any religious extremism, but a specifically Muslim version"; a former Foreign and Commonwealth Affairs minister argued that "it should be incumbent on those who profess Islam to challenge the fanatics who cite Islam as a justification for appalling acts of violence" (2006 and 2002, cited in Moosavi 2015, 655). The racist and Orientalist Othering of "barbarians," the Middle East, the "Muslim world," and other homogenized groups reified the boundaries—the inside/outside—of the liberal political community (and, indeed "civilization").

The identification of this racialized fault line, however, although important, doesn't tell us anything about how the political community is (re)produced *internally* around collective violence. As a complement to these existing understandings of exclusionary relations of negative contrast, seen in racist, civilizational frames post-9/11, this chapter argues that loyalty and solidarity are essential to understanding the violence(s) of the war on terror and within liberalism more broadly. The gendered political obligation to engage in violence, as reflected in social relations of support, bounds the political and produces the political community. It informs who is in, who is out, and who can be *made* to be in a righteous liberal polity.

I demonstrate this in two ways. First, the constitution of "support as the new service" shifts the normative structure of US and UK civil-military relations from one of femininized home-front care to a masculine logic of totalizing and unreflective martial loyalty. Support is a condition—even the definition—of belonging. Consequently, StT discourses (re)produce an idealized vision of the (amended) liberal polity. It is characterized not by failing obligations of heroic masculine combat or external imperial violence but by reciprocal martial solidarity. Support the troops also normatively redeem the polity. They (re)make it as a coherent entity worthy of violent defense.

Second, I show that this synonymity of support with political membership detaches gendered political obligation from the boundaries of the nation-state. Although superficially support appears to be only about internal civil-military relations, it also facilitates a stretching of what counts as internal. StT serves as an apoliticized vector for imperial relations that demand support—or even military service—without a corollary recognition of rights and belonging. Support can be projected (and imposed) upon racialized noncitizens and illiberal states, disciplining and extending the liberal order. The amended liberal political community—be it the US, UK, or the transnational liberal imperial order—normatively hangs together through gendered relations of seemingly spontaneous and reciprocal, yet fully irrefutable and experientially uneven, solidarity.

Support and the Production of the Liberal Polity

Support, as the previous chapter argued, is the new service. It offers a means of performing—and accessing—normative martiality and masculinity, of being a good person. The ideal-typical liberal structure of gendered civil-military relations, wherein a feminized home front depends upon a protective military and cares for them in exchange, has been transformed. It is now a relationship of all-encompassing masculine loyalty between a masculinized civil society and a more ambivalently gendered, but normatively martial, troops. Violent solidarity, as an expression of discursive martiality, produces and bounds, the political community.

Solidarity and Political Belonging

This is a complex and abstract idea. It is easiest to understand when contrasted with externally oriented notions of enmity. Consider the illustrative example of small-unit combat cohesion: how small infantry units "hang together" under fire on an active battlefield. Obviously, soldiers in the field aren't a literal empirical parallel to supporting the troops, but small-unit cohesion works as a conceptual analogy. It intuitively captures how gendered, violent solidarity helps produce groups regardless of the substance of external political dynamics of Othering.[1] I then analytically extrapolate this general dynamic to illustrate how supporting the troops makes up political community.

Small-unit combat cohesion refers to the notion that many soldiers are motivated to fight not by political or national affiliations but rather by affection for and obligation to "the man next to them" (King 2013, 24–39; MacKenzie 2015). Though the empirical validity and specific mechanisms of combat cohesion (i.e., how and why this happens) remain a matter of social scientific debate, it is a powerful narrative. A study of US Iraq veterans, for instance, cited "fighting for my buddies" as their primary combat motivator (Wong et al. 2003, 9). This intense cultivation of loyalty is tied to constructions of masculinity, shame, and obligation to the group (King 2013, 63–73). It relies on the ideological (if no longer literal) exclusion of values, characteristics, or practices associated with femininity and/or queerness as purportedly weak and vulnerable (King 2013, 70–73; Mackenzie 2015, 14–15). In this context, failing to adequality perform combat masculinity has high stakes. It endangers one's comrades, breaks solidarity, and risks being cast out of the group. Martial cohesion requires individuals to relinquish their rights and interests—even life—for the group. Membership is conditional upon the performance of normative masculinity.

The small group is constituted by two mutually reinforcing dynamics of violence. First, the small group is produced by its positioning within the context of war—in this case, the global war on terror—informed by overarching dynamics of racialized antagonism, Othering, and enmity. The small unit arrives at the battlefield following a *politics* of violence against a specific enemy (e.g., terrorists, the Taliban, etc.) (see Barkawi 2017). Second, once situated on the battlefield, the relational dynamics of war (i.e., immediate, kinetic violence) produce an *internal* cultivation of extreme loyalty that, crucially, pertains regardless of the substantive identity of the enemy (Barkawi 2017).

The interrelated imperatives of survival and masculinized, heroic loyalty hold the unit together beyond individual motivations relating to identity, patriotism, ideology, and so on—beyond the formal politics of war. Each dynamic—external enmity and internal solidarity—is key to defining the bounds, nature, purpose, and meaning of the group in relation to violence. It would be difficult to argue, however, that either (fighting or interpersonal loyalty) is absent, irrelevant, or reducible to the other. Simply knowing who the "enemy" is does not tell us as much about "us" as we might think. To extrapolate the logic of this analogy, dynamics of risk, threat, and exclusion must be balanced with consideration of how the political community relates to those who commit (and risk) violence on behalf of the whole.

Following these general dynamics, the transformation of military service into military support can be read as an extension of "fighting for the man next to you" to the entire polity.[2] Supporting the troops similarly bypasses engagement with enmity and the politics of war. Instead, within StT, obligation arises not from solely formal political membership in a nation-state (i.e., simple nationalism) but also solidarity and affection borne of proximity, circumstance, and interdependence. Cohesion—and solidaristic support— are not cultivated on the basis of the substantive cultural and/or political identification (e.g., patriotism, speaking French, etc.), but rather relations of normative obligation. Combat heroism within the small infantry unit is mirrored by the normatively martial, now masculinized/ing practice of support. Both are underpinned by an avoidance of the feminine and/or queer, as weak, dependent, dangerous, and so on.

Read back onto the polity, this leads to all countervailing concerns, such as perspectives on the war, political orientation, and substantive identities such as race, gender, class, and so forth, being subsumed within the universal need to support the troops in a time of war. In the words of a Vietnam veteran who disagreed with Iraq and disliked President Bush:

Vietnam was not supported back home, but you know what? I really didn't care. The guy I cared about was the guy next to me, the guy who was getting shot at and was going to help me survive. It's the same thing now. You have to take care of the people fighting over there. I'm all for the troops. I'm for every soldier. (Applebome 2004)

This dynamic of support is also seen in the tendency of embedded journalists, authorized by the Pentagon to cover Iraq and Afghanistan from the front, to report war stories solely from the viewpoint of deployed personnel (Carruthers 2011, 229). As these reporters were often the sole source of first-person news available to US and UK viewers, the perspectives of the media and the public were brought into alignment with that of the military (Carruthers 2011). The formal politics of the war on terror were stripped out in favor of a simulated and—via masculinized support—participatory experience of martiality.

Without overstretching the analogy, we can analytically transpose normative martial cohesion from the small unit of heteromasculine combat soldiers to a polity similarly made up of appropriately masculine citizens during wartime. Both bound, produce, and organize, via relations of gendered solidarity, the relevant group—be it a unit or a polity—in a manner related to, but distinct from, the politics of specific wars. Regardless of an individual's personal beliefs, they are interpellated, as a member of the polity, by normative structures of gendered political obligation that compel and presuppose support. Support bounds the political, [3] such that to be a member of the political community is, *by definition*, to be supporting the troops. A failure of masculinizing support is thus a betrayal of the political community.

As a form of discursive martiality, StT reflects and sets the limits of the existing social and political order, relationally, structurally, and normatively. The transformation of gendered political obligation within StT discourse therefore also implies a transformation of the political community; the amendment of the liberal military contract is also the amendment of the liberal polity. It informs who belongs (those to whom political obligation pertains), who is out (those who fail, refuse, or are not extended the expectation of obligation), and the terms upon which the community relates to itself.

Redeeming the Political Community

The major implication of this argument—that discursive martiality produces political community in a manner that does not mechanically follow from the politics of war—is that if the dynamic of solidarity changes, so does the nature of the political community.

Although StT discourse superficially preserves the form and logic of liberal contractualism (and binary heteropatriarchy), the bounds of the political have shifted. The amended liberal military contract attempts to alleviate gendered civilian anxiety and secure the normative gender and sexual relations of the "good" story of liberalism, by reconstituting previously feminized civilian support as a masculinized form of normative martiality. This very process of reconstitution, however, highlights the tenuousness of martial masculinity as the basis of political community—and means of arbitrating its normativity. A polity based on relations of masculine, reciprocal obligation for military service—to commit violence—and feminine home-front care is not the same as a polity based on the often-asymmetric masculine obligation to support the troops.

StT discourse both affirms and (re)makes the political community. The way this works can be understood with reference to Elaine Scarry's conceptualization of conflict. She argues that wars are not fought for political communities as they are, but as they are imagined, hoped, or believed to be. As Scarry puts it:

> If the democracy for which one dies existed in a world safe for democracy, one would not be dying to make the world safe for democracy. If the country for which one kills existed in a world in which there was an end of wars, one would not be killing to make a war that ends all wars. (1985, 130–31)

The collective use of force (re)produces not just the political community but also a type of idealized political community that normatively "hangs together" in a particular way. Discursive martiality, by bringing together the politics of war with the solidaristic formation of the political via violence, helps us understand the contingency of this process. The amended liberal military contract and related binary heteropatriarchal sex/gender order are empirically produced as common sense. Conceptually, however, we can imagine many ways of organizing gendered obligations around violence. A polity constituted in accordance with the gendered obligation of communitarian support, for instance, might resemble the apocryphal vision of ancient Sparta: a totalized, martial society where mothers sent their sons into battle preferring that they die rather than be defeated or captured (Redfield

1977, 149). The polity implied by altruistic relations of violent obligation would be horrifying—perhaps resembling the Hunger Games, wherein victimized combatants resolve, by violent proxy, the conflicts of ostensibly beneficent, masculinized patrons. All of which is to say: the amended liberal military contract is not an inevitability. The liberal polity is reified via StT discourse as continuous, (re)masculinized, coherent, and righteous.

This process is neither easy nor straightforward. The necessity of producing the political community—of insisting upon support, of seeking heteromasculinity—implicitly acknowledges it is a fiction. The polity is not already real/manifest as the basis for the actions done in its name. The political community produced by war (as safe, as democratic, as righteous), as well as within martial StT discourse (as masculine, solidaristic, disengaged from violence), is an aspirational, yet unacknowledged, normative project. The anxious refusal of the feminine and/or queer—of the temptation to shirk gendered political obligation—that characterizes civil-military relations can be read up a level, as a contestation over the nature of a good polity.

This slightly abstract point—that the (ostensibly) liberal, supportive polity is both belied and (re)produced by StT discourse—is best understood through Derrida's discussion of declarations of independence. Derrida asks, "who signs, and with what so-called proper name, the declarative act which founds an institution?" (1986, 8). The problem, as he sees it, is that the entity understood as signing a declaration of independence does "not exist as an entity, it does not exist, before this declaration, not as such" (Derrida 1986, 10). The polity that declares independence is theoretically created as a polity by the declaration. It paradoxically brings itself into being.

If the US and UK were really characterized by the mythical liberal military contract wherein all eligible (masculine) citizens serve, there would be no need to ameliorate the gendered civilian anxiety impelled by its nonperformance. There would be no need to redraft the terms of normative citizenship, and normative masculinity, as "military participation"—and no need to support the troops. The contestation over gendered political obligation seen within StT discourse is a "construct-substantiating process." The polity supports the troops not so much to annihilate an opponent as to "first 'make' and then 'make real' its own beliefs, its own territorial and ideological self-definition" (Scarry 1985, 132 and 140).

This discussion may seem to be over-reading a fairly discrete discourse. But it points us toward a significant political effect of StT discourse. If it's not—quite—able to fix the amended, gendered military contract (or gender itself), it is, by shifting the goalposts from service to support, able to redeem the normativity of the political community. Martiality is a "medium for evoking images of [ourselves] and the societies [we] live in"—for bringing about the idealized community (Ben-Ari 2004, 346; for original see Lutz 2001). Chapter 5 argued that figure of the troops facilitates the conduct of war by vanishing it from view, shifting our attention to relations of internal support. Complicity in the violence of the liberal state, which we would typically understand citizens as taking on as a function of their political membership and participation in democracy (see Chapter 8), is repackaged as a matter of masculine loyalty.

The support side of this equation similarly directs our attention inward, to the masculinized—and normative—redemption of supporters as good liberal and gendered subjects (as good people). This dynamic bolsters the violence of the liberal state in a slightly different way. In changing what it means to be a normative citizen, StT discourse also changes what it means to be a normative polity. Richard Ashley argues that "the sovereign figure of man . . . supplies the constitutive principle" of the state. The legitimacy of the state rests on the existence of reasoning man, while the (rational and violent) capacities of man are attributed to and exercised by the state (Ashley 1989, 265 and 300–301). This is, in essence, an internationalization of liberal social contract: the state navigating the anarchic international takes the place of the individual overcoming the state of nature (Ashley 1988, 256). The political community mirrors the idealized qualities of the normative, heteromasculine political subject. The breakdown of the liberal military contract is not just a crisis of normative masculinity for individual supporters but also a more generalized crisis as to the moral worth of the political community (see Mann 2013).

The substitution of masculinized support for masculinized service, in shifting the nature of the normative public subject, provides a new model for the polity. The material and structural conditions that produced the ideological inconsistencies of contemporary liberal warfare—inequitable racialized, gendered, and sexualized service, invasions of "choice," and so forth—are no longer the relevant benchmarks for civil-military relations. The normative failure of the polity implied by the fracture in the liberal military contract goes away. Instead, masculine normativity vis-à-vis force is concerned with what is owed to members of the internal community. If these obligations are discursively satisfied, it once again becomes possible to (re)imagine the liberal polity as itself a normative subject.

Within the global war on terror, the passive troops, normative supporters—and polity, along with them—are all able to be cast simultaneously as victims and saviors, overcoming the externalized calamity of war through martial solidarity. Parts of this construction come from the GWoT narrative with which we're already familiar: the US and UK experienced "attacks on our way of life" (Ali 2005, 62) by those who "hate our freedoms" (Esch 2010, 382–83). The sense of moral righteousness generated through negative contrast with the Orientalist tropes attributed to terrorists, however, also subtly relies on that same way of life being worth defending. It depends on the polity, and citizens, living up to their own story—part of which, this section has argued, is fulfilling the gendered political obligation of solidaristic violence. Both components are required to legitimate the violence of the US and UK as stemming from good political communities.

The alterations in discursive martiality found within StT discourse provide an opportunity for the US and UK, through support, to (re)make themselves as (hetero)masculine, moral, and righteous international actors (Mann 2006, 2013; Eisenstein 2007). Bluntly, once "we" are again produced as good people, "we," in turn, produce a good community that does not pursue violence, but whose preservation justifies it. The positive self-image of liberalism that validated the civilizational violence of colonialism (see Chapter 2) thus remains accessible, modified for a new form of war and a more (superficially) progressive political sensibility. The amended liberal military contract is the basis for the good story of liberalism, version 2.0. As Mann observes, "in the end, the real justification is not the reason for the war, but the subject that is constituted through it" (2006, 160) and the normative social relations that produce/sustain it.

Support and the Imperial Extension of Liberal Order

This section demonstrates how, counterintuitively, the internality of support the troops discourse, provides an effective warrant for imperial war by extending the request for (or imposition of) support beyond the territorial nation-state. Support becomes a means for allies to express their solidarity and bound the transnational liberal order. It also serves as a racialized vector for coloniality, articulating as an inequitable demand for loyalty from Othered states and individuals without the reciprocal recognition of political belonging.

Transnational Solidarity

Empirically, StT discourses—almost uniformly—fail to engage with the international. In keeping with the discourse's general deflection of war, external adversaries and/or the estimated (to date) 278,000 Iraqi, Pakistani, and Afghan civilians killed by the wars are rarely mentioned (Watson Institute 2021). Instead, the small but meaningful strand of StT discourse that acknowledges the international revolves around what are essentially alliance politics, re-read through the idiom of support for US and UK troops. A 2010 statement by UK Minister of Defence Fox announced:

> The British Government supports both the mission and the counter-insurgency strategy. I encourage Allies to demonstrate strategic patience and give time for the counter-insurgency strategy to work, but stress the need to be able to show significant progress, consolidating ISAF's hold in central Helmand, and accelerating the training of the Afghan security forces. We need to produce a stronger narrative alongside the political leadership we are providing to ensure that our troops get the support they deserve. (2010)

Fox rhetorically extends the logic of violent obligation for support (as a function of a shared mission and the deserving troops) beyond the UK to implicate the political leadership of allied NATO states. The collective subject implied by the "our" modifying our troops is unclear. It likely pertains to the UK, but in the context of the quotation, could also be read as referencing NATO allies, Afghanistan, or all three. The discourse does not construct the NATO political leadership as belonging to the same (territorial) polity as the troops; it clearly constructs those who are obligated as nation-states.

The use of the language of StT, however, suggests the allies are implicated by a broader liberal project/social order and expected to perform as such. This reflects a relational inflection to the strategic calculus that led not only the addressed NATO allies but also the UK itself to participate in the war on terror (and Iraq specifically). A sense of support, commonality, and, if you like, loyalty to the US—the "special relationship"—were arguably as important to spurring UK military action as any given commitment to the specific geopolitics of the war on terror (Ali 2005, 4–7; Dumbrell 2009). The invocation of support and, implicitly, collective moral character shifts the stakes of the discussion from a shared strategic goal or material national interest to a more nebulous projection of substantive similarity and affective solidarity. NATO allies are both invited to participate in—and subtextually shamed for a temptation to shirk—the normative masculinity of martial support.

This production of common community—if not a polity per se—is also articulated, albeit to opposing political ends, within the discourse of the antiwar movement.[4] The US NGO Military Families Speak Out (MFSO), for instance, drew on growing Canadian and Australian opposition to the war in Iraq to encourage its supporters to contact their congressional representatives, stating:

> Canada's House of Commons passed a nonbinding resolution calling on their government to stop the deportation of Iraq war resisters who came to Canada seeking refuge from participating in a war that they saw as illegal and immoral . . . The Australian government, once among the Bush administration's closest allies, is now standing up against the Iraq war . . . The world stands behind us as we demand that our own government bring all of our troops home from Iraq now, and give them the care they need when they get home. (MFSO 2008).

The quotation shows ambivalence in its (re)production of the supportive community. The reference to the Bush administration and "our" troops suggests a national frame of reference, yet Canada is commended for its service to endangered US military personnel. The governments of Canada and Australia are posited as standing with MFSO in supporting the safe return of the (presumably US) troops. The locus of political obligation is subtly shifted to Canada and Australia, standing in for the liberal international—with the US framed as potentially failing to support the troops. The reach of the liberal martial ideal is extended via political obligation to encompass "the world"—as represented, not incidentally, by settler colonial states—united in a normative project: protecting and caring for our troops.

This blurry extension of violent political obligation, and imperfect limning of the liberal polity(s), is not limited to formal politics. In a striking example, the UK Army Benevolent Fund (ABF) launched a US branch—the British Army Benevolent Fund America—with the following rationale:

> Given the current scale of operations in which the British Army is involved, demand has been increasingly placed on our charity to support soldiers and their young families through difficult times. We hope the American people

will be able to learn more about our charity and its work and support their allies by making a donation or attending our fundraising events. (2007)

While this statement slightly tempers the compulsory nature of support—it is requested rather than demanded—it is noteworthy for its assumption that individual Americans, rather than the state, would feel moved to support British troops. It is an invitation for US citizens to participate, via support, in not only British martiality but also, given the ABF's emphasis on its historical legacy as a service charity, World War II romanticism and colonial nostalgia (Basham 2016). This form of support relationally extends the boundaries of the British polity (or reads the US and UK together, into one) via political obligation. The commonality of the logics of political obligation between and across the US and UK (and liberal allies) speaks to the integrative potential of StT discourse's pluralistic solidarity in bounding and maintaining the martial, liberal order (see Jabri 2006).

These states—the US, UK, and others with pervasive support the troops practices, notably Canada and Australia—are also unified by their status as colonial states. These predominantly English-speaking states[5]—and, with the exception of the UK, White Dominion settler states—have frequently stood in for liberal internationalism and "civilization" (Vucetic 2011). During the war on terror, the US and associated allies frequently invoked a cosmopolitan understanding of war. They argued their actions were in defense of humanity, against the evils of terrorism and extremism (Odysseos 2007). As we saw in Chapter 2, however, the claims of liberal polities to universalism and pacifism (or at least restraint) are premised upon an elision of these same polities continual reproduction of, and within, racialized colonial hierarchies. Humanity, as throughout liberal modernity, is implicitly constructed as White, European, cisnormative, and heteromasculine—a model that is then universalized to all (Wynter 2003).

It is significant, then, that many (though not all) states exhibiting StT discourses—and projecting them transnationally—are colonial and normatively White (see Howell and Richter-Montpetit 2020). Americans supporting British troops indicates common mission, community, and normative project. The politics of the war on terror—namely US exceptionalism and the framing of Middle East/Central Asia as barbaric (Esch 2010)—reiterated and repackaged racialized, historical British imperial tropes in the language of neoconservatism (Said quoted in Ali 2005, 43). The constitution of StT as a project of internal support of a shared troops subtly reflects this blurring of the US and UK into a White, liberal imperial West. This, as with the domestic racial and sexual contracts that undergird the domestic liberal polity,[6] suggests that the solidarity owed to the transnational liberal project is produced not only by normative gender but also by race. Supporting the troops, in addition to a domestic rallying cry, is also a transnational practice for bounding the "good" political community in line with White imperialism.

Support produces the good community and functions as the racialized, civilizational frontier of the global war on terror (see Richter-Montpetit 2014). This double life of StT works by blurring the line, through the extension of obligation, between the domestic and international. By constituting multiple normative communities simultaneously (e.g., the family, the US, NATO, the world), StT discourse enables the military service of people(s) of color— and constitution of the troops as encompassing pluralistic difference (see Chapter 5)—to exist alongside the external racialization of support as normatively White solidarity.[7] The US and UK can be internally inclusive and multicultural (albeit under the racialized universalism of liberalism), while the liberal international can be conditioned by affective, ostensibly apolitical support that "just happens" to track racialized hierarchies.

The Persistence of Service

The racialized/ing dynamic of transnational martial support is further underscored by discourse that demands non-Western states and/ or noncitizens demonstrate martial solidarity with US and UK troops. Consider the following reprimand of the Turkish government by Secretary of State Powell for failing to adequately contribute to the US mission in Iraq. Powell warned Turkey that the US was looking for "full cooperation in the days ahead, full support for humanitarian efforts as well as an effort to support our troops in northern Iraq" (Kessler and Pan 2003). On the one hand, this statement, contextualized by war and the specter of territorial conquest, seems to be operational in nature. It works in the idiom of strategic—and often fairly transactional—state alliances. On the other hand, Powell invoked the idiom of StT rather than a more technical or geopolitical framing. He expressed his "lingering sense of disappointment" (Kessler and Pan 2003) in Turkey's past failures. Powell suggests Turkey is not living up to its contractual obligation(s), wherein the US provides aid in exchange for war participation.

Without overdrawing the implications of a single illustrative example, the passage reveals tensions in the transnationalization of political obligation. At one level, the oscillation between strategic and obligatory logics suggests a recognition that Turkey is not a priori expected to support coalition troops. Turkey, as constructed via colonial, Orientalist tropes of liminality vis-à-vis Europe and the West (Zarakol 2010), is on the outside of the normatively White liberal community. At the same time, the gendered dynamic of this exchange, wherein the less powerful partner is shamed for failing to perform appropriate support/gratitude, plays out the masculine logic of protection at the macro level. Turkey is implied to be insufficiently anxious about the violent political obligations expected—and extended—by the US. Recall Bush's infamous proclamation that the nations of the world "are either with us or against us" (CNN 2001).

During the early years of the war on terror, the Bush administration condemned the news network Al-Jazeera in similar Orientalist terms (Carruthers 2011, 249). Rumsfeld called Al-Jazeera's coverage "vicious, indefensible and inexcusable"; Paul Wolfowitz accused the network of "endangering the lives of American troops" (cited in Carruthers 2011, 249). Unlike allied states (and Pentagon-approved media), Al-Jazeera didn't benefit from a racialized assumption of commonality and community. Though press freedom is a principle of political liberalism, Al-Jazeera's editorial independence was instead posited as a threat to the troops (and an implicit betrayal of solidarity). Al-Jazeera, despite not "really" being a member of the liberal order, is still projected as having a responsibility to protect the troops. Support is necessary but, for racialized and colonial Others, insufficient for peer membership in the liberal imperial order.

This perpetuation of racialized and gendered imperial hierarchies via seemingly open and expansive extensions of political obligation also pertains to individuals and groups. A *Wall Street Journal* article, for instance, approvingly quotes an Iraqi soldier, Staff Sgt. Alaa Akram as praising the "American soldier" who "never worries about money" but is "worried about his country." Akram is framed as an ideal to which the Iraqi army should aspire (Taranto 2005). The *Journal* commentator notes, "It is nice to know that someone supports the troops" (Taranto 2005). This statement is a pointed rebuke to those who do not meet the speaker's standard for StT. It is also has racialized and colonial overtones, wherein the support of a citizen of a less powerful and (potentially) enemy state is deployed to shame the failure of US citizens that more closely approximate the gendered and racialized Western citizen ideal to appropriately perform support.

The one-liner also speaks to the naturalization of supporting the troops as a foundational, universalized obligation in the US. Taking a step back, there is something surreal about projecting support for coalition troops onto a citizen (even in an allied force) of an occupied state. This also implicitly highlights "support" as an articulation of racialized imperial loyalty. It seems unlikely that support for *opposing* (i.e., not US or UK) troops would be recognized as an intelligible normative stance akin to the generic masculine valorization of honor in battle. To borrow another example, during the GWoT, pro-US military video games proliferated and, though designed to boost enlistment, were frequently constructed as educational (Carruthers 2011, 262). Similar games produced by Hezbollah, depicting military actions against Israel, were condemned as promoting violent hatred (Carruthers 2011). Solidaristic martiality is not recognized as a universal, formal, or transferrable principle of political obligation. Instead, the implication is that if even the above Iraqi soldier can support the US troops, there is something particularly wrong with those Americans who do not.

The explicit approval offered for Akram's support, though condescending in tone, also suggests that non-nationals may opt, or be forcibly read, in to the polity through their recognition of the gendered (and racialized) terms of the amended liberal military contract. Though the recognition of the Iraqi soldier's support for US troops is less about him than the domestic audience, the proffering of support opens space—albeit one conditioned by stark differences in power—for claiming symbolic inclusion and participation. Much like the double-moves of StT discourse generally, the conditional extension/recognition of support simultaneously reinforces the colonial hierarchy existing between coalition and Iraqi troops while eroding the territorial nation-state/citizenship as the sole basis for political solidarity.

Though the example of Staff Sgt. Akram is small, its ideological deployment parallels broader narratives of support, solidarity, and affection ostensibly held by Iraqi and Afghan citizens for International Security Assistance Force (ISAF) and coalition troops. Think, for instance, of the insistence that the war in Afghanistan was not "only" about terrorism, but also about "liberating" Afghan women and girls from the "backwards" strictures of the Taliban (Hunt 2006; Khalid 2011). The much-circulated images of Iraqi citizens toppling the statue of Saddam Hussein served a similar function in enabling Western states to impose an affect of enthusiasm and support for coalition military action and troops upon civilians whose lives had been ir-reparably upended by the war (Major and Perlmutter 2005). The articulation of these racialized hierarchies in terms of support, rather than the geopolitics of the war, serves to further universalize the GWoT as undertaken on behalf of a participatory "humanity." It is a subtler articulation of the common colo-nial "belief in the need and the right to dominate others for their own good, others who are expected to be grateful" (Razack 2004, 10) and supportive.

This apoliticized, integrative operation of StT discourse is bolstered by the fact that, superficially, the extension (and claiming) of membership in the lib-eral international order via obligatory support mirrors the logic of minority groups joining domestic armed forces. It is possible to read support, as with older forms of martial service, as a declaration of equality and membership within the (domestic) liberal state (see Krebs 2006; Ware 2010, 2014). Under the terms of the amended liberal contract, wherein support replaces service, this should be true. And to some degree, it is: as wild as it is to project and expect support from citizens of occupied states, it also doesn't seem viable to *refuse* support from ostensible outsiders. The US and UK (and coalition forces) pragmatically rely on the seeming approbation of Afghans and Iraqis in order to legitimate their use of force—and risking of the troops' lives.

It also helps, as above, to read support for *these* troops as support for the violent imposition of the liberal international order more generally. Ideologically, the construction of support as ostensibly voluntary and spon-taneous, *independent* of pre-existing political relationships, makes it difficult to decline. It's not about politics; it's a matter of normative, moralized, mas-culinized solidarity. Turning down support from external (or racially "inap-propriate") supporters would be to admit that the theoretically open liberal polity conditioned by (somewhat) reciprocal relations of masculine/zing vi-olent obligation is not, in fact, universal. The mandatory acceptance of sup-port, however, should not be taken to imply that it has been—or can—be co-opted toward progressive ends.

The material dimensions of the transnationalized liberal martial contract, unsurprisingly, reveal the continued operation of violence within these neo-imperial dynamics of solidarity. Afghan and Iraqi translators and "locally engaged civilians" who assisted deployed US and UK forces, for instance, obviously exhibited masculine, martial loyalty. They also went above and beyond the bake sales and care packages support of the (re)masculinized home front (Baker 2010; Abramson 2014; Long 2013). For most of the war on terror, the US and UK offered various programs to, in theory, assist Iraqi and

Afghan civilians following their employment, ranging from financial support to expedited entry to the US and UK to permanent resettlement (Parliament of the United Kingdom 2018). This is in line with the classic tenets of the amended military contract. Martial support (which, of course, in an active warzone bleeds quickly into martial service) is reciprocally exchanged in return for political belonging.

The implementation of these programs through to the present, however, has been conditional and lacking. Both the US and UK resettlement programs put caps—which often aren't met, due to bureaucratic and logistical hurdles—on the number of people who can be resettled each year (Gibian 2019). Several visa tracks required either that individuals prove they are at risk of being killed (i.e., qualify as a refugee) or, based on a blanket assessment of the conflict (particularly in Afghanistan prior to the 2021 US withdrawal), simply assumed they are not (Parliament 2018). Under the Trump administration, the US went further, first cancelling these visas under the discriminatory "Muslim ban" (Surana and O'Toole 2017), then creating an exemption, but with dramatically fewer visas available per year (taken from the overall refugee quota) (Huetteman 2016). These hurdles were not popular. Media commentary in both states decried the inability of Iraqi and Afghan civilians to access visas (and safety) as "broken promises" and an immoral "abandonment" (Walsh 2009; Huetteman 2016). In the US, the NGO No One Left Behind was formed to pressure the government into "keeping our promises." US General Mattis stated it baldly: "we owe them support for their commitment" (Editorial Board 2019).

The contractual tenor and presumption of martial solidarity within these objections is clear. The civilians have fulfilled the political obligation of support to such a degree they are nearly read into the troops themselves. And yet . . . they are not. This came to a head in August 2021, when the US withdrew from Afghanistan, spurring a mass evacuation of Western citizens, vulnerable Afghan civilians, and Afghans associated with NATO, ISAF, and the US from the Kabul airport (Gaouette et al. 2021). Though over 120,000 people were airlifted from Kabul, up to an estimated 300,000 more—including Afghan translators and military contractors whose applications to leave for the US and UK had been delayed in the bureaucratic visa morass (Lang et al. 2021; Ingliss 2021; De Luce 2021; Parker et al. 2021)—were left behind. Those able to leave face extreme material hardships in attempting to restart life in the US and UK, as well as immigration systems that impose substantial obstacles to achieving permanent residency (Lang et al. 2021; Al-Jazeera 2021). Despite risking their lives for the US and UK's liberal imperial order, locally employed civilians are denied, both materially and symbolically, full and reciprocal membership within the political community.

This interruption of the masculine (normatively White) logics of masculine solidarity via support for the troops by racialized colonial hierarchies is even more apparent in the military service of noncitizens. In the UK, the legacies of the nineteenth-century imperial construction of "martial races" (Streets 2017) continue to pertain. Commonwealth nationals (subject to a shifting set of residency criteria), Nepalese Gurkhas, and Irish citizens are eligible to serve in the military (BBC 2018). As of 2012, approximately one in ten members of the UK armed forces were born outside the UK (Beckford 2012). Many of these soldiers are people of color from previously colonized states. British citizenship is technically possible, but not guaranteed, following the completion of service. The difficulties faced by these soldiers in achieving legal residency and/or citizenship is often cast in terms of a "betrayal" by the public of racialized, but, by dint of their military service, "deserving" soldiers (Ware 2010). Bundling racialized and "foreign" bodies in with the rest of "our boys" establishes their belonging and heroism, enabling them to be distinguished from "undesirable" economic migrants (or enemy combatants) who remain threateningly Other (Ware 2010).

A similar dynamic occurs in the US. In 2008, approximately 65,000 noncitizens were serving in the armed forces, the majority of whom were people of color from states within the United States' sphere of influence (notably, Mexico and the Philippines) (Batalova 2008; Zong and Batalova 2019). Naturalization and citizenship, though still far from simple, is easier in the US than UK (US Citizenship and Immigration Services n.d.). After 9/11, Bush issued an executive order enabling foreign-born military personnel to apply for naturalization after a year of service. This exchange of citizenship for service is, fairly obviously, not in line with the terms of the amended liberal martial contract but the original version. This extension of membership via *service* exposes the fact that membership via support, though seemingly inclusive of particularistic difference, does not actually pertain to everyone. Noncitizen civilians living in the US, though expected to support the troops, are not granted citizenship or recognized as normative members of the polity on the basis of support. Instead, noncitizen military personnel, particularly those identified/ing as Latinx and/or Dreamers, are frequently constructed as more deserving of support, services, and political membership than other "migrants" (Valdez 2016).[8] Whose support counts for membership is inflected by other normative categories—particularly race and coloniality.

Like liberalism writ large, the amended liberal military contract contains a double-standard. The purportedly voluntary, spontaneous nature of support and service facilitates coloniality and racialized coercion through appeals to a purportedly shared liberalism and individual accession to normative masculinity (and, less obviously, Whiteness). Martiality remains a mechanism for individual Others to opt into the community—and into being good. This support, however, is not sufficient to overcome the presumption of threat and externality. The pleasant martial solidarity of normatively White liberal states continues to rely on the labor of people(s) of color, who are invited to participate on the unequal terms of the original military contract. Or, almost the originary liberal contract since the granting of reciprocal rights and political membership is far from guaranteed. The liberal military contract—constituted by the sexual contract (Pateman 1988) and the racial contract (Mills 2014), premised upon the expropriation of people of color—is transnationalized to the liberal imperial order.

Support the troops discourse thus sets up a gendered, racialized logic of violent political obligation that maintains and legitimates imperial power relations. Hierarchy and dependency are reconstituted, simultaneously, in the idioms of liberal universalized inclusion and seemingly apolitical declarations of loyalty and solidarity. This shifts the war on terror from a matter of politics—of interests, negotiations, power, and so forth—among sovereign equals to a project of affective affinity. Framing complex geopolitical and imperial relations in terms of support once again sidesteps the central issue of war: maiming and killing. The material realities of imperial war are elided through the constitution of the purportedly inclusive, universal liberal polity as normatively worthy through the externalization of the burden of service, and violence, to racialized Others. The hands of liberalism remain clean.

Conclusion

So, how does the political community hang together? What does the new contract look like? I've sketched a situation where, in exchange for political membership (which may or may not include full civil and political rights, see Chapter 8) and a secure sense of normative masculinity, individuals must support the troops. The troops themselves are not constructed as sufficiently agential to be a party to the contract. Instead, they are the figurative site of affective investment and (a)political negotiation of gendered obligation for supportive civilians. When performed "correctly," these relations of gendered support redeem the masculinity, coherence, and normativity of the liberal polity. This masculinizing process of martial support is underwritten by the actual military service of sacrificial subjects of the transnational liberal order, including racialized non-nationals whose loyalty may otherwise be in doubt.

Supporting the troops disguises the fact that

> at least on our end of the thing, it is arguably the case that we have accepted the gift [of military service, of Others' suffering] merely by inhabiting a social order that is upheld by violence, by the dying of those who have gone before here and in foreign lands. (MacLeish 2013, 187)

The persistence of contractual framings of obligation under the amended martial contract, with their connotations of masculine heroism, autonomy, and voluntarism, obscure support's entangling with affective and structural forms of transnationalized coercion. Despite all explicit concerns regarding individualism and reciprocity, in modern liberal societies, it is racialized, gendered, and uneven "sacrifice, and not contract that is the most accurate way of framing the political relationship as it has been experienced" (Paul Kahn cited in Taussig-Rubbo, 84). Support is sacrifice disguised as a contract disguised as a spontaneous, voluntary relation of (a)political—and unconditional!—solidarity.

Although, empirically, I've drawn this account from the contemporary politics of the war on terror, the argument applies to liberalism more broadly. The production of the political community follows an integrative, colonizing (in more ways than one) logic to implicate "everyone"—all of humanity—in an ostensibly common, solidaristic project of protecting the troops. Relations of affective solidarity are crucial to (re)producing the liberal imperial order and obscuring its foundational dependence upon hierarchical, gendered, and racialized colonial violence(s). The liberal "political" is bounded by both the dynamics of exclusion and enmity with which we are already familiar *and* relations of violent solidarity.

The implications of this totalizing (re)production of the liberal "political" through relations of gendered, obligatory support for dissent are examined in the next chapter. Is it possible to oppose war—or refuse support—without being ejected from the political community? From being a "good" person?

8

The Meaning of Support
for War Opposition

This chapter examines the implications of the amendment of the martial liberal contract for dissent and resistance. We have seen that "the troops" and "support" are key to legitimating politics of contemporary war; support the troops (StT) discourses reflect and reproduce the gendered relations of violent obligation that bound the liberal political. Here, I return to the interplay between these dual components of discursive martiality: "politics," the formal contestations regarding power and governance in the public sphere, and "the political," the naturalized and invisibilized basis for social order. Rather than looking solely at discourses of support, however, I also examine discourses conventionally understood to oppose war and the valorization of the military.

In a context of mandatory support for the troops, what does it mean to dissent? Is it to oppose the wars the troops are fighting? Or is it to resist the call to support the troops—to contest the gendered martial contract? What is it possible to intelligibly and legitimately say? Analytically, I examine the way these two threads—antiwar dissent *and* resistance to the amended contract—articulate with respect to contextual, empirical understandings of "politics" during the global war on terror (GWoT). Dissent is discourse constructed as actively engaging in formal, recognizable "politics," typically articulated in terms of war opposition. Resistance, in contrast, comprises actions and practices that are not formally recognized as politics at all, but contest the bounds of "the political," of normality—in this case, liberal relations of gendered martial obligation.

Concretely, I focus on the discourse(s) of antiwar and peace organizations. As the center of dissent during the global war on terror—and with explicit political commitments to opposing the invasions of Iraq and Afghanistan (or war generally)—they are a logical point of entry for examining the limits of

Support the Troops. Katharine M. Millar, Oxford University Press. © Oxford University Press 2022.
DOI: 10.1093/oso/9780197642337.003.0008

democratic contestation under StT. As a trade-off, I am less able to see more radical and ad hoc practices, from handing out flyers at a memorial to failing to display a yellow ribbon. To attend to these silences within mainstream antiwar discourse (Dingli 2015; Enloe 1996), I examine a few instances of resistance that, as breaches of normatively expected conduct (Sokhi-Bulley 2013, 2; Foucault 1990), were singled out for commentary and condemnation in the public record.

My analysis proceeds in three steps. First, I demonstrate that, as implied by the hegemony of the amended military contract, StT is naturalized as apolitical. The very idea of "politics" in relation to the troops is constructed as inappropriate or immoral. Abstaining from politics, in contrast to typical democratic norms, is constituted as a masculine duty of normative civilian citizenship.

Second, the apoliticization of StT narrows the content of politics to positions on the wars in Iraq and Afghanistan— mostly war opposition. These protests are tenuously accepted as components of democratic discourse while simultaneously posited as inappropriate politicizations of the troops' plight. As a condition of this minimal acceptability, antiwar and peace groups frequently couch their war opposition with reference to the troops as insulation against critique and/or as explicitly on *behalf* of the troops. It does not transcend the strictures of amended gendered military contract.

Third, resistance to the amended liberal martial contract—refusing to support the troops or recognize that one is supposed to—is typically dismissed as simply offensive. Since StT is the foundation of the political, confronting the martial cannot be recognized as a matter of normal politics (Sokhi-Bulley 2013, 2–3, 6). Explicitly opposing the gendered martial contract is not on the table.

The Apoliticization of Supporting the Troops

This section examines how StT discourses frame the relationship between the troops, war, and the general category of something called "politics." As outlined in Chapter 7, the premise of political community has been transformed from an assumed obligation of military service to one of support. The logical corollary of this is the apoliticization of support for the troops within the public sphere. If the gendered, solidaristic obligations of support make up the political community, they cannot simultaneously be subject to debate within the politics they make possible.

This naturalized exemption of StT from politics is easy to observe empirically. StT discourses frequently valorize solidarity with the troops above democratic debate. This dynamic is evident, to take one example among many, in a congressional statement praising StT activities in schools:

> I learned that our young children, who have the same opinions that many of their parents do and many Members of Congress do, have a vitally important opportunity, *despite those opinions, to show what counts, and that is support for our troops* . . . Ultimately, I hope that that [sending emails to the troops from school] gave them a sense that they can engage in the great issues of our time, that they can venture an opinion, that that opinion counts, and that they can give some solace and some comfort to people who are fighting for their future. (Israel 2003, H2373)

Engagement in conventional democratic practice—voicing opinions and involvement in public affairs—though lauded, is subordinated to the greater obligation of "military" participation. Supporting the troops is "what counts." While emailing the troops is framed as "voicing an opinion" and giving young people agency in the context of war, none of the subsequently quoted emails express ambivalence about StT or doubts about the war. "Opinion" is a telling misnomer, insofar as it implies the existence of multiple positions (on what, exactly, is not clear), rather, all opinions support the troops.

This emphasis upon martial rather than democratic participation is also seen in the discursive production of support as explicitly apolitical. This is paradigmatically represented in the materials of the UK NGO Help for Heroes (H4H), which, in response to the FAQ, "Is H4H political?," responds:

> H4H is strictly non-political. We accept that wars happen under any government and seek to support those people wounded in war, not to comment on the reasons behind such conflicts. Wars are brutal and Servicemen and women are injured almost daily—we can't prevent this, but together, we can help those who are wounded in the service of our country to recover. (H4H 2010c; H4H 2009d)

This statement denies its own political nature—in the sense of participating in a powered public contestation—and implicitly casts the attachment of politics to StT as negative and inappropriate. It limits the ambit of politics to partisan, ideological opinions (on the war) by suggesting that conflict will "happen under any government." The quotation denies the democratic agency of the addressed public, as they "can't prevent" conflict. The call to StT reads "civilian" supporters into the discursive military, rather than the formal political sphere.

Similar distinctions between supporting the troops and politics are found throughout US StT discourse. The founder of a new veterans' support organization, Vets 4 Vets, for instance, insisted to the *New York Times* that although he "has roots in the antiwar movement," the veterans' group is "apolitical" (Downes 2008). This valorization of apoliticality is not limited to charitable organizations that might have a strategic interest in appealing to a broad constituency. A *Washington Post* article, entitled "At Walter Reed [a US military hospital], Mellencamp Shuts His Mouth and Sings," approvingly recounts the entertainer's decision to, in the author's words, "check[] his politics"—his outspoken opposition to the invasion of Iraq—to support the troops (Freedom du Lac 2007). Supporting the troops is not only naturalized as an obligation of citizenship, but politics—engaging in democratic debate—is also posited as something that would be *wrong*.

These passages are alarming for what they reveal about the meaning of the (re)constitution of normative masculinity—and citizenship—via martiality for democracy. Within conventional theories of liberalism, outlined in Chapter 2, the liberal masculine citizen possesses the civil and political rights to participate in democracy. The soldier, in contrast, agrees to renounce his individual rights to engage in governance (Hardt and Negri 2004, 17; Cowen 2008b) to preserve the democratic control of the armed forces (and liberal subordination of violence to politics). The conflation of normative martiality with supportive citizenship, however, subsumes democratic rights of participation to the gendered obligation of violence. The purported civilian is imbued with the same responsibilities of obedience, solidarity, and apolitical obligation as the soldier.

During the war on terror, the valorization of antidemocratic principles in relation to the military was supplemented by broader constraints placed upon civil liberties, such as the PATRIOT Act and related counterterrorism policies in the US and UK (Ali 2005, 67; Youngs 2010, 930). The vagueness of the war on terror, as a distant and seemingly enduring conflict, stymied the activated, individual agency that democracy and protest require (Youngs 931–32). In the absence of normative and social traction on the war, silence was constituted as a substantive, if paradoxical, obligation of normative public masculinity. Martiality is coming to supplant "the state as the arbiter of freedom, champion of the nation, model for social relations and author of its destiny" (Howard and Prividera 2008, cited in Dixon 2012, 118).

The Refusal of "Politics"

The explicit refusal to understand troop support as a matter of legitimate public politics is most apparent in practices of commemoration. The materiality of death and the specter of masculine martial sacrifice raise the affective and political stakes. In the UK, commemoration practices in Royal Wootton Bassett, where the bodies of British service personnel were repatriated from 2007 to 2011, became a locus of troop support (Jenkings et al. 2012). As bodies were transported in a procession through the town, people who lived there—and eventually, many others from across the country—would stop what they were doing and "pay their respects" (Freeden 2011, 1–10). Like StT generally, the apparent spontaneity and private nature of these aggregated, individual acts of grief reinforced the practice as morally right. It also performatively rebuked state authorities for failing to provide sufficiently grand commemorative rituals (Freeden 2011). Honoring the dead was framed by the mayor, locals, and national press as distinct and separable from the war. Perceived attempts to "politicize" the space of remembrance, be it by activists or politicians, were strongly resisted (Jenkings et al. 2012, 358–60; see also Morris 2009 and Daily Mail 2010).

The pervasiveness of this sentiment can also be observed in reactions to public figures for perceived failures to wear a commemorative poppy in the weeks prior to Remembrance Sunday. In 2011, for instance, FIFA infamously banned the English national football team from displaying poppies on their jerseys, under a general ban on political and religious messaging (Fox 2014). The UK press and prime minister decried FIFA, insisting there was nothing at all political about the poppy (Fox 2014). The apoliticization of "respect," which, in the post-9/11 era has frequently blurred into support for serving personnel (and their wars) (Basham 2016), is such that the *omission* of the poppy is read as an inappropriate politicization of the war dead.[1] Those who do not wear the poppy—or, in the case of former Labour leader Jeremy Corbyn (The Herald 2015; Jordan 2006), those who are perceived as wearing the poppy incorrectly—are constituted as failing in their duty to refrain from even implied criticism of the armed forces.

Similar attempts to parse "respect" and "politics" characterize commemoration in the US. "Freedom Walks" sponsored by the US Department of Defense from 2005 to 2008 to remember the 9/11 victims and support the troops deployed to Iraq and Afghanistan, for instance, incurred controversy. The DoD insisted the walks were a "non-political homage to the victims and a salute to veterans past and present, devoid of commentary on the merits of the war in Iraq" (Montgomery 2005). Others, including the *Washington Post* (which withdrew as an official sponsor of the first Walk) and antiwar groups, expressed concern that the event endorsed the war and was therefore political in nature.[2] The US national military cemetery at Arlington is likewise governed by a complex script of gendered and racialized mourning practices that seek to seal off commemoration from ongoing issues of justice, inequality, and democratic contestation (McElya 2016, 416). Memorial Day practices (Howard and Combs n.d.) have been critiqued for an increasing emphasis upon holidays and sales rather than solemn reflection (VFW n.d.). As a capitalist appropriation of martial sacrifice (Sanchez 2017; Anheuser-Busch 2017), Memorial Day is constituted as apolitical in the "wrong" way. The apoliticization of support is an extension of the depoliticization of conflict within war commemoration, wherein the "potentially contentious elements are stripped out" (Tidy 2015a, 228; Imber and Fraser 2011).

The obligation to perform ritualized acts of support and remembrance goes beyond affirming respective, public masculinity through the withdrawal from democratic debate. It also contains an undercurrent of "emphasized femininity" (Schippers 2007) that mirrors the obligations of care and social labor associated with the private sphere. In this case, however, it is not the archetypical rational, autonomous masculine actors of the public sphere to whom the feminine/ized subject is commended for caring (and expected to defer) but various figures of martiality—the soldier, the military, the troops, the war. The specter of the gendered "betrayal" of the Vietnam era troops by disloyal women and/or antiwar protestors helps produce StT as obviously moral. StT (re)constitutes the eschewal of democratic politics as a component of normative, public masculinity yet still acknowledges the potential for femininized duplicity in its concern with naturalizing support as apolitical. The framing of politics as dangerous and potentially treacherous blurs the gendered public-private divide, constituting politics as a form of disorderly and disruptive femininity (Managhan 2011a, 449). Refusing politics becomes another way of refusing association with the feminine—even if it means democratic abstention .[3]

Support and the Discursive Traps of War Opposition

In this section, I demonstrate that in addition to constructing politics as dangerous, negative, and feminine/ising, not all positions are treated as equally political within StT discourse. Though it is possible for supporting the war to be seen as a political position, as in the case of Freedom Walk, politics is largely read as synonymous with war opposition. A 2009 UK House of Lords statement provides a good example of this construction:

> I am confident that the whole of this House is fully behind our troops in Afghanistan and that this will continue to be the case. Sometimes I find it slightly difficult when noble Lords are critical of various aspects of the war. It is right that there is a space for people to question and be critical but, as my noble friend says, the important thing is that our troops, their families and those who are wounded should know that they have the full support of all parties represented in this House. (Baroness Royall of Blaisdon 2009, c662)

The quotation mirrors the previous distinction between the dual masculine obligations to support the troops and engage in democracy. While the speaker acknowledges that, technically, there should be space for debate, "what is important" is providing support for the troops, a clear hierarchy delegitimizes opposition to the war as political while naturalizing the apparently obvious moral rectitude of supporting the troops (and troops themselves).

The opprobrium attached to war opposition is even more apparent in US discourses. In an unusual example, a team of US competitive bridge players faced a year-long suspension and were accused by other bridge players of "treason" and "sedition" for displaying a handwritten sign that said "We did not vote for Bush" at an awards ceremony (Strom 2007). They contravened the expectation of martial, masculinity solidarity. Instead, the players inadvertently invoked feminized betrayal, ejecting themselves from the realm of legitimate dissent. Other bridge players noted it was common for competitors to wear "Support the Troops" buttons, but "they don't go after those people" (Strom 2007). Though the stakes in this example are relatively low, it demonstrates the extent to which the disciplining of political speech and normalization of StT extended beyond formal politics and conventionally authoritative social actors.

Together, these depictions of war opposition express the common notion—the assumption that inspired this book—that while the troops are deployed, it is "inappropriate" to voice dissent. A spokesperson for the UK Prime Minister's Office, for instance, stated:

> While he [Blair] recognized that there were differences of view over the war and that it was perfectly legitimate to ask questions about it, he nevertheless believed that at a time like this, it was important for the country to show support for the troops on the ground and the job they were doing. (Prime Minister's Office 2004)

Though the speaker concedes the existence of the right to debate the war, he frames it as a questionable choice. It is a failure of the martial stoicism that inflects public masculinity.

Other references to dissent reflect the "discursive legacy" of Vietnam (Coy et al. 2008) and the belief that active opposition to war provides "aid and comfort" to the enemy. The mainstream media, particularly but not exclusively within the US, was frequently criticized by the government (and political right) during the GWoT for covering the human cost of the wars on civilians. It was framed as a form of "sabotage" against the troops (Carruthers 2011, 233; on the BBC see Ali 2005, 28). A 2007 statement by a US senator provides a good example of this trope:

> To all of those who suggest that General Petraeus [the US commander in Iraq] should be called "General Betray Us," I have a message for you. You are giving aid and comfort to our enemies. We used to try people who did this as traitors . . . The Senate Democratic majority leader was quoted as saying no one wants us to succeed in Iraq more than Democrats. Well, I say . . . stand by your words. Let's focus on succeeding in Iraq and for once show a united support for our troops. (Bunning 2007)

Support for the war is rolled into support for the troops, while the notion that the failure to provide support might endanger the troops invokes altruistic, spontaneous structures of political obligation. The dependent troops and the disloyal should-be supporters who oppose the war are both constructed in accordance with feminized tropes of vulnerability and treachery, respectively (Huiskamp 2011, 291; Managhan 2011a). Dissent is framed as an excessive practice of a cowardly, ungrateful, or simply foolish civil society.

The passage "portray[s] the anti-war left as dangerous, feral, and shockingly, awesomely effective" (Gitlin 2003). This position, common to the organized yet unofficial political right (e.g., members of the conservative press, think tanks, pro-military advocacy groups, etc.), has existed throughout US (and, increasingly, UK) history, ranging from Vietnam and Northern Ireland through the GWoT to the present (Carruthers 2011, 243). It was (and is) e difficult to be recognized as a normatively masculine, martial subject—a "good" citizen—and oppose the wars in Iraq and Afghanistan. Opposition is outside the bounds of the liberal political set by the amended contract.

Which is not to say that no one tried. The now-stereotypical, even rote, phrase "support the troops, oppose the war" is premised upon the assertation that dissent (and politics) are not incommensurate with solidarity. An *Independent on Sunday* op-ed captures this (re)contextualization of StT, arguing:

> It is humbug for Mr Kennedy to turn round and pretend that he supports [the war] merely because it has started and our troops are involved. If you really want to support our boys, the truly patriotic course is to call for them to be removed speedily from the sands of Mesopotamia to the shores of Blighty. (Watkins 2003)

This quotation blends appeals to patriotism and the inseparability of the "warrior and the war," using the communitarian structure of masculine obligation to demand responsibility for, and express opposition to, the invasion of Iraq.

Similarly, a request for debate in the US House of Representatives demonstrates the framing of dissent as still, or equivalent to, StT:

> I rise with a humble spirit to salute the people of Iraq who have shown us the ability for a successful election and ask that we honor and support our troops, but *yet* [emphasis added] have an open and full debate on the redeployment of our troops on the floor of the House regarding Iraq. (Jackson-Lee 2006)

The amended contractual foundations of the liberal polity are explicitly stated, as the speaker acknowledges that support is required regardless of one's position on the war. The passage shows a common slide from supporting the troops, to supporting the war, to supporting a particular political administration, as even the request for debate (let alone its subsequent content) is implicitly recognized as a form of dissent. The congressperson is requesting to be temporarily exempted from the masculinized duty of democratic abstention of contemporary liberal political belonging.

Despite the universalizing dynamics of supporting the troops—and the virtual consensus regarding StT among US and UK politicians across the political spectrum—the framing of politics during the GWoT reveals substantial political and cultural polarization. Within StT discourse, as elsewhere, democratic politics *itself* is constructed as distasteful, elite, corrupt, and/or immoral (Vittori 2017, 57). Discursive martiality during the GWoT subtly furthered the dynamics of so-called culture war (see Hall 1994; Fairclough 2003). Positions assimilated to the norm of racialized, imperial, and capital power (e.g., war/troop support) are seen as neutral, and attempts to dispute them (e.g., war opposition) are framed as excessive special pleading. In addition to StT's reproduction of conservative, binary sexual and gender norms and racialized dynamics of violent solidarity, it also facilitates a denigration of democracy. Supporting the troops has resonances with populism (see Millar 2021).

Gendered Military Obligation and Antiwar Activism

In this context of non-democratic solidarity, the mainstream media monitored their coverage for "taste and tone," self-policing their coverage for appropriate martiality (Carruthers 2011, 258). The antiwar movement, given its historical association with feminine betrayal and masculine "shirking"— alongside the political left—was subject to intense suspicion. The production of both "politics" and the political via discursive martiality pushed (and pushes) antiwar groups into a catch-22. Contesting the obligatory nature of masculinized martial support would be an effective way of opposing war, yet the ability to dissent at all is premised upon accepting it. "Supporting the troops," as argued by Managhan, "became, more or less, a condition of legitimate dissent" (2011a, 442).

Mainstream antiwar and peace groups in the US and UK used StT discourses (to a greater or lesser degree) in their public materials. Organizations, networks, and coalitions founded specifically to oppose the wars in Iraq and Afghanistan—though existing in a lineage of mass antiwar movements—such as the Stop the War Coalition and Veterans for Peace in the UK, and United for Peace and Justice, CodePink, and Military Families Speak Out in the US, made the troops a focal point of their activism. Multi-issue organizations, such as the UK Campaign for Nuclear Disarmament, the Muslim Council of Britain, or the American Friends Service Committee in the US, though they acted in concert with the newer organizations and expressed concern for serving military personnel, did so less frequently. This partially attributable to the organizations' multiple mandates and lesser on-line presence during the GWoT.

Long-established organizations with stated commitments to pacifism, such as the Women's International League for Peace and Freedom and Peace and Social Witness in the UK, and Peace Action, Pax Christi, and the Friends Service Committee in the US, referred to the troops much less often. They did, however, participate in the major coalitions (Stop the War and United for Peace and Justice) that were the focal point for antiwar efforts, amplifying those groups' discourse supporting the troops. Organizations founded before Iraq and Afghanistan (and date back to the First World War when the originary gendered martial contract at least seemed operant) focus more on the prevention (and horrors) of war than the presumed peril of the troops.

That said, mainstream antiwar discourse of the GWoT largely reflects and reproduces the gendered logics of political obligation for violence we have seen throughout the book. The common antiwar declaration that the wars were "Not in My Name" (Stop the War Coalition n.d.), for instance, draws on a sense of common identity and collective implication in the mission— membership implied by "name"—to discredit claims of the war's necessity. It's an instance of communitarian antiwar discourse, characterized by calls for the polity to take responsibility for the wars in Iraq and Afghanistan—to engage, in other words, in politics.[4]

A parallel strain of antiwar discourse constructs the troops as heroes who deserve support. This common trope reifies the liberal, contractarian construction of political obligation as individualized and (imperfectly) reciprocal. In the US, for instance, United for Peace and Justice and CodePink consistently campaigned on the message that " 'supporting the troops' and 'ending the war' are one and the same" (see CP 2004; UfPJ 2003b, 2006). The troops belong to the same community as supporters and, like supporters, exist at some remove from the war; they are victimized by it. The discursive excision of war from military service within StT discourse enables antiwar groups to advocate "supporting the troops by ending the war" (or bringing them home—see below) without violating either the obligation of support or lapsing into normative incoherence.

The altruistic mode of gendered violent obligation is particularly congruent with war opposition. It portrays the troops in affective terms. CodePink, for instance, in establishing their antiwar bona fides, also reminded the public that they "lobb[ied] for veterans' rights under the banner "Love the Troops, Hate the War" (2006). Antiwar sentiment is proclaimed in the context of an interpersonal, affective idiom that reflects the language used by people with loved ones in the military, regardless of their position on the war. Again, the troops are posited as victims of conflict, or misfortune, who are reliant on the feminized loyalty and masculinizing protection of antiwar advocates.

Antiwar activists, as members of the political community, are also always-already citizen-supporters. Antiwar groups' claiming of their right to participation in political debate is also a claim to political membership. This, despite gendered suspicions as to potential treachery, also opens antiwar groups to the mandatory imposition/projection of support, even in instances when it is not explicitly offered. With few exceptions (see the following section), antiwar groups do not problematize the construction of support as a political obligation, nor the equation of martiality with normative masculine citizenship.

Instead, groups "strategically" conceded the hegemonic status of the heroic soldier (and support for the troops) (Woehrle et al. 2008, 30–39). Woehrle et al. (2008, 38) found that 94 percent of US peace groups' references to soldiers/the troops were positive; only 6 percent portrayed military personnel in a negative light. They sought to harness the discursive power of the troops by calling on the government to bring them home. A study of the UK press's treatment of antiwar groups and attitudes found that prior to the war, antiwar groups were portrayed positively. Once the invasion of Iraq began, however, a "support our boys consensus" was formed and the space for legitimate dissent was circumscribed (Murray et. al. 2008).

Voicing support for the troops is a "discourse trap" (Michaels 2013, 2) for large and/or pervasive mainstream antiwar groups (e.g., Campaign for Nuclear Disarmament [CND], CodePink). It is instrumentally useful in gaining a hearing—and modest veneer of social and political acceptability—for war opposition. StT tropes are (potentially) effective in opposing specific wars, in this case generating backlash to the invasions of Iraq and Afghanistan on behalf of the troops. This position of strategic accommodation—as well as genuine feelings of concern and affiliation—for the troops is congruent with pacifism: a politics that opposes specific wars, on principled grounds, but leaves open the possibility of ethical uses of force (in defense of self or Others) (Ceadel 1987; Dower 2009). It is also an exact parallel to the role of war, as used only when necessary and for moral ends, within the "good story" of liberalism. Though the democratic climate of the GWoT made war opposition seem and feel radical, this is a reformist, not revolutionary, position.

From the perspective of saving lives abroad, this is still an exigent political project. If performing the normative martiality and masculinity associated with troop support is required for ending violent and unjust imperials wars, it may be worth it. It would also be narcissistic to prioritize internal relationships to force—that is, the normative coherence of gendered structures of obligation toward violence—within the West over the safety, rights, and dignity of people endangered by liberal force abroad. This critical assessment of antiwar groups' engagement in support the troops discourse is not offered from an investment in an absolutist or purist approach to peace.

The Paradox of Antiwar Protest

The problem, rather, is that this doesn't work. While StT discourses are helpful in the short term, they curtail antiwar and peace groups' long-term ability to address the underlying normative structures that facilitate the collective use of force. Without contesting the synonymity of normative masculinity (and personhood) with martiality—that is, the production of the "the political" through relations of gendered violence—contesting specific wars offers diminishing returns.

The foundational nature of the amended contract is exemplified by its reification within what, initially, appears to be the most coherent counterdiscourse: "support the troops, bring them home." Variations on this phrase appear in both the US and UK.[5] Managhan calls it the "rallying cry of the mainstream American antiwar movement" (2011a, 441). A statement by US Congressperson Lee illustrates this trope:

The way we support our troops is by developing a plan to get them out of harm's way and to bring them home. To date, more than 1,600 American troops have given their lives, over 11,000 American troops have been injured, and over 17,000 innocent Iraqi civilians, including women and children, have died in a war that should never have started in the first place . . . We should send the signal that we support our troops, we love our troops, we value our troops, and we want them home. (2005, H4039–H4040)

This quotation is founded upon the presumption, discussed above, that StT was being equated with supporting the war (and the Bush administration). Lee attempts to resignify StT by debating its "true" meaning and turning it back against the pro-war Republican political establishment. A UK CND press release discussing the war in Afghanistan contains similar constructions, stating:

Thousands marched through London on Saturday 24th October, calling for troops to come home from Afghanistan. Eight years on from the invasion of Afghanistan the death toll amongst British troops is higher than ever, with an awful price being paid in the blood of Afghan civilians . . . With two thirds of people wanting British forces to withdraw, now is the time for the Government to bring the troops home. (CND 2009)

As above, the troops are constructed as victims, similar to Afghan civilians, of the war and government policy. Though the majority of supportive civilians are portrayed as holding an opinion on the war, the shift of blame to the "government," while effective, shifts accountability away from the democratic public. Due to its reification of the martial support of the amended contract, the counter-discourse of "bring them home" is not meaningfully counter-performative.

In this way, antiwar StT discourse reflects the tensions characterizing military families' antiwar activities. The family members of deceased combatants, such as Cindy Sheehan (US) and Rose Gentle (UK), are often posited as potent antiwar activists (Ase et al. 2019; Managhan 2011a). They "earn" their dissent the hardest way, through the military service and/or the injury or deaths of their loved ones (Managhan 2011a, 438–66; and Tidy 2015b). Grieving mothers' authority to dissent is premised upon their heteronormative "sacrifice" of their children through the traditional structure of gendered civil-military relations (Managhan 2011a; Tidy 2015b). In contrast to more straightforwardly civilian subjects, the dissent of the bereaved mother cannot be portrayed as stemming from cowardice or ignorance, or implicitly cast as a failure of their gendered political obligation(s). Instead, military family members somewhat perversely accrue the presumed legitimacy to engage in deliberative democratic debate that the amended military contract denies civilians.

The dependence of mothers' dissent upon the authority of war experience (i.e., fulfillment of liberal military contract), however, ends up reifying the gendered, sexualized (classed and racialized) power relations their antiwar rhetoric seeks to challenge (Tidy 2016, 14). The military mother is subject to what Managhan (2011a, 447) refers to as the "compulsory discursivity" of gendered martial grief. The essentialistic, heteropatriarchal valorization of a mother's love as (a) private and (b) above reproach are what enable the grieving mother to speak and oppose war. Grief is not seen as political, but rather an affective expression of loss.[6] For these same reasons, however, grieving mothers are also unable to be recognized as anything *other* than grieving mothers (Managhan 2011a, 447). It defangs their radical potential to challenge the liberal military and its gendered expectations of "appropriate" grief and mourning (Ase et al. 2019; Millar 2015; Rashid 2020).

Antiwar organizations encounter the same issue. Their ability to speak and be heard is premised upon their reification of martial masculine obligation: the same construct that necessitates their dissent in the first place. As we have seen throughout the book, "supporting the troops to support the war" and "supporting the troops to end the war" are both intelligible positions under the amended martial contract. This undermines the troops as a foundation for war opposition (or, really, a politics of violence of any kind). Wars can be fought for the troops or opposed for the troops (Millar, 2016a, 20). But the troops, not ethics in warfare or the rights and lives of distant Others, remain the animating rationale for collective action.

Resistance at the Margins

The account of dissent I've given this far is pretty grim. The metamorphosis of democratic, masculinizing obligation from deliberation to acquiescence enables the co-optation of dissent. Constituencies alienated from the universalized White, cis, heterosexual ideals of the liberal state were, previously, often (though not monolithically, of course) sources of war opposition. Consider, for instance, Black Americans' opposition to the war in Vietnam on anti-imperial and anti-racist grounds (Hall 2011), queer Americans' opposition to Gulf War military service on behalf of a heteronormative state (Enloe 2000), or even (some) suffragettes' opposition to masculinist wars of aggression (Millar 2019b). Now, however, as we saw in Chapter 5, support for the troops is cast in a universalized language of ostensible neutrality/naturalization. This renders virtually any given identity, affect, and position on the war—including direct opposition—commensurate with "the troops." The oft-observed "anaemic nature of the peace movement" (Harding and Kershner 2011, 79) during the GWoT can be at least partially attributed to its (re)production within the normative confines of StT.

When we move further from mainstream antiwar discourse, however, some (limited) space is held for resistance to the amended martial contract. The status of supporting the troops as the terms upon which intelligibly political speech is uttered, however, means that such resistance is often indirect. "We" may not always recognize it (or even necessarily *like* it) when we see it. In contrast to dissent, which articulates in the formal register of public politics and democratic contestation, resistance pokes at the bounds of social intelligibility, normativity, and normality. It works at the level of "the political," exposing the contours of discursive martiality. This section discusses key instances in which people engaged with the central silence within StT discourse—*not* supporting the troops—and the disciplining reactions that followed.

Subverting Compulsory Support: Resistance in the UK

In the UK, it is uncommon to refute (explicitly or otherwise) the naturalized presumption of supporting the troops (and the underlying gendered obligations to do so). Instead, contestations of *parts* of the apoliticized normative masculinity-martial solidarity nexus sneak in around the edges. Veterans for Peace (VfP) UK, for instance, criticized the Royal British Legion's late-2000s decision to frame its long-standing poppy campaign in terms of "support of 'our Heroes,'" arguing: "There is nothing heroic about being blown up in a vehicle. There is nothing heroic about being shot in an ambush and there is nothing heroic about fighting in an unnecessary conflict" (2010). This example decries the presumed heroism of the hegemonically masculine combat soldier and thus the basis for the contractual mode of political obligation.

In terms of an actual politics of confronting the martial contract, of course, the status of VfP as a veterans' organization renders this resistance incomplete. Veterans' war opposition is legitimated by the "soldiers' contract" between the state and military personnel (Schrader 2019, 16). When something is off in the bargain—such as risking soldiers' lives in ill-planned, under-resourced, and potentially illegal wars in Iraq and Afghanistan (Schrader 2019, 49–66)—soldiers are authorized to dissent. The soldiers' contract itself, however, is produced by underlying liberal martial contract: the gendered obligation of violence for *all* normatively masculine citizens. The dissent of antiwar, or more radically anti-militarism veterans and military personnel, just as with bereaved military families, is enabled by the same gendered violent obligations they oppose.

This is a good place to note that veterans and serving military personnel often themselves feel constrained by support the troops discourses (Millar 2016a). In my anecdotal experience, as well as the anthropological and ethnographic accounts of others (MacLeish 2013, Finkel 2013), service members often have an ambivalent relationship to StT, contesting or challenging it far more directly than most civilians. This opposition to supporting the troops, however, though undeniably powerful in refuting the presumption that this is something all military personnel desire and need, falls into the same gendered reification of the liberal military contract outlined above.[7] Legitimating opposition to the troops with reference to, in essence, the troops does not get around the central problem of mandatory masculine martial obligation. Resisting the gendered martial contract would still be necessary, though it might feel unkind, even if military personnel opposed it.

Neither veterans' antiwar/militarist activism nor the skepticism of military personnel towards StT can completely circumvent liberal discursive martiality. What these forms of resistance can do, however, is invite others to break the taboo of (even seeming to) criticize the troops. Veterans for Peace, in particular, is an example of activism attempting to turn the solidaristic tenets of normative masculinity against itself. VfP invites *more* people into the realm of martially authorized critique, insulating them from the specter of feminized/izing betrayal. It isn't able to obviate the martial contract, but it can level out some of the disciplining normative gender dynamics.

A 2004 CND protest conducted under the banner "Stop the Torture—Bring the Troops Home Now" offers a similar pathway for, if not confronting, working around the gendered martial solidarity project/expected under the contract. It asked Britons to "join us to protest about the shocking abuses in Iraq and to call for the withdrawal of the illegal aggressor force" (CND 2004). "Bringing the troops home" is reframed not as a supportive compulsion for the troops' sake but implied as a means of stopping the harm they cause to innocent Iraqis. The juxtaposition of the troops with torture produces them as violent (and potentially criminal) actors. The passage side-steps political obligation by removing the *troops*, rather than the protestors, from the normative liberal international order.

This quotation also provides a good example of a subtle oscillation in UK "bring them home" discourse. While much of it plays directly into the "protect" the troops frame, some offers a more ambiguous message, proclaiming "Troops Out!" (see CND 2007). The meaning of these references to the troops is left open, relying on the observer to determine whether such calls are on behalf of the troops themselves—or are a more instrumental, almost operational, means of ending the war. Given the legacy of the British antiwar movements' demand for "Troops Out!" of Northern Ireland, these exhortations have a tenor of anger and condemnation missing from "bringing them home."

The undecidability of such invocations of the troops—"Troops Out Now!"—subverts the compulsive hegemony of StT. It can be read, as I just did, as a continuity of leftist British antiwar activism and an anti-imperial politics. It can also be read in the context of broader troop support as an aggressive call for protection. As "Troops Out!" doesn't self-interpret through the direct invocation of obligation, those who encounter this version of "bring them home" must reflect upon what it really means. There is no particular social relationship implied between the person calling for "troops out" and the troops: the contract is missing. By attaching an open-ended politics to the troops, "troops out" facilitates resistance while also avoiding the hegemonic backlash that often shuts down more overt criticism.

Such disciplining is evident in the reactions to two prominent UK antitroop incidents—or, more accurately, what were constructed as "anti-troop" incidents. The charity Help for Heroes was founded with an initial mandate to raise money for a new military-specific rehabilitation center and swimming pool at Headley Court. Its inception was contextualized by a widely reported occurrence in which a member of the public purportedly verbally abused severely wounded soldiers swimming at a public leisure center (H4H 2007). The woman was said to have argued that the soldiers "hadn't paid" and might "scare children," sparking "widespread condemnation" (Harding et al. 2007). A Conservative MP reacted to the story by declaring, "it may well be that these people had paid for the use of the pool, but our soldiers have paid so much more for their country" (Daily Mail 2007).

The contrast of the member of the public, as a woman, to the masculinized service members underlines this point. The incident, implicitly, revolves around a failure to perform appropriately gendered respect. Their gendered positionality implicitly suggests that the soldiers served on her behalf, and thus she (and everyone else) owed them the best public services available (see Cowen 2008b). The former head of the Armed Forces went further, demanding the woman be "named and shamed," stating, "these people are beneath contempt and everything should be done to get their names and publish them in the press" (Harding et al. 2007). Boris Johnson, the future British prime minister, wrote a column about the incident as part of his campaign for the mayoralty of London, wherein he promised to show solidarity with the troops (Johnson 2007).

The woman, certainly uncompassionate in her remarks, was vilified for failing to recognize the moral worth of the troops and her obligation to support them. The fact that a local incident involving a small number of people, none of whom are public figures, was broadly reported in the national press, publicized by Help for Heroes, and met with opprobrium highlights the difficulty inherent to articulating critical constructions of the troops. The use of the phrase "these people" extrapolates from the woman in question to a presumably larger, undeserving group of people. Johnson also framed the incident in terms of class, with shades of the left-right culture war—a "yuppie" woman prioritizing her own comfort and routine above deference to the working-class and heroic injured soldiers (Johnson 2007). In forsaking masculinized, martial solidarity, the woman falls into feminized betrayal.

Condemnation was also levied in response to less polemical—or direct— challenges to StT. Rowan Williams, the archbishop of Canterbury, was frequently criticized for "not supporting the troops," implicitly impugning their honor or undermining their morale, throughout the GWoT. In 2004, the archbishops of York and Canterbury "rebuked" the US and UK governments for the coalition's treatment of prisoners (Gledhill 2004). Much of the reaction to the statement took the archbishops (and Church of England) to task for failing to recognize the "necessity of public support for our Armed Forces" and inappropriately articulating their "private" views in the public sphere (Times 2004).

The Archbishop's 2009 decision to ask for reflection upon the "wisdom of the decisions to go to war" during a remembrance service at St. Paul's similarly spurred outrage in the tabloid press (Kelly 2012, 730). The *Sun* argued that "they're soldiers, not politicians" and "we have to support our troops" (Kelly 2012; original Newton Dunn and Phillips 2009). The views of a prominent clergyperson, informed by religion (and sacral notions of obligation), were relegated to the "private," failing to earn recognition as political speech. This is fascinating as, given the official role of the Church of England within the British state, archbishops are to a large extent public figures. In contrast to typical liberal expectations of secularism, here, formally political views on the war are rendered private, whereas structurally private religion is constituted as public. The archbishop's challenge to the sacral public-private divide in the UK, for the sake of war opposition, risked being read as a betrayal of a private moral obligation to the troops.

These instances of commemoration, as argued by Kelly, are more visible acts of resistance than banal, everyday practices such as failing to display a yellow ribbon, which follow a similar logic of refusal. Perceived failures of support—or even of articulating support correctly—elicit public commentary and, as a result of the rigorousness with which their tenuous apolitical nature is policed, have indelible political undertones (Kelly 2012, 730–31). The intersection of insistent (a)politics and resistance suggests that the only refutations of StT sufficiently explicit to be "seen" are also subject to being dismissed as not only not political but also offensive. They are unintelligible as legitimate political acts, and their proponents, as disorderly women and men—as "bad people"—are not recognized as legitimately political subjects.

Just Offensive: Resistance in the US

These dynamics of sporadic, overt, and "offensive" resistance are also evident—in more dramatic fashion—in the US. A letter to the *New York Times'* "Ethicist" column, for instance, queries:

> We have heard a lot recently about how, even if we oppose the war in Iraq, once it was under way, we should support the troops. How is this ethical? Our troops are volunteers; they chose to enlist and fight where ordered. Is there an ethical obligation for those who oppose the war to support the troops? (Cohen 2003)

The writer identifies another significant silence in StT discourse: the implications of volunteering for military service. Soldiers could hypothetically, within liberal, individualist ideology, be responsible for the decision to serve and risk war. She challenges, in other words, the presumption that an (ostensibly) hypermasculine, individual choice to join the military produces a social debt. The passage resists the totalizing, amended liberal contract by openly questioning it, (re)politicizing "support."

A similar letter to a local paper, publicized by a *Wall Street Journal* columnist for the purpose of discrediting it, challenges contractual obligation explicitly, declaring:

> I do not support the troops who are willing to kill for their government, for the money it pays, for the education they may receive later—if they make it home alive with their brains intact—or any patriotism they claim to represent. A yellow ribbon should denote cowardice in the case of welcoming these people home . . . The willingness to kill, maim and torture for the government is not something to be proud of. (in Taranto 2004)

This is a direct refutation of the heroism of the hegemonically masculine combat soldier-citizen hero and the normative obligation to support the troops. The letter portrays soldiers as willing to commit violence for material gain—essentially, as mercenaries—and reads yellow ribbons negatively, as endorsing the military, state, and war.

Rather than confront this construction, the column's author congratulates the writer on her honesty, suggesting that this is the position "actually" held by all antiwar activists (Taranto 2004)—again, reading politics together with the imagined left. These activists, by implication, are just as self-evidently radical, offensive, and unfit for membership in the political community as the letter writer.

The Ethicist, similarly, answers the original query by chastising the author for "cast[ing] individual soldiers as the architects of the war you disdain" (Cohen 2003). He dismisses the complexity of precisely this point raised in the letter: enlistment means agreeing to potentially commit violence without a say in the matter. The columnist goes on to highlight the plethora of meanings associated with StT, noting that war opposition and StT are not mutually exclusive. He reads the author "back in" to the amended liberal military contract, by providing an irrefutable chain of equivalence: a "support" for every political inclination.

Similar to the UK, the most overtly transgressive resistance in the US occurs in a commemorative context. The most infamous of such activities were the protests of deceased service members' funerals by the Westboro Baptist Church (WBC), a small, radical religious group. WBC members picketed the 2006 funeral of Matthew Synder with signs that read "You're going to hell," "God hates you," "Thank God for dead soldiers," and "Fag Troops" (Grinberg 2010; Alito 2011). The WBC propounds a theodicy that holds up "the nation's deceased military personnel . . . as stunning, corporeal evidence that God is punishing this nation for its tolerance of homosexuality and other vices" (Brouwer and Hess 2007, 70).

Protesting a deceased soldier's funeral refuses to grant a veneer of the respect "owed" to those who undertake military service. The use of abusive homophobic rhetoric attempts to undermine the hegemonic, implicitly heterosexual masculinity of the combat soldier—and, through this figure, that of the collectivity that identifies with and honors him (see Mann 2013).[8] Through the WBC's framing of the troops' deaths as a symptom of what they perceive as the moral decay of the polity, they also performatively suggest an alternative structure of normative political obligation, one that suggests war ought to be welcomed and recognized as divine punishment. Within this worldview, their proselytizing protest activities are normatively required by, and for, the "righteous" community discursively constituted within their rhetoric. Obligation still pertains, but it is an obligation to oppose the troops.

These protests were met with virulent backlash. Indeed, these practices, due to their hateful treatment of LGBTQ+ people (as well as, in other contexts, in the promotion of hate against Catholics, atheists, Orthodox Christians, Jews, and Muslims) *are* offensive. This offensiveness reflects the ingraining of the amended liberal military contract and, more positively, respect for the rights and dignity of LGBTQ+ people. The prominence of these offensive acts within national discourse also reflects the tendency of the press to cover the most provocative discourses. Subtler acts of resistance, such as not clapping at a parade, are unobserved. As negative resistance—failing or refusing to engage— these practices do not actively contest, or provide an alternative narrative, to the amended military contract. Instead, as assimilated to "the political," support is projected/assumed in the absence of evidence to the contrary.

The extreme visibility of the WBC—a small group of 6 to 20 people (Brouwer and Hess 2007)—solidified the affective righteousness and normative commitment to the amended liberal military contract through collective revulsion. Matthew Snyder's family condemned the protests and filed a lawsuit for emotional distress against WBC, originally winning USD$5 million in damages (NBC News 2010). Media organizations, though distancing themselves from the group's message, filed amicus briefs defending the principle of free speech (Schogol 2010; NBC News 2010). Several prominent veterans' groups issued statements focusing on the media, rather than the WBC—a reflection of how self-evidently abhorrent WCB practices are perceived to be and a foreshadowing of US populist suspicions of the media—indicating disbelief that the WBC decision had implications for free speech and freedom of the press. They argued, "I have a job that requires me to be correct; why shouldn't the press be held to that same standard?" (Schogol 2010). "Correctness" refers not to factual accuracy, but martial appropriateness.

Not only was the WBC constructed as intolerable, but this abhorrence was extrapolated to those who might seem to be even remotely sympathetic to their activities—the media and the antiwar movement. A study of military bloggers' responses to the protests, for instance, found they tended to frame the WBC as synonymous with mainstream antiwar protestors. One blogger argued: "Every day, military members who support our troops that are in harms [sic] way, or who are involved in the war on terror and supporting America, go to work at the Pentagon. And every day they are met with protesters who try and undermine their morale" (Brouwer and Hess 2007, 79). A similar reaction accompanied a widely distributed photograph of a single protestor in San Francisco carrying a sign that stated "We support the troops when they shoot their officers" (see Taranto 2003; and McInnis 2003, H2846). This single instance, buoyed by its apparent reference to (predominantly apocryphal) Vietnam era anti-troop protest, was similarly framed as expressing what the antiwar movement "really" felt. This sweeping generalization underlined StT as not only exigent but also the only acceptable public stance. The seeming consensus of troop support facilitated—and, importantly, obscured—the growing left-right polarization of US politics during the global war on terror.

The rejection of the WBC from politics, as well as the political community, is seen in the subsequent spate of state and federal legislation restricting the right to protest at military funerals or federal cemeteries (Brouwer and Hess 2007). When signing the bill, Obama stated, "We have a moral sacred duty to our men and women in uniform . . . The graves of our veterans are hallowed grounds" (Wing 2013). In contrast to UK Archbishop Williams, whose "private" political views, in seeming to criticize the troops, were cast as inappropriately political, Obama draws on notions of the sacral in a political context to delegitimize the WBC's attempts to dissent. Obama's "private" religious beliefs, though he is a secular public figure, reinforce the obligation of support as a guardrail on the political.

Though the WBC protests were eventually ruled to be protected speech, the group was not recognized as socially intelligible. Although, in contrast to the UK pool incident, the WBC protests were public and conducted in the register of formal public "politics," including protest signs, messages directed at the state, and press releases, they were not constructed as political actors. Their refusal to validate the amended liberal military contract pushed them beyond the political. Snyder's father, for instance, stated, "They wanted their message heard, and didn't care who they stepped over," initially seeming to recognize a form of politics, before dismissing them as "a bunch of clowns" (Simmons 2007). Similarly, Chief Justice Roberts characterized the WBC's picketing as "certainly hurtful" noting "its contribution to public discourse may be negligible" (Liptak 2011).[9]

Together, the WBC and "shoot their officers" examples illustrate the subordination of the principles of deliberative democracy—including the toleration of highly offensive, dissenting speech—to "tasteful" martiality. In both the US and UK, the most visible resistance to the hegemonic intersection of gender, war, and political obligation—the bounds of the liberal "political"—fails to achieve intersubjective recognition as legitimate politics. Instead, it is cast as insulting or abusive.

Counter-Recruitment: A Meaningful Alternative?

The trick for legitimate, public dissent in the context of StT therefore seems to be either (a) a pragmatic acceptance of martial political obligation in the service of opposing specific wars or (b) attempting to inject some indeterminacy into the gendered contract without confronting it directly. Resistance to the masculine martial contract is not impossible but is often most evident as a breach of expectations of good conduct rather than a radical (re)vision of liberal violence. To that end, this section briefly examines one final alternative that goes beyond antiwar protest to the active contestation of martiality (usually framed by activists in terms of "militarism"): counter-recruitment discourse and practices.

The counter-recruitment movement, unlike the sporadic and often distasteful practices of resistance discussed above, is actively organized and purposively working to construct a coherent counter-narrative to heteromasculinity, martiality, and service. As observed by Rech, counter-recruitment in the US and UK arose, in part, as a reaction to the "largely ineffective modern anti-war movement" (2014, 246), implicitly identifying the antiwar movement's instrumental indebtedness to the contract. Counter-recruitment instead seeks to address, expose, and politicize the material and normative structures that encourage individuals to join the military, with the hope of stemming recruitment (Rech 2014, 246; Harding and Kershner 2011; Alison and Solnit 2007). The movement works toward these aims by distributing counter-propaganda ("jamming" recruitment materials); providing information about the material realities and experiences of military service to secondary school students; lawsuits; and lobbying (Rech 2014, 253–55; Harding and Kershner 2011; Alison and Solnit 2007; Tannock 2005). Counter-recruitment largely avoids the language and question of support, instead framing its critique of normative martiality as more effective antiwar opposition.

Counter-recruitment does, however, come into contact with StT discourse as a fellow traveler to more mainstream war opposition. A US Peace Action flyer calling on people to "support the troops by bringing them home," for instance, also contains a small sidebar explaining opportunities for the public to get involved with counter-recruitment activities (2007). CodePink, similarly, publicizes anti-recruitment FAQ, occupies recruitment centers, and encourages "creative, forceful tactics to confront a murderous, imperial, military machine that recruits youth like cannon fodder" (2008). Pax Christi provides links to the major US counter-recruitment campaigns (2005) organized by the American Friends Service Committee and the Fellowship of Reconciliation, each of which emphasizes "awareness of possible dangers of joining the military and false promises made by recruiters" (AFSC 2016; FoR 2016).

Peace and Social Witness issued a 2014 report titled "The New Tide of Militarisation" in the UK, where they explicitly noted the Royal British Legion's move to selling poppies under the auspices of supporting our troops as a discernible change from the past (PSW 2014, 6). Also in the UK, the NGO ForcesWatch was founded to address "unethical military recruitment" that uses "toys, computer games and military hardware and . . . ideas of steady employment, getting an education, having experiences that other young people do not have, and "self-discovery powered by the army" (ForcesWatch n.d.). Counter-recruitment opposes the propagation of cultural myths of brave men, "good" wars, and righteous liberalism.

In deconstructing and myth-busting the glamour of a military career and experience, these organizations encounter one more issue contextualizing anti-militarist dissent (and resistance): What do we do with all the people already in the military? Much of counter-recruitment discourse invokes the idea of the "economic draft," or "poverty draft," which holds that in an all-volunteer military, it is the poor, marginalized, rural, and members of racialized minorities that recruiters target for service due to their perceived lack of alternatives (see Marsical 2007). Peace Action argued that this draft "has unfairly burdened many of our nation's most vulnerable youth with fighting this war and enduring the long-term fallout of joblessness and Post-Traumatic Stress Disorder" (2007). Counter-recruitment organizations call out the inequitable racialized, classed, and gendered sacrifice that undergirds the constitution of "support as the new service" domestically (and, as we saw in Chapter 7, transnationally). "We" might all be produced by discursive martiality as ideal, normatively masculine supporters, but we're still not all in the institutional military. The amended contract can smooth this over ideologically, but materially, some will still serve. Counter-recruitment gets back to the paradox of liberal sacrifice.

Critiquing this dynamic is essential to raising awareness of the individual perils of military service and the complicity of supportive civilians in the suffering and hardship of military personnel. The construction of military recruitment as a form of deceptive predation, however, also frames those already in the military as victims of the system in a mode not dissimilar to that of the altruistic, paternalistic civil-military dynamic. As a result, while this form of resistance to literal military participation undermines the idea of the heroic, masculine soldier—and the foundational association of martiality with heteromasculine agency and citizenship—it is still congruent with a supportive orientation toward the troops.

Counter-recruitment discourses, in walking this fine line, tend not to explicitly address how people who are not in the institutional military should relate to the troops. This makes sense—it's not the central focus of their mission. In attempting to reduce and discourage recruitment, counter-recruitment activists, by necessity, take a far narrower and more literal reading of the meaning of the troops (as solely military personnel) than common to StT discourse as a whole. The efficacy of counter-recruitment in shading the amended martial contract stems at least in part from the movement's tangential interest in that form of gendered obligation. Due to its relatively robust institutional organization and shrugging off the question of support, counter-recruitment has the potential to offer a more effective form of resistance than the offensive examples provided above. At the same time, it is not quite able to shake the normative and affective confines of the amended, gendered military contract. The question of duties to military personnel is unresolved. Though the relationship between heteromasculinity, citizenship, and martiality is disrupted, the production of the political via solidaristic violence remains comparatively intact.

Conclusion

Support the troops discourses severely constrained the conditions of legitimate political dissent during the wars in Iraq and Afghanistan. Given the historical trajectory of support for the troops in both states, growing left-right political polarization, and a generalized populist suspicion of politics, there is little reason to believe this difficulty contesting war will not continue in the future. The moves to fix the gendered martial contract, intensified by the specific pressures of the global war on terror, have nearly entirely displaced "the troubled emancipatory rhetoric dating back to the Enlightenment" (Eisenstein 2007, xiv).

Normative citizenship masculinity has shifted the central political obligation of normative (masculine) citizenship from participation in deliberative, democratic politics to participation in the discursive military. Only those authorized by formal military service and/or proximity to combat—military personnel, military family members, and veterans—in a flip of the convention of the democratic control of the armed forces, are able to legitimately contest state violence. The substantive meaning of "politics," in turn, is limited to war opposition. Antiwar groups face a tense choice between pragmatically accommodating the tropes and gendered expectations of the amended liberal martial contract or risk being dismissed as insensible or irrelevant. At the edges of the political, there is some scope for resistance, expressed in practices and discourses that either bypass the gendered tenets of the amended martial contract or subtly call it into question through the articulation of less exhortative and more ambiguous protest ("Troops Out!").

Overall, however, supporting the troops, as entangled with the reconstitution of normative masculinity under the amended martial contract, has defied politicization. War opposition takes on a somewhat circular quality: StT is necessary for a fair hearing but also underlies the contemporary unthinkability of a more deliberative approach, and alternative ethical orientation, to conflict. As produced through discursive martiality, StT produces an apolitics of societal complicity in the killing, maiming, and endangerment of distant, often racialized Others.

9

Conclusion

From the beginning of the global war on terror in 2001 through to time of writing, late 2021, approximately 241,000 people have been killed in Afghanistan and Pakistan—including at least 71,000 civilians. In Iraq, it has been difficult to estimate the number of people killed since 2003. It has been verified that between 184,000 and 207,156 civilians died, though the true number is certainly higher (Watson Institute 2021). Over 7,000 US and 626 UK military personnel have been killed in Iraq, Afghanistan, and Pakistan. So have 8,000 contractors and over 173,000 allied military and police personnel (Watson Institute 2021; Sabbagh 2020). The Taliban regained social and political control of Afghanistan, leading to insecurity and uncertainty for millions of Afghans after 20 years of war. Iraq has seen the destruction of basic infrastructure—water, power, roads, and so on—and public services, such as health and education, accompanied by political violence and insecurity for civilians. The war on terror, in response to the rise of the Islamic State and continued relevance of al-Qaeda and al-Shabaab, among other groups, has expanded to Yemen, Syria, Somalia, Nigeria, Mali, and other less prominent theaters (Savell 2021).

To conclude the book, I could revisit the argument thus far. We've seen that supporting the troops is not an apolitical or natural phenomenon; rather, it is contested and contingent. It both reflects and papers over fractures in the liberal military contract: the gendered obligation of all good men—all good citizens—to serve in the military in wartime. I've unpacked the "good" story of naïve liberalism and used the analytic of "discursive martiality" to bypass the ideological loading of existing notions of "militarism." This enabled me to pull together the politics of the military, gender, and war within liberalism with the more deeply constitutive role solidaristic violence plays in producing "the political": the liberal social order.

From there, we saw that concern for the troops distances the political community from war; that supporting the troops addresses gendered civilian

Support the Troops. Katharine M. Millar, Oxford University Press. © Oxford University Press 2022.
DOI: 10.1093/oso/9780197642337.003.0009

anxiety arising from non-service by (re)masculinizing civilian supporters; and that the solidarity in relation to violence expressed in StT plays an important role in making the political community. The ability to frame violence in terms of internal solidarity obscures the unequal, racialized and colonial terms of the amended (and originary) liberal military contract. The nexus of normative martiality, masculinity, and citizenship within support, in turn, sharply limits the contemporary scope of democratic debate and war opposition. Supporting the troops is moral, natural, and apolitical. Discussing the war on terror is engaging in politics. Support is the new service; martial deference is the new democracy.

This summary is accurate. To properly conclude, however, we also need to look more bluntly at the normative and political stakes of that analysis. As indicated by the opening of this section, the central activity of the global war on terror was (and is) death, injury, and suffering. Supporting the troops didn't cause it. But it likely helped prolong it and certainly didn't constrain it. Supporting the troops enabled the publics of the US, UK, and the West to look away from the harms of war and back toward something more comfortable. It helped sever the relationship between democracy and the wars of democracies. Supporting the troops turned civilian complicity in the racialized killings of people abroad into a simpler, more palatable question of solidarity at home and across the transnational liberal order. Supporting the troops reveals it's not just negative relations of enmity that get people killed. It also takes loyalty, solidarity, and love.

The politics of supporting the troops served to legitimate, via depoliticization, the specific wars in Iraq and Afghanistan. The logic of supporting the troops furthers the reproduction of liberal political community via gendered obligations of solidaristic violence. Given these stakes—and the continued violences enacted in the name of liberalism and under the guise of the war on terror—the conclusion is left with (at least) two open questions. What does this mean? And, what do "we" do about it?

Supporting the Troops and the Legacies of the War on Terror

What supporting the troops means is primarily a question of how we read StT in context. It requires thinking about supporting the troops as a reflection of a specific historical period and in terms of its contemporary political legacy. What does supporting the troops tell us about the so-called global war on terror?

Supporting the troops, as argued throughout the book, as a discourse, social phenomenon, affect, and expression of obligation, predated 2001. The central characteristics of StT—a sense of vulnerability and victimhood, detachment from the violence of war, attempts to recapture normative masculinity, and disinterest in politics and democratic engagement—also reflect and were intensified by the particularities of the war on terror. The shock and grief that followed 9/11 created a "rally round the flag" effect (Mueller 1973) in the US and among its allies—notably the UK—that further cemented supporting the troops as not only natural and inevitable but also moral. The constitution of the United States—and, with it, the liberal West—as vulnerable and victimized following the September 11 attacks, a substantial challenge to existing ideas of US exceptionalism, intensified the constitution of the troops as similarly dependent, vulnerable, and victimized.

As the war on terror became less popular—particularly after the invasion of Iraq (and the subsequent revelation Saddam Hussein had not possessed weapons of mass destruction)—the troops offered an alternative focal point for affective investment and solidarity initially offered to the US (and UK) governments. This shift in normative focus from the war to the troops, combined with a comparative dearth of reporting on the wars' impact on civilians, facilitated the depoliticization—and prolongation—of the war on terror. The civilizational discourse of the war on terror that posited the US and allies as defending a universalized humanity also produced the feature of StT discourse most clearly specific to the post-9/11 era: the creeping framing of what had previously been understood as strategic questions of interests, alliances, and geopolitics in terms of (often affective) social relations of loyalty. Supporting the troops was transnationalized. It became a vehicle for soliciting (and coercing) gendered martial solidarity with a normatively White imperial liberal order while also eliding the material continuation of the unequal, racialized, and colonial hierarchies upon which that same order was, and is, based.

Within the US and UK, the war on terror heightened existing contradictions. The liberal martial contract continued to fracture. With distant wars and professional militaries, few men (and citizens) served in the wars and few civilians were called upon to make meaningful material wartime sacrifices. This coincided with broader transformations within Western masculinity across the twentieth century. Changes in the structure of the globalized economy, particularly during the 1990s, not only reduced the number of viable blue-collar jobs available in the US and UK but also challenged the previous hegemony of associated masculinized/izing values such as hard work, manual labor, self-sufficiency, and so on (Thobani 2010).

Those closely identified or identifying with the universalized Western, liberal subject (as masculine, cis, heterosexual, White, autonomous, physically brave, economically productive, etc.) found that the conventional economic and martial sources of meaning and authority were no longer available. Fewer people—with perhaps particular relevance to those identifying as men—were able to access or inhabit the existing ideal of normative public masculinity. The discomfort of this positionality was heightened by the increased martial (and economic) participation, during the same period, of people previously marginalized by this same hierarchicalized, gendered, racialized liberal order: women, queer people, people of color, people who are not citizens, and so forth.

This reading of structural transformation, of course, as articulated from the perspective of those identifying with the idealized liberal subject, is conservative (and potentially reactionary). In a manner that animates gendered civilian anxiety, it narrates a decline in privilege as a form of material and normative loss. Supporting the troops thus entered and was (re)produced within a moment of apparent challenge to conventional structures of social order (military service, racialized nationalism, a heteropatriarchal sex/gender system, etc.) within the US and UK. StT during the war on terror was a move to paper over a seeming crisis in public normative masculinity (Kimmell 2018). The domestic articulation of the discourse did so via a double-move not dissimilar to the blurring of solidarity and enmity via relations of affect and obligation internationally.

The reconstitution of support as the new service, as a masculinized/izing practice of normative martiality, blurred the lines between the civil and the martial in order to disavow the feminization that accrues to civilians in wartime. At the same time, StT re-anchored a binary, cisnormative heteropatriachal sex/gender order that, as the conventional sources of normative masculinity declined in material participation and social valorization, risked coming unmoored. It also, by incorporating all forms of particularistic difference—that is, race, gender, political belief, and so on—into an all-encompassing logic of affective support, sneakily diffused challenges to the idealization of the underlying heteromasculine, White, martial liberal subject.

The structural parts of this account—the fracturing of the liberal military contract, the transformation of binary, heteropatriarchal sex/gender order—are not unique to the war on terror. As I'll get into below, the masculinity-martiality-citizenship nexus is a constituent feature of liberalism. "Crises" in masculinity are recurrent social cycles. The specifics of these purported crises, however, as argued by Kimmell (2018), are significant in what they reveal as emergent critiques of culture and (usually) reactions to change, challenges to privilege, and a sense of foregone power. And it's the way StT responded to, modified, and projected this crisis into the future that is one of the more substantial legacies of the war on terror. Despite its integrative, universalizing liberal trappings, StT was also a precursor to, and bellwether for, the emergence of populism within the US and UK.

The war on terror saw substantial reductions in civil liberties via, among other mechanisms, the PATRIOT Act in the US and a suite of counterterrorism legislation in the UK. The broad definition of "terrorism" used by the Bush, Blair, and subsequent administrations facilitated unlawful detention of terrorist suspects, substantial extensions of policing and surveillance powers that disproportionately targeted people of color, and restrictions on protest (Human Rights Watch 2012). Support the troops discourses were not only produced within this context but also facilitated it; first, by constituting support as the primary duties of normative masculine citizens, and second, by defining "support" as apolitical, normal and natural. Support was negatively contrasted with engaging in politics, understood narrowly as either opposing the war or merely engaging in democratic debate regarding the war. Together, these factors—the formal laws of the war on terror and replacement of democratic debate with martial solidarity—created a strong curb to the formal, procedural aspects of democracy and the rule of law, legitimated via an affect-infused social norm against contesting the war.

The parsing of citizens from politics, in addition to enabling the killing of people abroad, furthered the denigration of democracy within the US and UK. Though support the discourses, as normatively martial, are cast in a tenor we might consider in some ways patriotic, they are also notably anti-state. Solidarity with the troops, when war is vanished as a matter of collective politics, is instead framed as articulating against the government, against elites, against an imagined army of traitorous non-supporters and, indeed, as against politics per se. The main locus for affective investment and relational solidarity is less the state, or even the nation, than the imagined figure of the troops themselves. The constitution of the troops as tragic heroes and victims is produced by and productive of a broader societal skepticism of, as well as disengagement from, government.[1]

StT is a liberal consensus: open-ended, integrative, and essential to the violent maintenance of liberal order. Its commonsense propagation during the war on terror by both the right and left also, however, diffused its anti-statist, anti-elitist undertones across the political spectrum. Put differently, the valorization of democratic disengagement constituted by StT discourse as a form of masculinizing martial obligation laid the groundwork for the overtly exclusionary, racialized, heteropatriarchal articulations of apolitical solidarity that make up contemporary right-wing populism in the US and UK. Supporting the troops did not cause Brexit or the election of Trump; it was produced within and reflective of the same broader sociopolitical context that brought them about. But the attitudes, affects, gendered normativity, racialized disregard for civilian deaths, and political skepticism normalized within StT discourses helped open the door.

Gendered Political Obligation and Liberalism

Given all that's happened in the 20 years since September 11, 2001—the hundreds of thousands of deaths, the rise of the surveillance state, the undermining of democracy, the racialized and racist politics that have accompanied the crisis in normative Western public masculinity—it's tempting to place StT in the past. It would be comforting to think of supporting the troops as an artifact of a series of misguided politics and bad wars.

As Louiza Odysseos has argued, however, the war on terror is neither novel nor exceptional. Rather, it is "an exceedingly exemplary manifestation of the paradox of liberal modernity and war: of the occurrence of ever more violent types of war within the very attempt to fight wars which would end 'war' as such" (2007, 137). What Bacevich (2005) has critiqued as the "forever wars," suggesting a new, interminable temporality to ostensibly pacifying liberal violence, are better understood as the "always-already and forever" wars. Neither the war on terror nor supporting the troops are breaks with liberalism. They're simply contemporary manifestations of the foundational continuity of politics with violence and the production of political community through violence within liberal orders.

Whether or not we expect to see supporting the troops in this specific manifestation again—and, honestly, we might—the fundamental questions it raises about who fights, what is owed to those who do, and how the political community hangs together, persist. The long arc of civil-military relations across the nineteenth and twentieth centuries tracks the forging, fracturing, and amendment of the gendered liberal military contract alongside an increasing valorization of the troops on gendered, sexualized, and racialized terms.

Supporting the troops demonstrates, yet again, that liberalism is mutable, robust, and adaptable to shifting gendered, sexualized, racialized, classed, and colonial hierarchies and ideals. It relies on these seemingly illiberal particularities and affective relations of loyalty, solidarity, and love, alongside conventional dynamics of enmity, for its (apparent) ideological coherence and longevity. These paradoxes are constitutive of liberalism. Consequently, as evidenced by the attempts of antiwar protestors to turn support the troops discourses to radical ends, it is challenging to transcend the strictures of the amended liberal military contract and normative binary sex/gender order. As solidaristic violence constitutes the political, we lack a politics of violence.

So, what is to be done?

There are a few obvious candidates. A return to conscription would alleviate the continuing inequities in military service (and access to normative martial masculinity) that spurred the fracture in the originary liberal military contract. Putting aside the fact that virtually no system of conscription has ever been universal or equitable, however, wouldn't challenge the production of the liberal polity through gendered relations of violent political obligation but would redouble it. The relationship between political belonging, masculinity, and martiality is untouched. A return to conscription, despite the projected aspirations of democratic peace theory, offers no traction upon racialized, imperial war. The solution to the tensions, failures, and violences of liberalism is not found in liberalism (Ndlovu-Gatsheni 2019).

There are other candidates in the existing political vocabulary. Fascism resolves virtually all the tensions in the gendered military liberal contract (to say nothing of liberalism generally). Its embrace of political homogeneity and propagation of xenophobia and racism offers, for those positioned in proximity to privilege, a clear pathway to normative martial heteromasculinity. That this isn't a politically or normatively desirable outcome goes without saying. But, given the way politics in the US, UK, and broader West have gone since the end of my 2010 period of analysis, it is important to note how the liberal, universalizing logics at work in StT can tip this way. The violent clarity of fascism is a tempting path for resolving crises.

Pacifism, in any of its many guises, offers another potential avenue of escape from the gendered political obligation of liberal violence. Pacifisms, of course, oppose violence and war per se (Ceadel 1987) on humanitarian and/or religious grounds. As we can infer from the fortunes of antiwar and anti-militarist protest during the global war on terror, however, pacifism is currently unintelligible under the terms of the amended liberal military contract. To oppose war is also, subtly, to impugn the normativity—or even necessity—of the troops (Millar 2016a). Pacifisms hold the potential to break through the self-legitimating tautologies of troop support because their normative commitments to nonviolence bypass the premise of the contract—but, as a consequence, they cannot be contemporaneously heard. Pacifisms also, more troublingly, may further the preservation the same liberal (White, heteropatriarchal, colonial) international order whose wars it would contest by denying the legitimacy of the violences of oppressed and expropriated peoples of color (see Rossdale 2019). By opposing violence without being able to contest the gendered military contract, pacifisms can actually serve the status quo.

As this incredibly schematic discussion has hopefully suggested, the solution to supporting the troops, as well as violent liberal solidarities, doesn't seem to lie in absolutist political commitments or, necessarily, existing ideological idioms (though feminism's confrontation of essentialist masculinities and rigid, cis-heteropatriarchal sex/gender binaries will likely help). The clarity that follows the apparent elimination of paradoxes comes with its own problems and power dynamics. Instead, confronting liberal war and violent solidarities probably requires something—or a suite of somethings—messier, less satisfying, and more partial.

What do we do about supporting the troops? We need a re-politicization of violence. All violence—the imperial wars of liberal order and the racialized, sexualized, and ableist violences of policing, surveillance (settler) colonialism, and austerity (please see, again, Howell 2018). This is not a naïve call for a return to the formal, electoral democracy from before the GWoT and StT discourses used heteropatriarchal norms to transform liberal political obligation from democratic participation to martial bystanding. It's not, in other words, an aspiration to revivify an idealized politics of the 1990s or 1960s. After all, it is those same gendered, sexualized, and racialised systems that facilitated and produced supporting the troops in the first place.

What I do mean, though, is almost similarly old school: placing opposition to the gendered liberal military contract back into a series of interlinked struggles for social justice, alongside and part of anti-colonial, anti-racist, labor, feminist, and queer liberatory work. This would move the gendered (and sexualized, racialized, etc.) terms of violent obligation, and use of violence itself, from bounding "the political" to a matter of politics. A contentious matter, but no longer the constitutive warrant for existing within the political community. Though fragmented, we have seen examples of how this might be done in the indeterminate antiwar discourse of "troops out!" campaigns, in counter-recruitment activism, in the continuing direct actions of anti-militarist protestors, and in the connection of war opposition with other issues of racial and social justice through broader coalitions.

If this book has shown nothing else, however, it is also that the political efficacy of such efforts relies on one more step. We (whoever that means, at this point) need to stop supporting the troops. No more clapping, no more magnets. Trying to contest liberal wars without taking on this expectation of troop support only further reifies the relationship between masculinity, violence, agency, and good personhood that underlie most modern theories of politics, practices of governance, and visions of the state (Millar 2019b). Refusing to support the troops, though seemingly small, works in the tenor of revolution, not reform.

There is no denying this is uncomfortable. Martiality and normative gender have a strong affective pull (Wegner 2021). It risks deeply hurting people's feelings—which matters more than our discipline cares to admit. Unpacking the expectation to support the troops cannot be accomplished without confrontation. It requires attempting to envision normative forms of gender, good personhood, and political belonging that don't rely on a willingness to engage in, approve of, or deny violence. It requires attempting to imagine different forms of solidarity, more attuned to relations of complicity and of harm, articulated with an understanding of ongoing and historical patterns of marginalization, hierarchy, and (in)justice.

Such a project doesn't require the callous treatment of serving military personnel or veterans, who arrive in those positions from an array of backgrounds, through complex circumstances, and for a variety of reasons. It also doesn't require a disregard for the suffering of their loved ones. It might require re-placing military personnel and veterans into a more robust social welfare system that doesn't parse its benefits and recognition on the basis of normative martial heroism (Cowen 2008b) but another form of solidarity. It does require shifting military personnel from the center of our moral, affective, and political reckoning with war, in favor of those killed and harmed by liberal violences.

In its fullest expression, the dismantling of the gendered liberal military contract probably also entails abolishing the military, alongside other institutional manifestations of the state capacity for force. Martiality and its formal expression in the military, as we've seen, are not a pathology of liberalism—an unaccountable "militarism"—but rather a core component of liberalism's long-standing ideological capacity for heroization, self-legitimation, coercion, and oppression. Abolishing the military, a barely thinkable, almost retro political aim, isn't likely to happen anytime soon. But it sets a vision for undermining the centrality of masculinized, violent agency as the definitive marker of modern political belonging.

As I close, I don't suggest that any of this is easy. It's hard; I'm nervous putting it forward. I was home in Canada, visiting my family, as I finished this book in the COVID-19 summer of 2021. When I went running, I saw the yellow ribbon magnets on the cars of my neighbors and my parents' friends. They're not the same magnets from 20 years ago, of course. But the magnets are a material reminder that as the war on terror is disavowed and its politics fade from collective memory, the social relations animated in supporting the troops persist.

Methodology

All studies, from inception through publication, remain works in the progress. This appendix works through the methodological, sourcing, and ethical/reflexive considerations that underlie this book. To transparently explain the choices and trade-offs that went into the construction of the study, it is written in a fair amount of detail. The appendix is an exercise in pedagogy. I discuss the challenges of conducting this study, how I managed them, and what my "solutions" mean for how the final arguments can be understood.[1] Throughout the research design and implementation process, my guiding principle was to produce the "best" account of support the troops (StT) discourse—selecting for breadth and depth of discourse, with an eye toward contestation—wherever analytically and practically possible. The result is a logically grounded, if slightly complex, methodological and sourcing process that goes above and beyond the methodological and epistemological requirements of a typical discourse analysis.

Methodology

As discussed in the Introduction, the book's central methodological approach is a form of thematically organized discourse analysis. I collected a very large corpus of texts to identify key patterns of meaning, contestations, and silences with in the broad "support the troops" discursive formation. I examined 3,258 paragraph-level units from approximately 6,000–9,000 pages of text. (Many, but not all, of the paragraph units were founded in longer documents that I briefly considered as context for the interpretation of the specific uses of support the troops discourse). These broad patterns, explicated in Chapter 4, were then used to contextualize subsequent close-readings and feminist interpretive analysis of particularly illuminating trends and quotations.

Thematically organized discourse analysis uses an iterative process of categorizing texts, working inductively from primary materials and deductively from the secondary literature (Taylor and Ussher 2001, 297). It captures patterns of meaning articulated within a discursive formation and interprets them within a broader conceptual, social, and political context. As with all discourse analysis, the aim is to analyze not only what is literally expressed in language but also to track key silences, elisions, and forms of implicit meaning. Language is understood not as directly conveying the intentions of a fully autonomous individuated subject, but rather as expressing meanings, connections, subjectivities, and power relations that are beyond the control of social actors. Discourse is conceptualized as intersubjective, constituting and making real the social world—including that inhabited by the researcher (2001, 310).

What thematic organization adds to discourse analysis is a way of structuring patterns of meaning within a body of texts, as well as bringing transparency and order to the analysis, without eliding the intersubjective nature of discourse writ large. The process of thematic organization and categorization itself is a form of interpretation. The researcher uses their own critical analytical insights and context from the literature to identify salient patterns of meaning and silence within a corpus. This is done without conceptualizing discursive themes as other mutually exclusive and/or reducible to each other. As articulated by Taylor and Ussher (2001, 302), discursive themes can, and do, overlap and contradict each other (potentially within the same text). The point of the analysis is not to resolve these contradictions, nor synthesize them into a neat whole, but to use the structured themes to pull out these tensions for further interrogation. Where thematic discourse analysis is messy, asymmetric, contradictory, and partial is often where we find the most important political stakes. Where the discourse fails to be "fixed" or internally consistent reveals processes of transformation and fracture in broader social discourses, processes, and structures. The tensions within "support the troops" discourse reveal the underlying fracture of both liberal civil-military relations and the instability of the heteronormative gender binary upon which civil-military relations are founded.

Thematically organized discourse analysis differs from other methods frequently used to analyze large volumes of text—notably quantitative content analysis. Quantitative content analysis aims to produce quantitative data amenable to statistical analysis (Schreier 2013, 172–73). Quantitative content analysis requires transforming texts into mutually exclusive, discrete, and fairly literal units of meaning that are reflective of rational and/or subjective intention. It is well-suited to determining efficient causal relations but cannot (and does not aim to) capture the more diffuse processes of social constitution, normalization, and (re)production I examine within this book.

Thematically organized discourse analysis is more analogous to qualitative content analysis, which refers to the systematic examination of a range of texts, via a process of categorization/coding, according to a structured set of principles. Qualitative content analysis is focused on understanding the meaning of language in context (see Mayring 2000). This process requires the exercise of contextually situated interpretation and to some degree maintains the interaction between researcher and text that informs discourse analysis (Hardy et al 2004, 1). Most qualitative content analysis, however, is designed to answer fairly closed research questions and adheres fairly rigidly to a process of either inductive or deductive textual analysis. It is less able to address open-ended questions of broad social constitution (Mayring 2000)—such as the conditions of normalization for StT discourses and the "work" the discourses perform—or accommodate the iterative processes of analysis such questions require.

Thematically organized discourse analysis lets me reconcile my ambition of understanding a broad discursive formation with the attention to nuance, marginal voices, and contingency required for meaningful interpretation. The volume of texts considered, selected to maximize the depth and breadth of StT discourse, also raises confidence that the corpus is plausibly representative of the major themes of the discursive formation writ large (see Fierke 2004). This is not to make false pretensions toward objectivity—which is neither plausible nor desirable within discourse analysis—but rather to highlight the unusual scope and scale of my study.

Thematically organized discourse analysis enables me to place my conceptual, critical, and political "bets" in approaching StT discourse: a commitment to feminist analysis, and an interest in the constitutive potential of violence. As StT discourse has not, to the best of my knowledge, been the subject of large-scale discourse analysis—nor a systematic content analysis of any kind—this ability to thematically map the discursive formation while maintaining a consistent critical analytical stance is particularly important. By considering two cases of StT discourse in the US and UK, over a 10-year period, and across media, civil society, and government actors, I have constructed the most comprehensive study of supporting the troops to date.

Method

As discussed in the Introduction, I identified, coded, and analyzed the textual corpus (discussed below) iteratively, moving between broad patterns of explicit meaning that structure the corpus and more implicit cross-cutting themes. First, I categorized each paragraph mentioning "support the troops" or an analogous phrase. Broadly, I qualified StT discourse on the basis of its use of the literal phrase "support the troops" or a contextually appropriate reflection upon the normative state of civil-military relations.

Previous studies of StT tended to be illustrative (i.e., using examples of StT discourse to further a broader critical point, see Stahl 2009) or empirically bounded to particular practice or actor (see Tidy 2015a on Help for Heroes or Kelly 2012 on militarism at sports events). Little was known about the content of StT discourse as a broader phenomenon; the literature tended to assume that what it meant to support the troops was either obvious or uniform. There were (and, to the best of my knowledge, currently are) no other studies of internal variation within StT discourse.

To address this empirical gap, I began by asking basic questions of the corpus. Who supports the troops? Why do they support the troops? Against whom do they support the troops? How? In which wars? I derived the answers inductively from the texts themselves, designing the resulting descriptive themes (e.g., we support the troops to support the war, because we love them, because we must, etc.) to be as open-ended as possible (Hardy et al. 2004, 21). I added new themes as significant "answers" emerged and dropped themes that were analytically unhelpful and/or, as the more critical process of interpretation came into play, unnecessary. I used the qualitative analysis software program NVivo to organize my analysis.

Many of these initial themes captured explicit meaning within the texts, such as that one could support the troops by paying taxes. I also relied on the context of the broader document to draw out more implicit meanings. For instance, the phrase "support the troops" is often exhortative and somewhat decontextualized (this is what leads to the assumption that its meaning is either obvious or unimportant). To determine "who" supports the troops, requires an attention to implicit meanings—most notably the social relations at work within a particular text—to determine who the intended "supporter" is imagined to be. Often, the answer is an unaddressed "everyone," an interpretive conclusion that requires taking into account the content of the text, its implied social relations, and its situation within a broader, normalized liberal social and cultural orientation towards civil-military relations. The patterns revealed by these explicit questions thus also reveal implicit subthemes and silences—such as a sort of moral pity for the troops and an absence of explicit refusals to support the troops.

This initial, descriptive mapping of often—though not exclusively—explicit patterns of meaning within support the troops discourse is an important empirical contribution in and of itself. It provides a robust basis with which to contextualize the more fine-grained, conceptually driven interpretation of implicit meanings in the balance of the study. In other words, in the absence of an existing body of detailed scholarship on the heterogeneity and contingency of StT discourses within which to ground (and offer a validity check for) my own interpretations of the politics of StT, I had to create that empirical basis myself. This commitment to empirical comprehensiveness, and the identification of broad, socially circulating patterns, thus gives my study a much broader and deeper empirical basis than common to discourse analysis.

The thematic organization of StT discourse also refutes the misperception—common when I began the study in 2011 and circulating today—that "supporting the troops" is (a) obvious in its meaning; (b) an uninteresting epiphenomenon of unpopular wars; (c) a "niche," propagandistic rhetoric far from "real" politics; or (d) some combination of all three. I conducted the descriptive mapping of StT discourse to demonstrate its pervasiveness and internal heterogeneity, establishing the importance of StT in and of itself. This thematically organized discourse analysis, presented in Chapter 4, provides a robust empirical context for subsequent critical, interpretive claims and is also a proof of concept of the study itself. StT is complex and contradictory; its tensions and elisions are politically significant.

Once the initial thematic analysis, contained in Chapter 4, was concluded, I used the patterns to pull out particular trends and silences for additional interpretation. This analysis, found in Chapters 5 to 8, is the majority of the study. These patterns helped me pick out, for instance, which constructions of StT were common, potentially hegemonic—for example, liberal understandings of obligatory support—which were less common—for example, supporting the troops because you love them—and how these themes contest and overlap with each other.

The frequency of a particular discursive theme, such as the idea that everyone must support the troops, is not taken as a proxy for its importance. Silences and rare statements are just as politically important—and potentially more analytically telling—within a discursive epistemology as prevalent themes. The meanings, as well as analytical implications, of silences, uncommon articulations, and dominant constructions are not arbitrary; they go together in contingent yet predictable ways. Given the empirical comprehensiveness of the study, common patterns can be taken to reflect socially circulating commonsense and underlying normative structures. Silences and less common tropes, in contrast, point to instances of the failures of that common sense, to alternative normative structures existing within the same time/place, and potential moments of transformation/consolidation.

Overall, I iteratively organize StT discourse into empirical themes and frequently explicit, dominant patterns of meaning, presented in Chapter 4. These patterns are then used to contextualize and inform the fine-grained analysis of the complex and contradictory array of implicit meanings, silences, and contestations that constitute the politics (and normative naturalization) of supporting the troops, explicated in Chapters 5 through 8.

Text Selection

This study examines primary materials—documents—produced for public dissemination by a range of social actors relevant to StT. I understand these documents as a form of discursive practice, in keeping with the poststructural understanding of "text" as encompassing virtually anything involved in communication (Hansen 2006, 23). This enables me to read materials ranging from political speeches to news articles to bumper stickers to protest signs (as long as they were produced and in some way archived by one of the social actors examined within the study) as analytically equivalent forms of political communication. I read the documents in context, taking the social authority of their source and form of distribution into account. The primary documents were also used to locate and consider social practices, such as the Yellow Ribbon Campaign, which encourages citizens to tie yellow ribbons on neighborhood trees and other everyday items, that extend beyond the literal document. These practices are used to contextualize the arguments and claims of the thematic discourse analysis. They are not incorporated into the discourse analysis as themselves primary materials. In this way, though I primarily use documents, I aim to ameliorate the risk of textual reductionism in my interpretation.

This expanded understanding of text also, importantly, facilitates the identification of potential "dissent" to the mythical liberal contract and/or StT. This is key to appropriately contextualizing diagnoses of "hegemonic" or "disciplining" discourses, as well as identifying their contradictions/limitations. Hansen and Weldes, respectively, argue that research should be broadened beyond officially "authoritative" texts likely to participate in the dominant discourse (e.g., policy documents and major newspapers). To help locate dissent, they suggest including nontraditional sources (often pejoratively referred to as "low data") such as travel writing, music, and other artifacts of popular culture (Weldes 2006, 177–78 and 181–83; Hansen 2006, 55). I incorporate the public texts of selected military and antiwar NGOs, including press releases, , images, protest signs, email chains, brochures, and so forth, to track the operation of StT discourse at a remove from formal political authority.

To do this, I use a modified version of Hansen's "intertextual" technique for identifying specific sources and limning the realm relevant documents. Intertextuality means that texts are understood to exist with "a shared textual space" and constantly in reference to each other (2006, 55; for original, see Kristeva 1980). These shared references—which may be literal, such as website links, or common metaphors—are used to identify additional texts. The basic principle holds that in following either explicit (e.g., quotations or direct references) or implicit (e.g. allusions, common symbolism, or conceptual similarity) linkages between texts, it is possible to map the various representations present in the discourse(s) and the interactions between them (Hansen 2006, 56–64). Once the new references became repetitive—either to new texts or of the same recurring themes—the discourse is saturated.

I do not incorporate all potential forms of StT discourse (and dissent). My data is limited to the social actors named in the study (the media, government, and select military and antiwar NGOs) *and* the social practices of troop support intertextually referenced within their public textual materials. More ad hoc resistance that fails to be represented within this "public culture" of supporting the troops, such as smaller civil society organizations, reddit posts, or individual failures to clap for the troops, fall outside the scope of analysis. It is my hope, however, that this study of the center of StT discourse may lay the groundwork for interrogating more marginal and/or radical practices of resistance.

Sourcing

It is neither theoretically necessary nor practically possible to exhaustively capture every public use of the phrase "support the troops." Instead, I used a stratified data collection strategy to examine the public materials of media, state, and selected military and antiwar NGOs (i.e., the "strata" within which data is collected). I selected both the relevant social actors (e.g. CodePink, *The Guardian*) and the specific documents from their publicly available materials in accordance with the principle of constructing a textual corpus of sufficient breadth and depth to identify general patterns of usage, themes, and contestation.

To select specific documents from these organizations, I searched for the phrase "support the troops"/"support our troops," or a contextually appropriate synonym. "Bring them home now!" and "help for heroes," for instance, are phrases that comment on the normative relationship between society and the military. They are a vital component—and potential source of contestation—of the phenomenon. All texts were publicly available at their time of production and intended for a public audience. (See Appendix 2 for specific organizations and sourcing procedures).

For a variety of reasons relating to the volume of StT discourse, institutional archival procedures, public secrecy laws, and the general accessibility of these texts, each strata within each case (media, government, and NGO) and organisation required a slightly different sourcing to gather the most accurate depiction of StT discourse possible. To cope with this unavoidable asymmetry in data availability and access, I developed detailed and organization-specific data collection and, where necessary, sampling procedures. This section outlines the challenges, solutions, and trade-offs encountered in each strata in detail. The timeframe for all texts is September 1, 2001, to January 1, 2011.

Newspapers

For both the US and UK, newspapers were the most straightforward source to collect. In keeping with the conventions of media analysis, I selected newspapers on the basis of importance to the dissemination of the discourse, understood as "national" newspapers with wide circulation and, collectively, political diversity.[2] For the UK, I included *The Guardian, The Telegraph, The Independent, The Observer, The Financial Times* and, due to its identification through intertextual references in both other papers and by NGOs, *The Sun* tabloid. For the US, I included the *New York Times*, the *Washington Post*, and the *Wall Street Journal*. As the United States lacks a national tabloid comparable to those in the UK, one was not included in this study, though a popular magazine, such as *US Weekly*, could be added to future projects. (I also considered two additional US newspapers, the *Chicago Sun-Times* and the *LA Times*, on the basis of regional representation, but an initial search found their use of StT discourse did not dramatically differ from the included papers. As a result, they were omitted).

I searched the selected newspapers in the Factiva database using term "'support the troops' OR 'support our troops'" for 2001–2010, inclusive. Articles using the phrase StT or SoT but referring to a non-national context (i.e., an article about US StT discourse in the UK press) were left in, as they obviously contributed to the dissemination of the discourse in the location of the press (i.e., the UK). Duplicates were removed. Due to the nature of mainstream media databasing, this stratum of data is complete universe of relevant texts. (In contrast to the balance of the US strata, the newspaper discourse was not sampled.)

State Documents

To analyze the use of StT discourse by conventional political authorities, I examined the records of legislative debates; press releases and public statements by the executive branch; and press releases, public documents, and public statements by the Ministry of Defence and Department of Defense. As archival practices and data availability differ between the two cases, I outline the individual text selection procedures below.

The primary limitation on data access for both the US and UK was, ironically, the (relatively) recent nature of the so-called global war on terror. Government documents in the United Kingdom—even those available publicly at the time—are not transferred to the national archive and made available for public use until 20 years after their initial creation.[3] Though there is a strong corpus of government texts available via other means, at least some potentially relevant documents may be archived and were unavailable during the time the research was conducted. (The earliest some of this material could be made available—even without delays due to the COVID-19 pandemic, would be the likely year of publication for this book.) The United States has a similar rule, wherein automatic declassification—relevant to StT discourse as it generally pertains to the military—is conducted on a 25-year time frame, such that any currently archived documents would not be available until 2026 (at the earliest).[4] This availability pertains to both physical and online archives.

Given that I am interested in publicly available, not secret, texts, these archival practices do not unduly constrain my analysis. I was able to access sufficient discourse through other means (discussed below). My attempt to work through the archives was a first step, for both efficiency and a means of due diligence—of checking the discourse I collected through other fora. The archives are not likely to contain any information that would shift the results of the study, but they would, if available, make it easier to identify the "universe" of potential documents. Until approximately 2007 or 2008, moreover, materials primarily disseminated online, such as department-specific press releases and statements, were not systematically archived (if at all). The absence of a single, unified database from which to select texts, with potentially relevant data dispersed among a number of online and physical archives in both the United States and the United Kingdom, also placed practical limitations upon searches due to my limited time and capacity for data collection.

I mention these constraints upon data collection primarily for the purposes of pedagogy and to be transparent about the "universe" from which I eventually selected texts. Discourse analysis does not require an exhaustive collection of all potentially relevant documents, nor do its subsequent claims rely upon sampling from a strictly bounded universe of texts. What discourse analysis does rely upon is confidence that the texts examined are plausibly representative of the discourse, its internal variations within a specific time and place, and some sense that meaningful contestation is not inadvertently excluded. Having sourced government discourse from "live" (as of 2011–2016) sites, and subsequently "checked" the texts available online against those archived in the Wayback Machine online internet archive (see below), I am confident that my corpus is representative of the patterns of meaning with StT discourse at the time. It does not systematically exclude analytically or politically significant contestations. The details of the text selection strategy for each case are below.

United Kingdom

I considered Hansard (the transcripts of the House of Lords and House of Commons) to incorporate the legislative branch; press releases and public statements of the Prime Minister's Office and Cabinet Office, to incorporate the executive; and press releases and public documents of the Ministry of Defence to account for the perspective of military officials.

The relevant portions of Hansard were identified by searching the phrase "support our troops" in the archive TheyWorkforYou.com. The site contains the complete legislative record of the United Kingdom but has a more flexible and accurate search function than the official Parliament site.[5] I used the paragraph as the general unit of analysis, but to bolster the strength of the interpretation, I considered the entire speech by each legislator for context. As such, references relating to the general normative relationship between society and the military not picked up by the specific phrase "support our troops," such as "support our armed forces" or "support the troops," were also analyzed.

I sourced the press releases, public statements and documents of the Prime Minister's Office, Cabinet Office, and Ministry of Defence from a number of websites: the live gov.uk Announcements website, the National Archive, the UK Web Archive, and the Wayback Machine (a not-for-profit digital archive). Announcements by the various UK government ministries and departments are centralized and disseminated by the live Announcements gov.uk website,[6] which was searched for the word "troops" (exact phrase searches were not possible on this site), which returned complete results for 2010 back to approximately 2008, with sporadic results for earlier years. This has slight implications for interpreting the frequency of UK government StT discourse, as it's not possible definitely determine whether the greater use of StT discourse from 2008 to 2010 (see Chapter 4) is due to the greater availability of 2008–2010 or a broader increase in StT discourse use at the time. Given that this aligns with the end of the Labour government and beginning of the Conservative government, which invested heavily in the explicit promotion of the armed forces and patriotism, it's reasonable to believe that while some usage from 2001–2007 may be missed, there was also an uptick in StT discourse from 2008 to 2010.

With respect to earlier versions of these websites, I identified the primary Prime Minister's Office (PMO) texts for inclusion using the websites currently archived as Records of the Prime Minister's Office (PREM) by the National Archives.[7] They are held by the UK Web Archive, which preserves important United Kingdom websites (beginning in 2004).[8] These websites—number10.gov, pm.gov.uk, number-10.gov—which linked to the relevant press releases, were keyword searched for the phrase "support the troops." I culled the results to only those referring to the normative relationship between the armed forces and society. Duplicates (of which there were many) were removed. The results provided by the UK Web Archive were subsequently checked (by office, keyword, and URL) against the listings of the UK Government Web Archive.[9] The materials referenced there are the same as those held by the UK Web Archive, but are indexed differently, making triangulated searches possible. Though the results were largely identical, relevant texts excluded by the parameters of the initial search were added to the corpus.

Existing Ministry of Defence records were identified in a similar way, searching all relevant archived URLs indexed in the UK Government Web Archive—mod.uk, https://www.gov.uk/government/organisations/ministry-of-defence, and operations.mod.uk/ with the keywords "support troops,"[10] and subsequently cross-checked with results within the UK Web Archive. Following the same procedure as the PMO records, duplicates and irrelevant results were discarded, and additional results identified were added. Searches of the UK Web Archive's Cabinet Office Archive, and associated pages in the UK Government Web Archive did not reveal any results for the phrases "support our/the troops."

To check for analytically significant excluded texts, I briefly examined the relevant UK government URLs within the nonprofit internet archive the Wayback Machine. Though a limited number of returned results were not encompassed in the existing corpus, the patterns and meanings of usage evident in the newly searched texts reflected those of the previously identified texts. Finally, in light of the sporadic internet archiving and 20(plus)-year archival release rule, I also filed freedom of information requests asking for all public texts utilizing the phrases "support the troops" or "support our troops" with the Cabinet Office/Ministry of Defence and the PMO. As the subsequent responses contained fewer results than those identified via the process described above and only one non-duplicate result, I am confident the compiled corpus is the best-possible representation of publicly available data.

I conducted these cross-checks for the UK government (and all other organizations, as described below) to increase my confidence in the comprehensiveness of the empirics. This detailed discussion of sourcing should not be read as constraining the power of my analysis. Instead, it demonstrates that the study goes above and beyond the methodological and epistemological requirements of typical discourse analysis to most powerfully support those same claims.

United States

For the US government, I incorporated the Congressional Record of the House of Representatives and the Senate (legislature), presidential press releases and public statements produced by the White House (executive), and press releases and public documents of the Ministry of Defense (military). The Department of Veterans' Affairs, though obviously relevant to the military, was excluded, due to both a comparative lack of access and need to manage the volume of relevant documents in the US case study.

For many reasons, including greater population and government size, greater societal awareness of the military, and the longer historical legacy of StT, the sourcing procedures applied to the UK case (where I began my analysis, to offset the US centrism of typical studies of liberal civil-military relations) returned a far larger number of results in the United States. The newspaper stratum, discussed above, for instance, returned approximately as many references to StT as the entire UK case (including all sources). As a result of the sheer time required to digitally identify, collect, and then analyze the data, sampling was required.

The keyword search of "support our troops" (which returned more accurate results than "support the troops") in the Congressional Record on the thomas.gov database returned,[11] for instance, 1,496 results. This count refers to the number of speeches in which the phrase was used, rather than instances of the phrase itself. One search result could include one reference to StT, or multiple—as was more often the case. While the entire universe of congressional references to StT is available, it was time prohibitive (and methodologically unnecessary) to analyze each instance.

I selected 300 search results (approximately the number of results identified in UK Hansard) using a random number generator to identify 20 percent of the results returned *for each year*. This preserves the relative frequency/year of results while ensuring that potential changes in meaning over time are included. The returned results were analyzed in context (by speech). Similar results not highlighted by the specific keyword search (such as "support our armed forces") were also included. The search is a way to identify relevant material, rather than exhaustively encompassing it. I then cross-checked the included results with another randomized sample to ensure that significant patterns of use were not omitted. As the secondary sample closely mirrored the first, the initial sample of the Congressional Record is discursively saturated.

As in the UK, sourcing the documents of the president and Department of Defense, due to the timing of archival accession and sporadic online archiving, was the greatest challenge. For the Bush administration (2001–2008), I sourced executive statements (press briefings, speeches, and other public statements) from the archived White House website, accessible via the George W. Bush Presidential Library website.[12] I searched the site for the terms "support the troops" (196 results) and "support our troops" (687 results). As with the Congressional Record, 20 percent of results for each year were collected using a random number generator (a procedure repeated for each US governmental database). This record was then checked against the Wayback Machine to ensure significant trends were not omitted. For the Obama administration (2009–2010), I used a similar procedure on the WhiteHouse.gov live site,[13] searching for "support our/the troops" and taking 20 percent for each year. I also ran a search of presidential speeches and documents using the LexisNexis database to further triangulate these results. This material, too, was checked against the Wayback Machine.

Statements from the Department of Defense (DoD) were sourced from the live site, defense.gov, using the search terms "support our/the troops," selecting 20 percent of returned results for each year. I also searched this site in the Wayback Machine, as the live site only contained results from 2006 onwards. I also examined the Wayback Machine[14] archive of the defunct DoD site AmericaSupportsYou.mil.[15] I searched the Wayback Machine, as with the NGOs (discussed below), by selecting the most-archived (by number of crawls) in each relevant month (or year, depending on the life of the site). The sampling strategy is based on search criteria rather than returned results due to the structure of the archive (which is not keyword searchable).[16] To further check for potentially relevant material, I also searched the Library of Congress collection of archived websites (searching defense. gov).[17]

Finally, I filed Freedom of Information requests for the relevant documents to the White House and DoD press offices. The requests were filed in May 2014; at time of writing, they have not been processed.[18]

Nongovernmental Organizations (NGOs)

To capture influential articulations of StT outside conventional sources of sociopolitical power, I examined the press releases, public statements/documents, brochures, and websites, and so forth of 10 (per case) key nongovernmental organizations. This includes military-related charitable organizations and prominent peace/antiwar groups (five each). For the UK, I examined Help for Heroes, the Royal British Legion, the Army Benevolent Fund (now The Soldiers' Charity), BLESMA: The Limbless Veterans' Charity, uk4uThanks!, Veterans for Peace UK, Stop the War Coalition, the Campaign for Nuclear Disarmament, the Women's International League for Peace and Freedom (WILPF) UK, and Peace and Social Witness UK. In the US, I looked at Birdies for the Brave, Operation Gratitude/Freedom Alliance, Disabled Veterans of America, Veterans of Foreign Wars, the Iraq and Afghanistan Veterans' Association, Military Families Against the War, ANSWER/United for Peace and Justice, Peace Action, CodePink, and the American Friends' Service Committee.

I selected NGOs using a combination of criteria. NGOs had to possess an approx. £100,000 annual budget, employ at least one staff member, and have registered charitable/advocacy status. I also selected NGOs on the basis of their importance to the overall phenomenon and representation of significant "strands" of StT discourse to reflect the depth and breadth of the discursive formation. With this in mind, I created a typological classification of relevant charitable and military-related NGOs. (The details of this typology, as well as the initial identification of NGOs, are discussed below.) Initially I planned to use the same typology for each country. Closer investigation revealed, however, that particular categories of NGOs were more important in one case than the other. As a result, the final charities included in the study were based on an evaluation of essentiality of particular organizations to each context, the relative importance of typological categorizations, and availability of data.

For each category, I identified and contacted two representative NGOs. I included the organization with the greatest access and/or data availability. (When neither responded, I either replaced the organizations with a third choice or used the online archives of the organization I considered to be more important/representative of that category.) I contacted each organization identified for potential inclusion (at least) three times—by letter and by two follow-up emails. As many NGOs do not undertake systematic record-keeping, many organizations did not respond to any requests or had no records beyond those available online to offer. As such, there is an unavoidable asymmetry in the materials analyzed across organizations. Long-standing and well-institutionalized organizations possess deep physical and online archives, while newer organizations keep no such archives.

As a result, the corpus has a slight lean in terms of the inclusion and volume of material analyzed toward more established organizations. My sense, however, is that this reflects their overall contribution to/prominence within StT discourse, as larger organizations have greater capacity for dissemination. Similarly, much like the government online archives, it is not possible to estimate how much material exists elsewhere (e.g., within internal archives) or no longer exists (due to poor online-archiving practices). The gathered corpus's ability to represent frequency of StT use over time, consequently, must be contextualized via secondary and media sources. Though I've taken all care to source from NGOs as logically and transparently as possible and am confident that no trends are systematically excluded, the discursive mapping is illustrative rather than exhaustive.

Due to the nature of the databases—generally the Wayback Machine, contemporary live sites, and physical archives—where the public statements of these organizations are stored, their materials are not available for keyword search. Similarly, as charitable organizations, unlike the press or politicians, have a branding incentive to generate their niche in the overall StT and/or peace space, they often do not use the literal phrase "support the troops" but a synonym. "Help for Heroes," for instance, as a phrase, mirrors StT in social positioning and meaning, yet the organization rarely invokes StT literally. While I paid close attention to invocations of StT (and "bring them home!" in relation to antiwar groups, which is discussed in Chapter 8), I also incorporated references to the normative relationship between society and the armed forces without the exact phrase.

I searched the current (live) website of each organization, as well as past website "captures" archived in the Wayback Machine. In sourcing the documents for UK NGOs, I looked at every capture of each website to check for relevance. As this proved highly time-consuming and unfruitful in terms of identifying new/diverse material, for the US, I looked at each organization's captures four times/year. As the Wayback Machine notes how many times a particular site was captured—with higher frequencies generating better results—dates with greater captures were selected preferentially. I also analyzed the public texts, statements, brochures and so forth provided by organizations willing/able to facilitate greater access to information—noted in Appendix 2—as well as those available in public archives.

I excluded duplicates unless identical materials were produced and disseminated more than once (i.e., identical flyers in subsequent years). As charitable organizations have a narrower public identity, organizational mission, and branding incentive to create a consistent message, saturation typically occurred within fewer documents/references that that of the press and state documents.

United Kingdom

I identified the military-related charities in the United Kingdom through an initial a search of the UK Charity Commission for all charities listing "promotion of armed forces efficiency" as one of their major goals/aims—arriving at a total of 420 (as of January 2013).[19] These organizations were culled in accordance with the criteria described above. Explicitly local/regional organizations were removed. "Trusts," which primarily distribute money to other organizations and lack a significant public profile and organizations without websites, were also removed.

This left a list of 64 candidates from which to select 5. These organizations were then organized into a typography by organizational purpose: family oriented, care for wounded, morale/care package, service specific, professional/advocacy, direct compensation, commemoration, reintegration/employment, all service (large general aid), and sports/recreation. Many organizations exhibit characteristics that fall into more than one category and were categorized according to their primary function.

Peace/antiwar organizations were harder to identify and sort in this way. As antiwar organizations often have multiple mandates (e.g., promotion of peace and protection of the environment), they lack a unifying descriptor in the UK Charity Commission and are less amenable to keyword search. That said, in contrast to military-related charitable organizations, about which, until very recently, relatively little had been written, there is a large existing literature on the discourse of peace and antiwar organizations. I therefore adapted a typology of peace/antiwar groups similar to that of Coy, Woehrle and Maney, in their 2008 *Social Problems* study of StT discourse and US peace groups. Coy et al. identify nine organization types, primarily by constituency, which I reduced to (an amended) five categories. The organizations selected to fill each typological category were identified via a survey of the existing literature on UK peace/antiwar movements (see Gillan et al. 2011), background consultations with politicians and activists, and a cross-referencing among the links of identified organizations to ensure that no significant organization was initially omitted. This resulted in a list of 23 organizations from which I drew the included 5.

United States

The US also lacks a searchable database for peace and antiwar groups. A 2013 search of the US 501c3 (registered charitable organizations, as classified by the US Internal Revenue Service) database returned 1,903 results for the word "peace" in organizational titles (more sophisticated searches of the database were precluded by weak search functions). This was not only huge but also excluded many significant organizations, such as CodePink, that don't explicitly reference "peace" in their names.[20] As peace/antiwar organizations are often considered advocacy/political NGOs rather than charitable organizations, moreover, they may be considered 501c4 organizations, and not listed in the compiled database.[21]

As in the UK case, I drew on the Coy et al. study (2008). This article provided an initial core of fourteen influential peace/antiwar organizations through which to identify via, again, consultations with activists, archivists, additional secondary literature, and cross-references between organizational websites, further organizations relevant to the US peace/antiwar organization universe. This resulted in the creation of a list of 30 organizations, from which the 5 included in the study were selected in accordance with the modified version of Coy et al.'s 2008 typology.

The selection process for military-related NGOs mirrored that of the UK. The primary exception to this similarity is the fact that as the 501c3 database was only searchable by keyword, rather than category/mission, the official charitable register was less useful in identifying a list of relevant organizations. (A 2013 search of the database revealed the term "troops" retrieves 101 organizations; "hero" 796; "military" 684; "veteran" 2,177, none of which catches those whose titles don't contain those terms, such as the American Legion.)

Instead, I generated an initial list of military-related charitable organizations from an extensive list of DoD registered and approved "community support organizations."[22] While this potentially limited the identification of marginal or dissenting groups, DoD approval is a strong indicator of organizational legitimacy and influence.[23] As the vast majority of military-related charitable organizations consider themselves to be apolitical in character, moreover, there is little reason to believe that major organizations of substantial importance to the StT phenomenon would be systematically excluded. (Many military-related charities also partner with the Ministry of Defence in the UK.)

This list was then culled to eliminate non-national groups and highly specific charities, such as Trees for Troops (which provides Christmas trees to families of serving military personnel)[24] or Sew Much Comfort (which produces adaptive clothing for wounded personnel).[25] I then cross-referenced this list of organizations through webpage linkages and media searches (given the lack of existing secondary literature) to identify potentially relevant organizations not found on the initial DoD list. This resulted in a list of 137 candidate organizations from which the final 5 were selected, following the military NGO typology discussed above. The details of all selected groups and the text sourcing logistics are summarized in Appendix 2.

Ethics and Reflexivity

From the perspective of what might be thought of as conventional research ethics, I encountered few obstacles in this study. I didn't conduct interviews or engage in participant observation; the military is an elite institution of state power. My work and findings do not generate what we might think of as conventional risks of harm to specific—and, particularly, marginalized and/or vulnerable—groups of people. Despite the absence of conventional ethics considerations, I include this section to show the complexities of what may superficially seem like "desk research."

To start with the basics, I am a civilian and I am not American or British. This doesn't disqualify me from undertaking this type of study or offering my assessment of the troubling gendered/ing politics of supporting the troops. But it does place me in an interesting position. For example, throughout my research I was frequently asked (not only by informational gatekeepers, such as archivists or receptionists, but also other scholars, friends, etc.) why, as a civilian, as a woman, as a Canadian, I chose to undertake this work. The question arises from genuine curiosity, not to mention small talk—but also reflects a key assumption of gendered civil-military relations that underlies the book: the martial is the realm of masculine activity and that (ideally combat) veterans are the authoritative source of war and military knowledge.

The questions— or, to be fair, perhaps my interpretation of the questions—were looking for a justification for my interest in the military, usually in the form of a family connection (or, rarely, veteran status myself). I did my best to answer these questions, particularly when related to processes of accessing information, transparently and directly. Since I was asking institutions—the state or NGOs—for copies of documents that were in the public sphere at time of their publication, the project did not raise substantial issues in terms of transparency, data access, privacy, or subsequent use of texts. What it raised was, as alluded to above, some layered interpersonal interactions between me, archivists, NGO staff, activists, and civil servants. There is a fine balance to strike between being forthright about the aim and questions of the research and respecting that its point of interrogation may not be shared by a particular person, organization, or audience. I did not know what my final argument or assessment of archived materials would be (particularly before I saw them). I was clear, however, that my sense was that the politics of StT was (and is) more complex than it is presented to be publicly.

To return to the question that became this reflection, if asked about my connection to the military, I sometimes mentioned that my grandfathers both served in World War II. I have an aunt who served in the Canadian Reserves. I have mixed feelings about this answer. I virtually never told the story from the preface. I also rarely pointed out the assumptions underlying the question. Usually I just talked about research interests.

This line of questioning also speaks to one of the central ethical issues underlying my analysis: the implications of my project for people in the armed forces and their families. The questions about my connection to the military—to check for expertise, for "insider" credentials—are, I think, best read in the context of a widespread, very genuine affective investment in the US and UK militaries.

In other words, people engaged with my work—either due to interest or skepticism—at least partially because they support the troops. Across the US and UK people worry about military personnel (as individual loved ones and an aggregate group); military personnel spend long periods of time away from home, are often wounded, and are sometimes killed. Support the troops comes from worrying about them. I don't find it incongruous to recognize—without endorsing the politics of StT or approving of the invasions of Iraq and Afghanistan—that supporting the troops is a profoundly meaningful personal and community practice. If it wasn't it wouldn't work nearly so well politically.

StT also intersects with race, class, and coloniality, as briefly discussed throughout the book, in complex ways. The way I collected, and examined StT discourse means that my corpus, and much of my analysis, mirrors the universalized/izing tendencies of ideological liberalism. Differences in the motivations for, and terms of service, for communities of color, women, and/or queer people—as well as the way "support" was practiced and experienced by those same groups—do not figure highly in the book. They appear as context, but not a distinct point of interrogation. Though this is in line with my research design, it is a significant critical and political limitation of the study. These differences are important (see for instance Marsical 1991), and I hope future work will take them up.

With regard to the affective politics of StT writ large, the point of critical scholarship is not to ascribe intentionality to individuals' use of and investments in supporting the troops, nor to judge the "appropriateness" of individual feelings of solidarity the troops (or love for friends and family). The entire aim of the book is to see what StT does in the aggregate. As I demonstrate, "the troops" are not synonymous with military personnel. It should be possible to empathetically care for and relate to individual soldiers without upholding the violent, often racist, generally colonial, gendered/ing architecture of liberal political obligation. The objects of critique are powerful state institutions and normative structures of liberal violence, racialized colonial hierarchies, and binary accounts of gender and sexuality, not people themselves.

The stakes of StT are such that the argument must be made (and democratic debate would be improved if the practice stopped). I also recognize that, the specifics of my analysis aside, this may be a hurtful argument to many people who exist in complex relationships to military personnel, deployments, and various forms of grief and loss. (It will also for many others, as indicated by Chapter 8, simply read as offensive, particularly as written by a civilian and noncitizen, but I care less about that.)

This empathy for loss and attentiveness to the complexity of actual social relations in the context of the military, however, is balanced by the project's stakes: the ways solidaristic, gendered feelings of obligation toward collective violence uphold liberal imperial wars abroad. Supporting the troops facilitates the killing of people abroad. Supportive solidarity obscures complicity. The more pressing ethical quandary of this book may well be, then, that in the context of the so-called global war on terror, which created so much harm, suffering, and death in Afghanistan, Iraq, and subsequent theaters, I focus on internal civil-military relations. I center the most powerful actors in my analysis. The self-referential nature of StT discourse, as well as my framing of it in terms of liberal obligation(s), means that the scale and experience of the global war on terror are absent from this book. So are the voices and perspectives of people who were (and continue to be) harmed. This is not a limitation of the study per se—it wasn't designed to address these questions—but it was a choice. My hope is that the connections I've drawn between supporting the troops, normative gender, and complicity within violence of liberal states still speaks to the death and suffering produced (and elided) by the so-called war on terror. But I also think it would be fair to ask questions about whose social relations, lives, and feelings "we" care about (and who I have posited that "we" to be) when examining the (re)production of liberal violence(s).

Summary of Primary Material Data Sources

Table A.1 Newspapers Summary Table

Country	Right of Center	Centrist	Left of Center	Tabloid	Sampling
US	*The Wall Street Journal*	*The Washington Post*	*The New York Times*	N/A	N/A
UK	*The Telegraph* *The Times*	*The Independent* *The Financial Times*	*The Guardian* *The Observer*	*Sun*	N/A

Table A.2 State Documents Summary Table

Country	Government Agency	Database	Keywords	Sampling
UK	**House of Commons and House of Lords**	TheyWorkForYou.com	"support our troops"	N/A
UK	**Office of the Prime Minister**	UK National Archive UK Web Archive UK Government Web Archive Wayback Machine Gov. of UK Announcements (live site) UK government Freedom of Information Request	"support our troops" or "support the troops"	N/A

(*continued*)

Table A.2 Continued

Country	Government Agency	Database	Keywords	Sampling
UK	Ministry of Defence	UK Web Archive UK Government Web Archive Wayback Machine Gov. of UK Announcements (live site) UK government Freedom of Information Request	"support our troops" or "support the troops"	N/A
US	House of Representatives and Senate	Congressional Record (THOMAS.gov)	"support our troops"	20% of all returned results for each year (approx. 300 total)
US	Office of the President	George W. Bush Presidential Library Archive WhiteHouse.gov Wayback Machine Lexis Nexis	"support our troops" or "support the troops"	20% of all returned results for each year, for each database
US	Department of Defense	AmericaSupportsYou.mil Defense.gov OurMilitary.mil	"support the troops" or "support our troops"	20% of all returned results for each year (live site); most-crawled/archived results for Wayback Machine

Table A.3 Military-Related NGOs by Country

Organization Type	United States	United Kingdom
Sports	**Birdies for the Brave** Live site Materials provided by NGO Wayback Machine	N/A
"Morale-raising"/ Care Packages	**Operation Gratitude/** **Freedom Alliance** Live site Materials provided by NGO Wayback Machine	**Uk4uThanks!** Live site Wayback Machine
Wounded	**Disabled Veterans of** **America** Live site Materials provided by NGO Wayback Machine	**BLESMA** Live site Wayback Machine
Service Specific	N/A	**Army Benevolent Fund** (now the Soldiers' Charity) Live site Wayback Machine
All Service	**Veterans of Foreign Wars** Live site Wayback Machine Institutional physical archives	**Royal British Legion** Live site Wayback Machine
Iraq/ Afghanistan-Specific	**Iraq and Afghanistan** **Veterans** Live site Wayback Machine	**Help for Heroes** Live site Wayback Machine

Table A.4 Peace/Antiwar NGOs by Country

Organization Type	United States	United Kingdom
Veteran/Military Associated	**Military Families Against the War** Live site Archived material (Swarthmore Peace Collection) Wayback Machine	**Veterans for Peace UK** Live site Wayback machine
Cyber/Mass Organizing	**ANSWER/United for Peace and Justice** Live site Archived materials (Swarthmore Peace Collection) Wayback Machine	**Stop the War Coalition** Live site Archived materials (Bishopsgate Institute) Wayback Machine
Pacifist	**Peace Action** Live site Archived materials (Swarthmore peace collection Wayback Machine	**Campaign for Nuclear Disarmament** Live site Wayback Machine Personal materials held by activists
Women	**CodePink** Live Site Archived materials (Swarthmore Peace Collection) Wayback Machine	**WILPF UK** Live site Correspondence with archivists Wayback Machine
Religious	**American Friends Service Committee** Live site Archived materials (AFSC archive) Wayback Machine	**Peace and Social Witness UK** Live site Wayback Machine

Notes

Chapter 1

1. When I began this study in 2011, practitioners and academics challenged its premise on these grounds. There was little interesting about supporting the troops from their perspective. It was simply an epiphenomenon of the unpopularity of the war in Iraq. What else, they implied, did I expect? What else were people supposed to do? Great question.
2. The term/category of the "West" is imbued in Othering racialized colonial power dynamics and hierarchies. I use it here to denote the connections between liberalism and the civilizational claims to superiority at work in liberal imaginaries and for its typical association with a particular constellation of states (i.e., the "White Dominions" of the British Empire and Europe).
3. The situation isn't limited to liberal democratic and/or Western societies. In wars with conscription there have generally been more people outside the armed forces than in (Feaver and Gelpi 2011).
4. The terms "liberal" and "democracy" are contested. For the purposes of this project, I use the term "liberal democracy" to refer to states with democratic elections, the rule of law, and individual rights. The critiques made herein apply to these societies as they are rather than an "ideally" liberal society as it may be.
5. Austria, Cyprus, Denmark, Estonia, Lithuania, Finland, Greece, Norway, Sweden, and Switzerland.
6. This is not to say that no strain of liberal thought could ever account for military service—particularly voluntary service. Rather, if we accept this reading of the obligation of military service, it is difficult to reconcile with the ideological commitments of those states generally considered to be practicing, if imperfect, liberal democracies (Jahn 2011).
7. Liberalism is a universalizing (and colonizing) ideology that calls to, and projects itself on, all modern subjects. I use "we" to provide an experience of how supporting the troops may interpolate the reader. It also reflects my positionality as a White settler citizen, highly privileged within the liberal international order. I recognize this use of a shared "we" may also be experienced as alienating by readers from communities against whom liberal violences are directed and/or whose identities are not valued or recognized within the racialized cisheteropatriarchal structures of liberalism. Thank you for engaging with the book anyway. I hope you will yet find something of value.
8. See Appendixes A and B for details on methodology, sourcing, and data collection.
9. Thanks to Eleanor Knott for her guidance for this section.

10. The specific documents were identified by the use of the phrase "support the troops" or variations (e.g., "support our boys") and/or language similarly commenting on the normative civil-military relationship.
11. This period includes the initial invasion of Iraq and the majority of heavy operations in Afghanistan. It captures the "peak" political salience of StT discourse and its initial decline within the US and the ascendance of StT discourse in the UK as attention turned from Iraq to Afghanistan.

Chapter 2

1. This, of course, is not the entire story. The universalism of liberalism was reserved for those meeting the appropriate standard of rationality to count as a potential citizen, excluding women, colonized peoples, and peoples of color for virtual all classical liberals and much of history.
2. The evolution of critical thought on militarism is far more sophisticated than possible to fairly represent here (see Mabee and Vucetic 2018; Rossdale 2019; Stavrianakis and Stern 2018; Eastwood 2018). The critique of militarism as inadvertently legitimating the violences of liberalism I offer here is important in its own right. It is substantially simplified and abbreviated here. In making this argument, it is important to recognize the decades and volumes of feminist security and militarism scholarship—revealing the gendered nature of liberal militarism, the contingent nature of the civil-military divide, the salience of the everyday to the legitimation of liberal violences—to all current critical understandings of liberal violence(s), including mine. As Howell (2018) argues, however, the tight linkages between gender and militarization within this work has, unfortunately, led to a collapse of violence into militarism, with a corresponding inattention to the ways liberalism is also constituted through racialized, classed, colonial, and ablest violence that might exist beyond the normative (and intuitive) bounds of "militarism." Correspondingly she—and I, later in this chapter—argue for a move past the normatively loaded "militarism" toward a more open and relational concept of what Howell calls "martial politics" that I refer to as "discursive martiality." Though this critique is somewhat new, it has also been staged in full elsewhere. For a fuller exegesis, see Howell 2018, 2019; the responses to Howell in the *International Journal of Feminist Politics* in 2019 (Mackenzie et al.), my 2016 book chapter and 2020 *Security Dialogue* article, and Cowen n.d.; Tidy 2019; Stuurman 2020; and Manchanda 2022.
3. Martial politics is a corrective to a strain of predominantly White feminist militarism scholarship that has a tendency to inadvertently reify some of liberalism's positive self-mythologizing, particularly the distinction between civil and military, and violence and politics (Howell 2018, 121).
4. Neglecting the relationship between state violence and chattel slavery, marginalization of disabled people, the extermination and expropriation of Indigenous people also helps maintain the distinction between violence and politics within liberalism,

by denying that these are violences at all. They are, instead, domestic matters of *politics*.

5. Aspects of this discussion are drawn from my 2019(b) article in the *Review of International Studies*.

6. Women of color, obviously, exist at the intersection of the contracts and are thus doubly excluded from the initial workings of the contract. For the relationship between gender and race in contemporary social contract theorizing, see Pateman and Mills 2009.

7. During much of early European conscription, from which many of the romanticized democratic "nations in arms" myths stem, only propertyless men were subject to conscription in actuality. As colonial subjects of color were also frequently subject to conscription, this historical archetype perhaps pertains most directly to elite White officers and governors (Cowen 2008a, 190).

8. Put differently, the "soldiers' contract," as outlined by Schrader, mediates between the social contract, the state, and literal military personnel (2019, 16), while the liberal military contract exists prior to it and, more broadly, refers to the foundational obligation for citizens to engage in violence (i.e., *become* military personnel).

9. The wars of liberal polities have, from colonialism to slavery to the wars of the twentieth century, relied upon the expropriation, oppression, and killing of those peoples—generally of color—who were not (and in many cases, still now are not) regarded as citizens. There is more than one foundational, exclusionary paradox at work in the layered contracts of the liberal polity (see Barkawi 2017 and Chapter 7).

10. The military, as an existing thing, is a matter of politics; its production *as* that thing, reflects the bounds of the political.

11. Though the point is slight, this is what distinguishes my use of discursive martiality from Howell's 2018 "martial politics." I am examining dynamics of violent inclusion and solidarity, whereas Howell is concerned with internal relations of warlike exclusion.

Chapter 3

1. OED, 2018.

2. The many Black soldiers and veterans who served in the Union forces in the Civil War were virtually entirely absent from contemporaneous commemorations—and are not well represented in the popular imaginary of the Civil War today (Grant 2009, 249–50).

3. Nearly 3 million colonial troops also fought for the UK in the Second World War, including just over 1.4 million men from India (the largest volunteer army in history) and 134,000 from other colonies. Though soldiers from the so-called White dominions were to some degree acknowledged in contemporaneous discourse and popular memory, until recently the contributions of imperial soldiers of color were elided. They did not figure greatly into the British imaginary of "domestic" or "British"

civil-military relations as participants. Similarly, soldiers of color did not greatly inform the imagined, heroic British soldier, other than as a point of contrast—or perhaps loyal subject in need of racialized supervision (BBC 2003–2005. See also Parsons 2000; Barkawi 2006).

4. All such subjectivities retained the unmarked hegemonic Whiteness and heterosexuality that characterize the universalized modern European (or Eurocentric) political subject.

5. The oversupply of well-intentioned socks was a matter of (humorous) contention.

6. This romanticized image of a righteous war against uncomplicated evil is not, of course, the entire story. Feminist historians have demonstrated at length the ways in which World War II armed forces engaged in the exploitation of women, sexual violence in conflict, homophobia, racism, and anti-Semitism (Enloe 2020).

7. On the racist origins and implications of military standardized tests, see Howell 2018.

8. The endurance of the martial expectation for young men, however, is seen in the questions these deferrals or National Guard assignments raised for Vietnam-aged US politicians such as George W. Bush, Clinton, Trump, etc. (Schmidt 1988).

9. The *Daily Mirror* toned down its use of jingoistic rhetoric. For the mainstream press, see Shaw 1996, 99–117.

Chapter 4

1. Attempting to parse these utterances into mutually exhaustive, single-meaning categories misrepresents the complexity of the support the troops phenomenon and violates the epistemological assumptions of discourse analysis. See Appendix 1.

2. Including antiwar groups in the StT discursive formation is an analytical and political choice—and not an uncontroversial one. I include antiwar groups alongside pro-military organizations to play out the empirical and, less obviously, political continuities between seemingly opposite articulations of StT discourse and dissent. This was initially done at the research design phase to capture contestation, but subsequent analysis revealed it to instead reiterate the nearly inescapable nature of discourse's demands for support. See Chapter 8.

3. The exception to this is the Liberal Democratic Party's official opposition to the invasion of Iraq—though this quickly transformed into support for the troops once the war began.

4. Those framed as opposing the war and/or actively engaged in protest.

5. Though the "Americans" category captures some references to Americans supporting UK troops, most of this discourse derives from UK newspaper articles discussing American support for US troops or UK actors noting this support approvingly.

6. Elected or aspirant public officials not constructed as representing the state. "Right" and "Left" refer to discourse that explicitly references the political spectrum.

7. Rare exceptions to this are discourses connecting troop support to the experiences of Black communities within the US (see Chapter 5) and discourses connecting pro-troop, antiwar politics to family relationships (see Chapter 8).

8. Labour accounts for the vast majority of these references in the UK, while the Republican Party does so for the US, aligning with their time spent in government during the GWoT.

9. Schoolchildren were provided with materials to organize a Freedom Walk commemorating 9/11 and honoring GWoT soldiers. ASY also arranged for high-profile US celebrities to record messages of support for the troops (and, occasionally, paid appearance fees) (Inspector General 2008).

10. UK polls indicate that in February 2003, 52 percent of Brits opposed the war in Iraq, whereas in the US, the first poll where a majority of Americans indicated disapproval of the war was not registered until June 2005 (Travis and Black 2003; Milibank and Deane 2005).

11. "Don't" captures references that (a) suggest the troops ought not to be supported; (b) satirize mass support for the troops; or (c) accuse someone else of not supporting the troops. See Chapter 8.

12. "Domestic dissent," read as war opposition or, more rarely, opposition to the troops, was also, though much less commonly, constituted as a threat to the troops in the US and UK, generally for its potential to undermine morale. See Chapters 5 and 8.

Chapter 5

1. This chapter draws upon and expands on my 2019 *Security Dialogue* article examining the politics of "the troops" in the United States from 2001 to 2010.

2. The constitution of the troops as "active" was read broadly—as basically any instance in which they were associated with a verb that implied positive agency (e.g., fighting, asking for help) rather than passive existence (e.g., suffering).

3. In the UK, it is approximately three times more common (and nearly twice as common in the US) than the next most frequent activity—asking or thanking for support.

4. This dynamic, like the soldier, is archetypical, rather than representing any actual conditions of ideally unconstrained enlistment by actual individuals.

5. In a cisnormative heteropatriarchal gender order, upon which, I argue liberalism rests, this is figuratively true. "Everyone" is captured by this twinned dynamic of explicitly inclusive empirical sex/gender and relational gendering of the troops-society relationship. Nonbinary and genderqueer people and subjectivities, however, are excluded from this frame. They are not currently intelligible within a naturalized sexually dimorphic gender order as either a broad social structure or military policy. The US military, in its halting efforts toward (and then away from, and back toward again) greater equality for trans service members, has, thus far, explicitly eschewed policies that recognize nonbinary sex/gender, instead forcing personnel to identify

as male or female. In the UK, the terms of military service for nonbinary and gender-queer people are unclear; service by trans people is legally recognized and protected, but nonbinary gender identity specifically does not yet have legal status in the UK. Genderqueer, nonbinary, and gender fluid people are able to serve in the UK military but are subject to declaring their sex/gender for the purposes of billeting and dress, etc. (see Belkin 2017; UK Ministry of Defence 2019; Embser-Herbert 2017).

6. Insofar, again, as service members express trans identities that can be made to sit neatly with the military's ideological and institutional reliance on the cisnormative heteropatriarchal sex/gender binary (Belkin 2017).

7. Though approximately 7.5 percent of the UK armed forces identify as "Black and minority ethnic" (BAME), most of these soldiers are not UK born, instead, they are members of Commonwealth states, such as Fiji (Government of the United Kingdom 2019; Greene 2016).

8. There are many instances wherein this universalized, White Western male subject-soldier does not hold empirically (Kuntsman 2008). The diplomat-soldier, or migrant-soldier, or queer-soldier, however, continues to refer to a universalized, indi-viduated figure that, in turn, continues to legitimate the state as the purveyor of vio-lence (Ware 2010).

Chapter 6

1. The obverse of this belief, that the warrior is inseparable from the war, typifies com-munitarian StT discourse and is discussed in the next section.

2. MacLeish reads this dynamic as akin to Marcel Mauss's gift, wherein military service is "given" by soldiers to civilians but cannot be reciprocated, producing social disloca-tion and normative discomfort (2013).

3. During the GWoT, the UK government changed its previous recommendation against wearing military uniforms off-duty (a reaction to IRA-related safety concerns in the 1970s and 1980s) to encourage uniforms in public to raise the profile of the army (BBC 2013).

4. A *Washington Post* article notes that "warrior" has become a common form of ad-dress within the US military, giving the example of an automatic message sent by a Marine public affairs officer: "Warriors, I will be out of the office until Monday" (Henderson 2007).

5. It also conveys imperial nostalgia in referencing a time characterized by British co-lonial preeminence and "unproblematic" gender roles, when men went to war and women worked on the home front.

6. For more on the subjectification of military personnel within charitable StT dis-course, see Millar 2016a.

7. Similar patterns also characterize UK StT discursive formation—the iterated nature of the column just makes it the simplest illustration of the politics.

8. Bacevich (2005, 108) makes a similar point, arguing that "support for" has replaced "service with" as the standard of good US citizenship. What I contend is that while this is commonly read as passive or apathetic, support ought to be understood as active, participatory, and political.

Chapter 7

1. I'm basically using a Weberian ideal-type of solidaristic relations of group formation under violence, concretized into the heuristic example of small-unit combat cohesion, and then comparing it to the messier dynamics at work in supporting the troops in order to simplify the argument.
2. Stahl (2009, 558) makes a similar point but locates it in the citizen's willingness to "authorize state violence," rather than a form of apoliticized military participation.
3. By "the political," I refer to the "establishment of that very social order which sets out a particular, historically specific account of what counts as politics and defines other areas of social life as not politics" (Edkins 1999, 2).
4. The global/transnational character of the antiwar movement is well-established. On links between the US, UK, and Australian peace movements in post-9/11 era, see Gillan and Pickerill 2008.
5. New Zealand did not to generate a significant StT movement during the GWoT, an interesting avenue for future work.
6. See Pateman and Mills 2009, Chap. 2.
7. On the racialized production of civilian support for martial actors in the GWoT, see Millar 2020 and Grove 2019.
8. This uneven distribution of political membership is also reflected in the warping of liberal understandings of multiculturalism during the GWoT. As argued by Youngs (2010 934–45), counterterrorism policies and Islamophobic discourses positioned Muslim citizens not as contingent members of the liberal polity. Their ability to "opt out" of enmity, in a manner similar to the generation of "deservingness" by racialized military personnel earlier, was conditioned upon an acceptance of surveillance, a disavowal of "extremism," and a willingness to be instrumentalized in a civilizational narrative of liberal pluralism.

Chapter 8

1. In 2001 BBC Worldservice presenters did not wear poppies on the rationale that Remembrance Day was UK specific and the emblem was inappropriate for an international audience. Subsequent criticism argued British heroism ought to be projected to the world (Wells 2001).
2. The inclusion of Toby Keith performance of a song called "I Raq and I Roll" in the program likely didn't help (Montgomery 2005).

3. It is also a way of refusing queerness, as in relation to politics; the civilian is constituted as simultaneously a normatively masculine martial actor and as an always-already suspicious source of potential feminized/izing betrayal. It is a refusal of the blurring of civil/military and masculine/feminine.

4. Given the opprobrium attached to democratic processes during the GWoT, it's not surprising that this form of obligation, which left open space to blame conventionally authoritative, agential masculinized/citizens for the wars, was by far the least common among antiwar groups.

5. In the US, this was the favored phrase of United for Peace and Justice, Military Families Speak Out, and CodePink. In the UK, the Stop the War Coalition (and associated group Military Families Against the War) and CND were substantial proponents of the call to "bring them home."

6. The politicized grief of military mothers during the GWoT is an example of broader maternal antiwar activism and/or pacifism. This form of political mobilization instrumentalizes essentialist sex/gender roles—and women's association with mothering and peace—to resist state violence in the name of their children. For more on material pacifism, see Tidy 2015b, Tidy 2016; Ase et al 2019; Managhan 2011a, Managhan 2012; Knudson 2009; Leitz 2014, Liddington 1991; Foss and Domenici 2014, among others.

7. Military personnel's opinions on and relationships to StT discourses and associated heroizing practices bears further and future study.

8. It also underlines the continued salience of homophobia as a strategy of insult and denigration in the United States. None of those whose funerals were protested identified as LGBTQ+ (though that, of course, is beside the point) in Brouwer and Hess 2007, 70.

9. I make this point in relation to the construction of the WBC and its implications for general resistance to StT, not to validate the group's politics or positions. The WBC is homophobic, transphobic, Islamophobic, anti-Semitic, and anti-Catholic and characterized as a hate group by the Southern Poverty Law Centre (Wing 2013).

Chapter 9

1. The logic of depoliticization via valorization seen in StT also characterizes moves to recognize health workers during COVID-19. Calls to "Clap for Heroes" once again transformed an issue of public concern and political exigency (then, war, now, a pandemic) into a matter of privatized, individuated affection and solidarity. Not dissimilar to soldiers, health workers are made exploitable and disposable via heroization.

Appendix 1

1. Thanks to Eleanor Knott for her help framing this section (and general epistemological therapy).

2. For the left-right placement of US mainstream media: The Pew Research Center, "Ideological Placement of Each Source's Audience," October 20, 2014, available online at http://www.journalism.org/2014/10/21/political-polarization-media-habits/pj_14-10-21_mediapolarization-08/. For the political orientation of UK mainstream media: Stoddard, Katy, "Newspaper Support in UK General Elections," *The Guardian*, May 4, 2010, http://www.theguardian.com/news/datablog/2010/may/04/general-election-newspaper-support.

3. The National Archives, "Twenty-Year Rule," Government of the United Kingdom, https://www.nationalarchives.gov.uk/about/our-role/transparency/20-year-rule/.

4. The US Department of Justice, "Declassification: Frequently Asked Questions," http://www.justice.gov/open/declassification/declassification-faq. The sporadic availability of such press releases, speeches, and statements was confirmed by archivists at the US National Archive, which has not yet accessioned the relevant records. (Personal communication, September 17 and 18, 2014.)

5. See TheyWorkForYou.com, "Home"; and the Parliament of the United Kingdom, "Hansard," http://www.parliament.uk/business/publications/hansard/

6. Government of the United Kingdom, "Announcements," https://www.gov.uk/government/announcements?departments[]=ministry-of-defence.

7. UK National Archive, "PREM – Records of the Prime Minister's Office," http://discovery.nationalarchives.gov.uk/browse/r/h/C1512.

8. UK Web Archive, "Home," http://www.webarchive.org.uk/ukwa/.

9. The National Archives, "UK Government Web Archive: Home," http://www.nationalarchives.gov.uk/webarchive/.

10. Due to technical difficulties in the UK Government Web Archive search functions at the time the research was conducted, a search for the exact phrase "support the troops" was not possible. I searched for texts containing "support" and "troops" and then culled according to the rules discussed earlier.

11. The Library of Congress, "THOMAS," http://thomas.loc.gov/home/thomas.php.

12. George W. Bush Presidential Library, "The White House" (archived 2009), http://georgewbush-whitehouse.archives.gov/.

13. White House, "The White House: President Barack Obama," https://www.whitehouse.gov/, now the Obama presidential library online: https://www.archives.gov/findingaid/presidential-library-explorer/list/bho.

14. The Library of Congress directs researchers to the Wayback Machine for some of its contracted records preservation. Library of Congress, "Webarchiving FAQs," http://www.loc.gov/webarchiving/faq.html#faqs_04.

15. See, e.g., AmericaSupportsYou.mil, "About Us," archived January 9, 2008, http://web.archive.org/web/20080109011111/http://www.americasupportsyou.mil/americasupportsyou/.

16. Given the amount of time I spent manually checking online archives, if another scholar were to attempt a similarly comprehensive discourse analysis, I'd recommend learning to code and webscrape. The method I used was up to the task, but given improvements in the digital tools available, there is a simpler (and much, much faster) way to go about the logistics of data collection.

17. Library of Congress web archive, http://loc.gov/websites/collections/. Particularly the Department of Defense Community Relations archive, http://webarchive.loc.gov/all/*/www.ourmilitary.mil/.

18. Though they do send me a nice email every once and a while telling me they're still working on it.

19. Government of the United Kingdom, "The Charity Commission," https://www.gov.uk/government/organisations/charity-commission.

20. These results were generated at the time of sourcing, in 2013. As of 2015, the Internal Revenue Service no longer publishes a list of 501c3 organizations or supports a searchable online database. Internal Revenue Service, "Search for Charities," http://www.irs.gov/Charities-&-Non-Profits/Search-for-Charities.

21. For the distinction between 501c3 and 501c4 organizations in the US tax code, please see ProPublica, "Many Types of Nonprofits," https://projects.propublica.org/nonprofits/ctypes.

22. Department of Defense, "Community Support Organizations," http://www.ourmilitary.mil/comprehensive-list-of-community-support-groups.

23. For the DoD criteria for NGO approval, see Department of Defense, "Criteria for Listed Organizations," http://www.ourmilitary.mil/comprehensive-list-of-community-support-groups.

24. Christmas Spirit Foundation, "Trees for Troops," http://www.christmasspiritfoundation.org/dnn/default.aspx#&panel1-7.

25. Sew Much Comfort, "Home," http://www.sewmuchcomfort.org/.

Bibliography

Abramowitz, Michael, and Robin Wright. 2007. "Bush to Add 21,500 Troops in an Effort to Stabilize Iraq." *Washington Post*. January 11. http://www.washingtonpost.com/wpdyn/content/article/2007/01/10/AR2007011002437.html.

Abramson, N. 2014. "Wasting My Time in the Waiting Line: Solutions for Improving the Afghanistan and Iraq Special Immigrant Visa Programs." *Virginia Journal of International Law*. 55, no.2: 483–522.

Achter, Paul. 2010. "Unruly Bodies: The Rhetorical Domestication of Twenty-First-Century Veterans of War." *Quarterly Journal of Speech*. 96, no.1: 46–68.

Adams, Michael. 1994. *The Best War Ever: America and World War II*. Baltimore: Johns Hopkins Press.

Adams, Michael. 1998. "The 'Good War' Myth and the Cult of Nostalgia." *Midwest Quarterly*. 40, no.1: 59–74.

Agerholm, Harriet. 2017. "British Army Targets Recruitment of Young Working Class, Military Document Reveals." *Independent*. July 10. https://www.independent.co.uk/news/british-army-targets-young-working-class-recruitment-military-marketing-drive-campaign-uk-a7833086.html.

Agostino, Katerina. 1998. "The Making of Warriors: Men, Identity and Military Culture." *Journal of Interdisciplinary Gender Studies*. 3, no.2: 560–75.

Al-Jazeera. 2021. "Where Does the World Stand on Afghan Refugees? Al-Jazeera. August 19, 2021. https://www.aljazeera.com/news/2021/8/18/which-countries-will-take-in-afghan-refugees-and-how-many.

Ali, Tariq. 2005. *Rough Music: Blair/Bombs/Baghdad/London/Terror*. London: Verso.

Alison, Aimee, and David Solnit. 2007. *Army of None: Strategies to Counter Military Recruitment, End War and Build a Better World*. London: Seven Stories Press.

Alito, Samuel. 2011. "Dissent: Supreme Court of the United States Albert Snyder, Petitioner V. Fred W. Phelps, Sr., et al." March 2. https://www.law.cornell.edu/supct/html/09-751.ZD.html.

Alves, Jaime Amparo. 2018. *The Anti-Black City: Police Terror and Black Urban Life in Brazil*. Minneapolis: University of Minnesota Press.

American Friends Service Committee. (AFSC). 2016. "Counter-Recruitment." http://afsc.org/resource/counter-recruitment.

America Supports You. 2004. "Homepage." AmericaSupportsYou.mil. November 28. http://web.archive.org/web/20041128011845/http://www.americasupportsyou.mil/.

America Supports You. 2008. "About Us." AmericaSupportsYou.mil. January 9. http://web.archive.org/web/20080109011111/http://www.americasupportsyou.mil/americasupportsyou/.

America Supports You. 2005. "Show Your Support." AmericaSupportsYou.mil. 28 September. https://web.archive.org/web/20050928202114/http://americasupportsyou.mil/americasupportsyou/support/help.html.

American Legion. N.d. "Blue Star Banner." https://www.legion.org/troops/bluestar.

Amin-Khan, Tariq. 2012. "New Orientalism, Securitisation and the Western Media's Incendiary Racism." *Third World Quarterly*. 33, no.9: 1595–610.

Anderson, Benedict. 2006. *Imagined Communities: Reflections on the Origin and Spread of Nationalism*. London: Verso Books.

Anderson, Zoe. 2011. "Empire's Fetish: Sexualised Nationalism and Gendering of the Falklands War." *National Identities*. 13, no.2: 189–204.

Anheuser-Busch. 2017. "Budweiser Sets Goal of Raising $1 Million for Folds of Honor via Limited Edition Patriotic Packaging." May 23. https://www.anheuser-busch.com/newsroom/2017/05/budweiser-sets-goal-of-raising--1-million-for-folds-of-honor-via.html.

Applebome, Peter. 2004. "Ensuring Wounded Troops the Comfort of Family." *New York Times*. December 19.

Armed Forces Covenant. N.d. "Support and Advice: Businesses." https://www.armedforcescovenant.gov.uk/support-and-advice/businesses/.

Armed Forces Press Service. 2008. "'Very Important Patriots' Recognized for Efforts." October 15. https://web.archive.org/web/20081112113900/http://www.americasupportsyou.mil/AmericaSupports You/Content.aspx?ID=44987705&SectionID=1.

Army Benevolent Fund [The Soldier's Charity] (ABF). 2003. "Homepage." June 21. http://web.archive.org/web/20030621060723/http://www.armybenfund.org/.

Army Benevolent Fund [The Soldier's Charity] (ABF). 2007. "BABFA Launches in US." June 22. http://web.archive.org/web/20070622011928/http://www.armybenfund.org/news_pages/BABFAlaunc h.html.

Army Doctrine Publication. 2000. "Vol. 5: Soldiering—The Military Covenant." February. DGD&D/18/34/71, Army Code No. 71642.

Asad, Talal. 2007. *On Suicide Bombing*. New York: Columbia University Press.

Asal, Victor, Conrad, Justin, and Toronto, Nathan, 2017. "I Want You! The Determinants of Military Conscription." *Journal of Conflict Resolution*. 61, no.7: 1456–81.

Åse, Cecilia, Monica Quirico, and Maria Wendt. 2019. "Gendered Grief: Mourners' Politicisation of Military Death." In *Gendering Military Sacrifice* edited by Åse, Cecilia and Maria Wendt, 145–76. Abingdon: Routledge.

Ashe, Fidelma. 2007. *The New Politics of Masculinity: Men, Power and Resistance*. Routledge.

Ashley, Richard. 1988. "Untying the Sovereign State: A Double Reading of the Anarchy Problematique." *Millennium*. 17, no.2: 227–62.

Ashley, Richard. 1989. "Living on Border Lines: Man, Poststructuralism, and War." In *International/Intertextual Relations: Postmodern Readings of World Politics*, edited by James Der Derian and Michael J. Shapiro. 259–321. Lexington: Lexington Books.

Associated Press. 2003. "Supporters of Iraq War Stage Rallies." *Washington Post*. March 24. A25.

Bacevich, Andrew. 2005. *The New American Militarism: How Americans Are Seduced by War*. Oxford: Oxford University Press.

Baker, Catherine. 2018. *Unsung Heroism?: Show Business and Social Action in Britain's Military Wives Choir(s)*. London: Routledge.

Baker, Catherine, Victoria Basham, Sarah Bulmer, Harriet Gray, and Alexandra Hyde. 2016. "Encounters with the Military: Toward a Feminist Ethics of Critique?" *International Feminist Journal of Politics*. 18, no.1: 140–54.

Baker, Mona. 2010. "Interpreters and Translators in the War Zone: Narrated and Narrators." *The Translator*. 16, no.2: 197–222.

Barkawi, Tarak. 2006. "Culture and Combat in the Colonies: The Indian Army in the Second World War." *Journal of Contemporary History*. 41, 325–55.

Barkawi, Tarak. 2011. "From War to Security: Security Studies, the Wider Agenda, and the Fate of the Study of War. Millennium." *Millennium: Journal of International Studies*. 39, no.3: 701–16.

Barkawi, Tarak. 2017. *Soldiers of Empire*. Cambridge: Cambridge University Press.

Barkawi, Tarak, and Mark Laffey, eds. 2001. *Democracy, Liberalism, and War: Rethinking the Democratic Peace Debate*. Boulder: Lynne Rienner.

Barrett, Frank. 1996. "The Organizational Construction of Hegemonic Masculinity: The Case of the US Navy." *Gender, Work & Organization*. 3, no.3: 129–42.

Basham, Victoria. 2009a. "Effecting Discrimination: Operational Effectiveness and Harassment in the British Armed Forces." *Armed Forces and Society*. 35, no.4: 728–44.

Basham, Victoria. 2009b. "Harnessing Social Diversity in the British Armed Forces: The Limitations of 'Management' Approaches." *Commonwealth & Comparative Politics*. 47, no.4: 411–29.

Basham, Victoria. 2013. *War, Identity and the Liberal States: Everyday Experiences of the Geopolitical in the Armed Forces*. Abingdon: Routledge.

Basham, Victoria. 2016. "Gender, Race, Militarism and Remembrance: The Everyday Geopolitics of the Poppy." *Gender, Place & Culture*. 23, no.6: 883–96.

Basham, Victoria. 2018. "Liberal Militarism as Insecurity, Desire and Ambivalence: Gender, Race and the Everyday Geopolitics of War." *Security Dialogue*. 49, no.1–2: 32–43.

Batalova, Jeanne. 2008. "Immigrants in the U.S. Armed Forces in 2008." Migration Policy Institute. May 15. https://www.migrationpolicy.org/article/immigrants-us-armed-for ces-2008

BBC. 1999. "UK Military Gay Ban Illegal." September 27. http://news.bbc.co.uk/1/hi/uk/ 458625.stm

BBC. 2003. "Anti-War Rally Makes Its Mark." February 19. http://news.bbc.co.uk/1/hi/ uk/2767761.stm.

BBC. 2003–2005. "WW2 People's War: Timeline 1939–1945." https://www.bbc.co.uk/hist ory/ww2peopleswar/timeline/factfiles/nonflash/a6651218.shtml.

BBC. 2006. "First Veterans' Day Takes Place." June 27. http://news.bbc.co.uk/1/hi/uk/ 5119404.stm.

BBC. 2009a. "UK Ends Military Operations in Iraq." April 30. http://news.bbc.co.uk/2/hi/ uk/8026136.stm.

BBC. 2009b. "Helicopter Shortage a 'Scandal.'" July 19. http://news.bbc.co.uk/1/hi/uk_p olitics/8157978.stm.

BBC. 2010. "David Cameron Launches Tory 'Big Society' Policy." July 19. http://www.bbc. co.uk/news/uk-10680062.

BBC. 2011a. "UK Military Deaths in Afghanistan." October 5. http://www.bbc.co.uk/ news/uk-10634173.

BBC. 2013. "Woolwich Attack Will Not Stop Soldiers Wearing Uniforms." May 23. http:// www.bbc.co.uk/news/uk-22642441.

BBC. 2015. "Iraq Profile—Timeline." August 1. http://www.bbc.com/news/world-mid dle-east-14546763.

BBC. 2016. "Women to Serve in Close Combat Roles in the British Military." July 6. http:// www.bbc.co.uk/news/uk-36746917.

BBC. 2018. "Armed Forces: Recruits Don't Need to Have Lived in Britain." November 5. https://www.bbc.co.uk/news/uk-46092838.

Beamish, Thomas D. et al. 1995. "Who Supports the Troops? Vietnam, the Gulf War, and the Making of Collective Memory." *Social Problems*. 42, no.320: 344–60.

Beckford, Martin. 2012. "One in Ten Members of Armed Forces Was Born Abroad." *The Telegraph*. October 1. https://www.telegraph.co.uk/news/uknews/defence/9577167/One-in-ten-members-of-Armed-Forces-was-born-abroad.html.

Belkin, Aaron. 2017. "Queerly Misguided Decisions (Not) to Collude with the Imperial State Are (Not) Straightforward." Unpublished working paper.

Bell, D. S. 2003. "Mythscapes: Memory, Mythology, and National Identity." *The British Journal of Sociology*. 54, no.1: 63–81.

Bell, Duncan. 2014. "What is liberalism?." *Political Theory*. 42, no.6: 682–715.

Bell, Duncan. 2016. *Reordering the World: Essays on Liberalism and Empire*. Princeton: Princeton University Press.

Bell, Vikki. 1999. "Mimesis as Cultural Survival: Judith Butler and Anti-Semitism." *Theory, Culture and Society*. 16, no.2: 133–61.

Ben-Ari, Eyal. 2004. "The Military and Militarization in the United States." *American Ethnologist*. 31, no.3: 340–48.

Berinsky, Adam et al. 2011. "Revisiting Public Opinion in the 1930s and 1940s." *PS: Political Science & Politics*. 44, no.3: 515–20.

Berlant, Lauren. 1997. *The Queen of America Goes to Washington City: Essays on Sex and Citizenship*. Durham: Duke University Press.

Best, Geoffrey. 1998. *War and Society in Revolutionary Europe 1770–1870*. Guernsey: McGill-Queen's University Press.

Bhambra, Gurminder. 2007. *Rethinking Modernity: Postcolonialism and the Sociological Imagination*. New York: Springer.

Biden, Jill. 2009. "It's as Simple as Saying 'Thanks.'" Whitehouse.gov. https://www.whitehouse.gov/blog/2009/07/09/it-can-be-simple-saying-thanks.

Bigo, Didier, and Anastassia Tsoukala. 2008. "Understanding (In)Security." In *Terror, Insecurity, and Liberty: Illiberal Practices of Liberal Regimes After 9/11*, edited by Didier Bigo and Anatassia Tsoukala. 1–9. Abingdon: Routledge.

Billig, Michael. 1995. *Banal Nationalism*. London: Sage Publications Ltd.

Blachford, Kevin. 2020. "Liberal Militarism and Republican Restraints on Power: The Problems of Unaccountable Interventions for American Democracy." *Critical Military Studies*, 1–16.

BLESMA (Blind and Limbless Ex-Servicemen's Association). 2008. "2007 Annual Report." April 23.

BLESMA (Blind and Limbless Ex-Servicemen's Association). 2016. "Our History." https://blesma.org/about-us/our-history/.

Blieseman de Guevara, Berit. 2016. "Myth in International Politics: Ideological Delusion and Necessary Fiction." In *Myth and Narrative in International Politics: Interpretive Approaches to the Study of IR* edited by Berit Blieseman de Guevara, 15–47. Basingstoke: Palgrave MacMillan.

Bond, Brian. 1998. *War and Society in Europe 1870–1970*. Guernsey: McGill-Queen's University Press.

Boon, Kevin Alexander. 2005. "Heroes, Metanarratives, and the Paradox of Masculinity in Contemporary Western Culture." *The Journal of Men's Studies*. 13, no.3: 301–12.

Boose, Linda. 1993. "Techno-Muscularity and the 'Boy Eternal': From the Quagmire to the Gulf." In *Gendering War Talk*, edited by M. Cooke and A. Woollacott. 67–101. Princeton: Princeton University Press.

Born, Hans. 2006. "Democratic Control of Armed Forces." In *Handbook of the Sociology of the Military*, edited by Giuseppe Caforio and Marina Nuciari, 151–65. Boston: Springer.

Boyer, Peter J. 2003. "The New War Machine Tommy Franks and the Military's Future." *New Yorker*, 54–71. June.

Bradner, Eric. 2015. "U.S. Military Opens Combat Positions to Women." CNN. December 3. http://edition.cnn.com/2015/12/03/politics/u-s-military-women-combat-positions/.

Bremner, Robert H. 1988. *American Philanthropy*. Chicago: University of Chicago Press.

Brighton, Shane. 2011. "Three Propositions on the Phenomenology of War." *International Political Sociology*. 5, no1: 101–4.

Bristol Douglas W., Jr., and Heather Marie Stur, eds. 2017. *Integrating the US Military: Race, Gender, and Sexual Orientation since World War II*. Baltimore: Johns Hopkins University Press.

Brothers, Carolyn. 1996. *War and Photography: A Cultural History*. London: Routledge.

Brouwer, Daniel, and Aaron Hess. 2007. "Making Sense of 'God Hates Fags' and 'Thank God for 9-11': A Thematic Analysis of Milbloggers' Responses to Reverend Fred Phelps and the Westboro Baptist Church." *Western Journal of Communication*. 71, no.1: 69–90.

Brown, Larissa. 2015. "Top brass echo Harry's call to bring back National Service: Former Army chiefs say reintroduction would 'benefit' the country." *Daily Mail*. 18 May. https://www.dailymail.co.uk/news/article-3085652/Top-brass-echo-Harry-s-call-bring-National-Service-Former-Army-chiefs-say-reintroduction-benefit-country.html.

Brown, Melissa. T. 2012. *Enlisting Masculinity: The Construction of Gender in US Military Recruiting Advertising During the All-Volunteer Force*. Oxford: Oxford University Press.

Brown, Wendy L. 1998. *Manhood and Politics: A Feminist Reading in Political Theory*. London: Rowman and Littlefield.

Bunning, Jim. 2007. Departments of Transportation, Housing and Urban Development and Related Agencies Appropriations Act. US Congressional Record. September 11. S11372. Thomas.loc.gov.

Burns, Conrad. 2003. Honoring Our Armed Forces. US Senate Congressional Record. April 3.

Burrell, Ian. 2003. "Morgan's Dilemma." *The Independent*. April 8.

Bush, George W. 2001. "Address to the Nation on Homeland Security from Atlanta." *Government Publishing Office*. November 8. Weekly Compilation of Presidential Documents. 37, no.45: 1614–18. Available at: https://www.govinfo.gov/content/pkg/WCPD-2001-11-12/html/WCPD-2001-11-12-Pg1614.htm.

Butler, Judith. 1990. *Gender Trouble*. New York: Routledge.

Butler, Judith. 2006. *Precarious Life: The Power of Mourning and Violence*. London: Verso.

Butterworth, Michael, and Stormi Moskal. 2009. "American Football, Flags, and 'Fun': The Bell Helicopter Armed Forces Bowl and the Rhetorical Production of Militarism." *Communication, Culture & Critique*. 2: 411–33.

Cahn, Dianna. 2016. "Experts: Military has Uphill Battle Against Sexual Assault, Harassment and Hazing." *Stars and Stripes*. April 26. https://www.stripes.com/news/us/experts-military-has-uphill-battle-against-sexual-assault-harassment-and-hazing-1.406397

Calhoun, Craig. 1993. "Nationalism and Civil Society: Democracy, Diversity and Self-Determination." *International Sociology* 8, no.4: 387–411.

Campaign Against the War flyer, dated 10 Wednesday 1990, provided by Jeremy Corbyn, MP, from his personal files.

Campaign for Nuclear Disarmament (CND). 2003. "CND Sadness over Casualties." March 21. http://web.archive.org/web/20030418155937/http://www.cnduk.org/press2/press133.htm.

Campaign for Nuclear Disarmament (CND). 2004. "Homepage." May 21. http://web.archive.org/web/20040521045542/http://www.cnduk.org/.

Campaign for Nuclear Disarmament (CND). 2007. "National Demonstration to Call for 'No Trident' and 'Troops Out of Iraq.'" February 22. http://www.cnduk.org/cnd-media/item/67-national-demonstration-to-call-for-no-trident-and-troops-out-of-iraq.

Campaign for Nuclear Disarmament (CND). 2009. "Afghanistan Demo? Bring the Troops Home." October 27. http://www.cnduk.org/component/k2/item/765-afghanistan-demo-?-bring-the-troops- home?qh=YTozOntpOjA7czo2OiJ0cm9vcHMiO2k6 MTtzOjc6Iid0cm9vcHM.

Campaign for Nuclear Disarmament (CND). 2010. "CND Calls for Troops Out of Afghanistan as NATO Leaders Debate the War." November 2. http://www.cnduk.org/cnd-media/item/1046-cnd-calls-for-troops-out-of-afghanistan-as-nato-leaders-debate-the-war.

Campbell, David. 1992. *Writing Security: United States Foreign Policy and the Politics of Identity.* Minneapolis: University of Minnesota Press.

Card, David, and Thomas Lemieux. 2001. "Going to College to Avoid the Draft: The Unintended Legacy of the Vietnam War." *American Economic Review.* 91, no.2: 97–102.

Carpenter, Les. 2015. "Report Highlights the Obscene Price of NFL's Paid Patriotism." *The Guardian.* November 15. http://www.theguardian.com/sport/blog/2015/nov/05/report-highlights-the-obscene-price-of-nfls-paid-patriotism.

Carruthers, Susan L. 2011. *The Media at War.* London: Macmillan.

Carter, April. 1998. "Liberalism and the Obligation to Military Service." *Political Studies.* 46, no.1: 68–81.

Castle, Stephen. 1991. "Parties Hold the Line on Land War." *Independent on Sunday.* (24 February).

Ceadel, Martin. 1987. *Thinking About Peace and War.* Oxford: Oxford University Press.

Ceadel, Martin. 2009. "The Pacifisms of the Peace Movement." In *Pacifism's Appeal.* 63–80. Cham: Palgrave Macmillan.

Césaire, Aimé. 2001. *Discourse on Colonialism.* New York: New York University Press.

Chalabi, Mona. 2017. "Over a Third of Enlisted US Military Personnel Are Racial Minorities." *The Guardian.* October 19. https://www.theguardian.com/news/datablog/2017/oct/19/us-military-personnel-race-minorities-data.

Chambers, Luke. 2014. "Afghanistan: The Public Verdict." YouGov. April 4. https://yougov.co.uk/topics/politics/articles-reports/2014/04/04/afghanistan-final-verdict.

Chan, Sue. 2003. "Massive Anti-War Outpouring." CBS News. https://www.cbsnews.com/news/massive-anti-war-outpouring/.

Choi, Seung-Whang, and Patrick James. 2003. "No Professional Soldiers, No Militarized State Disputes?: A New Question for Neo-Kantianism." *Journal of Conflict Resolution.* 47, no.6: 796–816.

Chomsky, Noam. 2002. *Media Control: The Spectacular Achievements of Propaganda.* Vol. 7. New York: Seven Stories Press.

CIA World Factbook. N.d. "Military Service Age and Obligation." CIA. https://www.cia.gov/the-world-factbook/field/military-service-age-and-obligation/.

Clymer, Adam, 1991. "WAR IN THE GULF: Public Opinion; Poll Finds Deep Backing While Optimism Fades." *New York Times*. January 22. http://www.nytimes.com/1991/01/22/us/war-in-the-gulf-public-opinion-poll-finds-deep-backing-while-optimism-fades.html.

CNN. 2001. "You Are Either with Us or Against Us." November 6. http://edition.cnn.com/2001/US/11/06/gen.attack.on.terror/.

Coates, Ta-Nehisi. 2011. "I Support Some of the Troops . . ." *The Atlantic*. September 23. https://www.theatlantic.com/national/archive/2011/09/i-support-some-of-the-troops/245561/.

Cockburn, Cynthia. 2000. "The Anti-Essentialist Choice: Nationalism and Feminism in the Interaction Between Two Women's Projects." *Nations and Nationalism*. 6 no.4: 611–29.

CodePink (CP). 2004. "Four Activists Arrested During Mayor Bloomberg's 'NYC Welcomes the Protestors' Press Conference." August 18. http://www.codepinkalert.org/Press_Room_Press_Releases.shtml.

CodePink (CP) . 2006. "Commemorate Four Years of CODEPINK Rabble-Rousing by Giving Peace a Vote." October 2. http://www.codepink4peace.org/article.php?id=1248.

CodePink (CP). 2008. "Military Recruiting FAQs." April 29. http://www.codepink4peace.org/article.php?id=3911.

CodePink (CP). 2010. "Love the Troops, Hate the War!" Protest Sign. Swarthmore Peace Archives, Pennsylvania.

Cohen, Randy. 2003. "The Way We Live Now." *New York Times*. (20 April). Page 29, Column 3.

Coker, Christopher. 2012. "The Collision of Modern and Post-Modern War." In *The Oxford Handbook of War*, edited by Yves Boyer and Julian Lindley-French. 57–68. Oxford: Oxford University Press.

Cole, Timothy. 2005. "The Political Rhetoric of Sacrifice and Heroism and US Military Intervention." In *Bring 'Em On: Media and Politics in the Iraq War*, edited by L. Artz and Y. R. Kamalipour. 139–54. Lanham: Rowman and Littlefield.

Colvile, Oliver. 2010. "Hansard Remarks, HC Deb." November 25. c503.

Connell, Raewyn. 1990. "The State, Gender, and Sexual Politics." *Theory and Society*. 19, no.5: 507–44.

Connell, Raewyn. 1995. *Masculinities*. Berkeley: University of California Press

Cooper, Nicola, and Martin Hurcombe. 2009. "The Figure of the Soldier." *Journal of War and Culture Studies*. 2, no.2: 103–04.

Cornell, Caroline. 2010. "The Housewife's Battle on the Home Front: Women in World War II Advertisements." *The Forum: Journal of History*. 2, no.1: 8: 28–42.

Cornish, Paul. 2003. "Myth and Reality: US and UK Approaches to Casualty Aversion and Force Protection." *Defense Studies*. 3, no.2: 121–28.

Cornish, Paul. 2012. "The Changing Relationship Between the Armed Forces and Society." In *The Oxford Handbook of War*, edited by Yves Boyer and Julien French, 559–73. Oxford: Oxford University Press.

Coronado Eagle and Journal. 1941. "Bundles for Britain Becomes Bundles for Blue Jackets." 30 December 30. 29, no.50. Accessed via California Digital Newspaper Collection at UCR Center for Biographical Studies and Research. https://cdnc.ucr.edu/?a=d&d=CJ19411230.2.9&e=-------en--20--1--txt-txIN--------1

Cowen, Deborah. 2008a. "The Soldier and Social Citizenship." In *Recasting the Social in Citizenship*, edited by Elgin F. Isin. 187–209. Toronto: University of Toronto Press.

Cowen, Deborah. 2008b. *Military Workfare: The Soldier and Social Citizenship in Canada.* Toronto: University of Toronto Press.

Cowen, Deborah. N.d. "Militarism? A Mini-Forum." Society & Space. http://societyandspace.com/material/discussion-forum/militarism-a-mini-forum/.

Coy, Patrick G. et al. 2008. "Discursive Legacies: The US Peace Movements and 'Support the Troops.'" *Social Problems.* 55, no.2: 161–89.

Cree, Alice. 2020. "'People Want to See Tears': Military Heroes and the 'Constant Penelope' of the UK's Military Wives Choir." *Gender, Place & Culture.* 27, no.2: 218–38.

Cummings, Elisabeth. 2003. Saluting our Troops. March 26. Congressional Record. H2394. THOMAS.loc.gov.

Dahlgreen, Will. 2015. "Memories of Iraq: Did We Ever Support the War?" YouGov. https://yougov.co.uk/topics/politics/articles-reports/2015/06/03/remembering-iraq

Daily Mail. 2007. "Wounded Iraq Veterans Driven Out of Pool When Told They Might Scare Children." November 22. http://www.dailymail.co.uk/news/article-495910/Wounded-Iraq-veterans-driven-public-pool-told-scare-children.html.

Dahl Christensen, Tea. 2015. "The Figure of the Soldier: Discourses of Indisputability and Heroism in a New Danish Commemorative Practice." *Journal of War & Culture Studies.* 8, no.4: 347–63.

Dallas Voice. 2020. "Election 2020—Democrats for President: Joe Biden on LGBTQ Issues." February 29. https://dallasvoice.com/election-2020-democrats-for-president-joe-biden-on-lgbtq-issues/

D'Amico, Francine. 2000. "Citizen-Soldier? Class, Race, Gender Sexuality, and the US Military." In *States of Conflict: Gender, Violence and Resistance,* edited by Susie Jacobs. 105–20. London: Zed Books.

Dancy, Steve. 2008. "Heroes First Year Sees £12.5 in the Kitty. This Is Hampshire." October 6. http://web.archive.org/web/20081023193535/http://www.helpforheroes.org.uk/inthemedia.html.

Dandeker, Christopher, and Mady W. Segal. 1996. "Gender Integration in Armed Forces: Recent Policy Developments in the United Kingdom." *Armed Forces & Society.* 23, no.1: 29–47.

DataBlog. 2011. "Army Cuts: How Have UK Armed Forces Personnel Numbers Changed over Time?" *The Guardian.* https://www.theguardian.com/news/datablog/2011/sep/01/military-service-personnel-total#data.

Davey, Monica. 2003. "For Parishioners, Right or Wrong Takes a Back Seat to Prayer." *New York Times.* March 24. 15, col. 2.

Davidson, Janet. 2016. "Humility and 'Having a Good Time': Prince Harry Brings His Royal Rapport to Toronto." CBC. May 1. http://www.cbc.ca/news/canada/prince-harry-invictus-games-military-support-toronto-1.3554153.

Dean, Jodi. 2016. *Crowds and Party.* London: Verso Books.

De Luce, Dan. 2021. "U.S. Official: 'Majority' of Afghan Allies Who Applied for Special Visas Left Behind in Afghanistan." NBC News. 1 September. https://www.nbcnews.com/news/world/small-fraction-america-s-afghan-allies-made-it-out-afghanistan-n1278141.

Delay, Thomas, Representative. 2003. Conference Report on H.R. 1559, Emergency Wartime Supplemental Appropriations Act, 2003. 12 April. Pp. H3204. Congressional Record Vol. 149, No. 60.

Della Porta, Donatella. 2012. "Chapter 11—Comparative Analysis: Case-Oriented Versus Variable-Oriented Research." In *Approaches and Methodologies in the Social Sciences,* edited by Donatella Della Porta and Michael Keating, 198–222. Cambridge: Cambridge University Press.

Department of Defense. N.d. "Community Support Organizations." http://www.ourmilit ary.mil/comprehensive-list-of-community-support-groups.

Department of Defense. N.d. "Criteria for Listed Organizations." http://www.ourmilitary. mil/review-process-for-listed-organizations/.

Derrida, Jacques. 1986. "Declarations of Independence." *New Political Science*. 7, no.1: 7–15.

DeYoung, Karen. 2009. "Obama Sets Timeline for Iraq Withdrawal, Calling It Part of Broader Middle East Strategy." *Washington Post*. February 28. http://www.washing tonpost.com/wp-dyn/content/article/2009/02/27/AR2009022700566.html.

Dingli, Sophia. 2015. "We Need to Talk About Silence: Re-Examining Silence in International Relations Theory." *European Journal of International Relations*. 21, no.4: 721–42.

Dixon, Paul. 2000. "Britain's 'Vietnam Syndrome'? Public Opinion and British Military Intervention from Palestine to Yugoslavia." *Review of International Studies*. 26, no.1: 99–121.

Dixon, Paul. 2012. *The British Approach to Counterinsurgency: From Malaya and Northern Ireland to Iraq and Afghanistan*. Abingdon: Palgrave MacMillan.

Dixon, Paul. 2012. "Bringing It All Back Home: The Militarisation of Britain and the Iraq and Afghanistan Wars." In *The British Approach to Counterinsurgency*, edited by Paul Dixon, 112–46. London: Palgrave Macmillan.

Dodds, Norman. 1973. "Voluntary Recruitment." *Military Review*. 53, no.6: 77–85.

Dodds, Klaus-John. 1993. "War Stories: British Elite Narratives of the 1982 Falklands/ Malvinas War." *Environment and Planning D: Society and Space*. 11, no.6: 619–40.

Doty, Roxanne Lynn. 1993. "Foreign Policy as Social Construction: A Post-Positivist Analysis of US Counterinsurgency Policy in the Philippines." *International Studies Quarterly*. 37, no.3: 297–320.

Dower, Nigel. 2009. *The Ethics of War and Peace*. Cambridge: Polity.

Downes, Lawrence. 2008. "Veterans, Alone Together, Share Stories They Can't Tell You." *New York Times*. October 6.

Doyle, Michael W. 2005. "Three Pillars of the Liberal Peace." *American Political Science Review*. 99, no.3: 463–66.

Dumbrell, John. 2009. "The US–UK Special Relationship: Taking the 21st-Century Temperature." *The British Journal of Politics and International Relations* 11, no.1: 64–78.

Duncanson, Clare, 2009. "Forces for Good? Narratives of Military Masculinity in Peacekeeping Operations." *International Feminist Journal of Politics*. 11, no.1: 63–80.

Duncanson, Clare. 2013. *Forces for Good? Military Masculinities in Iraq and Afghanistan*. Hampshire: Palgrave MacMillan.

Earlam, Katie. 2012. "Royalty, Sports Stars and Celebrities Honour British Troops at Millies 2012." *The Sun*. December 6. https://www.thesun.co.uk/archives/news/318766/ royalty-sports-stars-and-celebrities-honour-british-troops-at-millies-2012/.

Eastwood, James. 2018. "Rethinking Militarism as Ideology: The Critique of Violence After Security." *Security Dialogue*. 49, nos.1–2: 44–56.

Edgerton, David.1991. "Liberal Militarism and the British State." *New Left Review* 185 no.1: 138–69.

Editorial Board. 2019. "Opinion: Iraqis Who Helped the United States During the War Shouldn't Be Abandoned." *Washington Post*. November 5. https://www.washingtonp

ost.com/opinions/iraqis-who-helped-the-united-states-during-the-war-shouldnt-be-abandoned/2019/11/05/f8f72a4c-ff2b-11e9-8bab-0fc209e065a8_story.html

Edkins, Jenny. 1999. *Post-Structuralism and International Relations*. Boulder: Lynne Reiner.

Edwards, Tim. 2003. "Sex, Booze and Fags: Masculinity, Style and Men's Magazines." *The Sociological Review*. 51, no.1: 132–46.

Eikenberry, Karl, and David M. Kennedy. 2013. "Americans and Their Military, Drifting Apart." *New York Times*. May 26. http://www.nytimes.com/2013/05/27/opinion/americans-and-their-military-drifting-apart.html?_r=0.

Eisenstein, Zillah. 2007. *Sexual Decoys: Gender, Race and War in Imperial Democracy*. London: Zed Books.

Elshtain, Jean Bethke. 1995. *Women and War*. Chicago: Chicago University Press.

Embser-Herbert, M. Sheridan. 2017. "Transgender Military Service: A Snapshot in Time." In *The Palgrave International Handbook of Gender and the Military*, edited by Clare Duncanson and Rachel Woodward, 177–94. Palgrave Macmillan, London.

Enloe, Cynthia. 1993. *The Morning After: Sexual Politics at the End of the Cold War*. Berkeley: University of California Press.

Enloe, Cynthia. 1996. "Margins, Silences and Bottom Rungs: How to Overcome the Underestimation of Power in the Study of International Relations." In *International Theory: Positivism and Beyond*, edited by Steve Smith, Ken Booth, and Marysia Zalewski. 186–202. Cambridge: Cambridge University Press.

Enloe, Cynthia. 2000. *Maneuvers: The International Politics of Militarizing Women's Lives*. Berkeley: University of California Press.

Enloe, Cynthia. 2004. *The Curious Feminist: Search for Women in a New Age of Empire*. Berkeley: University of California Press.

Enloe, Cynthia. 2007. *Globalization and Militarism: Feminists Make the Link*. New York: Rowman and Littlefield Publishers, Inc.

Enloe, Cynthia. 2010. "Gender Relations as Causal in Miltarization and War: A Feminist Standpoint." *International Feminist Journal of Politics*. 12, no.2: 139–57.

Enloe, Cynthia. 2015. The Recruiter and the Sceptic: A Critical Feminist Approach to Military Studies. *Critical Military Studies*. 1, no.1: 3–10.

Enloe, Cynthia. 2020. "COVID-19: 'Waging War' Against a Virus Is NOT What We Need to Be Doing." Women's International League for Peace and Freedom. March 23. https://www.wilpf.org/covid-19-waging-war-against-a-virus-is-not-what-we-need-to-be-doing/.

Erenberg, Lewis A., and Hirsch, Susan E. 1996. *The War in American Culture: Society and Consciousness During World War II*. Chicago: University of Chicago Press.

Esch, Joanne. 2010. "Legitimizing the 'War on Terror': Political Myth in Official-Level Rhetoric." *Political Psychology*. 31, no.3: 357–91.

Ewing, Margaret. Hansard. HC Deb, 21 February 1991, c482.

Fairclough, Norman. 2003. "Political Correctness': The Politics of Culture and Language." *Discourse & Society*. 14, no.1: 17–28.

Feaver, Peter D., and Christopher Gelpi. 2011. *Choosing Your Battles: American Civil-Military Relations and the Use of Force*. Princeton: Princeton University Press.

Fellowship of Reconciliation. (FoR). 2016. "Counter-Recruitment News." http://forusa.org/tags/counter-recruitment.

Field, Connie. 1987. *The Life and Times of Rosie the Riveter* [videorecording]. Produced and Directed by Publish Info Los Angeles, CA: Direct Cinema Ltd. Cited in A. Standlee,

"Shifting Spheres: Gender, Labor and the Construction of National Identity in US." 2008. Working paper presented at the American Sociological Association Conference. August. Boston.Available at: https://www.researchgate.net/profile/Alecea-Standlee/publication/238450983_Shifting_Spheres_Gender_Labor_and_the_Construction_of_National_Identity_in_US_Propaganda_during_the_Second_World_War/links/571a26de08aee3ddc568eec9/Shifting-Spheres-Gender-Labor-and-the-Construction-of-National-Identity-in-US-Propaganda-during-the-Second-World-War.pdf

Fierke, Karin. 2004. "World or Worlds? The Analysis of Content and Discourse." *Qualitative Methods*. 2, no.1: 36–38.

Finkel, David. 2013. *Thank You for Your Service*. New York: Sarah Crichton Books.

Fischer, Mia. 2014. "Commemorating 9/11 NFL-Style: Insights into America's Culture of Militarism." *Journal of Sport and Social Issues*. 38, no.3: 199–221.

Fletcher, Kim. 2003. "Why the Pen Is Joining Forces with the Sword." 21 March. *The Telegraph*.

Flyvbjerg, Bent. 2006. Five misunderstandings about case-study research. *Qualitative inquiry*. 12, no.2: 219–45.

ForcesWatch. N.d. "What's the Problem?" http://www.forceswatch.net/what_why.

Forrester, Katrina. 2014. "Citizenship, War, and the Origins of International Ethics in American Political Philosophy 1960–1975." *The Historical Journal*. 57, no.3: 773–801.

Foss, Karen A., and Kathy L. Domenici. 2001. "Haunting Argentina: Synecdoche in the Protests of the Mothers of the Plaza de Mayo." *Quarterly Journal of Speech*. 87, no.3: 237–58.

Foucault, Michel. 1976. *The Archaeology of Knowledge*. Translated by Alan Sheridan Smith. London: Harper & Row.

Foucault, Michel. 1980. *Power/knowledge: Selected Interviews and Other Writings, 1972–1977*. New York: Vintage.

Foucault, Michel. 1984. *The Foucault Reader*. Edited and translated by Paul Rabinow. New York: Pantheon Books.

Foucault, Michel. 1990. *The History of Sexuality*. Vol 1: *An Introduction*. Translated by R. Hurley. New York: Vintage.

Fountain, Ben. 2013. *Billy Lynn's Long Halftime Walk*. London: Canongate.

Foweraker, Joe, and Roman Krznaric. 2000. "Measuring Liberal Democratic Performance: An Empirical and Conceptual Critique." *Political Studies*. no.48: 4.

Fox, Liam. 2007. Uncorrected Minutes of Evidence Taken Before the Defence and Foreign Affairs Committees on 11 January. House of Commons 209–i, Session 2006–07. Theyworkforyou.com.

Fox, Liam. 2010. "Increasing Afghan Training Effort—the Moral Duty of NATO Allies." UK Ministry of Defence Press Release. June 11. https://www.gov.uk/government/news/increasing-afghan-training-effort-the-moral-duty-of-nato-allies.

Fox, James. 2014. "Poppy Politics: Remembrance of Things Present." In *Cultural Heritage Ethics: Between Theory and Practice*, edited by Constantine Sandis, 21–30. Cambridge: Open Book.

Frazer, Elizabeth. 1999. *The Problems of Communitarian Politics*. Oxford: Oxford University Press.

Frazer, Elizabeth, and Nicola Lacey. 1993. *The Politics of Community: A Feminist Critique of the Liberal-Communitarian Debate*. Hemel Hempstead: Harvester Wheatsheaf.

Freeden, Michael. 2009. *Liberal Languages: Ideological Imaginations and Twentieth-Century Progressive Thought*. Princeton: Princeton University Press.

Freeden, Michael. 2011. "The Politics of Ceremony: The Wootton Bassett Phenomenon." *Journal of Political Ideologies*. 16, no.1: 1–10.

Freeden, Michael. 2015. *Liberalism: A Very Short Introduction*. Oxford: Oxford University Press

Freedland, Jonathan. 2003. "Dilemmas of War." *The Guardian*. March 19.

Freedom du Lac, J. 2007. "At Walter Reed, Mellencamp Shuts His Mouth and Sings." *Washington Post*. April 23.

Freedom House. 2018. "Table of Countries 2018." https://freedomhouse.org/report/free dom-world-2018-table-country-scores.

French, David. 2005. "The Nation in Arms II: The Nineteenth Century." In *The Oxford History of Modern War*, edited by Charles Townshend. 2nd ed. 55–73. Oxford: Oxford University Press.

French, David. 2012. *Army, Empire, and Cold War: The British Army and Military Policy, 1945–1971*. Oxford: Oxford University Press.

French, Henry, and Mark Rothery. 2019. "Male Anxiety Among Younger Sons of the English Landed Gentry, 1700–1900." *The Historical Journal*. 62, no.4: 967–95.

Frist, William. 2003. Supporting Our Troops. Congressional Record. April 7. THOMAS. loc.gov.

Gallup. 2010. "Iraq." https://news.gallup.com/poll/1633/iraq.aspx.

Gaouette, Nicole, Jennifer Hansler, Barbara Starr, and Oren Liebermann. 2021. "The Last US Military Planes Have Left Afghanistan." CNN. August 31. https://edition.cnn.com/ 2021/08/30/politics/us-military-withdraws-afghanistan/index.html.

Gartner, Scott S., Gary M. Segura, and Michael Wilkening. 1997. "All Politics Are Local: Local Losses and Individual Attitudes Toward the Vietnam War." *Journal of Conflict Resolution*. 41, no.5: 669–94.

George W. Bush Presidential Library. N.d. "The White House" (archived 2009). http:// georgewbush-whitehouse.archives.gov/.

Gibian, Rebecca. 2019. "The US Promised Thousands of Foreign Interpreters Special Immigrant Visas. Now They're Trapped." *The World*. September 19. https://www.pri. org/stories/2019-09-19/us-promised-thousands-foreign-interpreters-special-immigr ant-visas-now-they-re.

Gillan, Kevin et al. 2011. *Anti-War Activism: New Media and Protest in the Information Age*. Basingstoke: Palgrave MacMillan.

Gillan, Kevin, and Jenny Pickerill. 2008. "Transnational Anti-War Activism: Solidarity, Diversity and The Internet in Australia, Britain and the United States After 9/11." *Australian Journal of Political Science*. 43, no.1: 59–78.

Gitlin, Todd. 2003. "The War's Over, but the Fighting's Getting Worse." *Washington Post*. May 4.

Gledhill, Ruth. 2004. "Archbishops accuse Blair of double standard." *The Times*. 30 June. Available at: https://www.thetimes.co.uk/article/archbishops-accuse-blair-of-double-standards-rcr69vphvm7.

Goldberg, Matthew S. 2017. "Casualty Rates of US Military Personnel During the Wars in Iraq and Afghanistan." *Defence and Peace Economics*. 29, no.1: 44–61.

Goldin, Claudia. D. 1991. "The Role of World War II in the Rise of Women's Employment." *The American Economic Review*. 81, no.4:741–56

Gootman, Elissa. 2003. "A Chorus of Support in Times Sq." *New York Times*.

Government of the United Kingdom. N.d. "Announcements." Gov.uk. https://www.gov. uk/government/announcements?departments[]=ministry-of-defence.

Government of the United Kingdom. N.d. "The Charity Commission." Gov.uk. https://www.gov.uk/government/organisations/charity-commission.

Government of the United Kingdom. 2019. "Armed Forces Workforce." Gov.uk. February 27. https://www.ethnicity-facts-figures.service.gov.uk/workforce-and-business/workforce-diversity/armed-forces-workforce/latest.

Grant, John. 2014. "On Critique of Political Imaginaries." *European Journal of Political Theory*. 13, no.4: 408–26.

Grant, Peter. 2008. "'An Infinity of Personal Sacrifice': The Scale and Nature of Charitable Work in Britain During the First World War." *War & Society*. (October 27), no.2: 67–88.

Grant, Peter. 2014. *Philanthropy and Voluntary Action in the First World War: Mobilizing Charity*. London: Routledge.

Grant, Susanne-Mary. 2009. "A Season of War: Warriors, Veterans and Warfare in American Nationalism." In *Nations and Their Histories*, edited by Susanne Carvalho and François Gemenne, 237–54. London: Palgrave Macmillan.

Gray, Harriet. 2016. "Domestic Abuse and the Public/Private Divide in the British Military." *Gender, Place & Culture*. 23, no.6: 912–25.

Gray, Robert. 1982. "The Falklands Factor." *Marxism Today*. July 8–12.

Grayzel, Susan R. 2012. *At Home and Under Fire: Air Raids and Culture in Britain from the Great War to the Blitz*. Cambridge: Cambridge University Press.

Green, Elna C. 2006. "Protecting Confederate Soldiers and Mothers: Pensions, Gender, and the Welfare State in the US South, a Case Study from Florida." *Journal of Social History*. 30, no.4: 1079–104.

Greene, Balissa. 2016. "The Experience of Foreign and Commonwealth Soldiers in the British Army: An Exploration and Methodological Commentary." Doctoral dissertation, London School of Economics and Political Science (LSE).

Greenwald, Maurine W. 1990. *Women, War, and Work: The Impact of World War I on Women Workers in the United States*. Ithaca: Cornell University Press.

Gregory, Adrian. 1994. *The Silence of Memory: Armistice Day 1919–1946*. Oxford: Berg.

Greiner, Bernd. 2014. "Heroism and Self-Sacrifice: The Vietnam War as a Case in Point." In *Heroism and the Changing Character of War*, edited by Sibylle Schieprs, 108–19. London: Palgrave Macmillan.

Gribble, Rachael et al. 2020. "British Social Attitudes Survey: Armed Forces." https://www.bsa.natcen.ac.uk/latest-report/british-social-attitudes-29/armed-forces/introduction.aspx.

Grinberg, Emanuella. 2010. "Dead Marine's Father Ordered to Pay Protestors Legal Costs." CNN. March 31. http://edition.cnn.com/2010/CRIME/03/30/westboro.baptist.snyder/.

Gronemeyer, Marianne. 2010. "Helping." In *The Development Dictionary: A Guide to Knowledge as Power*, edited by Wolfgang Sachs, 2nd edn, 55–74. London: Zed Books.

Grove, Nicole Sunday. 2019. "Weapons of Mass Participation: Social Media, Violence Entrepreneurs, and the Politics of Crowdfunding for War." *European Journal of International Relations*. 25, no.1: 86–107.

Gullace, Nicolette. 1997. "White Feathers and Wounded Men: Female Patriotism and the Memory of the Great War." *Journal of British Studies*. 36, no.2: 178–206.

Haddad, Tareq. 2019. "Veterans 'Uncomfortable' with 'Thank You for Your Service,' Ask for More Civilian Support This Veterans Day." *Newsweek*. November 9. https://www.newsweek.com/veterans-thank-you-service-veterans-day-support-1470776.

Hale, Hannah. 2012. "The Role of Practice in the Development of Military Masculinities." *Gender, Work and Organization*. 19, no.6: 699–722.

Hall, Sarah. 2003. "Kennedy in Doldrums after Battering on Iraq." *The Guardian*. June 30.

Hall, Simon. 2011. *Peace and Freedom: The Civil Rights and Antiwar Movements in the 1960s*. Pittsburgh: University of Pennsylvania Press.

Hall, Stuart, ed. 1997. *Representation: Cultural Representations and Signifying Practices*. Vol. 2. Thousand Oaks: Sage.

Hall, Stuart. 1994. "Some 'Politically Incorrect' Pathways Through PC." In *The War of the Words: The Political Correctness Debate*, edited by S. Dunant. 164–84. London: Virago Press.

Hallifax, Stuart. 2010. " 'Over by Christmas': British Popular Opinion and the Short War in 1914." *First World War Studies*. 1,no.2: 103–21.

Haltiner, Karl W. 2006. "The Decline of the European Mass Armies." In *Handbook of the Sociology of the Military*, edited by Giuseppe Caforio and Marina Nuciari, 361–84. Boston: Springer.

Hammond, Richard, and Thomas Curran. 2002. *A History of Memorial Day: Unity, Discord and the Pursuit of Happiness*. New York: Lang.

Hansen, Len. 2006. *Security as Practice: Discourse Analysis and the Bosnian War*. Trowbridge: Routledge.

Hansen, Len. 1996. "Slovenian Identity: State-Building on the Balkan Border." *Alternatives*. 21, no.4: 473–95.

Harding, Scott, and Seth Kershner. 2011. "'Just Say No': Organizing Against Militarism in Public Schools." *Journal of Sociology and Social Welfare*. 38, no.2: 79–109.

Harding, Thomas et al. 2007. "Disabled Veterans Jeered at Swimming Pool." *The Telegraph*. November 22. http://www.telegraph.co.uk/news/uknews/1570130/Disabled-veterans-jeered-at-swimming-pool.html.

Hardt, Michael, and Antonio Negri. 2004. *Multitude: War and Democracy in an Age of Empire*. New York: Penguin Press.

Hardy, Cynthia et al. 2004. "Discourse Analysis and Content Analysis—Two Solitudes?" *Qualitative Methods*. 2, no.1: 19–22.

Harman, Harriet. 2010. UK Hansard. HC Deb. May 25, c39. TheyWorkForYou.org.

Harris, Carol. 2011. "Women Under Fire in World War Two." BBC. https://www.bbc.co.uk/history/british/britain_wwtwo/women_at_war_01.shtml.

Harris, Jose. 1992. "War and Social History: Britain and the Home Front During the Second World War." *Contemporary European History*. 1, no.1: 17–35.

Harrison, John. 2009. "Anti-War Campaigners Remember 201 Dead." *St Albans and Harpenden Review*. August 22. http://web.archive.org/web/20090914084240/http://stopwar.org.uk/content/view/1459/27/.

Hass, Kristin Ann. 1998. *Carried to the Wall: American Memory and the Vietnam Veterans Memorial*. Berkley: University of California Press.

Heilbronn, Lisa. 1994. "Yellow Ribbons and Remembrance: Mythic Symbols of the Gulf War." *Sociological Inquiry*. 64, no.2: 151–78.

Help for Heroes (H4H). N.d. "FAQs." http://www.helpforheroes.org.uk/how-we-help/about-us/faqs/.

Help for Heroes (H4H). 2007. "Help for Heroes Launch Speech." October 13. http://web.archive.org/web/20071013051452/http://helpforheroes.org.uk/launchspeech.html.

Help for Heroes (H4H). 2008. "Bake a Cake and Change the World." September 5. http://web.archive.org/web/20080905125534/http://www.helpforheroes.org.uk/bake_a_cake.html.

Help for Heroes (H4H). 2009a. "2008 Annual Report." http://www.helpforheroes.org.uk/Publications/Annual-Reports/2008/#29/z.

Help for Heroes (H4H). 2009b. "CEO Report—Annual Review." http://web.archive.org/web/20101014144955/http://www.helpforheroes.org.uk/CEO_Report.html.

Help for Heroes (H4H). "Frequently Asked Questions." 2009c. FAQ. http://www.helpforheroes.org.uk/how-we-help/about-us/faqs/.

Help for Heroes (H4H). 2009d. "Welcome to Help for Heroes." http://web.archive.org/web/20090531155220/http://www.helpforheroes.org.uk/index_sub.html.

Help for Heroes (H4H). 2009e. "Sergeant's Decisive Action Saves Platoon." May. http://web.archive.org/web/20090517020059/http://www.helpforheroes.org.uk/inthemedia_12_08.html.

Help for Heroes (H4H). 2010a. "Chairman's Introduction." October 14. http://web.archive.org/web/20101014145034/http://www.helpforheroes.org.uk/mark_wright_opening.html.

Help for Heroes (H4H). 2010b. "Messages of Support." February 10. http://web.archive.org/web/20100210053314/http://www.helpforheroes.org.uk/messagesofsupport.html.

Help for Heroes (H4H). 2010c. "FAQ." http://web.archive.org/web/20100510072044/http://www.helpforheroes.org.uk/faqs.html#3.

Help for Heroes (H4H). 2016. "Online Shop." http://shop.helpforheroes.org.uk/.

Henderson, Kristin. 2007. "What Should That Mean to the Rest of Us?" *Washington Post.* July 22.

Henry, Marsha. 2015. "Parades, Parties and Pests: Contradictions of Everyday Life in Peacekeeping Economies." *Journal of Intervention and Statebuilding.* 9, no.3: 372–90.

Herald, The. 2015. "Corbyn Tackled by Simon Danczuk MP After Refusing to Rule Out Wearing a White Poppy on Remembrance Sunday." September 15. https://www.heraldscotland.com/news/13720166.corbyn-tackled-by-simon-danczuk-mp-after-refusing-to-rule-out-wearing-a-White-poppy-on-remembrance-sunday/.

Higate, Paul. 2003. "Soft Clerks and Hard Civvies: Pluralizing Military Masculinities." In *Military Masculinities: Identity and the State*, edited by Paul Higate. 27–42. London: Praeger.

Higate, Paul, and John Hopton. 2004. "War, MIlitarism, and Masculinities." In *Handbook of Studies on Men and Masculinities*, edited by Michael S. Kimmel, Jeff Hearn, and Robert W. Connell. 432–47. Thousand Oaks: Sage.

Hindess, Barry. 2001. "The Liberal Government of Unfreedom." *Alternatives.* 26, no.2: 93–111.

Hobbes, Thomas. 1985. *Leviathan.* Harmondsworth: Penguin.

Hobbes, Thomas. 1986. *Leviathan or the Matter Form and Power of a Commonwealth, Ecclesiastical and Civil.* London: Routledge.

Hobhouse, L. 1964. *Liberalism.* Oxford: Oxford University Press.

Hobsbawm, Eric. 2020. *The Age of Extremes: 1914–1991.* London: Hachette UK.

Hobson, John M. 2012. *The Eurocentric Conception of World Politics: Western International Theory, 1760–2010.* Cambridge: Cambridge University Press.

Horton, John. 2010. *Political Obligation.* Basingstoke: Palgrave Macmillan

Houngnikpo, Mathurin C. 2010. *Guarding the Guardians: Civil-Military Relations and Democratic Governance in Africa.* Farnham: Ashgate.

House of Commons Library. 2014. "Research Briefing: Defense Personnel Statistics," SN/SG/02183. https://researchbriefings.files.parliament.uk/documents/SN02183/SN02183.pdf

Howard, Brian, and Sydney Combs. N.d. "The Facts Behind Memorial Day's Controversial History." National Geographic. https://www.nationalgeographic.com/culture/holidays/reference/memorial-day/

Howard, Michael. 2009. *War in European History*. Oxford: Oxford University Press.

Howard, Michael. 2018. *War and the Liberal Conscience*. London: Hurst.

Howell, Alison. 2018. "Forget 'Militarization': Race, Disability and the 'Martial Politics' of the Police and of the University." *International Feminist Journal of Politics*. 20, no.2: 117–36.

Howell, Alison. 2019. "Remember 'Militarization'? In Defense of 'Martial Politics' and Foregrounding Race and Disability" In an We Really 'Forget' Militarization? A Conversation on Alison Howell's Martial Politics." *International Feminist Journal of Politics*. 21, no.5: 816–36.

Howell, Alison, and Melanie Richter-Montpetit. 2020. "Is Securitization Theory Racist? Civilizationism, Methodological Whiteness, and Antiblack Thought in the Copenhagen School." *Security Dialogue*. 51, no.1: 3–22.

Howell, Thomas. 1997. "The Writers' War Board: US Domestic Propaganda in World War II." *The Historian*. 59, no.4: 795–813.

Hrywna, M. 2013. "New Veterans' Charities Race Past Broader Sector." *The Non-Profit Times*. December 2. http://www.thenonprofittimes.com/news-articles/new-veterans-charities-race-past-broadersector/.

Hsiao, Lisa. 1989. "Project 100,000: The Great Society's Answer to Military Manpower Needs in Vietnam." *Vietnam Generation*. 1, no.2: 4.

Huebner, Andrew. 2011. *The Warrior Image: Soldiers in American Culture from the Second World War to the Vietnam Era*. Chapel Hill: University of North Carolina Press.

Huetteman, Emmarie. 2016. "'They Will Kill Us': Afghan Translators Plead for Delayed U.S. Visas." *New York Times*. August 9. https://www.nytimes.com/2016/08/10/us/politics/afghan-translators-military-visas.html; https://www.pri.org/stories/2019-09-19/us-promised-thousands-foreign-interpreters-special-immigrant-visas-now-they-re.

Huiskamp, Gerald. 2011. "'Support the Troops!': The Social and Political Currency of Patriotism in the United States." *New Political Science*. 33, no.3: 285–310.

Human Rights Watch. 2012. "In the Name of Security: Counter-Terrorism Laws Worldwide Since 2001." https://www.hrw.org/report/2012/06/29/name-security/counterterrorism-laws-worldwide-september-11#.

Hunt, Krista. 2006. "'Embedded Feminism' and the War on Terror." In *En) Gendering the War on Terror: War Stories and Camouflaged Politics*, edited by Krista Hunt and Kim Rygiel, 51–71. London: Routledge.

Huntington, Samuel P. 1981. *The Soldier and the State: The Theory and Politics of Civil–Military Relations*. Cambridge: Harvard University Press.

Hutchings, Kimberly. 2008. "Making Sense of Masculinity and War." *Men and Masculinities*. 10, no.4: 389–404.

Hyde, Alexandra. 2016. "The Present Tense of Afghanistan: Accounting for Space, Time and Gender in Processes of Militarisation." *Gender, Place & Culture*. 23, no.6: 857–68.

Icasualties.org. N.d. "Total Casualties from 2001 to 2020." http://icasualties.org.

Iggulden, Caroline, and Tom Newton Dunn. 2008. "It's Great to Celebrate Britain's Real Heroes." *The Sun*. September 16.

Ignatieff, Michael. 2001. *Human Rights as Politics and Idolatry*. Princeton: Princeton University Press 2001.

Inglis, Shelley. 2021. "Perilous Situation for Afghan Allies Left Behind Shows a Refugee System That's Not Up to the Job." *The Conversation*. https://theconversation.com/peril ous-situation-for-afghan-allies-left-behind-shows-a-refugee-system-thats-not-up-to-the-job-166442.

Initiative Solidaritat. 2018. "Home Page." https://solidaritaet-mit-soldaten.de.

Inspector General. 2008. "The America Supports You Program." December 12. Report No. D-2009-032. US Department of Defense. http://www.wired.com/images_blogs/ dangerroom/files/asy_final_report.pdf.

Imber, Mark, and Trudy Fraser. 2011. "From Flanders to Fallujah: Rethinking Remembrance." *Journal of War & Culture Studies*. 4, no.3: 383–97.

Internal Revenue Service. N.d. "Search for Charities." Irs.gov. http://www.irs.gov/Charit ies-&-Non-Profits/Search-for-Charities.

Ipsos. 2007. "Political Commentary—The 'Falklands Factor' Revisited." April 10. https:// www.ipsos.com/ipsos-mori/en-uk/political-commentary-falklands-factor-revisited.

Iraq and Afghanistan Veterans Association. (IAVA). 2007. "Vets Address Presidential Commission." May 15. https://web.archive.org/web/20080410230110/http://www. iava.org/component/option,com_/Itemid,67/option,content/task,view/id,2457/.

Iraq and Afghanistan Veterans Association. (IAVA). 2008. "Landmark Week for Vets' Legislation." October 15. https://web.archive.org/web/20081015122830/http://www. iava.org/component/option,com_/Itemid,67/option,content/task,view/id,2824/.

Isaacs, Arnold. 2007. "Facts About the Vietnam War, Part II: The Draft Was a Moral Disgrace." War on the Rocks. September 12. https://warontherocks.com/2017/09/facts-about-the-vietnam-war-part-ii-the-draft-was-a-moral-disgrace/.

Isenberg, N. 2017. *White Trash: The 400-Year Untold History of Class in America*. New York: Penguin.

Israel, Steve. 2003. Urging Americans to Participate in the 'E-Mail Our Troops' Project. US Congressional Record. March 26. H2373. Thomas.loc.gov.

Jabri, Vivienne. 1996. *Discourses on Violence*. Manchester: Manchester University Press.

Jabri, Vivienne. 2006. "War, Security and the Liberal State." *Security Dialogue*. 37, no.1: 47–64.

Jackson-Lee, Sheila Representative. 2006. Victory in Iraq Resolution. US Congressional Record. December 16. H11908. Thomas.loc.gov.

Jahn, Beate. 2005. "Kant, Mill, and Illiberal Legacies in International Affairs." *International Organization*. 59, no.1: 177–207.

Jahn, Beate. 2009. "The Tragedy of Liberal Democracy." In *Statebuilding and Intervention: Policies, Practices and Paradigms*, edited by David Chandler, 210–29. Abingdon: Routledge.

Jahn, Beate. 2011. *Liberal Internationalism: Theory, History, and Practice*. Abingdon: Palgrave MacMillan.

Jahn, Beate. 2012. "Rethinking Democracy Promotion." *Review of International Studies*. 38, no.4: 685–705.

Jahn, Beate. 2013. *Liberal Internationalism: Theory, History, Practice*. Abingdon: Palgrave Macmillan UK.

Jahn, Beate. 2016. *The Cultural Construction of International Relations: The Invention of the State of Nature*. New York: Springer.

Janowitz, Morris. 1964. "The Military in the Political Development of New Nations." *Bulletin of the Atomic Scientists*. 20, no.8: 6–10.

Jefferson, Robert F. 2008. *Fighting for Hope: African American Troops of the 93rd Infantry Division in World War II and Postwar America*. Baltimore: JHU Press.

Jeffries, John W. 2018. *Wartime America: The World War II Home Front*. Rowman and Littlefield.

Jenkings, Neal et al. 2012. "Wootton Bassett and the Political Spaces of Remembrance and Mourning." *Area*. 44, no.3: 356–63.

Jensen, Kimberly. 2008. *Mobilizing Minerva: American Women in the First World War*. Champaign: University of Illinois Press.

Jensen, Kimberly. 2019. "A 'Disloyal' and 'Immoral' Woman 'In Such a Responsible Place': M. Louise Hunt's Refusal to Purchase a Liberty Bond, Civil Liberties, and Female Citizenship in the First World War." *Peace & Change*. 44, no.2: 147.

Jessop, Bob. 2012. "Liberalism, Neoliberalism, and Urban Governance: A State-Theoretical Perspective." *Antipode*. 34, no.3: 453.

Joaquim, Joanne. 2016. Marketing Officer at Berwick Offray. Personal email communication, April 11.

Johnson, Boris. 2007. "How, as Mayor, I Would Help Out Brave Troops." *The Spectator*. December 15. https://www.spectator.co.uk/2007/12/how-as-mayor-i-would-help-our-brave-troops/

Johnson, Chalmers. 2004. *The Sorrows of Empire: Militarism, Secrecy, and the End of Republic*. New York: Metropolitan Books.

Jones, Heather. 2014. "The Great War: How 1914–18 Changed the Relationship Between War and Civilians." *The RUSI Journal*. 159, no.4: 84–91.

Jordan, David. 2006. "Poppies and Presenters." BBC. November 10. https://www.bbc.co.uk/blogs/theeditors/2006/11/poppies_and_presenters.html.

Kant, Immanuel, 1991 [1795]. *Kant's Political Writings*. 2nd ed. Edited by Hans Reiss. Translated by H. B. Nisbet. Cambridge: Cambridge University Press.

Kaplan, Amy. 1990. "Romancing the Empire: The Embodiment of American Masculinity in the Popular Historical Novel of the 1890s." *American Literary History*. 2, no.4: 659–90.

Kayal, Michele. 2005. "Even in Paradise of Turquoise Waters, Absence and Stress Take Their Toll." *New York Times*. January 28.

Keegan, John. 1999. *The First World War*. New York: Alfred A Knopf.

Keene, Jennifer D. 2014. "Americans Respond: Perspectives on the Global War, 1914–1917." *Geschichte und Gesellschaft*. 40, no.2: 266–86.

Kelly, John. 2012. "Popular Culture, Sport and the 'Hero'-ification of British Militarism." *Sociology*. 47, no.4: 722–38.

Kelly, Ryan et al. 2010. "The Military and the Transition to Adulthood." *The Future of Children*. 20, no.1: 181–207.

Kerber, Linda. K. 1998. *No Constitutional Right to be Ladies: Women and the Obligations of Citizenship*. New York: Hill and Wang.

Kessler, Glen, and Phillip Pan. 2003. "Powell Tries to Keep Turks Out of N. Iraq; Secretary Ties Aid to Cooperation." *Washington Post*. April 2, A27.

Khalid, Maryam. 2011. "Gender, Orientalism and Representations of the 'Other' in the War on Terror." *Global Change, Peace & Security*. 23, no.1: 15–29.

Khalid, Maryam. 2014. "'Gendering Orientalism': Gender, Sexuality, and Race in Post-9/11 Global Politics." *Critical Race & Whiteness Studies*. 10, no.1: 1–18.

Khalid, Maryam. 2015. "Feminist Perspectives on Militarism and War: Critiques, Contradictions, and Collusions." In *The Oxford Handbook of Transnational Feminist Movements*, edited by Rawwida Baksh and Wendy Harcourt, 632–50. Oxford: Oxford University Press.

Khalid, Maryam. 2017. *Gender, Orientalism, and the "War on Terror": Representation, Discourse, and Intervention in Global Politics*. Abingdon: Routledge.

Kier, Elizabeth. 1999. *Imagining War: French and British Military Doctrine Between the Wars*. Princeton: Princeton University Press.

Kierkegaard, Soren. 1980. *Concept of Anxiety*. Princeton: Princeton University Press.

Kimball, Jeffrey. 2008. "The Enduring Paradigm of the 'Lost Cause': Defeat in Vietnam, the Stab-in-the-Back Legend, and the Construction of a Myth." In *Defeat and Memory*, edited by Jenny Maclead, 233–50. London: Palgrave Macmillan.

Kimmel, Michael. 2017. *Manhood in America*. New York: Oxford University Press.

Kimmel, Michael S. 2018. "The Contemporary "Crisis" of Masculinity in Historical Perspective." In *The Making of Masculinities*, edited by Harry Brod, 121–53. London: Routledge.

King, Anthony. 2013. *The Combat Soldier*. Oxford: Oxford University Press.

Kinsella, Helen A. 2005. "Securing the Civilian: Sex and Gender in the Laws of War." In *Power in Global Governance*, edited by Michael Barnett and Raymond Duvall. 249–72. Cambridge: Cambridge University Press.

Knudson, Laura. 2009. "Cindy Sheehan and the Rhetoric of Motherhood: A Textual Analysis." *Peace & Change*. 34 no.2: 164–83.

Krebs, Ronald R. 2006. *Fighting for Rights: Military Service and the Politics of Citizenship*. Ithaca: Cornell University Press.

Krishna, Sankaran. 2001. "Race, Amnesia, and the Education of International Relations." *Alternatives*. 26, no.4: 401–24.

Kristeva, Julia. 1980. *Desire in Language: A Semiotic Approach to Literature and Art*. New York: Columbia University Press.

Kruzel, John. 2007. "America Supports You: Pennsylvania Vet Receives Brotherly Love." American Forces Press Service. January 3. http://archive.defense.gov/news/newsarti cle.aspx?id=2587.

Kulman, Linda, Rick Newman, and Mark Mazzetti. 2001. "Covering All Bases." *US News & World Report*, November 19, 44.

Kuntsman, Adi. 2008. "The Soldier and the Terrorist: Sexy Nationalism, Queer Violence." *Sexualities*. 11, nos. 1–2: 142–70.

Kurpius, Gary, and Paul Morin. 2007. "Show Our Troops the Money." *Washington Post*. April 12, A15.

Lai, Brian, and Dan Reiter. 2005. "Rally 'Round the Union Jack? Public Opinion and the Use of Force in the United Kingdom. 1948–2001." *International Studies Quarterly*. 49, no.2: 255–72.

Lainer-Vos, Dan. 2014. "Masculinities in Interaction: The Coproduction of Israeli and American Jewish Men in Philanthropic Fundraising Events." *Men and Masculinities*. 17, no.1: 43–66.

Lang, Hardin et al. 2021. "After the Airlift: Protection for Afghan Refugees and Those Who Remain at Risk in Afghanistan." Refugees International. https://www.refugeesin ternational.org/reports/2021/9/7/after-the-airlift-protection-for-afghan-refugees-and-those-who-remain-at-risk-in-afghanistan.

Larsen, Lotte. 1994. "The Yellow Ribboning of America: A Gulf War Phenomenon." *Journal of American Culture.* 17, no.1: 11–22.

LaSalle University. N.d. "Advertising for Military Recruitment." Digitial Visual Archive. https://digitalcommons.lasalle.edu/military_advertisements_visual_history/#.

Lasswell, Harrold D., 1941. "The Garrison State." *American Journal of Sociology.* 46, no.4: 455–68.

Lau, Richard R., Thad A. Brown, and David O. Sears. 1978. "Self-Interest and Civilians' Attitudes Toward the Vietnam War." *Public Opinion Quarterly.* 42, no.4: 464–82.

Law Enforcement Equipment Program. (LEEP). 2008. "Take the LEEP for America." July 27. http://web.archive.org/web/20080727025657/http://www.lawenforcementequip mentprogram.org/.

LeBalanc, Paul. 2017. "The Countries That Allow Transgender Troops to Serve in Their Armed Forces." CNN. July 27. https://edition.cnn.com/2017/07/27/us/world-transgen der-ban-facts/index.html.

Lee, Barbara. 2005. National Defense Authorization Act for Fiscal Year 2006. US Congressional Record. House of Representatives. May 25. H4039–H4040. Thomas.loc. gov.

Leff, Mark H. 1991. "The Politics of Sacrifice on the American Home Front in World War II." *The Journal of American History.* 77, no.4: 1296–318.

Leitz, Lisa. 2014. *Fighting for Peace: Veterans and Military Families in the anti–Iraq War Movement.* Minneapolis: University of Minnesota Press.

Levine, Philippa. 1994. "Venereal Disease, Prostitution, and the Politics of Empire: The Case of British India." *Journal of the History of Sexuality.* 4, no.4: 579–602.

Lewis, Holly. 2012. "The Wars of Air and Electricity." *Public.* 10, 13–23.

Library of Congress. N.d. "THOMAS." http://thomas.loc.gov/home/thomas.php.

Library of Congress. N.d. "Webarchiving FAQs." http://www.loc.gov/webarchiving/faq. html#faqs_04.

Library of Congress. N.d. "Web Archive." http://loc.gov/websites/collections/.

Liddington, Jill. 1991. *The Road to Greenham Common: Feminism and anti-Militarism in Britain Since 1820.* Syracuse: Syracuse University Press.

Liptak, Adam. 2011. "Justice Rules for Protestors at Military Funerals." *New York Times.* March 2. http://www.nytimes.com/2011/03/03/us/03scotus.html.

Liu, James Hou-fu, ed. 2005. *New Zealand Identities: Departures and Destinations.* Wellington: Victoria University Press.

Llwyd, Elfyn. 2010. UK Hansard. HC Deb. May 26. c226. TheyWorkforYou.com.

Locke, John. 1980. *Second Treatise of Government.* Indianapolis: Hackett.

Long, Heather. 2013. "Britain and the US Have Betrayed Their Troops Iraqi and Afgan Interpreters." *The Guardian.* September 27. https://www.theguardian.com/commentisf ree/2013/sep/27/afghan-interpreter-visas-janis-shinwari.

Losurdo, Domenico. 2014. *Liberalism: A Counter-History.* London: Verso Trade.

Lowe, Lisa. 2015. *The Intimacies of Four Continents.* Durham: Duke University Press.

Lunch, William, and Peter Sperlich. 1979. "American Public Opinion and the War in Vietnam." *The Western Political Quarterly.* 32, no.1: 21–44.

Lutz, Amy. 2008. "Who Joins the Military?: A Look at Race, Class, and Immigration Status." *Journal of Political and Military Sociology.* 36, no.2: 167–88.

Lutz, Catherine. 2001. *Homefront: A Military City and the American Twentieth Century.* Boston: Beacon Press.

Lutz, Catherine. 2002. "Making War at Home in the United States: Militarization and the Current Crisis." *American Anthropologist*. 104, no.3: 723–35.

Mabee, Bryan. 2016. "From 'Liberal War' to 'Liberal Militarism': United States Security Policy as the Promotion of Military Modernity." *Critical Military Studies*. 2, no.3: 242–61.

Mabee, Bryan, and Srdjan Vucetic. 2018. "Varieties of Militarism: Towards a Typology." *Security Dialogue*. 49, no. 1–2: 96–108.

MacAskill, Ewen. 2015. "British Army Reluctant to Post Troops on UK Streets After Terror Attack." The Guardian. July 26. https://www.theguardian.com/uk-news/2015/jul/26/british-army-reluctant-post-troops-uk-terror-attack.

MacLeish, Kenneth. 2013. *Making War at Fort Hood: Life and Uncertainty in a Military Community*. Princeton: Princeton University Press.

MacLeish, Kenneth T. 2019. "How to Feel about War: On Soldier Psyches, Military Biopolitics, and American Empire." *BioSocieties*. 14, no.2: 274–99.

MacKenzie, Megan. 2015. *Beyond the Band of Brothers: The US Military and the Myth that Women Can't Fight*. Cambridge: Cambridge University Press.

MacKenzie, Megan, Thomas Gregory, Nisha Shah, Tarak Barkawi, Toni Haastrup, Maya Eichler, Nicole Wegner, and Alison Howell. 2019. "Can We Really "Forget" Militarization? A Conversation on Alison Howell's Martial Politics." *International Feminist Journal of Politics*. 21. no.5: 816–36.

Major, Lesa Hatley, and David D. Perlmutter. 2005. "The Fall of a Pseudo-Icon: The Toppling of Saddam Hussein's Statue as Image Management." *Visual Communication Quarterly* 12, nos.1–2: 38–45.

Managhan, Tina. 2011a. "Grieving Dead Soldiers, Disavowing Loss: Cindy Sheehan and the Im/possibility of the American Anti-War Movement." *Geopolitics*. 16, no.2: 438–66.

Managhan, Tina. 2011b. "Highways, Heroes, and Secular Martyrs: The Symbolics of Power and Sacrifice." *Review of International Studies*. 31, no.1: 97–118.

Managhan, Tina. 2012. *Gender, Agency and War: The Maternalized Body in US Foreign Policy*. London: Routledge.

Manchanda, Nivi. 2022. "The Janus-faced Nature of Militarization." *Critical Military Studies*. 1–5.

Mann, Bonnie. 2006. "How America Justifies Its War: A Modern/Postmodern Aesthetics of Masculinity and Sovereignty." *Hypatia*. 21, no.4: 147–63.

Mann, Bonnie. 2013. *Sovereign Masculinity: Gender Lessons from the War on Terror*. Oxford: Oxford University Press.

Mann, Michael. 1987. The Roots and Contradictions of Modern Militarism. *New Left Review Series*. 162 (March–April): 35–50

Marsical, George. 1991. "In the Wake of the Gulf War: Untying the Yellow Ribbon." *Cultural Critique*. 19: 97–117.

Marsical, Jorge. 2007. "The Poverty Draft." *Sojourners Magazine*. June. https://sojo.net/magazine/june-2007/poverty-draft.

Marten, James A. 2011. *Sing Not War: The Lives of Union & Confederate Veterans in Gilded Age America*. Chapel Hill: University of North Carolina Press.

Martin de Almagro, Maria. 2019. "Borders, Boundaries, and Brokers: The Unintended Consequences of Strategic Essentialism in Transnational Feminist Networks." In *Intersectionality in Feminist and Queer Movements*, edited by Elizabeth Evans and Éléonore Lépinard, 29–45. Abingdon: Routledge.

Marx, Karl. 1843 [1975]. *On the Jewish Question*. New York: Norton.

Massie, Allan. 2004. "SNP Shows True Colours Over Troop Support." *The Sunday Times.* August 14. Scotland News 18.

Mayring, Philip. 2000. "Qualitative Content Analysis." *Forum: Qualitative Social Research.* 1, no.2: Art. 20. https://www.qualitative-research.net/index.php/fqs/article/view/1089/2386

McCabe, Brian J. 2010. "Public Opinion on 'Don't Ask, Don't Tell.'" *New York Times.* November 30. https://fivethirtyeight.blogs.nytimes.com/2010/11/30/public-opinion-on-dont-ask-dont-tell/.

McCain, John. 2008. "Remarks at a Campaign Event in Ohio." *Washington Post.* September 29. http://www.washingtonpost.com/wp-dyn/content/article/2008/09/29/AR200809 2901431.html.

McCartney, Helen. 2010. "The Military Covenant and Civil-Military Relations in Britain." *International Affairs.* 86, no.2: 411–28.

McElya, Micki. 2016. *The Politics of Mourning: Death and Honor in Arlington National Cemetery.* Cambridge: Harvard University Press.

McGarry, Ross, and Neil Ferguson. 2012. "Exploring Representations of the Soldier as Victim: From Northern Ireland to Iraq." In *Representations of Peace and Conflict*, edited by Steven Gibson and Simon Mollan, 120–42. London: Palgrave Macmillan.

McGarry, Ross, and Sandra Walklate. 2011. "The Soldier as Victim." *British Journal of Criminology.* 51, no.6: 901–17.

McInnis, Scott. 2003. "America." US Congressional Record. April 7. H2846. Thomas.loc. gov.

McLeod, Douglas, Eveland, William P., and Nancy Signorielli. 1994. "Conflict and Public Opinion: Rallying Effects of the Persian Gulf War." *Journalism & Mass Communication Quarterly.* 71, no.1: 20–31.

Melin, J. 2016. "Desperate Choices: Why Black Women Join the US Military at Higher Rates Than Men and All Other Racial and Ethnic Groups." *New England Journal of Public Policy.* 28, no.2: 8.

Michel, Jean-Baptiste et al. 2011. "Quantitative Analysis of Culture Using Millions of Digitized Books." *Science.* 331, no.6014: 176–182.

Michaels, Jeffrey H. 2013. *The Discourse Trap and the US Military: From the War on Terror to the Surge.* London: Palgrave MacMillan.

Mignolo, Walter. 2011. *The Darker Side of Western Modernity: Global Futures, Decolonial Options.* Durham: Duke University Press.

Milibank, Dana, and Claudia Deane. 2005. "Poll Finds Dimmer View of Iraq War." *Washington Post.* June 8. http://www.washingtonpost.com/wp-dyn/content/article/2005/06/07/AR2005060700296.html.

Military Families Speak Out. 2008. Australia and Canada Speak Out Against the War– Tell Congress to Follow Their Lead! (5 June). Available at: http://www.mfso.org/article.php?id=1211 via Wayback Machine. Accessed 3 January 2016.

Mill, J.S. 2009. *Collected Works.* Vol. 1. London: Routledge.

Millar, Katharine M. 2015. "Death Does Not Become Her: An Examination of the Public Construction of Female American Soldiers as Liminal Figures." *Review of International Studies.* 41 no.4: 757–79.

Millar, Katharine M. 2016a. "'They Need Our Help': Non-governmental Organizations and the Subjectifying Dynamics of the Military as Social Cause." *Media, War & Conflict.* 9, no.1: 9–26.

Millar, Katharine M. 2016b. "Mutually Implicated Myths: The Democratic Control of the Armed Forces and Militarism." In *Myth and Narrative in International Politics: Interpretive Approaches to the Study of IR*, edited by Berit Bliesemann de Guevara. 173–93. Basingstoke: Palgrave MacMillan.

Millar, Katharine M. 2019a. "The Plural of Soldier Is Not Troops: The Politics of Groups in Legitimating Militaristic Violence." *Security Dialogue*. 50, no.3: 201–19.

Millar, Katharine M. 2019b. "What Do We Do Now? Examining Civilian Masculinity/ies in Contemporary Liberal Civil-Military Relations." *Review of International Studies*, 45, no.2: 239–59.

Millar, Katharine M. 2021. "What Makes Violence Martial? Adopt a Sniper and Normative Imaginaries of Violence in the Contemporary United States." *Security Dialogue*. 52, no.6: 493–511.

Millar, Katharine. M., and Joanna Tidy. 2017. "Combat as a Moving Target: Masculinities, the Heroic Soldier Myth, and Normative Martial Violence." *Critical Military Studies*. 3, no.2: 142–60.

Milliken, Jennifer. 1999. "The Study of Discourse in International Relations: A Critique of Research and Methods." *European Journal of International Relations*. 5, no.2: 225–54.

Mills, Charles W. 2014. *The Racial Contract*. Ithaca: Cornell University Press.

Mirlees, Tanner. 2015. "The Canadian Armed Forces 'Youtube War': A Cross-Border Military-Social Media Complex." *Global Media Journal*. 8, no.1: 71–93.

Mitchell, Ellen. 2018. "Court Rules Against Trump Administration on Transgender Military Ban." The Hill. July 18. https://thehill.com/policy/defense/397702-court-rules-against-trump-admin-on-transgender-military-ban.

Mitchell, Timothy. 1991a. "The Limits of the State: Beyond Statist Approaches and Their Critics." *American Political Science Review*. 85, no.1: 77–96.

Mitchell, Timothy. 1991b. *Colonizing Egypt*. Berkley: University of California Press.

Montgomery, David. 2005. "On Freedom Walk, Many Bridges to Cross." *Washington Post*. September 12.

Moore, Gwen. 2004. Reimbursing Members of United States Armed Forces for Certain Transportation Expenses. Congressional Record. March 30. H1690. THOMAS.loc.gov.

Moore, Sarah. 2008. *Ribbon Culture: Charity, Compassion, and Public Awareness*. Basingstoke: Palgrave MacMillan.

Moosavi, Leon. 2015. "Orientalism at Home: Islamophobia in the Representations of Islam and Muslims by the New Labour Government." *Ethnicities*. 15, no.5: 652–74.

Moseley, Alexander. 2005. "John Locke's Morality of War." *Journal of Military Ethics*. 4, no.2: 119–28.

Mueller, John E. 1973. *War, Presidents, and Public Opinion*. New York: Wiley.

Murray, Craig et al. 2008. "Reporting Dissent in Wartime: British Press, Iraq and the 2003 Anti-War Movement." *European Journal of Communication*. 23, no.1: 7–27.

Mycock, Andrew. 2014. "The First World War Centenary in the UK: 'A Truly National Commemoration'?" *The Round Table*. 103, no.2: 153–63.

Natanel, Katherine. 2016. "Border Collapse and Boundary Maintenance: Militarisation and the Micro-Geographies of Violence in Israel–Palestine." *Gender, Place & Culture*. 23, no.6: 897–911.

National Archives. N.d. "Twenty-Year Rule." Government of the United Kingdom. http://www.nationalarchives.gov.uk/about/20-year-rule.htm.

National Archives. N.d. "UK Government Web Archive: Home." http://www.nationalarchives.gov.uk/webarchive/.

National Army Museum. N.d. "The Troubles." https://www.nam.ac.uk/explore/troub les-1969-2007.

National Executive Committee Emergency Resolution on the Gulf Memorandum, 30 January 1991, provided by Jeremy Corbyn, MP, from his personal files.

NBC News. 2010. "Supreme Court Weighs Arguments in 'Thank God for Dead Soldiers' Case." October 6. http://www.nbcnews.com/id/39531700/ns/politics/t/supreme-court-weighs-arguments-over-thank-god-dead-soldiers-funeral-protest/#.V1Qt 0PkrLIU.

Ndlovu-Gatsheni, Sabelo. 2019. Keynote address at *Millennium: Journal of International Studies* conference, London School of Economics, London (derived from personal notes).

Neumann, Iver B. 2008. "Discourse Analysis." In *Qualitative Methods in International Relations: A Pluralist Guide*, edited by Audie Klotz and Deepa Prakash. 61–77. Chippenham and Eastbourne: Palgrave MacMillan.

Newall, V. 1976. "Armistice Day: Folk Tradition in an English Festival of Remembrance." *Folklore.* 87/ no.2: 226–29.

News.com.au. 2015. "Parades to Welcome Home Soldiers Who Served in Afghanistan to Be Held Around Australia Today." News Corp Australia Network. March 21. http://www.news.com.au/national/parades-to-welcome-home-soldiers-who-served-in-afgh anistan-to-be-held-around-australia-today/story-fncynjr2-1227272380731.

New York Times. 1970. "One-Third of Americans Killed in Vietnam are Draftees." February 11. https://www.nytimes.com/1970/02/12/archives/onethird-of-americans-killed-in-vietnam-war-are-draftees.html

New York Times. 2011. *Timeline of Major Events in Iraq War.* (21 October). Available at http://www.nytimes.com/interactive/2010/08/31/world/middleeast/20100831-Iraq-Timeline.html?_r=0#/#time111_3263. Accessed 13 August 2015.

Newton Dunn, Tom, and Martin Phillips. 2009. "A Disgrace, Your Grace." *The Sun.* October 10. http://www.thesun.co.uk/sol/homepage/news/campaigns/our_boys/2675 598/Archbishop-of-Canterburys-war-rant-mars-troops-tribute.html.

Niva, Steve. 1998. "Tough and Tender: New World Order Masculinity and the Gulf War." In *The "Man" Question in International Relations.* 1st ed., edited by Marysia Zalweski and Jane Parpart, 102–28. Abingdon: Routledge.

No One Left Behind. N.d. "Press." https://nooneleft.org/press/.

Norpoth, Helmut. 1987. "Guns and Butter and Government Popularity in Britain." *American Political Science Review.* 81, no.3: 949–59.

Odysseos, Louiza. 2007. "Crossing the Line? Carl Schmitt on 'Spaceless Univeralism' of Cosmopolitanism and the War on Terror." In *The International Political Thought of Carl Schmitt: Terror, Liberal War and the Crisis of Global Order*, edited by L. Odysseos and F. Petito. 124–43. London: Routledge.

Office for National Statistics. 2014. "Population and Migration, Government of United Kingdom." Office for National Statistics. June 5. http://www.ons.gov.uk/ons/guide-method/compendiums/compendium-of-uk-statistics/population-and-migration/index.html.

Office of the White House Press Secretary. 2010. Remarks by the President in Address to the Nation on the End of Combat Operations in Iraq. August 31. https://www.whi tehouse.gov/the-press-office/2010/08/31/remarks-president-address-nation-end-com bat-operations-iraq.

Ogg, Frederic A. 1918. "The British Representation of the People Act." *The American Political Science Review*. 12, no.3: 498–503.

Oneal, John R., Frances H. Oneal, Zeev Maoz, and Bruce Russett. 1996. "The Liberal Peace: Interdependence, Democracy, and International Conflict, 1950–85." *Journal of Peace Research*. 33, no.1: 11–28.

Operation Gratitude. (OpGrat.) 2006. "Homepage." March 15. http://web.archive.org/web/20060315033602/http://www.opgratitude.com/.

Oregon Military Families Speak Out. 2009. "Funds Raised to Buy Proper Scope for Soldier." November. Available in Swarthmore College Peace Collection Archives, Pennsylvania. DG-253, Acc. 2013–069.

Orwig, Marcy L. 2017. "Persuading the Home Front: The Communication Surrounding the World War I Campaign to 'Knit' Patriotism." *Journal of Communication Inquiry*. 41, no.1: 60–82.

Overy, Richard. 2005. "Total War II: The Second World War." In *The Oxford History of Modern War*, edited by Charles Townshend. 2nd ed. 138–57. Oxford: Oxford University Press.

Papayanis, Alena. 2010. "Everybody's Coming Back a Hero: Reflections and Deflections of Heroism in the Gulf." *Journal of War & Culture Studies*. 3, no.2: 237–48.

Parashar, Swati. 2018. "Discursive (In)securities and Postcolonial Anxiety: Enabling Excessive Militarism in India." *Security Dialogue*. 49, nos.1–2: 123–35.

Paris, Michael. 2000. *Warrior Nation: Images of War in British Popular Culture, 1850–2000*. London: Reaktion.

Parker, George, Helen Warrell, and Robert Wright. 2021. "UK Leaves Over 1,000 Afghans Behind with Airlift Set to End." *Financial Times*. August 27. https://www.ft.com/content/5cd260c6-e57a-4798-8837-44da6efaef24.

Parliament of the United Kingdom. N.d. "Hansard." http://www.parliament.uk/business/publications/hansard/.

Parliament of the United Kingdom. 2018. "Lost in Translation? Afghan Interpreters and Other Locally Employed Civilians." May 26. https://publications.parliament.uk/pa/cm201719/cmselect/cmdfence/572/57209.htm

Parry, Katy. 2011. "Images of Liberation? Visual Framing, Humanitarianism and British Press Photography During the 2003 Iraq Invasion." *Media, War, and Culture*. 33, no.8: 1185–202.

Parsons, Gerald E. 1981. "Yellow Ribbons: Ties with Tradition." *Folklife Center News*. 4, no.2: n.p.

Parsons, Gerald E. 1991. "How the Yellow Ribbon Became a National Folk Symbol." *Folklife Center News* 13, no.3: 9–11.

Parsons, Timothy. 2000. "Dangerous Education? The Army as School in Colonial East Africa." *The Journal of Imperial and Commonwealth History*. 28, no.1: 112–34.

Pateman, Carole. 2007 [1985]. *The Problem of Political Obligation: A Critique of Liberal Theory*. Cambridge: Polity Press.

Pateman, Carole. 1987 [1988]. "The Patriarchal Welfare State." In *Democracy and the Welfare State*, edited by Amy Gutman, 231–61. Princeton: Princeton University Press. (working paper version at http://bev.berkeley.edu/ipe/Pateman%20the%20Patriarchal%20Welfare%20State.pdf)

Pateman, Carole. 1988. *The Sexual Contract*. Redwood City: Stanford University Press.

Pateman, Carole, and Elizabeth Grosz. 2013. *Feminist Challenges: Social and Political Theory*. Abingdon: Routledge.

Pateman, Carole, Charles Wade Mills, and Charles Wright Mills. 2009. *Contract and Domination*. London: Polity.

Patten, Eileen, and Kim Parker. N.d. "Women in the U.S. Military: Growing Share, Distinctive Profile." Pew Social and Demographic Trends. https://www.pewresearch.org/wp-content/uploads/sites/3/2011/12/women-in-the-military.pdf.

Pax Christi. (PC). 2005. "The Organizer." December 28. http://www.paxchristiusa.org/news_the_organizer_story.asp?id=342.

Peace and Social Witness. (PSW). 2010. "Remembrance Day in Britain." http://www.quaker.org.uk/remembrance-day.

Penn-Barwell, J. G., S. A. Roberts, M. J. Midwinter, and J. R. Bishop, 2015. "Improved Survival in UK Combat Casualties from Iraq and Afghanistan: 2003–2012." *Journal of Trauma and Acute Care Surgery*. 78, no.5: 1014–20.

Perry, Keisha-Khan Y. 2013. *Black Women Against the Land Grab: The Fight for Racial Justice in Brazil*. Minneapolis: University of Minnesota Press.

Peter, Tom A. 2016. "Finally, A Realistic Iraq War Novel." *The New Republic*. August 2. https://newrepublic.com/article/135730/finally-realistic-iraq-war-novel.

Peterson, V. Spike. 2010. "Gendered Identities, Ideologies, and Practices in the Context of War and Militarism." In *Gender, War, and Militarism: Feminist Perspectives*, edited by L. Sjoberg and S. Via. 17–29. Boulder: Praeger

Pew Research Center. 2014. "Ideological Placement of Each Source's Audience." October 20. http://www.journalism.org/2014/10/21/political-polarization-media-habits/pj_14-10-21_mediapolarization-08/.

Piehler, G. Kurt. 2004. *Remembering War the American Way*. Washington, DC: Smithsonian Books.

Pienaar, John. 1991. Crisis in the Gulf–Labour Leader Kinnock Accused of Stifling Dissent. *The Independent*. (19 February).

Poutvaara, Panu, and Andreas Wagener. 2011. "Ending Military Conscription." CESifo DICE Report. February. https://www.cesifo-group.de/DocDL/dicereport211-rr1.pdf.

Prime Minister's Office. (PMO). 2004. Press Briefing—3:45pm Wednesday 28 April 2004. http://www.webarchive.org.uk/wayback/archive/20080303155920/http://www.pm.gov.output/Page5720.asp.

Prividera, Laura, and John Howard. 2006. "Masculinity, Whiteness, and the Warrior Hero: Perpetuating the Strategic Rhetoric of U.S. Nationalism and the Marginalization of Women." *Women and Language*. 29, no.2: 29–37.

Proctor, Tammy M. 2010. *Civilians in a World at War, 1914–1918*. New York: New York University Press.

ProPublica. N.d. "Many Types of Nonprofits." https://projects.propublica.org/nonprofits/ctypes.

Quandt, Katie Rose. 2015. "This Chart Sums Up the Pentagon's Paid Patriotism Program." *The Guardian*. November 6. http://www.slate.com/articles/sports/sports_nut/2015/11/paid_patriotism_the_pentagon_gave_50_sports_teams_taxpayer_money_to_honor.html.

Rahbek-Clemmenson, Jon et al. 2012. "Conceptualizing the Civil Military Gap: A Research Note." *Armed Forces and Society*. 38, no.4: 669–78.

Ralph, Jason. 2013. *America's War on Terror: The State of the 9/11 Exception from Bush to Obama*. Oxford: Oxford University Press.

Rao, Rahul. 2014. "Queer Question." *International Feminist Journal of Politics*. 16, no.2: 199–217.

Rashid, Maria. 2020. *Dying to Serve: Militarism, Affect, and the Politics of Sacrifice in the Pakistan Army*. Stanford: Stanford University Press.

Rashid, Maria. 2021. "'Appropriate'ing Grief: Mothers, Widows and the (un) Grievability of Military Weath." *NORMA*, 17, no.1: 52–66.

Razack, Sherene. 2004. *Dark Threats and White Knights: The Somalia Affair, Peacekeeping and the New Imperialism*. Toronto: University of Toronto Press.

Rech, Matthew. 2014. "Recruitment, Counter-Recruitment and Critical Military Studies." *Global Discourse*. 4, no.23: 244–62.

Rech, Matthew. 2015. "Geography, Military Geography and Critical Military Studies." *Critical Military Studies*. 1, no.1: 47–60.

Redfield, James. 1977. "The Women of Sparta." *The Classical Journal*. 73, no.2: 146–61.

Reese, Stephen D., and Seth C. Lewis. 2009. "Framing the War on Terror: The Internalization of Policy in the US Press." *Journalism*. 10, no.6: 777–97.

Reid, Harry. 2010. Federal Aviation Administration Extension Act of 2010. Congressional Record. December 14. P. S90s00. THOMAS.loac.gov.

Renwick, Aly. 2016. "Something in the Air: The Rise of the Troops Out Movement." In *The Northern Ireland Troubles in Britain*, edited by Graham Dawson, Jo Dover, and Stephen Hopkins, 111–26. Manchester: Manchester University Press.

Reuters. 2015. "2014 Deadliest Year for Civilians in Iraq Since 2006–7 Bloodshed—UN." January 2. http://uk.reuters.com/article/2015/01/02/uk-mideast-crisis-iraq-deaths-idUKKBN0KB0K320150102.

Richler, Noah. 2012. *What We Talk About When We Talk About War*. Fredericton: Goose Lane Editions.

Richter-Montpetit, Melanie. 2007. "Empire, Desire and Violence: A Queer Transnational Feminist Reading of the Prisoner 'Abuse' in Abu Ghraib and the Question of 'Gender Equality'." *International Feminist Journal of Politics*. 9, no.1: 38–59.

Richter-Montpetit, Melanie. 2014. "Beyond the Erotics of Orientalism: Lawfare, Torture and the Racial-Sexual Grammars of Legitimate Suffering." *Security Dialogue*. 45, no.1: 43–62.

Robathan, Andrew. 2010a. Land Warfare Conference. June 8. https://www.gov.uk/government/speeches/2010-06-08-land-warfare-conference.

Robathan, Andrew. 2010b. House of Commons Debate. HC Deb. November 25. c505. TheyWorkForYou.com.

Rodrigo, Chris Mills. 2019. "Poll: Majority of Americans Say Transgender People Should be Allowed in Military." The Hill. January 29. https://thehill.com/homenews/news/427516-poll-majority-of-americans-believe-transgender-people-should-be-allowed-in-the.

Roper, Michael. 1994. *Masculinity and the British Organization Man Since 1945*. Oxford: Oxford University Press.

Ros-Lehtinen, Ileana. 2007. Debate on Iraq War Resolution. Congressional Record. February 16. H1830. THOMAS.loc.gov.

Rossdale, Chris. 2019. *Resisting Militarism. Direct Action and the Politics of Subversion*. Edinburgh: Edinburgh University Press.

Royall, Baroness of Blaisdon. 2009. UK Hansard. HL Deb. November 30. c662. Theyworkforyou.gov.

Royal British Legion. 2003. "Can You Help Us?" http://web.archive.org/web/20031025134856/http://www.britishlegion.org.uk/helpus/index.asp.

Royal British Legion. 2007. "It's Time to Honour the Covenant." October 10. http://web. archive.org/web/20071010045139/http://www.britishlegion.org.uk/news/index. cfm?fuseaction=newsdetail&asset_id=517232.

Royal British Legion. 2010a. "Gordon Brown Pledges to "do his bit" for British Armed Forces." March 16. http://web.archive.org/web/20100425182258/http://www.britishleg ion.org.uk/about-us/media-centre/news/campaigning/gordon-brown-pledges-to-do-his-bit-for-british-armed-forces/.

Royal British Legion. 2010b. "It's Time to Do Your Bit." February 27. http://web.archive. org/web/20120530032140/http://e-activist.com/ea-campaign/clientcampaign.do?ea. client.id=145&ea.campaign.id=4388.

Ruddick, Sara. 1980. "Maternal Thinking." Feminist Studies. 6, no 2: 342–67.

Runyan, Anne Sisson, and V. Spike Peterson. 2014. Global Gender Issues in the New Millennium. Boulder: Westview Press.

Sabbagh, Dan. 2020. "UK Soldiers 12% More likely to Die in 'War on Terror' Than US Troops." The Guardian. December 4. https://www.theguardian.com/uk-news/2020/ dec/04/uk-soldiers-more-likely-die-us-troops-war-terror.

Said, Edward. 1978. Orientalism. London: Penguin.

Sanchez, Mark. 2017. "MLB Callously Uses Fallen Soldiers to Sell Hats." New York Post. May 29. https://nypost.com/2017/05/29/mlb-callously-uses-fallen-soldiers-to-sell-hats/.

Sands, Sarah. 2008. "The Brave Wears a Uniform, the Coward Wears a Suit." The Independent. March 9. http://www.independent.co.uk/voices/commentators/sarah-sands/sarah-sands-the-brave-wear-a-uniform-the-coward-wears-a-suit-793361.html.

Santino, Jack. 1992. "Yellow Ribbons and Seasonal Flags: The Folk Assemblage of War." The Journal of American Folklore. 105, no.415: 19–33.

Sasson-Levy, Orna. 2003. "Military, Masculinity, and Citizenship: Tensions and Contradictions in the Experience of Blue-Collar Soldiers' Identities." Global Studies in Culture and Power. 10, no.3: 319–45.

Sasson-Levy, Orna. 2008. "Individual Bodies, Collective State Interests: The Case of Israeli Combat Soldiers." Men and Masculinities. 10, no.3: 296–321.

Savell, Stephanie. 2021. "United States Counterterrorism Operations 2018–2020." Watson Institute. https://watson.brown.edu/costsofwar/files/cow/imce/papers/2021/US%20C ounterterrorism%20Operations%202018-2020%2C%20Costs%20of%20War.pdf.

Scarry, Elaine. 1985. The Body in Pain: The Making and Unmaking of the World. Oxford: Oxford University Press.

Schaffer, Ron. 2004a. "Beware the Wobbly Wheel Scam." Washington Post. September 19.

Schaffer, Ron. 2004b. "Drivers Ticked Off at Missing Kickoff." Washington Post. September 26.

Schaffer, Ron. 2004c. "Reader Decries Symbolic Patriotism on Cars." Washington Post. October 14.

Schaffer, Ron. 2004d. "Now a Word From Nissan Pavilion." Washington Post. October 21.

Schippers, Mimi. 2007. "Recovering the Feminine Other: Masculinity, Femininity, and Gender Hegemony." Theory and Society. 36, no.1: 85–102.

Schmidt, William. 1988. "Some Now in Congress Joined Reserve or Guard." New York Times. August 20. https://www.nytimes.com/1988/08/20/us/some-now-in-congress-joined-reserve-or-guard.html.

Schogol, Jeff. 2010. "Media Groups Side with Westboro Protestors in Court Case." *Stars and Stripes*. July 16. https://web.archive.org/web/20100804212844/http://www.vfw.org/index.cfm?fa=news.newsDtl&did=5545/.

Schrader, Benjamin. 2019. *Fight to Live, Live to Fight: Veteran Activism After War*. Albany: State University of New York Press.

Schreier, Margrit. 2013. "Qualitative Content Analysis." In *The SAGE Handbook of Qualitative Data Analysis*, edited by Uwe Flick. 170–83. London: SAGE.

Searle, Geoffrey Russell. 2004. *A New England?: Peace and War, 1886–1918*. Vol. 6. Oxford: Oxford University Press.

Secretary of Defense Employer Support Freedom Award. 2016. "Homepage." http://www.freedomaward.mil/.

Sengupta, Kim. 2004. "Your Country Would Really Quite Like You." *The Independent*. March 4.

Sennott, Charles. 2010. "Countries Where Gays Do Serve Openly in The Military." Huffington Post. April 5. https://www.huffingtonpost.com/2010/02/03/countries-where-gays-do-s_n_448317.html.

Sew Much Comfort. N.d. "Home."http://www.sewmuchcomfort.org/.

Shaw, Martin. 1988. *Dialectics of War*. London: Pluto.

Shaw, Martin. 1996. *Civil Society and Media in Global Crises: Representing Distant Violence*. London: Pinter.

Shaw, Martin. 2013. "Twentieth-Century Militarism: A Historical Sociological Framework." In *Militarism and International Relations: Political Economy, Security, Theory*, edited by A. Stavrianakis and J. Selby, 19–32. London: Routledge.

Sheehan, James. 2009. *Where Have All the Soldiers Gone? The Transformation of Modern Europe*. Boston: Houghton Mifflin.

Sherwood, Harriet. 2018. "Indians in the trenches: Voices of Forgotten Army Are Finally to Be Heard." *The Guardian*. October 27. https://www.theguardian.com/world/2018/oct/27/armistice-centenary-indian-troops-testimony-sacrifice-british-library

Shulte, Brigid. 2006. "Doing Battle for the Grunts; Virginia Group Seeks to Protect US Troops on the Frontline." *Washington Post*. February 2, T03.

Shy, John W. 1990. *A People Numerous and Armed: Reflections on the Military Struggle for American Independence*. Detroit: University of Michigan Press.

Silvestri, Lisa 2013. "Surprise Homecomings and Vicarious Sacrifices." *Media, War, & Conflict*. 6, no.2: 101–15.

Simmons, A. John. 1981. *Moral Principles and Political Obligations*. Princeton: Princeton University Press.

Simmons, Melody. 2007. "Marine's Father Sues Church for Cheering Son's Death." *New York Times*. October 26. http://www.nytimes.com/2007/10/26/us/26funeral.html?_r=0.

Simons, Geoff. 1997. *The Vietnam Syndrome: Impact on US Foreign Policy*. New York: Springer.

Skocpol, Theda. 1993. "America's First Social Security System: The Expansion of Benefits for Civil War Veterans." *Political Science Quarterly*. 108, no.1: 85–116.

Skocpol, Theda. 1995. *Protecting Soldiers and Mothers*. Cambridge: Harvard University Press.

Small, Melvin. 1988. *Johnson, Nixon, and the Doves*. New Brunswick: Rutgers University Press.

Sokhi-Bulley, Bal. 2013. "Counter Conduct or Resistance? The Disciplining of Dissent in the Riot City of London." Research Working Paper No. 2014-07. Queen's University Belfast.

Soldier On. N.d. "About Us." https://www.soldieron.org.au/how-we-help/about-soldier-on/.

Soldiers', Sailors' and Airmen's Family Association. SSAFA Newsletter, 1990 Annual Report, provided by Juliet Chaplin, SSAFA archivist.

Sparrow, B., and D. S. Inbody. 2005. "Supporting Our Troops? US Civil-Military Relations in the Twenty-first Century." Annual Meeting of the American Political Science Association, Marriott Wardman Park, Omni Shoreham, Washington Hilton, Washington, DC. September.

Spiers, Edward. 1992. *The Late Victorian Army: 1868–1902*. Manchester: Manchester University Press.

Stachowitsch, Saskia. 2013. "Military Privatization and the Remasculinization of the State: Making the Link Between the Outsourcing of Military Security and Gendered State Transformations." *International Relations*. 27, no.1: 74–80.

Stafford Branch. "The Military Wives Single." The Royal British Legion. 2010. Wayback Machine. http://branches.britishlegion.org.uk/branches/stafford/the-military-wives-single.

Stahl, Roger. 2009. "Why We 'Support the Troops': Rhetorical Evolutions." *Rhetoric & Public Affairs*. 12, no.4: 553–70.

Stavrianakis, Anna, and Jan Selby. 2013. "Militarism and International Relations in the Twenty-First Century." In *Militarism and International Relations: Political Economy, Security, Theory*, edited by Anna Stavarianakis and Jan Selby. 3–18. Abingdon: Routledge.

Stavrianakis, Anna, and Maria Stern. 2018. "Militarism and Security: Dialogue, Possibilities and Limits." *Security Dialogue*. 49, nos.1–2: 3–18.

Stevens, K. E. 2016. "Flight of the White Feather: The Expansion of the White Feather Movement Throughout the World War One British Commonwealth." MA thesis, Georgia Southern University.

Stevenson, Charles. 2006. *Warriors and Politicians: US Civil-Military Relations Under Stress*. Abingdon: Routledge.

Stoddard, Katy. 2010. "Newspaper Support in UK General Elections." *The Guardian*. May 4. http://www.theguardian.com/news/datablog/2010/may/04/general-election-newspaper-support

Stoler, Ann L. 1989. "Making Empire Respectable: The Politics of Race and Sexual Morality in 20th-Century Colonial Cultures." *American Ethnologist*. 16, no.4: 634–60.

Stop the War Coalition (StWC). N.d. "Not in My Name/Don't Attack Iraq!" Photograph of Protest Signs. Bishopsgate Institute Archives, London.

Stop the War Coalition (StWC). 2009a. "Reports on Stop the War Naming the Dead Events." September 14. http://web.archive.org/web/20090914084240/http://stopwar.org.uk/content/view/1459/27/.

Stop the War Coalition (StWC). 2009b. "Anti-War Protesters Mark Tragic Milestone for Victims of Conflict." August 28. http://web.archive.org/web/20090914084240/http://stopwar.org.uk/content/view/1459/27/.

Strachan, Hew. 2003. The Civil-Military 'Gap' in Britain. *Journal of Strategic Studies*. 26 no.2: 43–63.

Streets, Heather. 2017. *Martial Races: The Military, Race and Masculinity in British Imperial Culture, 1857–1914*. Manchester: Manchester University Press.

Strom, Stephanie. 2007. "Display of Anti-Bush Sign Has Competitive Bridge World in an Uproar." *New York Times*. November 14.

Sturken, Marita. 1997. *Tangled memories: The Vietnam War, the AIDS Epidemic, and the Politics of Remembering*. Berkley: University of California Press.

Stuurman, Ziyanda. 2020. "Policing Inequality and the Inequality of Policing: A Look at the Militarisation of Policing Around the World, Focusing on Brazil and South Africa." *South African Journal of International Affairs*. 27, no.1: 43–66.

Summers, Anne. 1976. "Militarism in Britain Before the Great War." *History Workshop Journal*. 2: 104–23.

Surana, Kavitha, and Molly O'Toole. 2017. "For Iraqi Military Interpreters, Trump Travel Ban Chaos Is 'Life and Death.'" *Foreign Policy*. February 6. https://foreignpolicy.com/2017/02/06/for-iraqi-military-interpreters-trump-travel-ban-chaos-is-life-and-death/

Swanson, Al. 2003. "Patriotism Boosts American Flag Sales." UPI. March 28. http://www.upi.com/Top_News/2003/03/28/Patriotism-boosts-American-flag-sales/5600104 8885689/.

Sylvester, Christine, ed. 2013. *War as Experience: Contributions from International Relations and Feminist Analysis*. Abingdon: Routledge.

Tannock, Stuart. 2005. "Is 'Opting Out' Really an Answer? Schools, Militarism, and the Counter-Recruitment Movement in the Post—9/11 United States." *Social Justice*. 32, no.3: 163–78.

Taranto, James. 2003. "Best of the Web Today—March 24 2003: What Do Sgt. Asan Akbar and the D.C. Sniper Suspect Have in Common?" *Wall Street Journal*. March 24.

Taranto, James. 2004. "Best of the Web Today—August 31 2004; Can a Missouri Dem Win a Seat After Taking a Stand for Gay Marriage?" *Wall Street Journal*. August 31.

Taranto, James. 2005. "Best of the Web Today—February 16 2005; The Dan Rather Scandal Isn't Over. Can CBS News Be Saved? Plus NPR Man Whines About 'Support the Troops' Exhortations!" *Wall Street Journal*. February 16.

Taylor, Charles. 2004. *Modern Social Imaginaries*. Durham and London: Duke University Press.

Taylor, Gary W., and Jane M. Ussher. 2001. "Making Sense of S&M: A Discourse Analytic Account." *Sexualities*. 4, no.3: 293–314.

Taylor, Philip. 1992. *War and the Media: Propaganda and Persuasion in the Gulf War*. Manchester: Manchester University Press.

Taylor-Norton, Richard. 2009. "Rights Charter Planned for Armed Forces." *The Guardian*. December 17. http://www.theguardian.com/uk/2009/dec/17/rights-charter-planned-armed-forces.

Telegraph, The. 2011. "Sir Richard Dannatt Calls for Military Charities to Work." January 15. http://www.telegraph.co.uk/news/uknews/defence/8261482/Sir-Richard-Dannatt-callsfor-military-charities-to-work-together.html.

TheyWorkForYou.com. N.d. "Home."

Thobani, Sunera. 2010. "Vigilante masculinity and the 'War on Terror.'" In *Islam in the Eyes of the West: Images and Realities in an Age of Terror*, edited by Tareq. Y Ismael and Andrew Rippen. 64–85. London: Routledge.

Tickner, J. Ann. 1988. "Hans Morgenthau's Principles of Political Realism: A Feminist Reformulation." *Millennium: Journal of International Studies*. 3, no.17: 429–40.

Tickner, J. Ann. 2001. *Gendering World Politics*. Columbia: New York.

Tidy, Joanna. 2015a. "Forces Sauces and Eggs for Soldiers: Food, Nostalgia and the Rehabilitation of the British Military." *Critical Military Studies*. 1, no.3: 220–32.

Tidy, Joanna. 2015b. "Gender, Dissenting Subjectivity and the Contemporary Military Peace Movement in Body of War." *International Journal of Feminist Politics*. 17, no.3: 454–72.

Tidy, Joanna. 2016. "The Gender Politics of 'Ground Truth' in the Military Dissent Movement: The Power and Limits of Authenticity Claims Regarding War." *International Political Sociology*. 10, no.2: 99–114.

Tidy, Joanna. 2019. "War Craft: The Embodied Politics of Making War." *Security Dialogue*. 50, no.3: 220–38.

Tilly, Charles. 1995. "The Emergence of Citizenship in France and Elsewhere." *International Review of Social History*. 40, no.S3: 223–36.

Times, The. 2004. "Church, State and War: Is the Archbishop's Involvement in the Row over Iraqi PoW's Justified?" July 2, T41.

Tosh, John. 1994. "What Should Historians Do with Masculinity? Reflections on Nineteenth-Century Britain." *History Workshop*. 38: 179–202.

Townsend, Mark. 2009. "MoD Under Fire for All-Male Toy Soldiers Promotional." *The Guardian*. May 3. https://www.theguardian.com/uk/2009/may/03/ministry-defence-male-toy-soldiers.

Travis, Alan, and Iain Black. 2003. "Blair's Popularity Plummets." *The Guardian*. February 18. http://www.theguardian.com/uk/2003/feb/18/politics.iraq.

Tuleja, Tad. 1994. "Closing the Circle: Yellow Ribbons and the Redemption of the Past." *Journal of American Culture*. 17, no.1: 23–30.

UK Government Coalition. 2010. "The Coalition." https://assets.publishing.service.gov.uk/government/uploads/system/uploads/attachment_data/file/78977/coalition_programme_for_government.pdf.

UK Ministry of Defence. 2010. "X-Factor Contestants Honour British Service Personnel." November 26. https://www.gov.uk/government/news/x-factor-contestants-honour-british-service-personnel.

UK Ministry of Defence. 2014. "Diversity Dashboard." https://www.gov.uk/government/collections/mod-diversity-dashboard-index.

UK Ministry of Defence. 2019. "JSP 889: Policy for the Recruitment and Management of Transgender Personnel in the Armed Forces." https://assets.publishing.service.gov.uk/government/uploads/system/uploads/attachment_data/file/847173/JSP889.pdf.

UK National Archives. N.d. "PREM—Records of the Prime Minister's Office." http://discovery.nationalarchives.gov.uk/browse/r/h/C1512.

UK Parliament. N.d. "National Service." https://www.parliament.uk/about/living-heritage/transformingsociety/private-lives/yourcountry/overview/nationalservice/.

UK Web Archive. N.d. "Home." http://www.webarchive.org.uk/ukwa/.

uk4uThanks!. 2009. "2008 Christmas Box." January. http://web.archive.org/web/20100123031741/http://www.uk4u.org/2008ChristmasBox.aspx.

uk4uThanks!. 2010. "Getting Your Family Involved with uk4u Thanks!" http://www.uk4u.org/.

United for Peace and Justice (UfPJ). 2003a. "Songs and Chants for Peace." May 12. https://web.archive.org/web/20030512141608/http://www.unitedforpeace.org/article.php?id=224.

United Kingdom Ministry of Defence. 2012a. Sign the Armed Forces Covenant and Make Your Promise. 11 March. Available at: https://www.gov.uk/government/publications/community-covenant-pledge. Accessed 6 April 2016.

United Kingdom Ministry of Defence. 2012b. Army Related Charities. Available at http://www.army.mod.uk/welfare-support/23202.aspx. Accessed 26 June 2012.

United Kingdom Ministry of Defence. 2012c. Armed Forces Covenant–Ideas for Best Practice. Available at: https://www.gov.uk/government/uploads/system/uploads/atta chment_data/file/504663/20160301

United Kingdom Ministry of Defence. 2022. Armed Forces Day. Available at: https://www.armedforcesday.org.uk/about/. Accessed 10 June 2022.

United for Peace and Justice (UfPJ). 2003b. "Bring Them Home for the Holidays." December 7. https://web.archive.org/web/20031207083012/http://unitedforpeace. org/calendar.php?calid=648.

United for Peace and Justice (UfPJ). 2005. "UFPJ Rejects Future Work with ANSWER." December 12. http://www.unitedforpeace.org/article.php?id=3162.

United for Peace and Justice (UfPJ). 2006. "Let's 'Stamp' Out the War in Iraq." May 24. http://www.unitedforpeace.org/article.php?id=3277.

US Citizenship and Immigration Services. N.d. "Naturalization Through Military Service." https://www.uscis.gov/military/naturalization-through-military-service.

US Department of Justice. 2020. "Declassification: Frequently Asked Questions." November 6. http://www.justice.gov/open/declassification/declassification-faq.

Vagts, Alfred. 1959. *A History of Militarism*. New York: Meridian.

Valdez, Ines. 2016. "Punishment, Race, and the Organization of US Immigration Exclusion." *Political Research Quarterly*. 69, no.4: 646–47.

Vergun, David. 2016. "Survival Rates Improving for Soldiers Wounded in Combat, Says Army Surgeon General." US Army. August 24. https://www.army.mil/article/173 808/survival_rates_improving_for_soldiers_wounded_in_combat_says_army_surg eon_general.

Veterans of Foreign Wars (VFW). N.d. "Patriotic Days." https://www.vfw.org/commun ity/community-initiatives/patriotic-days; https://warontherocks.com/2020/05/this-memorial-day-lets-finally-start-having-an-honest-national-conversation-about-milit ary-service/.

Veterans of Foreign Wars (VFW). 2003. "Loyalty Day/Support the Troops Speech." April 30. https://web.archive.org/web/20030430113912/http://www.vfw.org/index.cfm?fa= what.leveld&did=1066.

Veterans of Foreign Wars (VFW). 2004. "Kerry: Keeping Faith with America's Veterans." https://web.archive.org/web/20040901013202/http://www.vfw.org/index.cfm?fa= news.newsDtl&did=2114.

Veterans of Foreign Wars (VFW). 2005a. "War Protests Will Devastate Morale." December 28. https://web.archive.org/web/20051228234136/http://www.vfw.org/index.cfm?fa= news.newsDtl&did=2802.

Veterans of Foreign Wars (VFW). 2005b. "Now Through Veterans Day WalMart Honoring Military with Wall of Honor." October 25. Ahttps://web.archive.org/web/20051228234 119/http://www.vfw.org/index.cfm?fa=news.newsDtl&did=2906.

Veterans of Foreign Wars (VFW). 2006. "Veterans Day 2006." December 26. https://web. archive.org/web/20061226204022/http://www.vfw.org/index.cfm?fa=news.news Dtl&did=3669.

Veterans of Foreign Wars (VFW). 2008a. "VFW Applauds American Airlines for Waiving Luggage Fee." September. https://web.archive.org/web/20080909202534/http://www.vfw.org/index.cfm?fa=news.newsDtl&did=4663.

Veterans of Foreign Wars (VFW). 2008b. "VFW National Convention: A Letter to Veterans." August 27. https://web.archive.org/web/20080909203404/http://www.vfw.org/index.cfm?fa=news.newsDtl&did=4689.

Veterans for Peace UK (VfP UK). 2010. "The Subversion of Armistice Day." November 11. http://veteransforpeace.org.uk/2010/the-subversion-of-armistice-day/.

Victoria and Albert Museum. N.d. "What Did YOU do in the Great War, Daddy?" {http://collections.vam.ac.uk/item/O74621/daddy-what-did-you-do-poster-lumley-savile/}

Vinovskis, Maria A. 1989. "Have Social Historians Lost the Civil War? Some Preliminary Demographic Speculations." *The Journal of American History*, 76, no.1: 34–58.

Vittori, Davide. 2017. "Re-conceptualizing populism: Bringing a multifaceted concept within stricter borders." *Revista Española de Ciencia Política*. 44, 43–65. Doi: https://doi.org/10.21308/recp.44.02.

Vucetic, Srdjan. 2011. *The Anglosphere: A Genealogy of a Racialized Identity in International Relations*. Redwood City: Stanford University Press.

Walker, R. B. 1990. "Security, Sovereignty, and the Challenge of World Politics." *Alternatives*. 15, no.1: 3–27.

Walsh, Nick Paton. 2009. "Britain's 'Broken Promises' to Afghan Translators." Channel Four News. November 16. https://www.channel4.com/news/british-armys-broken-promises-to-afghan-translators.

Walzer, Michael. 1970. *Obligations: Essays on Disobedience, War, and Citizenship*. Cambridge: Harvard University Press.

Ward, Andrew. 2007. Yellow Ribbons Dwindle with War Support. *The Financial Times*. (2 March). Available at http://www.ft.com/cms/s/0/4793da48-c8f7-11db-9f7b-000b5df10621.html. Accessed 7 April 2016.

Ware, Vron. 2010. "Whiteness in the Glare of War: Soldiers, Migrants and Citizenship." *Ethnicities*. 10, no.3: 313–30.

Ware, Vron. 2014. *Military Migrants: Fighting for YOUR Country*. Basingstoke: Palgrave MacMillan.

Washington Post. 2006. "You're So Glad to Have a Show." 14 May. A10.

Watkins, Alan. 2003. "On the Eve of War—He May Have the Sympathy Vote. But Not Mine." *Independent on Sunday*. March 16.

Watson, Elton. 2010. *Pimps, Wimps, Studs, Thugs and Gentlemen: Essays on Media Images of Masculinity*. Jefferson, NC: McFarland.

Watson Institute. 2021. "Iraqi Civilians" and "Afghan Civilians" November. https://watson.brown.edu/costsofwar/costs/human/civilians/iraqi and https://watson.brown.edu/costsofwar/costs/human/civilians/afghan.

Weber, Cynthia. 2016. *Queer International Relations*. Oxford: Oxford University Press.

Wegner, Nicole. 2021. "Ritual, Rhythms, and the Discomforting Endurance of Militarism: Affective Methodologies and Ethico-Political Challenges." *Global Studies Quarterly*. 1, no.3: ksab008.

Weldes, Jutta. 2006. "High Politics and Low Data: Globalization Discourses and Popular Culture." In *Interpretation and Method: Empirical Research Methods and the Interpretive Turn*, edited by Dvora Yanow and Peregrine Schwartz-Shea. 176–86. London: M.E. Sharpe.

Wells, Matt. 2001. "BBC in Row over Ban on Poppies." *The Guardian*. November 3. https://www.theguardian.com/media/2001/nov/03/uknews.

Westbrook, Robert B. 1990. "'I Want a Girl, Just Like the Girl that Married Harry James': American Women and the Problem of Political Obligation in World War II." *American Quarterly*. 42, no.4: 587–614.

WhiteHouse.org. 2012. "Joining Forces, Government of the United States." WhiteHouse.gov. June 25. http://www.whitehouse.gov/joiningforces.

WhiteHouse.org. 2015. "The White House: President Barack Obama." WhiteHouse.gov. August 15. https://www.whitehouse.gov/.

Whitford, Margaret. 2000. "Introduction." In *The Irigaray Reader*, edited by Margaret Whitford, 1–15. Oxford: Blackwell.

Wibben, Annick. 2018. "Why We Need to Study (US) Militarism: A Critical Feminist Lens." *Security Dialogue*. 49, nos.1–2: 136–48.

Wilcox, Lauren. 2009. "Gendering the Cult of the Offensive." *Security Studies*. 18, no.2: 214–40.

Wilkerson, Isabella. 1991. "WAR IN THE GULF: THE TROOPS; Blacks Wary of Their Big Role as Troops." *New York Times*. January 25. https://www.nytimes.com/1991/01/25/us/war-in-the-gulf-the-troops-blacks-wary-of-their-big-role-as-troops.html.

Willis, John. 1975. "Variations in State Casualty Rates in World War II and the Vietnam War." *Social Problems*. 22, no.4: 558–68.

Wing, Nick. 2013. "Honoring America's Veterans Act Signed by Obama, Restricting Westboro Military Funeral Protests." The Huffington Post. March 5. http://www.huffingtonpost.com/2012/08/06/honoring-americas-veterans-act-obama_n_1748454.html.

Winter, J. M. 1977. "Britain's 'Lost Generation' of the First World War." *Population Studies*. 31, no.3: 449–66.

Woehrle, Lynne et al. 2008. *Contesting Patriotism: Culture, Power, and Strategy in the Peace Movement*. Plymouth: Rowman and Littlefield.

Wong, Leonard et al. 2003. "Why They Fight: Combat Motivation and the Iraq War." Carlisle Barracks, Strategic Studies Institute. US Army War College, Pennsylvania. http://www.strategicstudiesinstitute.army.mil/pdffiles/pub179.pdf.

Wood, James. 2007. "Anglo-American Liberal Militarism and the Idea of the Citizen Soldier." *International Journal*. 62 no.2: 403–22.

Woodward, Rachel. 1998. "'It's a Man's Life!': Soldiers, Masculinity and the Countryside." *Gender, Place and Culture: A Journal of Feminist Geography*. 5, no.3: 277–300.

Woodward, Rachel. 2014. "Military Landscapes: Agendas and Approaches for Future Research." *Progress in Human Geography*. 38, no.1: 40–61.

Woodward, Rachel, and K. Neil Jenkings. 2011. "Military Identities in the Situated Accounts of British Military Personnel." *Sociology*. 45, no.2: 252–68.

Woodward Rachel, Trish Winter, and K. Neil Jenkings. 2009. "Heroic Anxieties: The Figure of the British Soldier in Contemporary Print Media." *Journal of War and Culture Studies*. 2, no.2: 211–23.

Wool, Zoë H. 2014. "Critical Military Studies, Queer Theory and the Possibilities of Critique." *Critical Military Studies*. 1, no.1: 23–37.

Worsencroft, J. C. 2011. *Salvageable Manhood: Project 100,000 and the Gendered Politics of the Vietnam War*. Salt Lake City: University of Utah.

Wyatt, Caroline. 2012. "Communicating War: The Poacher's Perspective." In *The Oxford Handbook of War*, edited by Yves Boyer and Julien Lindley-French. 631–46. Oxford: Oxford University Press.

Wynter, Sylvia. 2003. "Unsettling the Coloniality of Being/Power/Truth/Freedom: Towards the Human, After Man, Its Overrepresentation—An Argument." *CR: The New Centennial Review*. 3, no.3: 257–337.

Young, Iris Marion. 2003. "The Logic of Masculinist Protection: Reflections on the Current Security State." *Signs: Journal of Women in Culture and Society*. 29, no.1: 1–25.

Young, Valerie. J. 2018. "The World War One Gold Star Soldiers from Adams County." *Adams County History*. 24, no.1: 3

Youngs, Gillian. 2010. "The 'New Home Front' and the War on Terror: Ethical and Political Reframing of National and International Politics." *International Affairs*. 86, no.4: 925–37.

Yuval-Davis, Nira. 2010. "Theorizing Identity: Beyond the 'Us' and 'Them' Dichotomy." *Patterns of Prejudice*. 44, no.3: 261–80.

Zarakol, A. 2010. *After Defeat: How the East Learned to Live with the West*. Cambridge: Cambridge University Press.

Zevnik, Andreja. 2017. "From Fear to Anxiety: An Exploration into a New Socio-Political Temporality." *Law and Critique*. 28, no.3: 235–46.

Zizek, Slavoj. 2007. "Anxiety: Kierkegaard with Lacan." *Annual of Psychoanalysis*. 35: 179–89.

Zong, Jie, and Jeanne Batalova. 2019. "Immigrant Veterans in the United States. Migration Policy Institute. May 16. https://www.migrationpolicy.org/article/immigrant-veterans-united-states-2018

Index

For the benefit of digital users, indexed terms that span two pages (e.g., 52–53) may, on occasion, appear on only one of those pages.